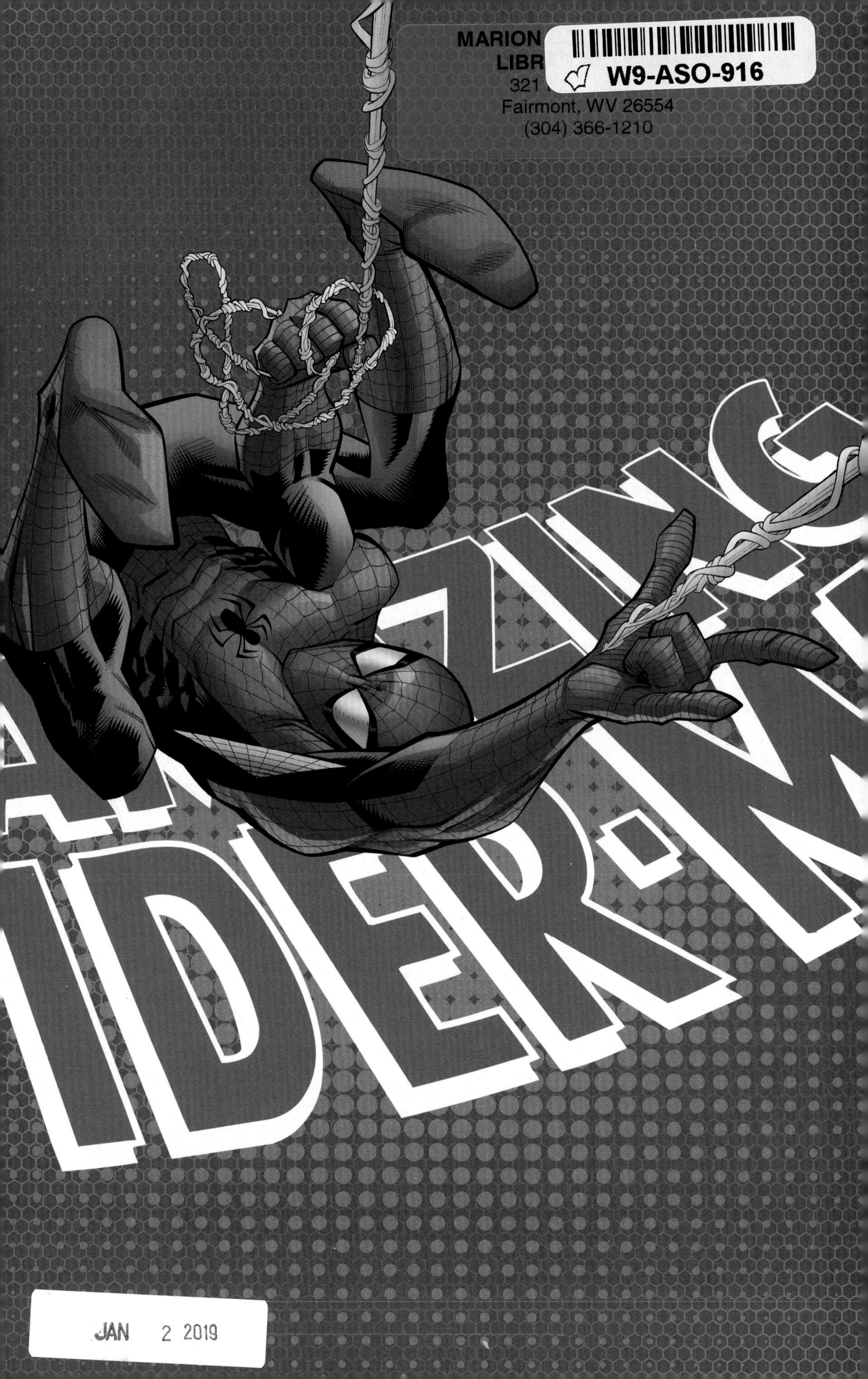
ZING
IDER

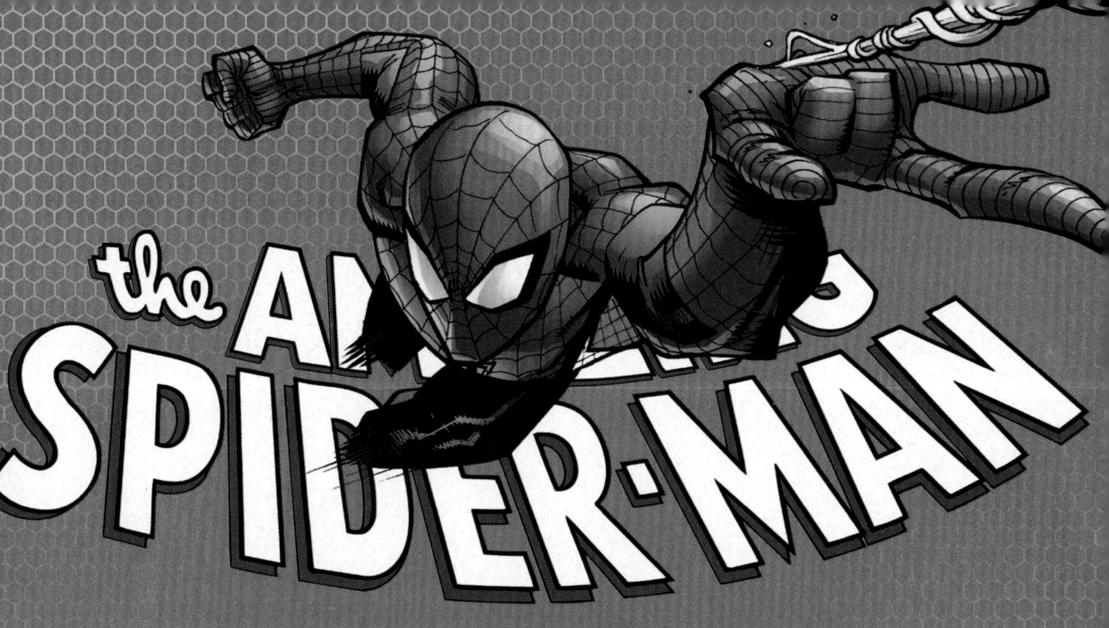
the
SPIDER-MAN

BACK TO BASICS

WRITER **NICK SPENCER**

PENCILER **RYAN OTTLEY**

INKER **CLIFF RATHBURN**
WITH **RYAN OTTLEY** (#5, PP. 13-20)

COLORIST **LAURA MARTIN**
COLOR ASSISTANTS, #4 **PETE PANTAZIS & JASEN SMITH**

#1 MYSTERIO STORY

PENCILER **HUMBERTO RAMOS**

INKER **VICTOR OLAZABA**

COLORIST **EDGAR DELGADO**

LETTERER **VC's JOE CARAMAGNA**
COVER ART **RYAN OTTLEY & LAURA MARTIN**
ASSISTANT EDITOR **KATHLEEN WISNESKI**
EDITOR **NICK LOWE**
SPECIAL THANKS **MATT FRACTION, SALVADOR LARROCA & ANTONIO RUIZ**

SPIDER-MAN CREATED BY STAN LEE & STEVE DITKO

COLLECTION EDITOR **JENNIFER GRÜNWALD** • ASSISTANT EDITOR **CAITLIN O'CONNELL** • ASSOCIATE MANAGING EDITOR **KATERI WOODY**
EDITOR, SPECIAL PROJECTS **MARK D. BEAZLEY** • VP PRODUCTION & SPECIAL PROJECTS **JEFF YOUNGQUIST**
SVP PRINT, SALES & MARKETING **DAVID GABRIEL** • BOOK DESIGNER **JAY BOWEN**

EDITOR IN CHIEF **C.B. CEBULSKI** • CHIEF CREATIVE OFFICER **JOE QUESADA**
PRESIDENT **DAN BUCKLEY** • EXECUTIVE PRODUCER **ALAN FINE**

AMAZING SPIDER-MAN BY NICK SPENCER VOL. 1: BACK TO BASICS. Contains material originally published in magazine form as AMAZING SPIDER-MAN #1-5 and FREE COMIC BOOK DAY 2018 (AMAZING SPIDER-MAN/GUARDIANS OF THE GALAXY) #1. First printing 2018. ISBN 978-1-302-91231-4. Published by MARVEL WORLDWIDE, INC., a subsidiary of MARVEL ENTERTAINMENT, LLC. OFFICE OF PUBLICATION: 135 West 50th Street, New York, NY 10020. **Printed in Canada.** DAN BUCKLEY, President, Marvel Entertainment; JOHN NEE, Publisher; JOE QUESADA, Chief Creative Officer; TOM BREVOORT, SVP of Publishing; DAVID BOGART, SVP of Business Affairs & Operations, Publishing & Partnership; DAVID GABRIEL, SVP of Sales & Marketing, Publishing; JEFF YOUNGQUIST, VP of Production & Special Projects; DAN CARR, Executive Director of Publishing Technology; ALEX MORALES, Director of Publishing Operations; DAN EDINGTON, Managing Editor; SUSAN CRESPI, Production Manager; STAN LEE, Chairman Emeritus. For information regarding advertising in Marvel Comics or on Marvel.com, please contact Vit DeBellis, Custom Solutions & Integrated Advertising Manager, at vdebellis@marvel.com. For Marvel subscription inquiries, please call 888-511-5480. **Manufactured between 10/5/2018 and 11/6/2018 by SOLISCO PRINTERS, SCOTT, QC, CANADA.**

10 9 8 7 6 5 4 3 2 1

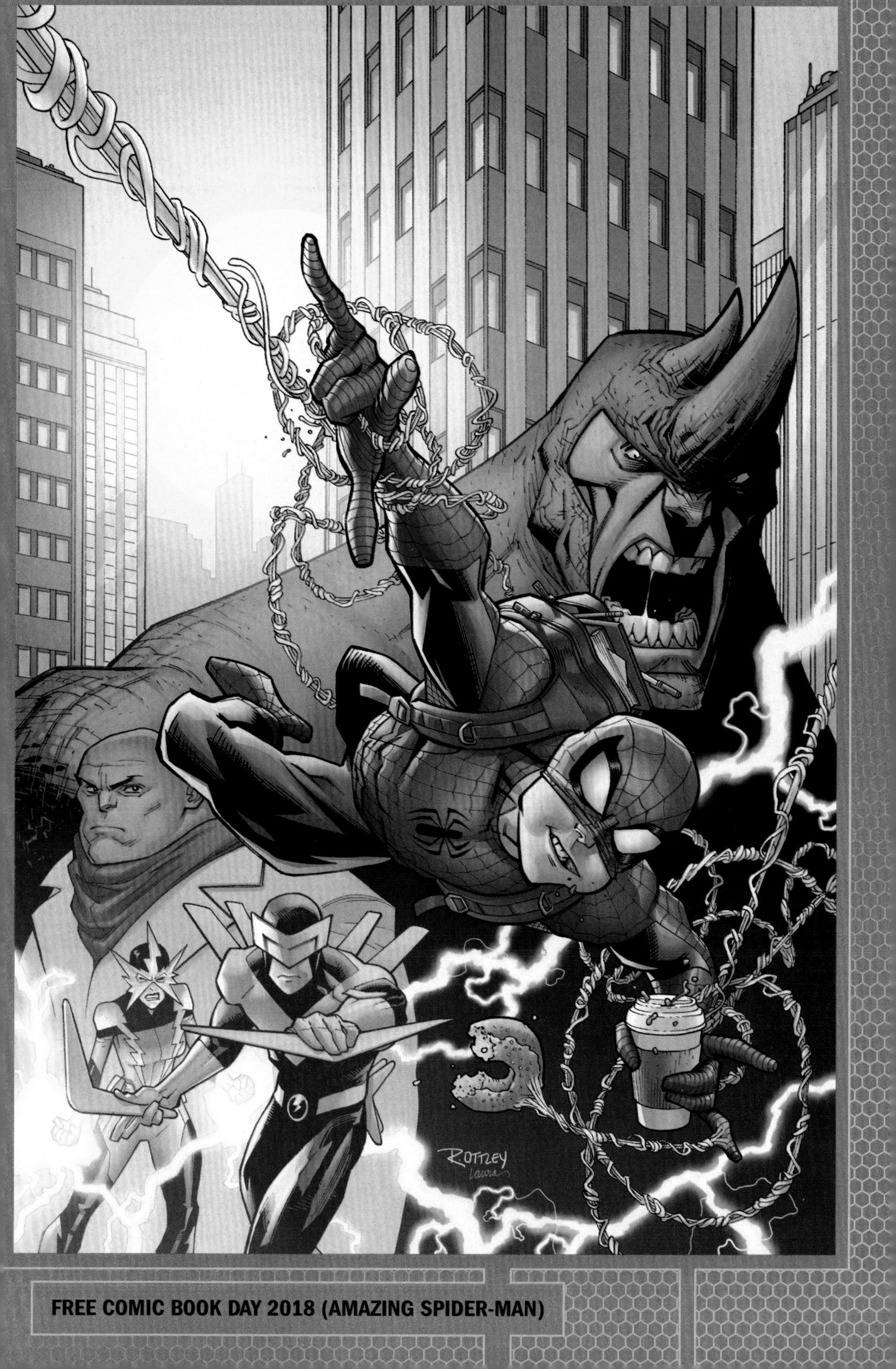

FREE COMIC BOOK DAY 2018 (AMAZING SPIDER-MAN)

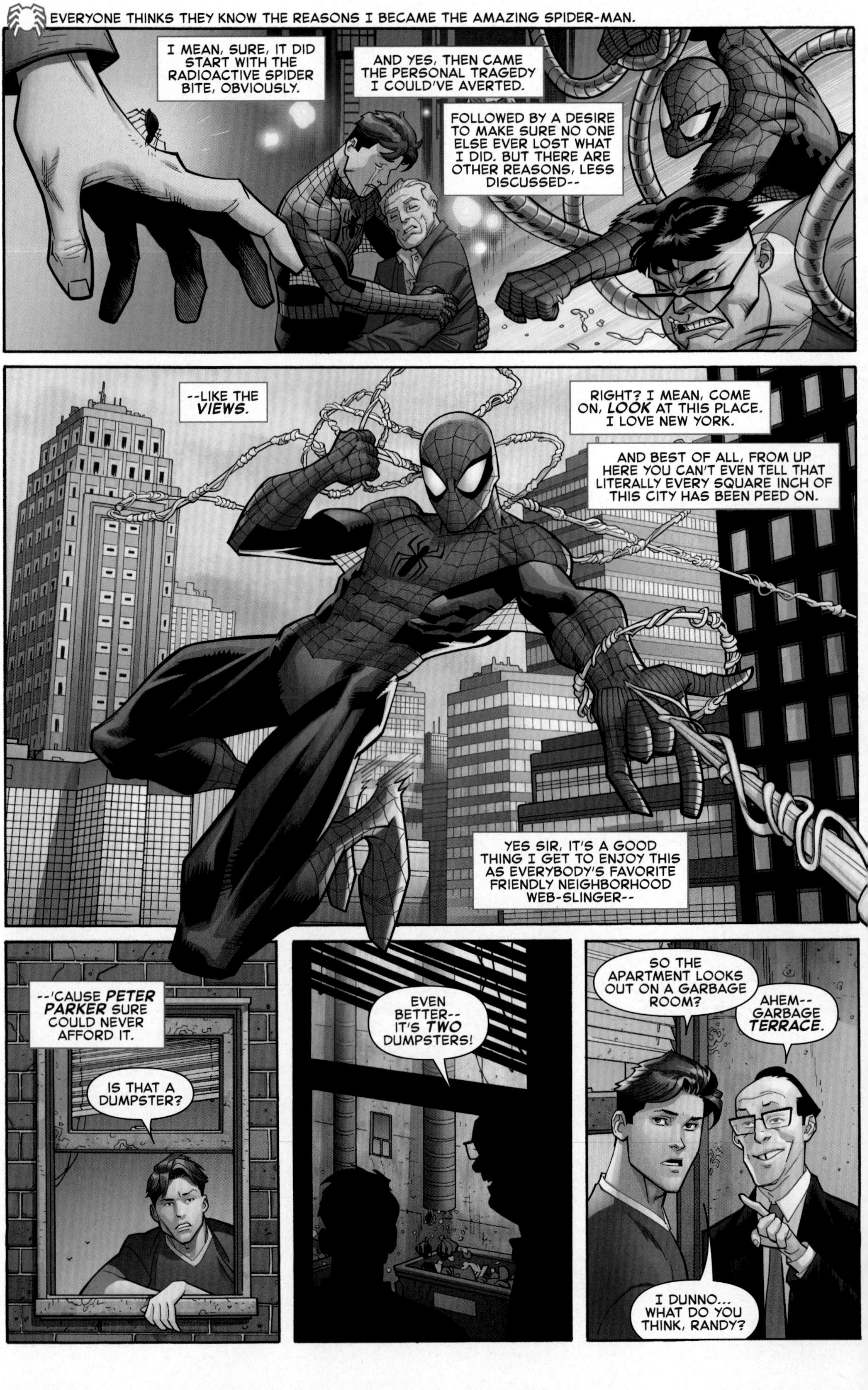
EVERYONE THINKS THEY KNOW THE REASONS I BECAME THE AMAZING SPIDER-MAN.
I MEAN, SURE, IT DID START WITH THE RADIOACTIVE SPIDER BITE, OBVIOUSLY.
AND YES, THEN CAME THE PERSONAL TRAGEDY I COULD'VE AVERTED.
FOLLOWED BY A DESIRE TO MAKE SURE NO ONE ELSE EVER LOST WHAT I DID. BUT THERE ARE OTHER REASONS, LESS DISCUSSED--
--LIKE THE VIEWS.
RIGHT? I MEAN, COME ON, LOOK AT THIS PLACE. I LOVE NEW YORK.
AND BEST OF ALL, FROM UP HERE YOU CAN'T EVEN TELL THAT LITERALLY EVERY SQUARE INCH OF THIS CITY HAS BEEN PEED ON.
YES SIR, IT'S A GOOD THING I GET TO ENJOY THIS AS EVERYBODY'S FAVORITE FRIENDLY NEIGHBORHOOD WEB-SLINGER--
--'CAUSE PETER PARKER SURE COULD NEVER AFFORD IT.
IS THAT A DUMPSTER?
EVEN BETTER-- IT'S TWO DUMPSTERS!
SO THE APARTMENT LOOKS OUT ON A GARBAGE ROOM?
AHEM-- GARBAGE TERRACE.
I DUNNO... WHAT DO YOU THINK, RANDY?

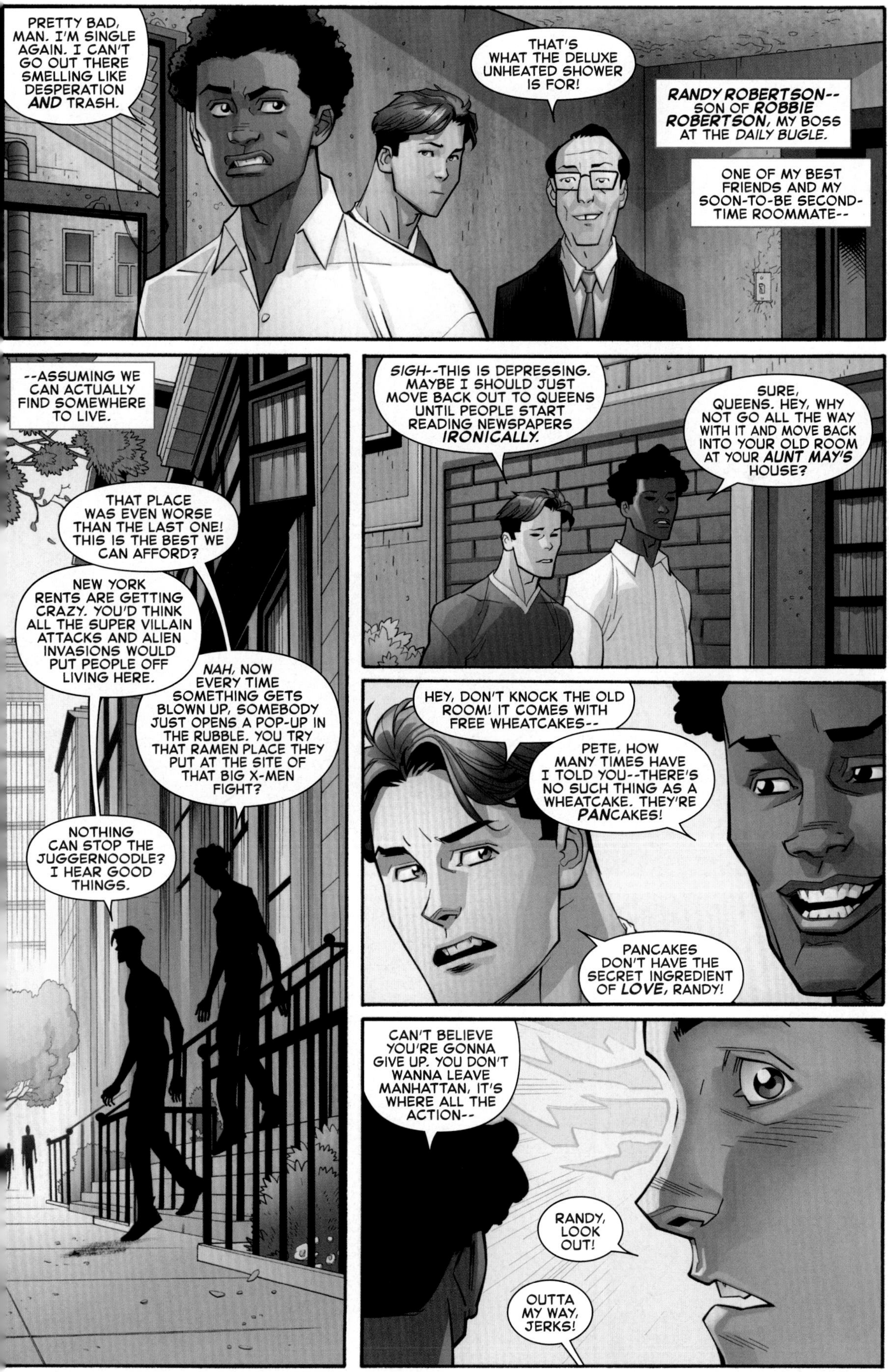

PRETTY BAD, MAN. I'M SINGLE AGAIN. I CAN'T GO OUT THERE SMELLING LIKE DESPERATION **AND** TRASH.
THAT'S WHAT THE DELUXE UNHEATED SHOWER IS FOR!
RANDY ROBERTSON-- SON OF ***ROBBIE ROBERTSON***, MY BOSS AT THE *DAILY BUGLE.*
ONE OF MY BEST FRIENDS AND MY SOON-TO-BE SECOND-TIME ROOMMATE--
--ASSUMING WE CAN ACTUALLY FIND SOMEWHERE TO LIVE.
THAT PLACE WAS EVEN WORSE THAN THE LAST ONE! THIS IS THE BEST WE CAN AFFORD?
NEW YORK RENTS ARE GETTING CRAZY. YOU'D THINK ALL THE SUPER VILLAIN ATTACKS AND ALIEN INVASIONS WOULD PUT PEOPLE OFF LIVING HERE.
NAH, NOW EVERY TIME SOMETHING GETS BLOWN UP, SOMEBODY JUST OPENS A POP-UP IN THE RUBBLE. YOU TRY THAT RAMEN PLACE THEY PUT AT THE SITE OF THAT BIG X-MEN FIGHT?
NOTHING CAN STOP THE JUGGERNOODLE? I HEAR GOOD THINGS.
SIGH--THIS IS DEPRESSING. MAYBE I SHOULD JUST MOVE BACK OUT TO QUEENS UNTIL PEOPLE START READING NEWSPAPERS ***IRONICALLY.***
SURE, QUEENS. HEY, WHY NOT GO ALL THE WAY WITH IT AND MOVE BACK INTO YOUR OLD ROOM AT YOUR ***AUNT MAY'S*** HOUSE?
HEY, DON'T KNOCK THE OLD ROOM! IT COMES WITH FREE WHEATCAKES--
PETE, HOW MANY TIMES HAVE I TOLD YOU--THERE'S NO SUCH THING AS A WHEATCAKE. THEY'RE ***PAN***CAKES!
PANCAKES DON'T HAVE THE SECRET INGREDIENT OF ***LOVE,*** RANDY!
CAN'T BELIEVE YOU'RE GONNA GIVE UP. YOU DON'T WANNA LEAVE MANHATTAN, IT'S WHERE ALL THE ACTION--
RANDY, LOOK OUT!
OUTTA MY WAY, JERKS!

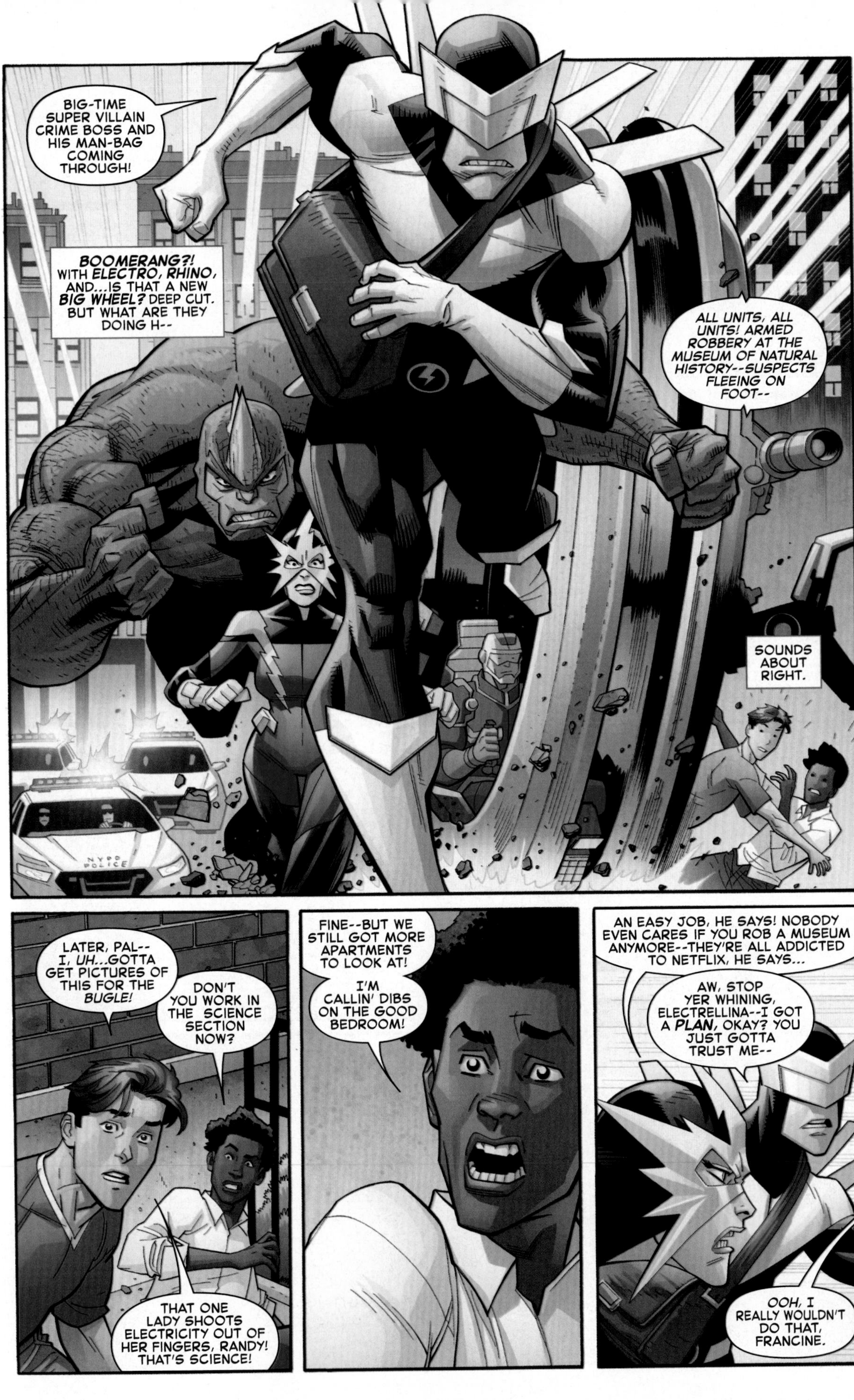
BIG-TIME SUPER VILLAIN CRIME BOSS AND HIS MAN-BAG COMING THROUGH!
BOOMERANG?! WITH ELECTRO, RHINO, AND...IS THAT A NEW BIG WHEEL? DEEP CUT. BUT WHAT ARE THEY DOING H--
ALL UNITS, ALL UNITS! ARMED ROBBERY AT THE MUSEUM OF NATURAL HISTORY--SUSPECTS FLEEING ON FOOT--
SOUNDS ABOUT RIGHT.
NYPD POLICE
LATER, PAL--I, UH...GOTTA GET PICTURES OF THIS FOR THE BUGLE!
DON'T YOU WORK IN THE SCIENCE SECTION NOW?
THAT ONE LADY SHOOTS ELECTRICITY OUT OF HER FINGERS, RANDY! THAT'S SCIENCE!
FINE--BUT WE STILL GOT MORE APARTMENTS TO LOOK AT!
I'M CALLIN' DIBS ON THE GOOD BEDROOM!
AN EASY JOB, HE SAYS! NOBODY EVEN CARES IF YOU ROB A MUSEUM ANYMORE--THEY'RE ALL ADDICTED TO NETFLIX, HE SAYS...
AW, STOP YER WHINING, ELECTRELLINA--I GOT A PLAN, OKAY? YOU JUST GOTTA TRUST ME--
OOH, I REALLY WOULDN'T DO THAT, FRANCINE.

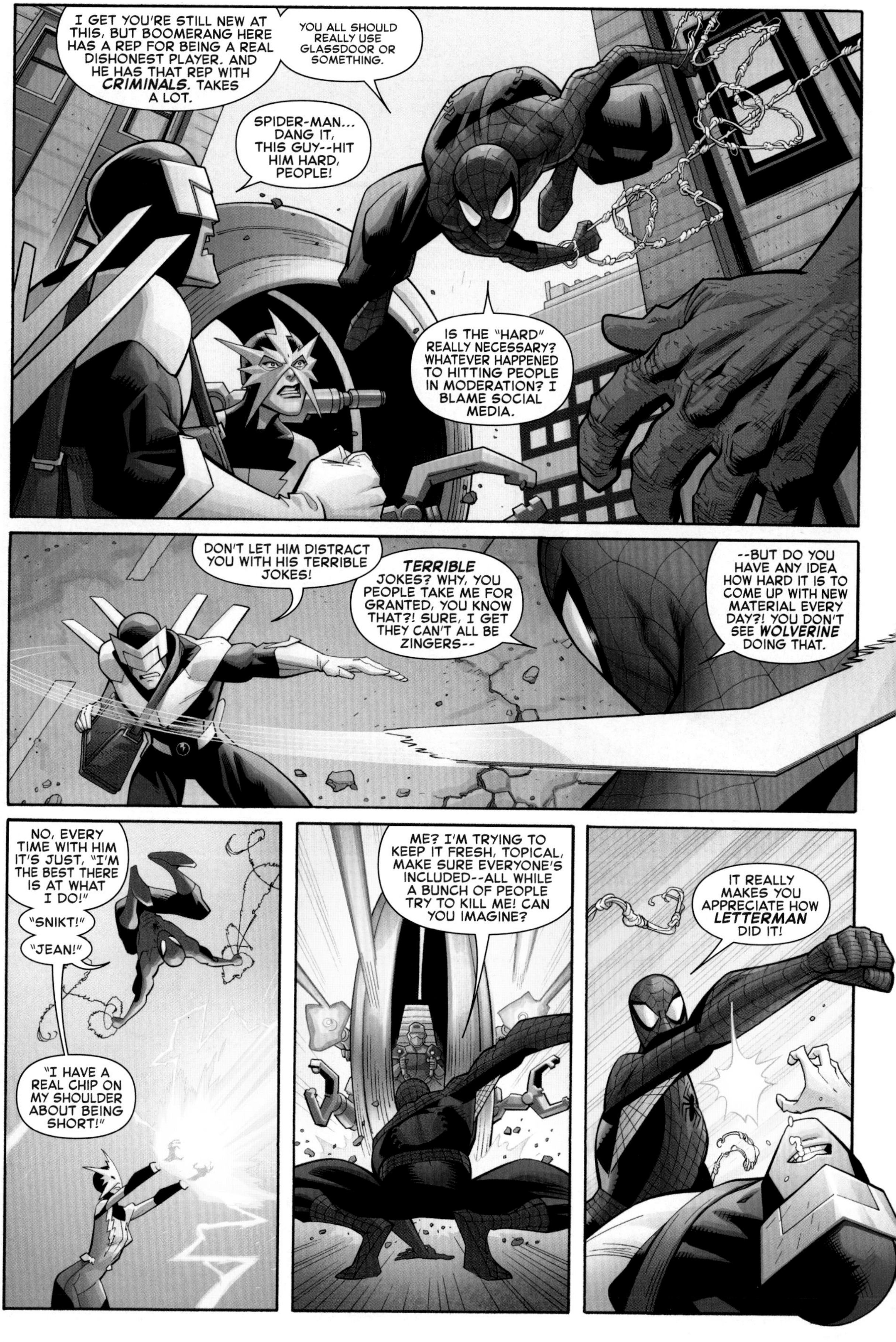
I GET YOU'RE STILL NEW AT THIS, BUT BOOMERANG HERE HAS A REP FOR BEING A REAL DISHONEST PLAYER. AND HE HAS THAT REP WITH CRIMINALS. TAKES A LOT.
YOU ALL SHOULD REALLY USE GLASSDOOR OR SOMETHING.
SPIDER-MAN... DANG IT, THIS GUY--HIT HIM HARD, PEOPLE!
IS THE "HARD" REALLY NECESSARY? WHATEVER HAPPENED TO HITTING PEOPLE IN MODERATION? I BLAME SOCIAL MEDIA.
DON'T LET HIM DISTRACT YOU WITH HIS TERRIBLE JOKES!
TERRIBLE JOKES? WHY, YOU PEOPLE TAKE ME FOR GRANTED, YOU KNOW THAT?! SURE, I GET THEY CAN'T ALL BE ZINGERS--
--BUT DO YOU HAVE ANY IDEA HOW HARD IT IS TO COME UP WITH NEW MATERIAL EVERY DAY?! YOU DON'T SEE WOLVERINE DOING THAT.
NO, EVERY TIME WITH HIM IT'S JUST, "I'M THE BEST THERE IS AT WHAT I DO!"
"SNIKT!"
"JEAN!"
"I HAVE A REAL CHIP ON MY SHOULDER ABOUT BEING SHORT!"
ME? I'M TRYING TO KEEP IT FRESH, TOPICAL, MAKE SURE EVERYONE'S INCLUDED--ALL WHILE A BUNCH OF PEOPLE TRY TO KILL ME! CAN YOU IMAGINE?
IT REALLY MAKES YOU APPRECIATE HOW LETTERMAN DID IT!

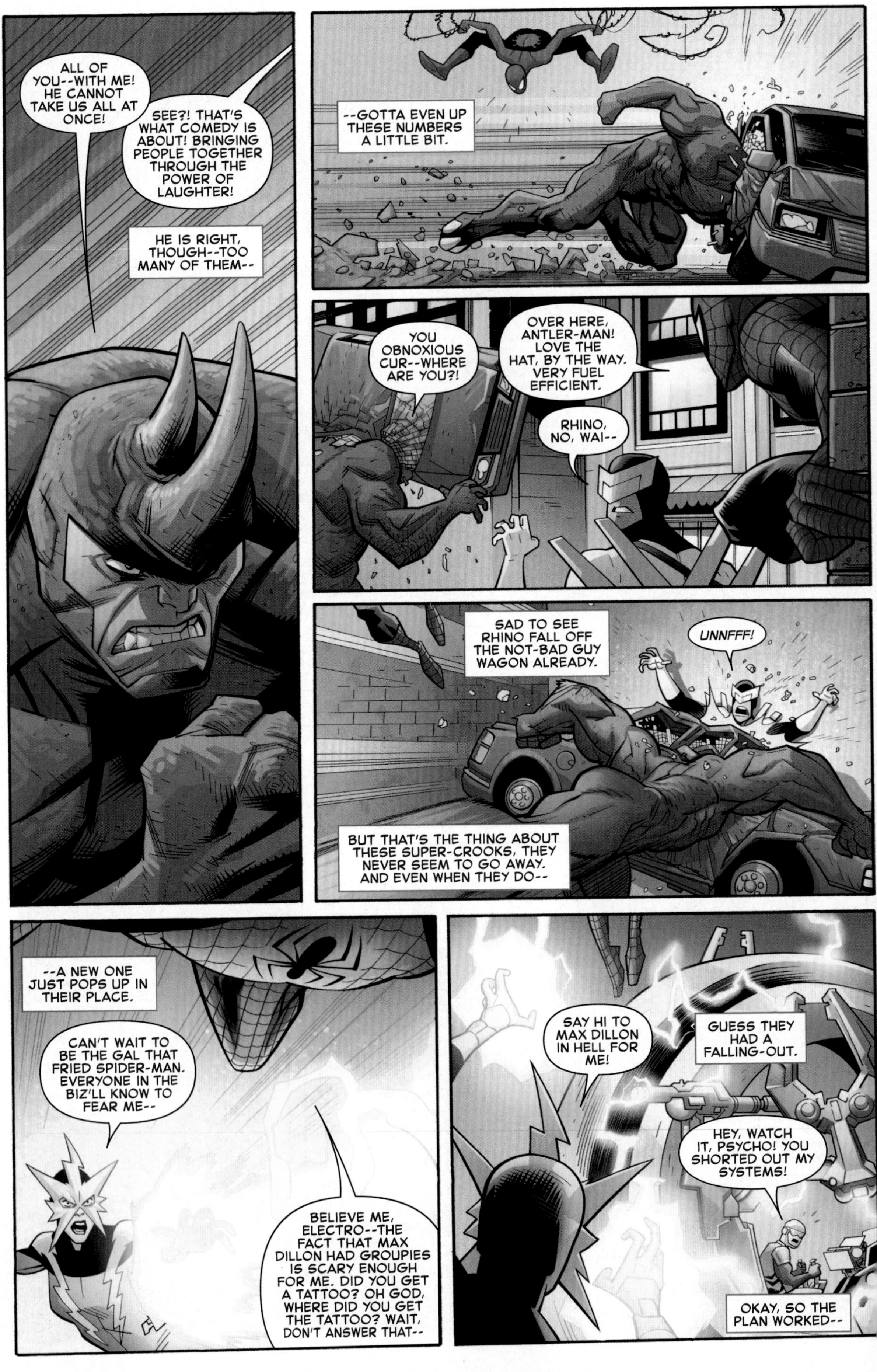

ALL OF YOU--WITH ME! HE CANNOT TAKE US ALL AT ONCE!
SEE?! THAT'S WHAT COMEDY IS ABOUT! BRINGING PEOPLE TOGETHER THROUGH THE POWER OF LAUGHTER!
HE IS RIGHT, THOUGH--TOO MANY OF THEM--
--GOTTA EVEN UP THESE NUMBERS A LITTLE BIT.
YOU OBNOXIOUS CUR--WHERE ARE YOU?!
OVER HERE, ANTLER-MAN! LOVE THE HAT, BY THE WAY. VERY FUEL EFFICIENT.
RHINO, NO, WAI--
SAD TO SEE RHINO FALL OFF THE NOT-BAD GUY WAGON ALREADY.
UNNFFF!
BUT THAT'S THE THING ABOUT THESE SUPER-CROOKS, THEY NEVER SEEM TO GO AWAY. AND EVEN WHEN THEY DO--
--A NEW ONE JUST POPS UP IN THEIR PLACE.
CAN'T WAIT TO BE THE GAL THAT FRIED SPIDER-MAN. EVERYONE IN THE BIZ'LL KNOW TO FEAR ME--
BELIEVE ME, ELECTRO--THE FACT THAT MAX DILLON HAD GROUPIES IS SCARY ENOUGH FOR ME. DID YOU GET A TATTOO? OH GOD, WHERE DID YOU GET THE TATTOO? WAIT, DON'T ANSWER THAT--
SAY HI TO MAX DILLON IN HELL FOR ME!
GUESS THEY HAD A FALLING-OUT.
HEY, WATCH IT, PSYCHO! YOU SHORTED OUT MY SYSTEMS!
OKAY, SO THE PLAN WORKED--

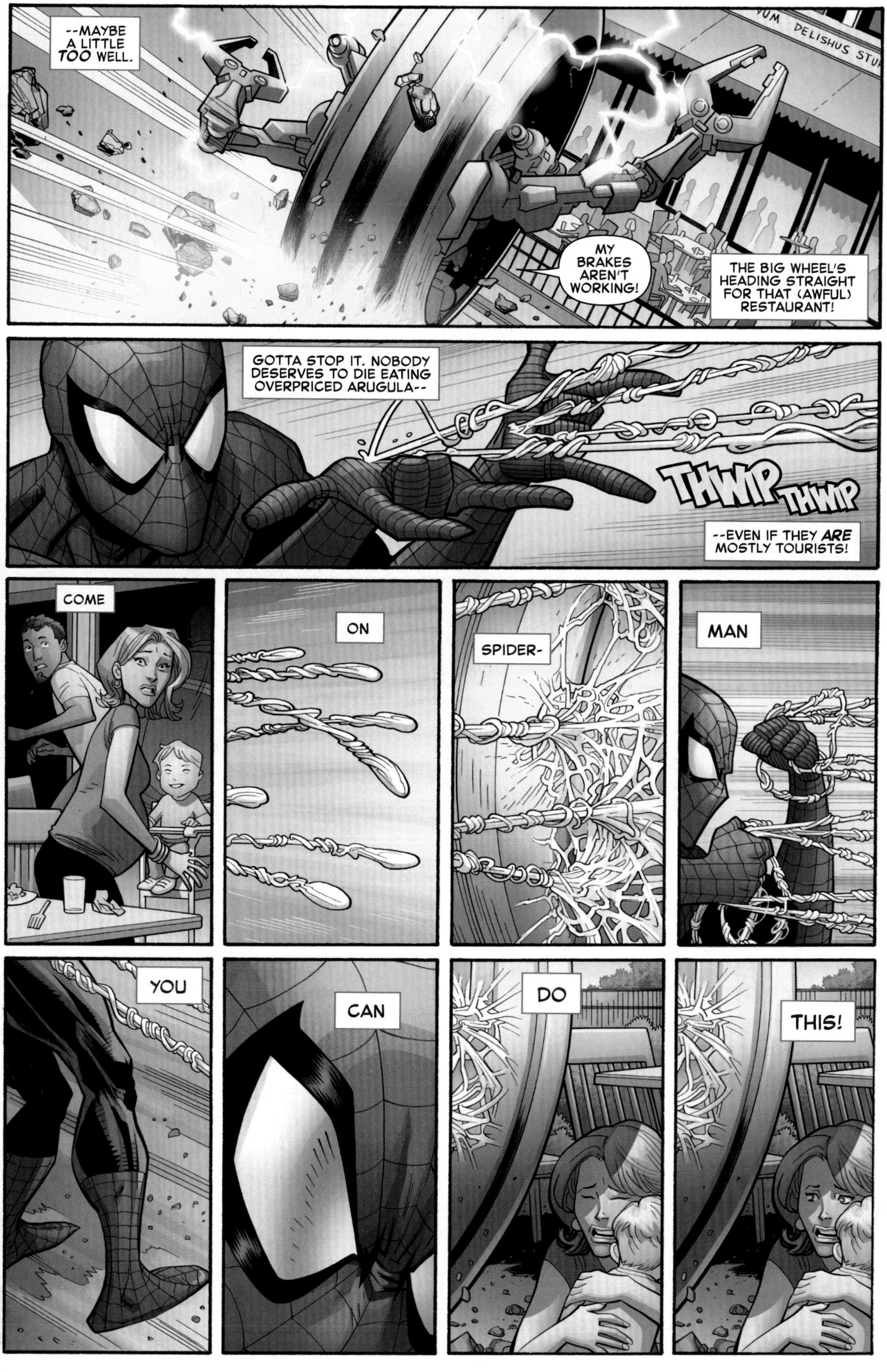
--MAYBE A LITTLE *TOO* WELL.
YUM DELISHUS STU
MY BRAKES AREN'T WORKING!
THE BIG WHEEL'S HEADING STRAIGHT FOR THAT (AWFUL) RESTAURANT!
GOTTA STOP IT. NOBODY DESERVES TO DIE EATING OVERPRICED ARUGULA--
THWIP THWIP
--EVEN IF THEY *ARE* MOSTLY TOURISTS!
COME
ON
SPIDER-
MAN
YOU
CAN
DO
THIS!

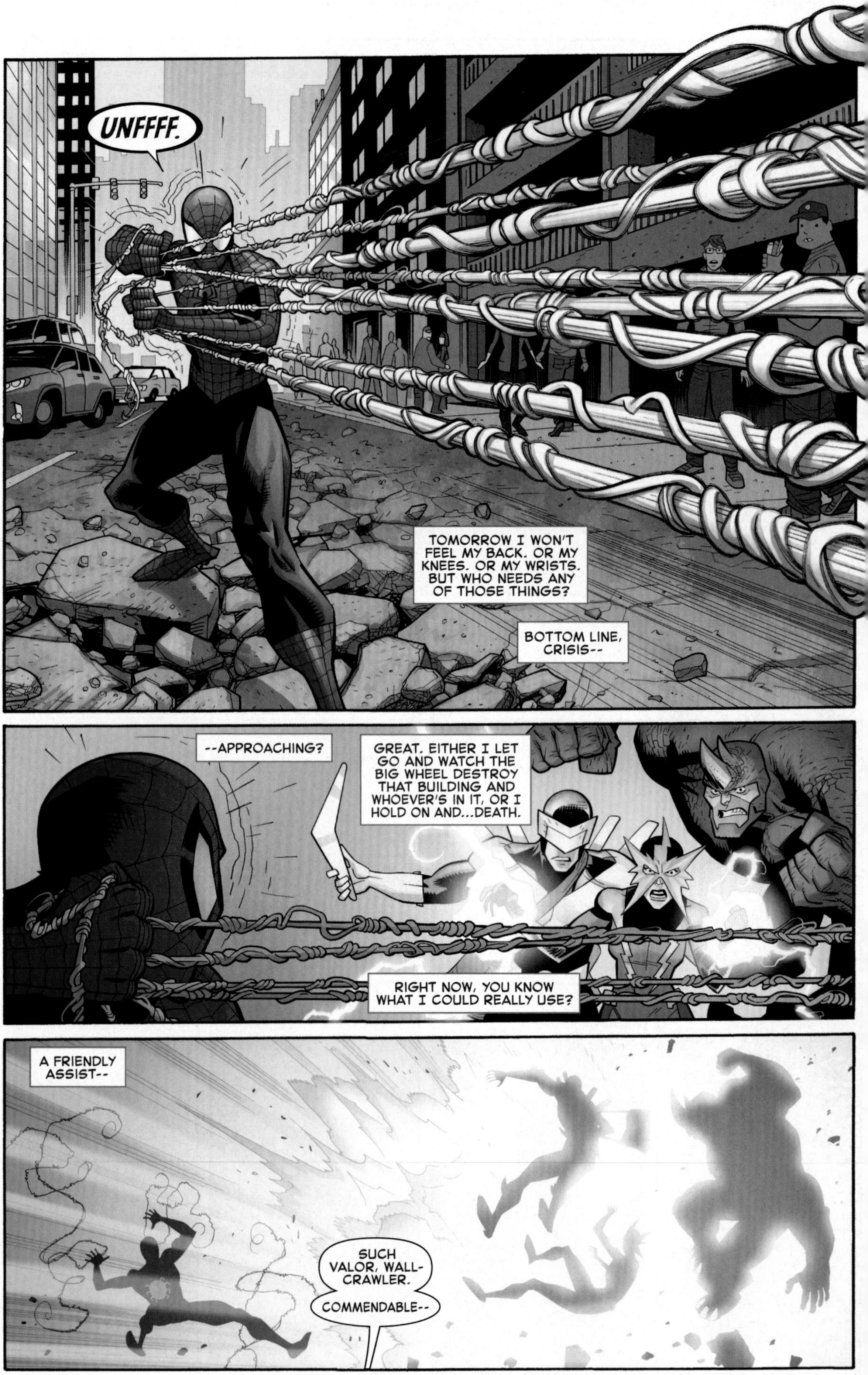
UNFFFF.
TOMORROW I WON'T FEEL MY BACK. OR MY KNEES. OR MY WRISTS. BUT WHO NEEDS ANY OF THOSE THINGS?
BOTTOM LINE, CRISIS--
--APPROACHING?
GREAT. EITHER I LET GO AND WATCH THE BIG WHEEL DESTROY THAT BUILDING AND WHOEVER'S IN IT, OR I HOLD ON AND...DEATH.
RIGHT NOW, YOU KNOW WHAT I COULD REALLY USE?
A FRIENDLY ASSIST--
SUCH VALOR, WALL-CRAWLER.
COMMENDABLE--

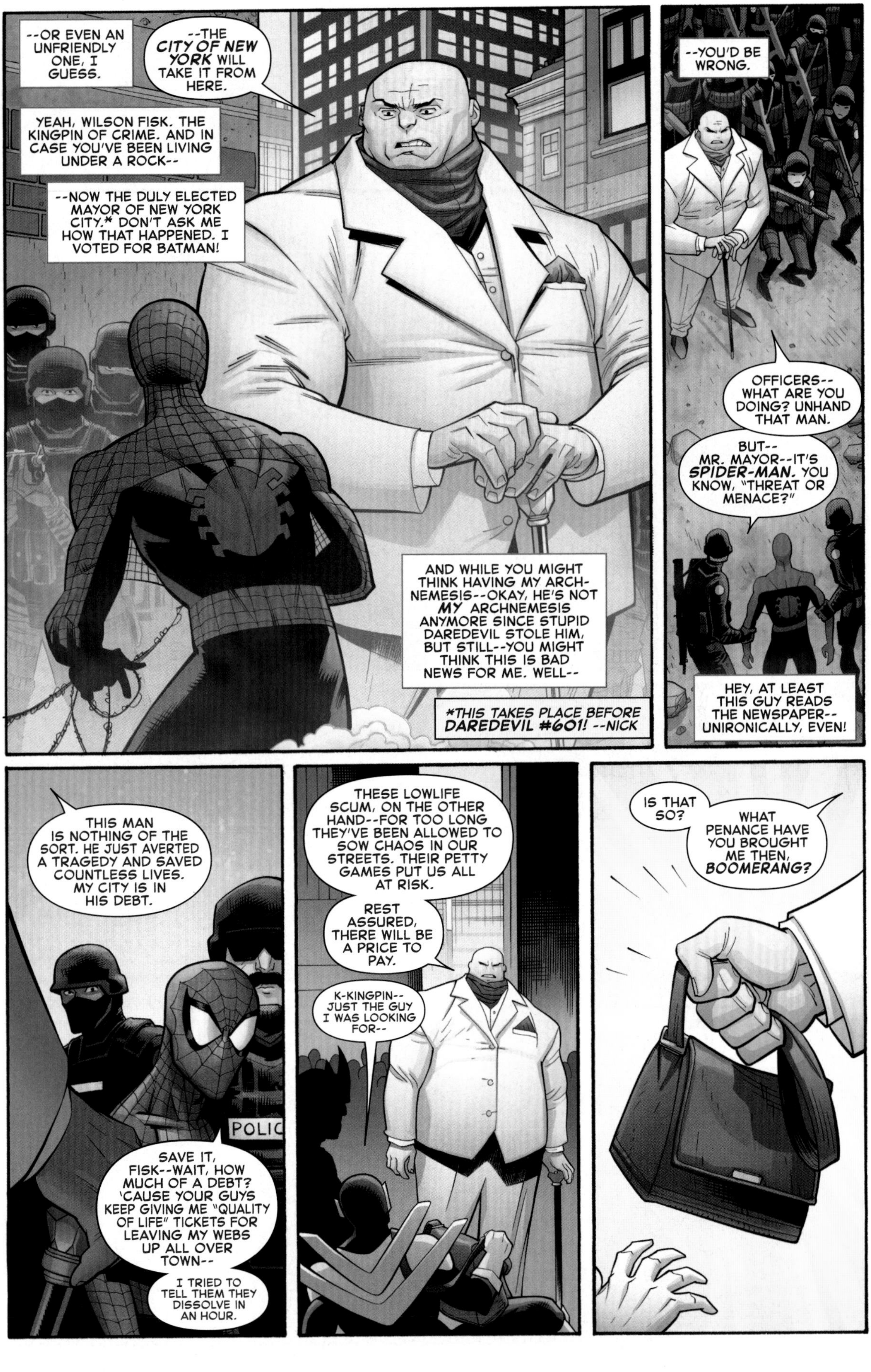
--OR EVEN AN UNFRIENDLY ONE, I GUESS.
--THE CITY OF NEW YORK WILL TAKE IT FROM HERE.
YEAH, WILSON FISK. THE KINGPIN OF CRIME. AND IN CASE YOU'VE BEEN LIVING UNDER A ROCK--
--NOW THE DULY ELECTED MAYOR OF NEW YORK CITY.* DON'T ASK ME HOW THAT HAPPENED. I VOTED FOR BATMAN!
AND WHILE YOU MIGHT THINK HAVING MY ARCH-NEMESIS--OKAY, HE'S NOT MY ARCHNEMESIS ANYMORE SINCE STUPID DAREDEVIL STOLE HIM, BUT STILL--YOU MIGHT THINK THIS IS BAD NEWS FOR ME. WELL--
*THIS TAKES PLACE BEFORE DAREDEVIL #601! --NICK
--YOU'D BE WRONG.
OFFICERS--WHAT ARE YOU DOING? UNHAND THAT MAN.
BUT--MR. MAYOR--IT'S SPIDER-MAN. YOU KNOW, "THREAT OR MENACE?"
HEY, AT LEAST THIS GUY READS THE NEWSPAPER--UNIRONICALLY, EVEN!
THIS MAN IS NOTHING OF THE SORT. HE JUST AVERTED A TRAGEDY AND SAVED COUNTLESS LIVES. MY CITY IS IN HIS DEBT.
POLIC
SAVE IT, FISK--WAIT, HOW MUCH OF A DEBT? 'CAUSE YOUR GUYS KEEP GIVING ME "QUALITY OF LIFE" TICKETS FOR LEAVING MY WEBS UP ALL OVER TOWN--
I TRIED TO TELL THEM THEY DISSOLVE IN AN HOUR.
THESE LOWLIFE SCUM, ON THE OTHER HAND--FOR TOO LONG THEY'VE BEEN ALLOWED TO SOW CHAOS IN OUR STREETS. THEIR PETTY GAMES PUT US ALL AT RISK.
REST ASSURED, THERE WILL BE A PRICE TO PAY.
K-KINGPIN--JUST THE GUY I WAS LOOKING FOR--
IS THAT SO?
WHAT PENANCE HAVE YOU BROUGHT ME THEN, BOOMERANG?

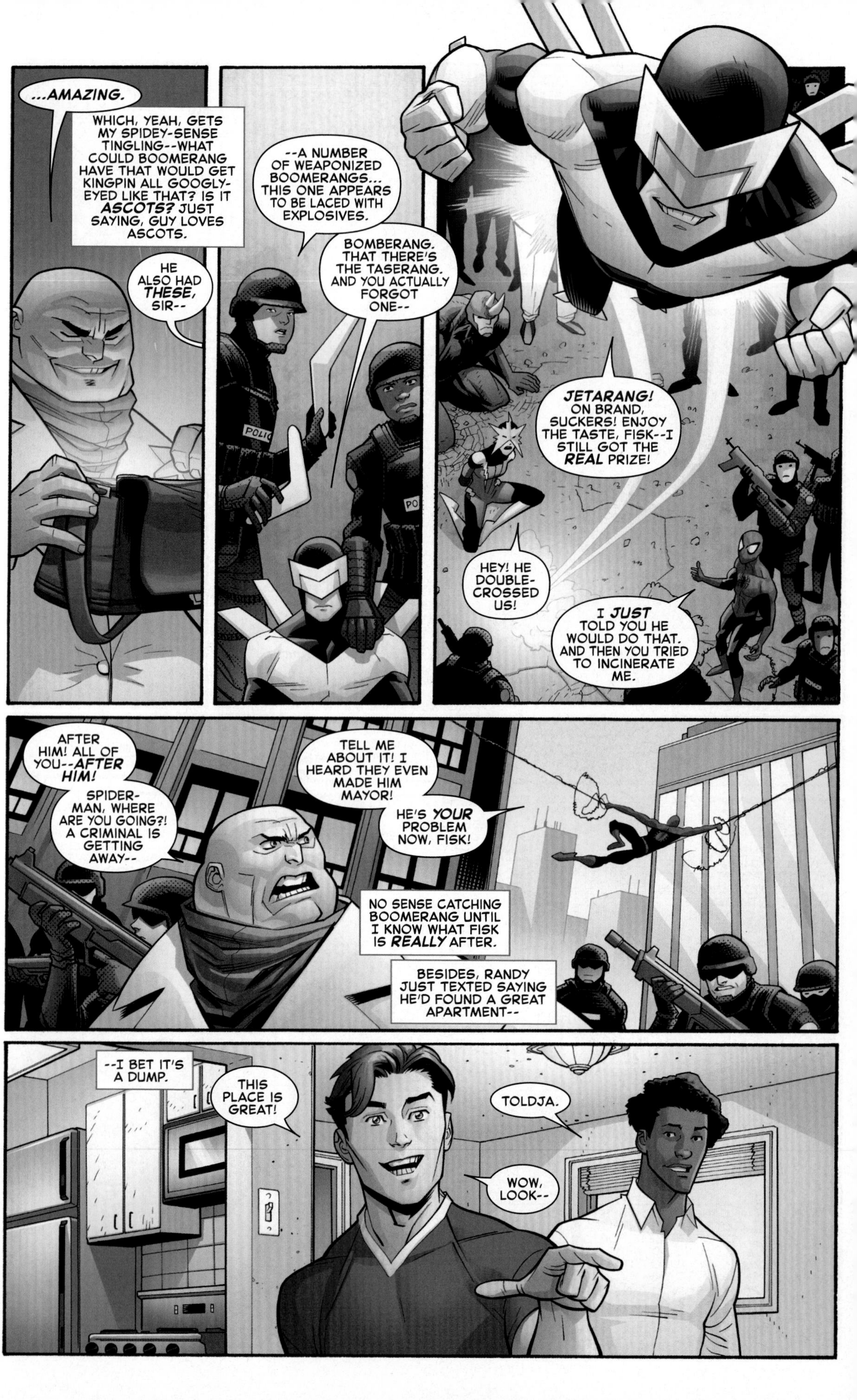
...AMAZING.
WHICH, YEAH, GETS MY SPIDEY-SENSE TINGLING--WHAT COULD BOOMERANG HAVE THAT WOULD GET KINGPIN ALL GOOGLY-EYED LIKE THAT? IS IT ASCOTS? JUST SAYING, GUY LOVES ASCOTS.
HE ALSO HAD THESE, SIR--
--A NUMBER OF WEAPONIZED BOOMERANGS... THIS ONE APPEARS TO BE LACED WITH EXPLOSIVES.
BOMBERANG. THAT THERE'S THE TASERANG. AND YOU ACTUALLY FORGOT ONE--
JETARANG! ON BRAND, SUCKERS! ENJOY THE TASTE, FISK--I STILL GOT THE REAL PRIZE!
HEY! HE DOUBLE-CROSSED US!
I JUST TOLD YOU HE WOULD DO THAT. AND THEN YOU TRIED TO INCINERATE ME.
AFTER HIM! ALL OF YOU--AFTER HIM!
SPIDER-MAN, WHERE ARE YOU GOING?! A CRIMINAL IS GETTING AWAY--
TELL ME ABOUT IT! I HEARD THEY EVEN MADE HIM MAYOR!
HE'S YOUR PROBLEM NOW, FISK!
NO SENSE CATCHING BOOMERANG UNTIL I KNOW WHAT FISK IS REALLY AFTER.
BESIDES, RANDY JUST TEXTED SAYING HE'D FOUND A GREAT APARTMENT--
--I BET IT'S A DUMP.
THIS PLACE IS GREAT!
TOLDJA.
WOW, LOOK--

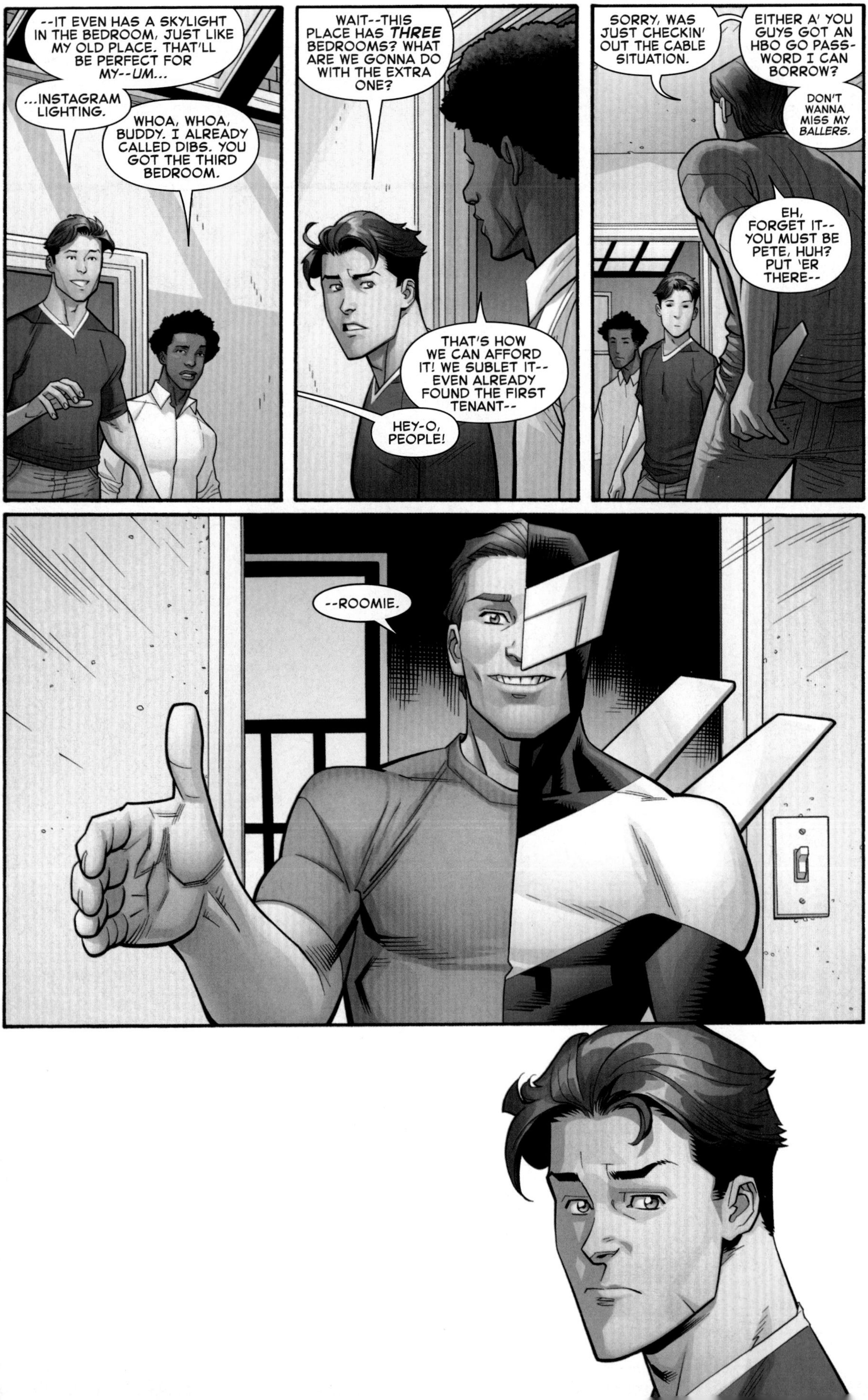
--IT EVEN HAS A SKYLIGHT IN THE BEDROOM, JUST LIKE MY OLD PLACE. THAT'LL BE PERFECT FOR MY--UM...
...INSTAGRAM LIGHTING.
WHOA, WHOA, BUDDY. I ALREADY CALLED DIBS. YOU GOT THE THIRD BEDROOM.
WAIT--THIS PLACE HAS THREE BEDROOMS? WHAT ARE WE GONNA DO WITH THE EXTRA ONE?
THAT'S HOW WE CAN AFFORD IT! WE SUBLET IT--EVEN ALREADY FOUND THE FIRST TENANT--
HEY-O, PEOPLE!
SORRY, WAS JUST CHECKIN' OUT THE CABLE SITUATION.
EITHER A' YOU GUYS GOT AN HBO GO PASS-WORD I CAN BORROW?
DON'T WANNA MISS MY BALLERS.
EH, FORGET IT--YOU MUST BE PETE, HUH? PUT 'ER THERE--
--ROOMIE.

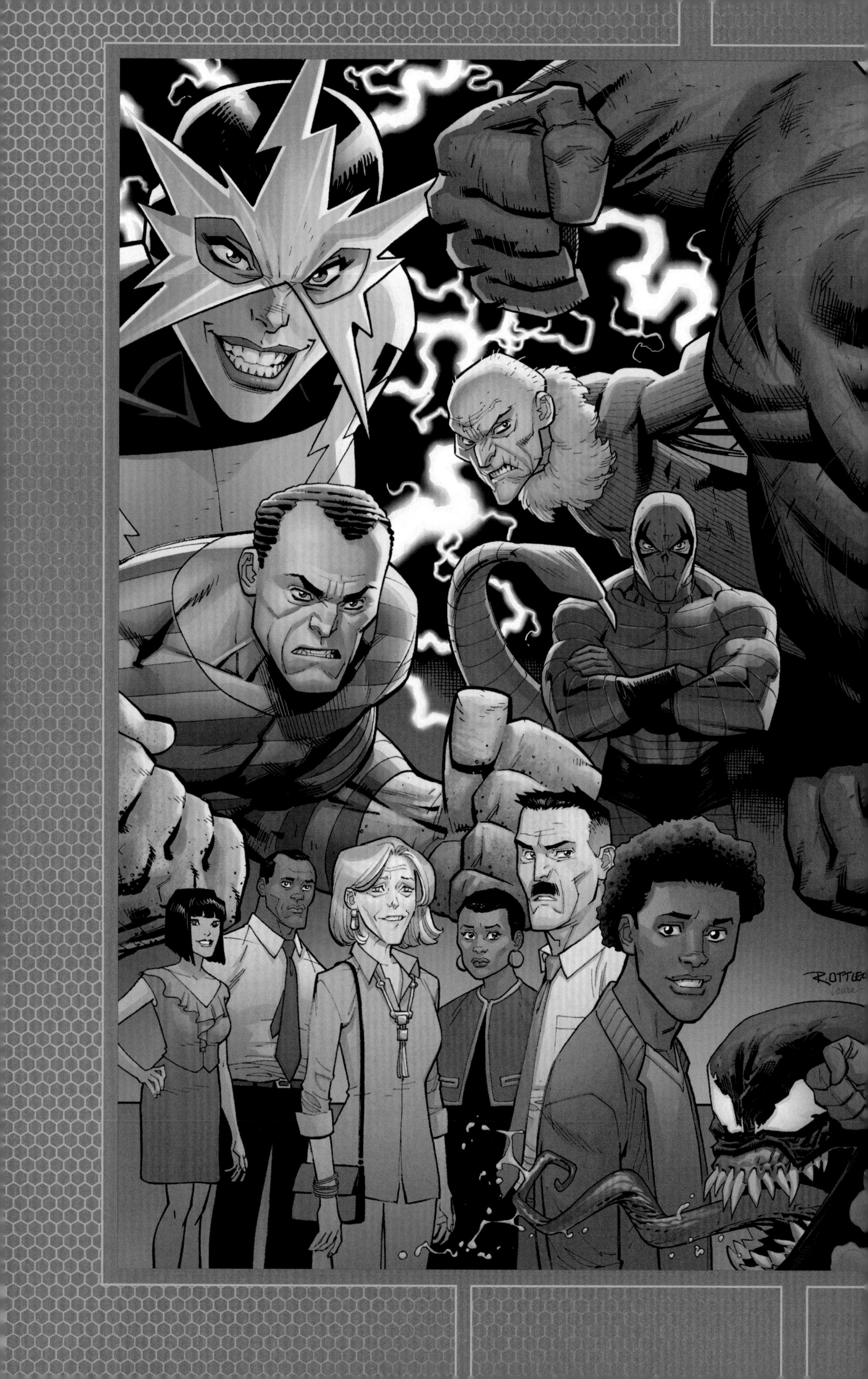

1

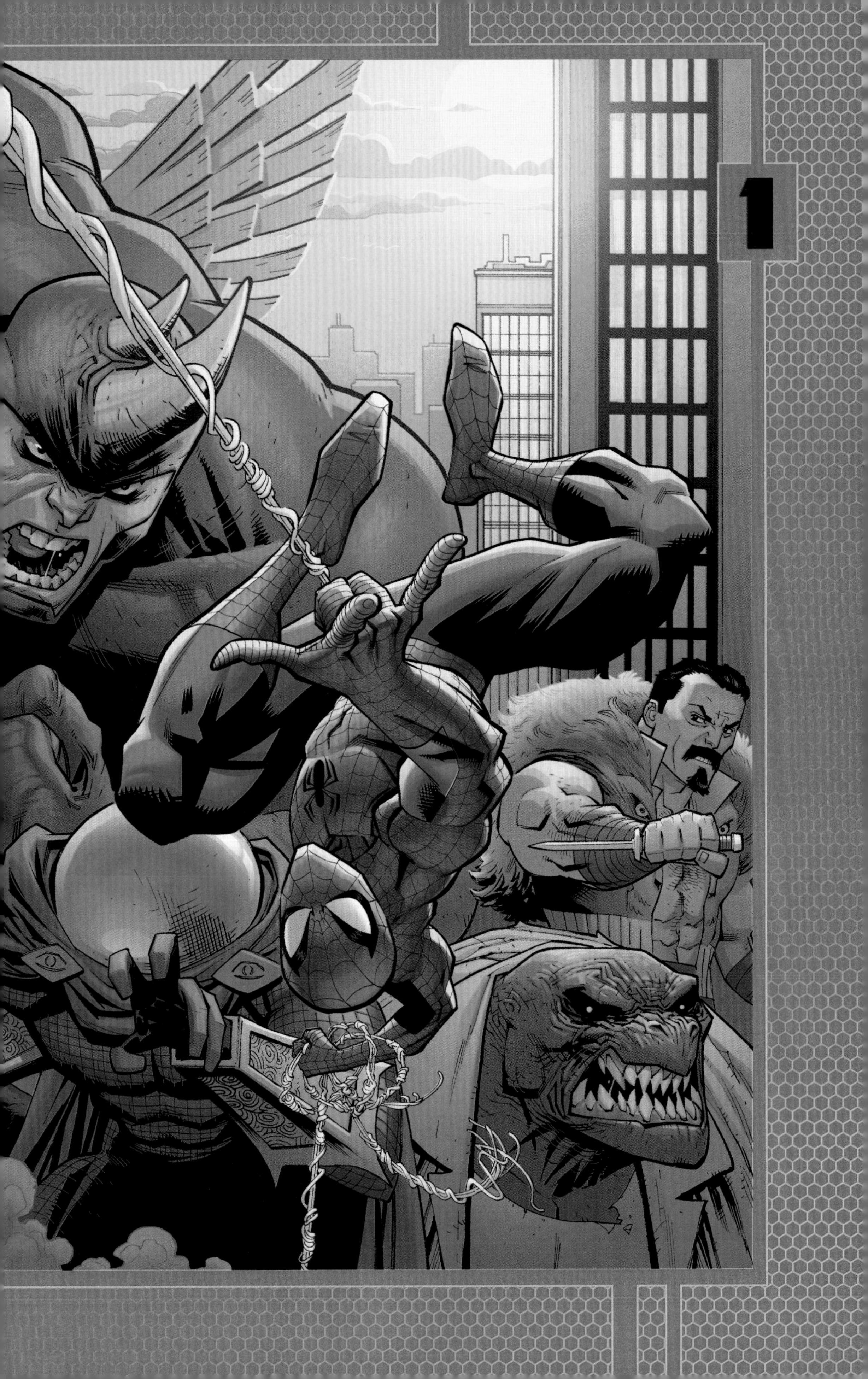

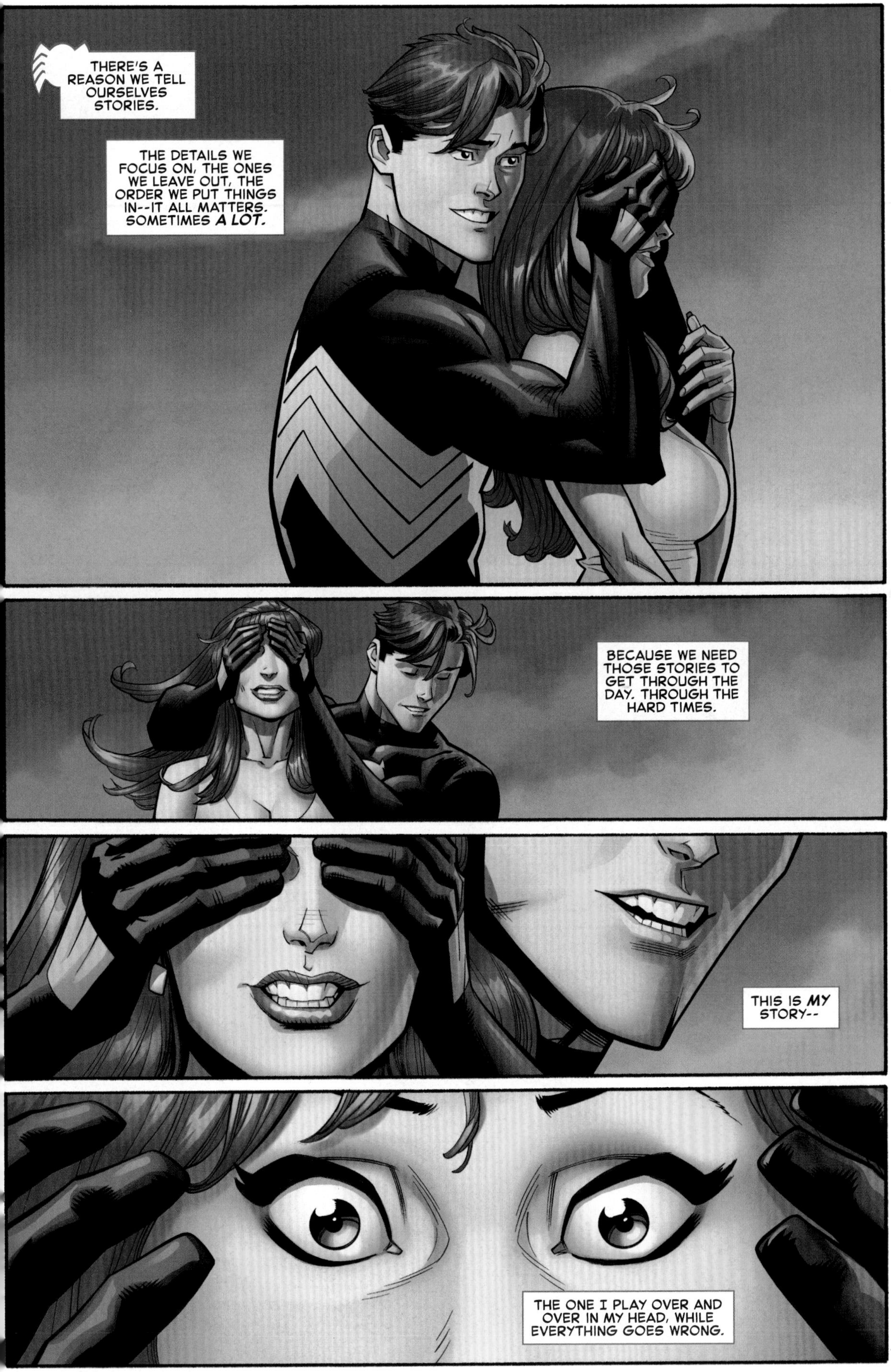
THERE'S A REASON WE TELL OURSELVES STORIES.
THE DETAILS WE FOCUS ON, THE ONES WE LEAVE OUT, THE ORDER WE PUT THINGS IN--IT ALL MATTERS. SOMETIMES *A LOT.*
BECAUSE WE NEED THOSE STORIES TO GET THROUGH THE DAY. THROUGH THE HARD TIMES.
THIS IS *MY* STORY--
THE ONE I PLAY OVER AND OVER IN MY HEAD, WHILE EVERYTHING GOES WRONG.

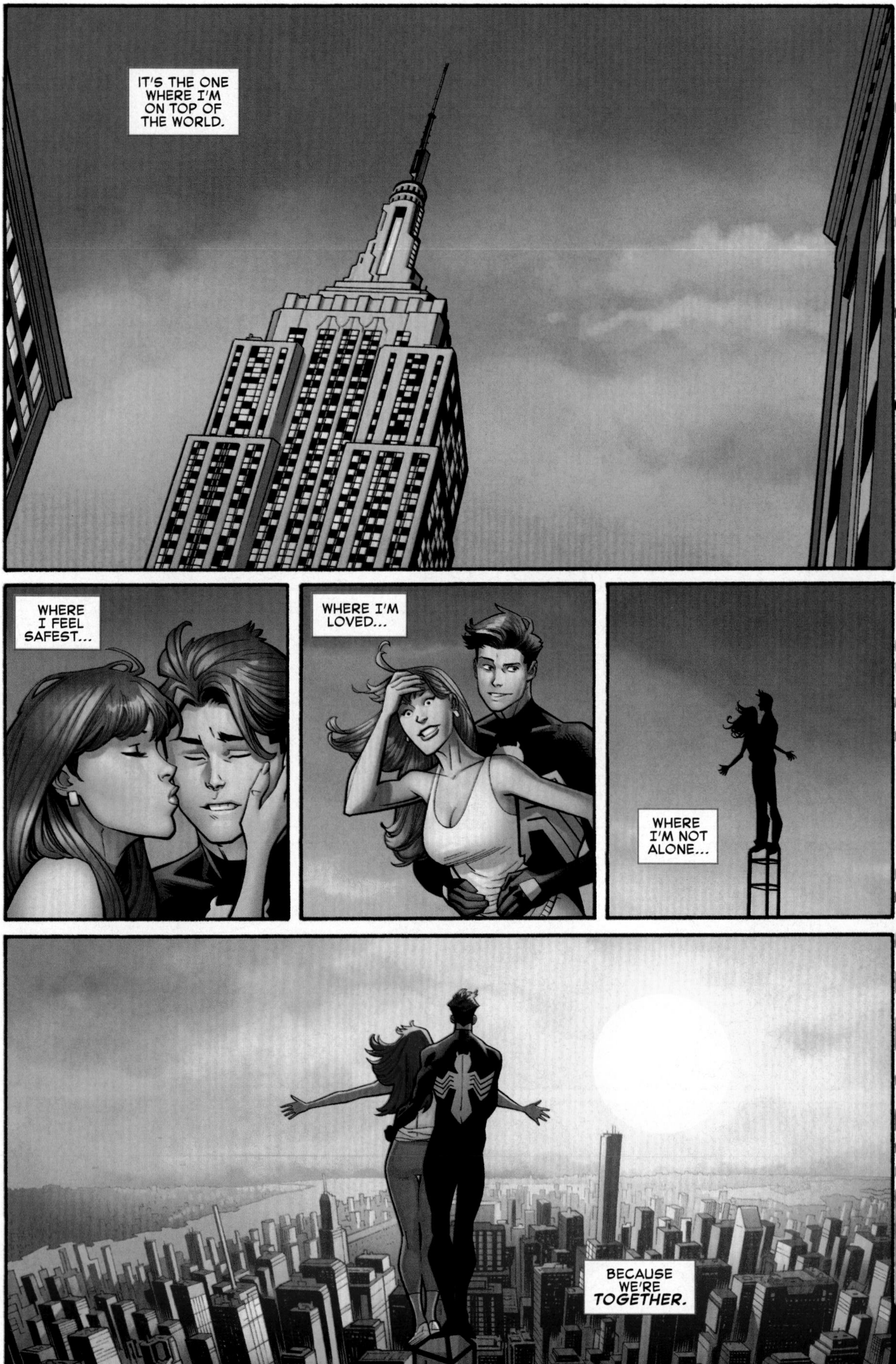
IT'S THE ONE WHERE I'M ON TOP OF THE WORLD.
WHERE I FEEL SAFEST...
WHERE I'M LOVED...
WHERE I'M NOT ALONE...
BECAUSE WE'RE TOGETHER.

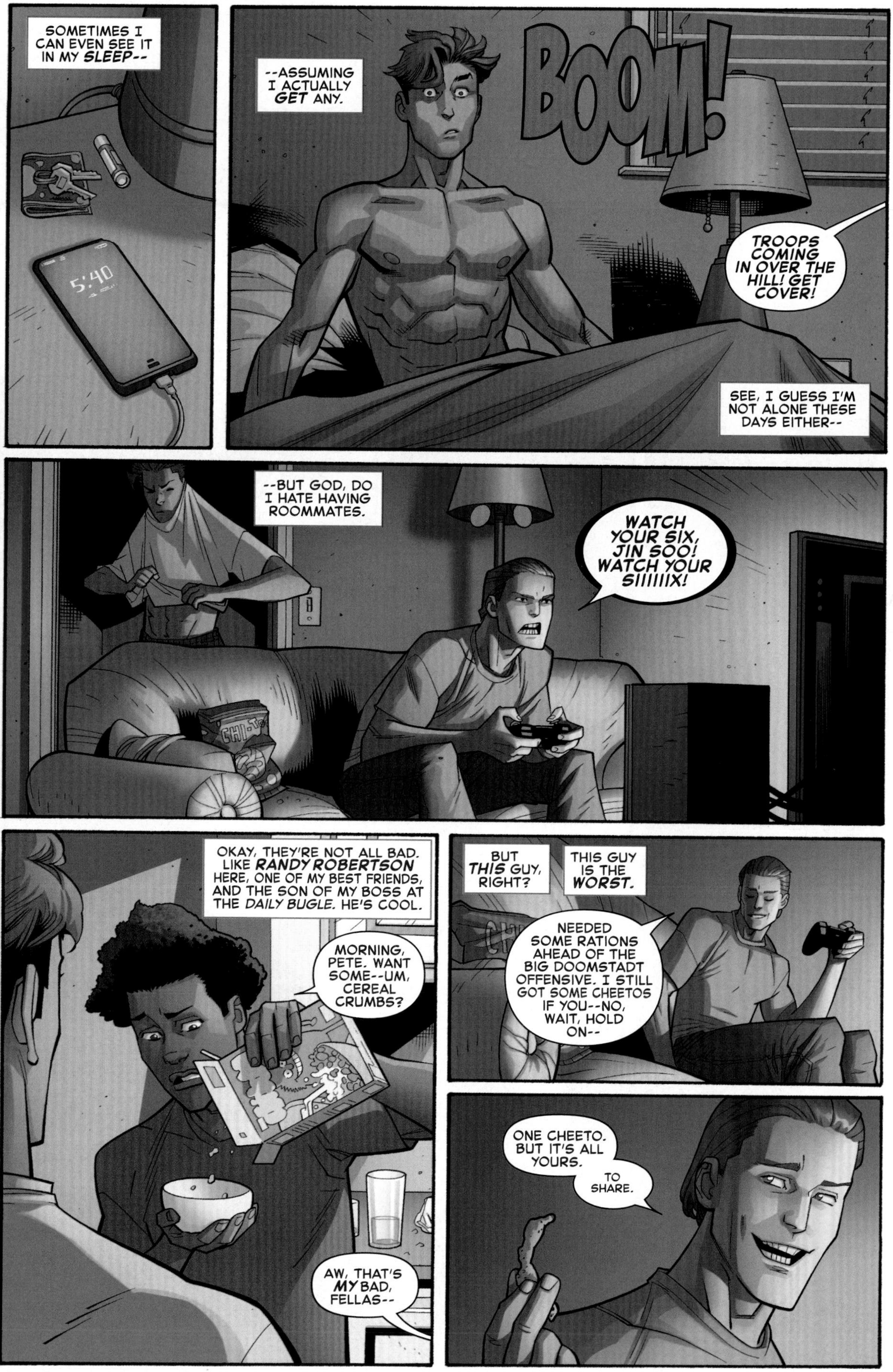

SOMETIMES I CAN EVEN SEE IT IN MY SLEEP--
5:40
--ASSUMING I ACTUALLY GET ANY.
BOOM!
TROOPS COMING IN OVER THE HILL! GET COVER!
SEE, I GUESS I'M NOT ALONE THESE DAYS EITHER--
--BUT GOD, DO I HATE HAVING ROOMMATES.
WATCH YOUR SIX, JIN SOO! WATCH YOUR SIIIIIIX!
OKAY, THEY'RE NOT ALL BAD. LIKE RANDY ROBERTSON HERE, ONE OF MY BEST FRIENDS, AND THE SON OF MY BOSS AT THE DAILY BUGLE. HE'S COOL.
MORNING, PETE. WANT SOME--UM, CEREAL CRUMBS?
AW, THAT'S MY BAD, FELLAS--
BUT THIS GUY, RIGHT?
THIS GUY IS THE WORST.
NEEDED SOME RATIONS AHEAD OF THE BIG DOOMSTADT OFFENSIVE. I STILL GOT SOME CHEETOS IF YOU--NO, WAIT, HOLD ON--
ONE CHEETO. BUT IT'S ALL YOURS.
TO SHARE.

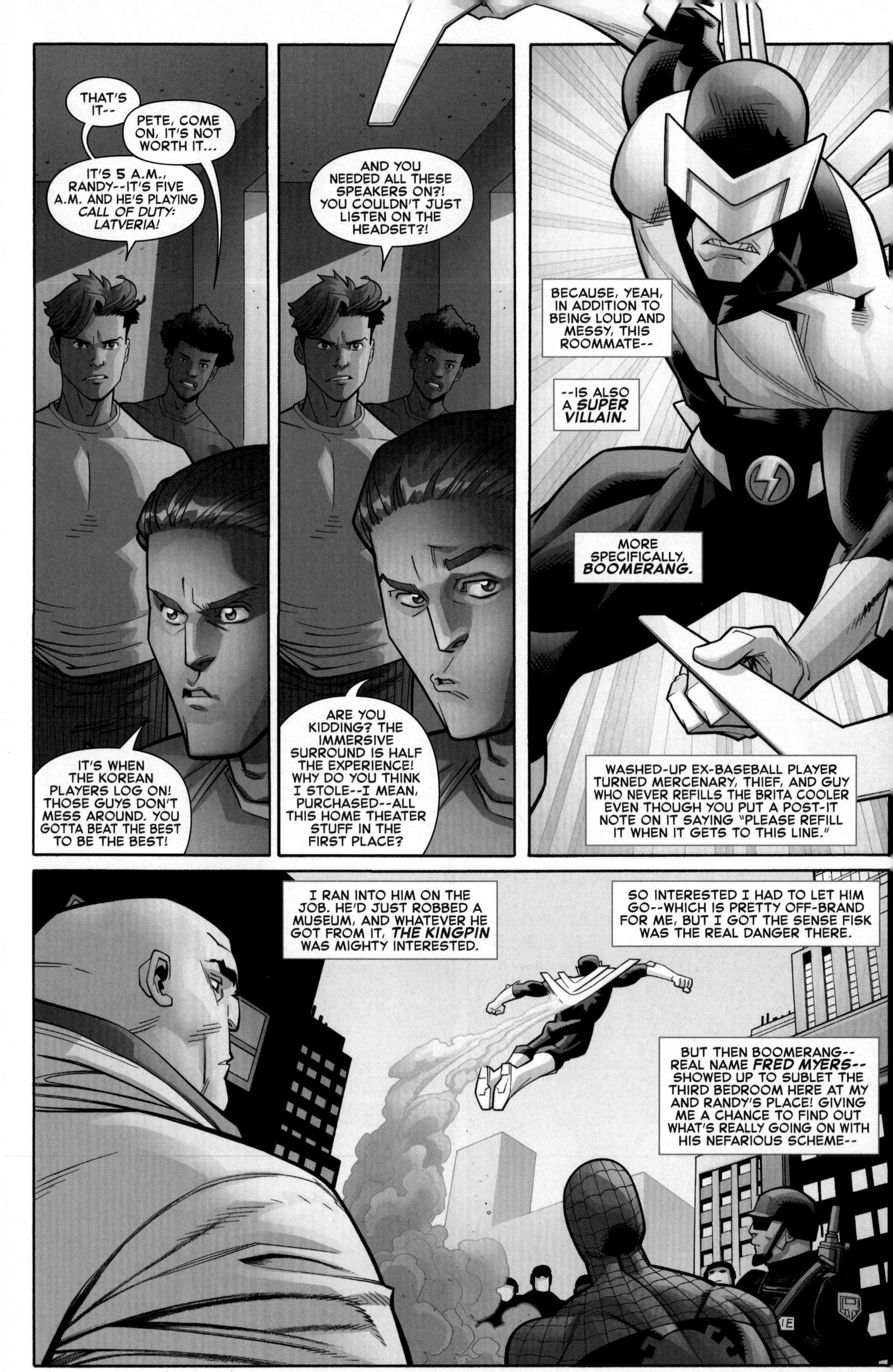
THAT'S IT--
PETE, COME ON, IT'S NOT WORTH IT...
IT'S 5 A.M., RANDY--IT'S FIVE A.M. AND HE'S PLAYING CALL OF DUTY: LATVERIA!
IT'S WHEN THE KOREAN PLAYERS LOG ON! THOSE GUYS DON'T MESS AROUND. YOU GOTTA BEAT THE BEST TO BE THE BEST!
AND YOU NEEDED ALL THESE SPEAKERS ON?! YOU COULDN'T JUST LISTEN ON THE HEADSET?!
ARE YOU KIDDING? THE IMMERSIVE SURROUND IS HALF THE EXPERIENCE! WHY DO YOU THINK I STOLE--I MEAN, PURCHASED--ALL THIS HOME THEATER STUFF IN THE FIRST PLACE?
BECAUSE, YEAH, IN ADDITION TO BEING LOUD AND MESSY, THIS ROOMMATE--
--IS ALSO A SUPER VILLAIN.
MORE SPECIFICALLY, BOOMERANG.
WASHED-UP EX-BASEBALL PLAYER TURNED MERCENARY, THIEF, AND GUY WHO NEVER REFILLS THE BRITA COOLER EVEN THOUGH YOU PUT A POST-IT NOTE ON IT SAYING "PLEASE REFILL IT WHEN IT GETS TO THIS LINE."
I RAN INTO HIM ON THE JOB. HE'D JUST ROBBED A MUSEUM, AND WHATEVER HE GOT FROM IT, THE KINGPIN WAS MIGHTY INTERESTED.
SO INTERESTED I HAD TO LET HIM GO--WHICH IS PRETTY OFF-BRAND FOR ME, BUT I GOT THE SENSE FISK WAS THE REAL DANGER THERE.
BUT THEN BOOMERANG--REAL NAME FRED MYERS--SHOWED UP TO SUBLET THE THIRD BEDROOM HERE AT MY AND RANDY'S PLACE! GIVING ME A CHANCE TO FIND OUT WHAT'S REALLY GOING ON WITH HIS NEFARIOUS SCHEME--

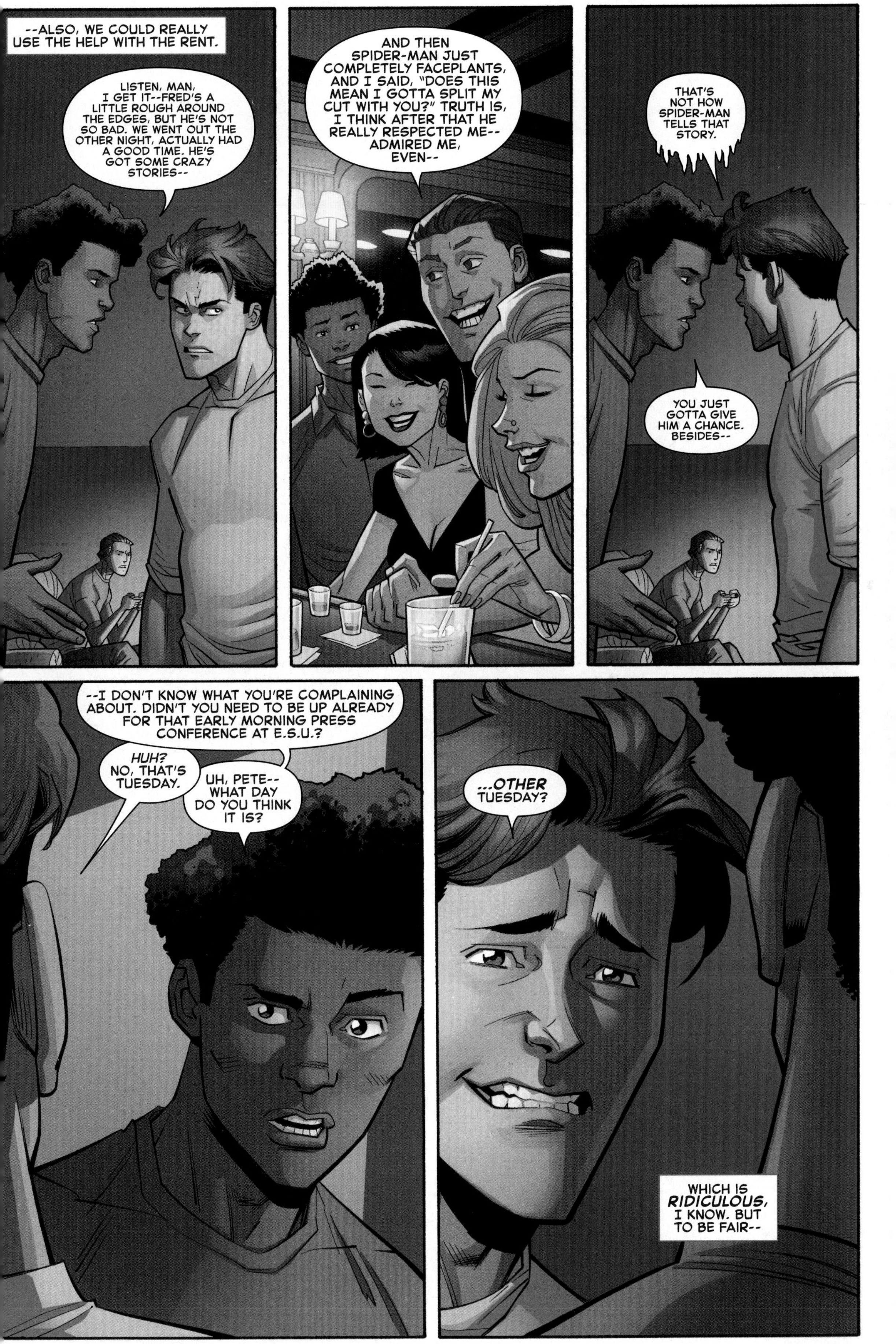
--ALSO, WE COULD REALLY USE THE HELP WITH THE RENT.
LISTEN, MAN, I GET IT--FRED'S A LITTLE ROUGH AROUND THE EDGES, BUT HE'S NOT SO BAD. WE WENT OUT THE OTHER NIGHT, ACTUALLY HAD A GOOD TIME. HE'S GOT SOME CRAZY STORIES--
AND THEN SPIDER-MAN JUST COMPLETELY FACEPLANTS, AND I SAID, "DOES THIS MEAN I GOTTA SPLIT MY CUT WITH YOU?" TRUTH IS, I THINK AFTER THAT HE REALLY RESPECTED ME--ADMIRED ME, EVEN--
THAT'S NOT HOW SPIDER-MAN TELLS THAT STORY.
YOU JUST GOTTA GIVE HIM A CHANCE. BESIDES--
--I DON'T KNOW WHAT YOU'RE COMPLAINING ABOUT. DIDN'T YOU NEED TO BE UP ALREADY FOR THAT EARLY MORNING PRESS CONFERENCE AT E.S.U.?
HUH? NO, THAT'S TUESDAY.
UH, PETE--WHAT DAY DO YOU THINK IT IS?
...OTHER TUESDAY?
WHICH IS RIDICULOUS, I KNOW. BUT TO BE FAIR--

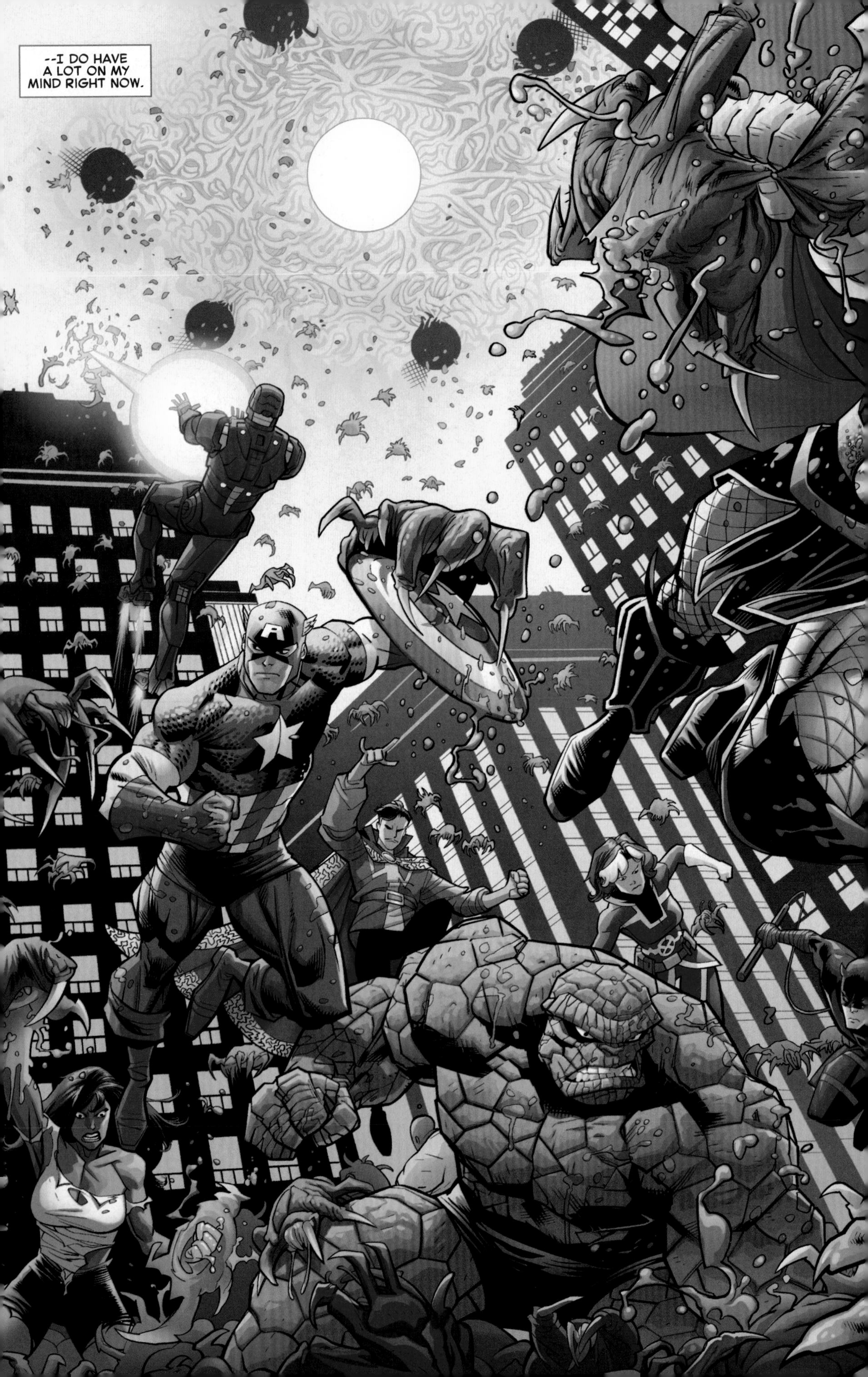
--I DO HAVE A LOT ON MY MIND RIGHT NOW.

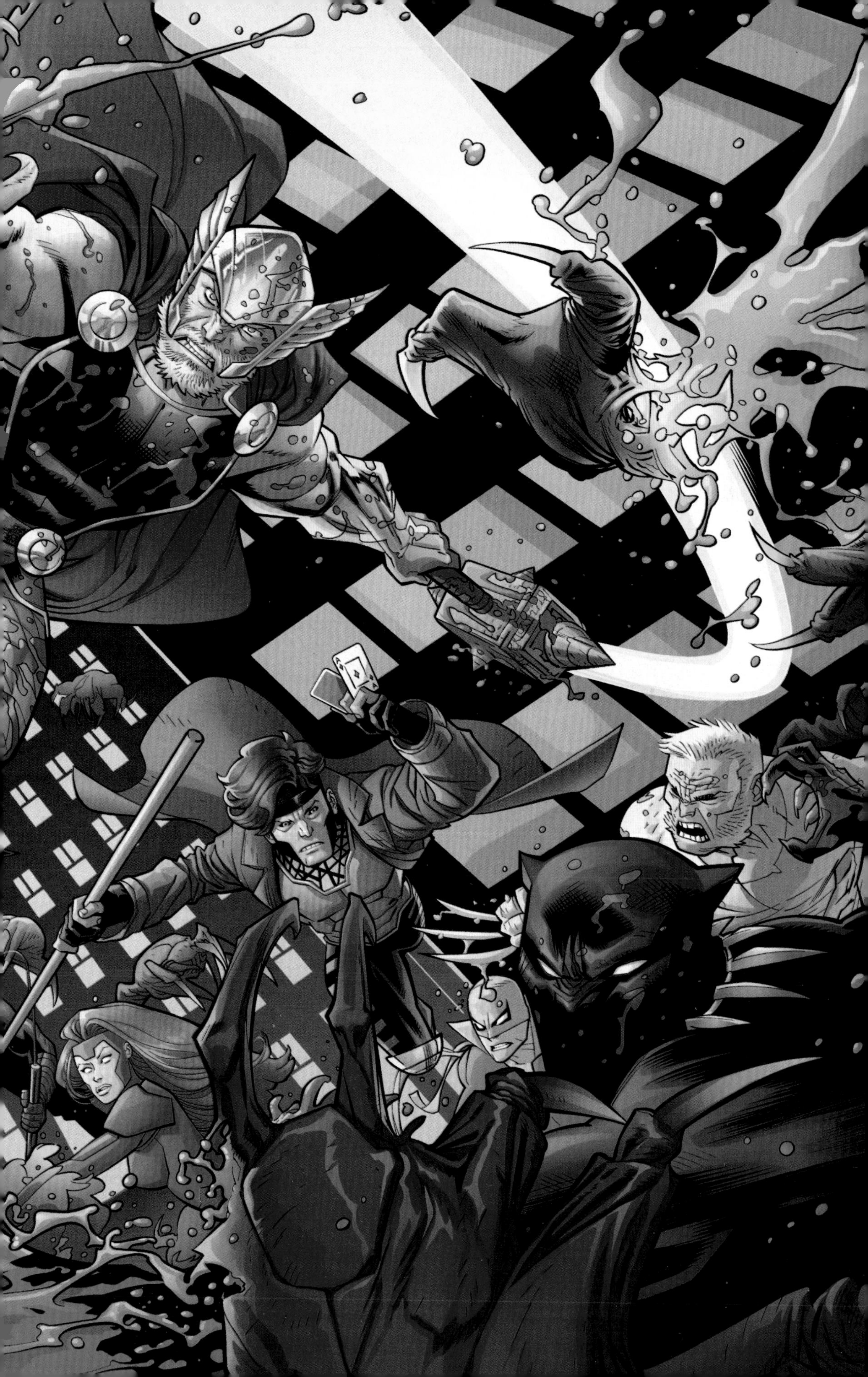

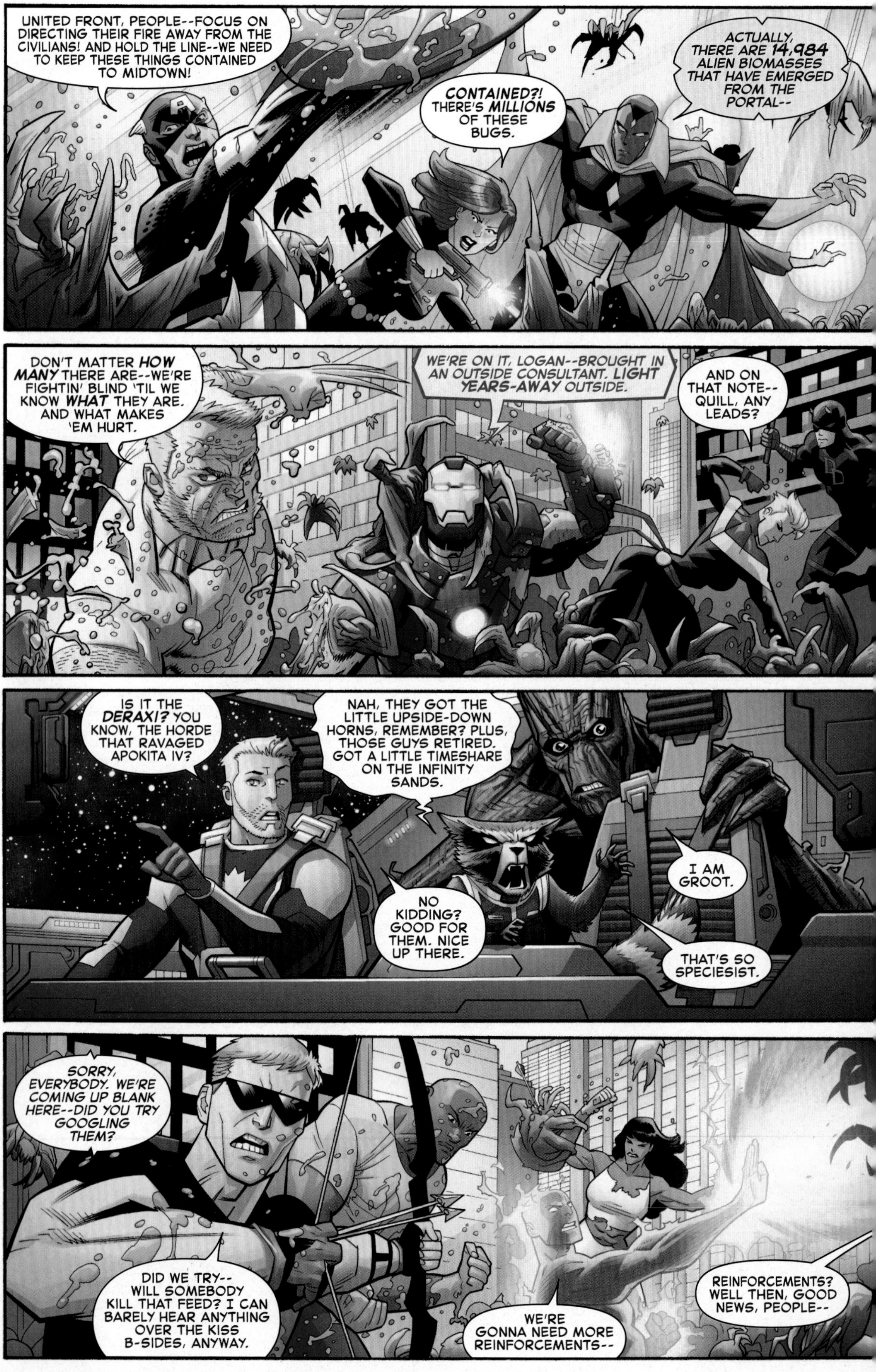

UNITED FRONT, PEOPLE--FOCUS ON DIRECTING THEIR FIRE AWAY FROM THE CIVILIANS! AND HOLD THE LINE--WE NEED TO KEEP THESE THINGS CONTAINED TO MIDTOWN!
CONTAINED?! THERE'S MILLIONS OF THESE BUGS.
ACTUALLY, THERE ARE 14,984 ALIEN BIOMASSES THAT HAVE EMERGED FROM THE PORTAL--
DON'T MATTER HOW MANY THERE ARE--WE'RE FIGHTIN' BLIND 'TIL WE KNOW WHAT THEY ARE. AND WHAT MAKES 'EM HURT.
WE'RE ON IT, LOGAN--BROUGHT IN AN OUTSIDE CONSULTANT. LIGHT YEARS-AWAY OUTSIDE.
AND ON THAT NOTE-- QUILL, ANY LEADS?
IS IT THE DERAXI? YOU KNOW, THE HORDE THAT RAVAGED APOKITA IV?
NAH, THEY GOT THE LITTLE UPSIDE-DOWN HORNS, REMEMBER? PLUS, THOSE GUYS RETIRED. GOT A LITTLE TIMESHARE ON THE INFINITY SANDS.
NO KIDDING? GOOD FOR THEM. NICE UP THERE.
I AM GROOT.
THAT'S SO SPECIESIST.
SORRY, EVERYBODY. WE'RE COMING UP BLANK HERE--DID YOU TRY GOOGLING THEM?
DID WE TRY-- WILL SOMEBODY KILL THAT FEED? I CAN BARELY HEAR ANYTHING OVER THE KISS B-SIDES, ANYWAY.
WE'RE GONNA NEED MORE REINFORCEMENTS--
REINFORCEMENTS? WELL THEN, GOOD NEWS, PEOPLE--

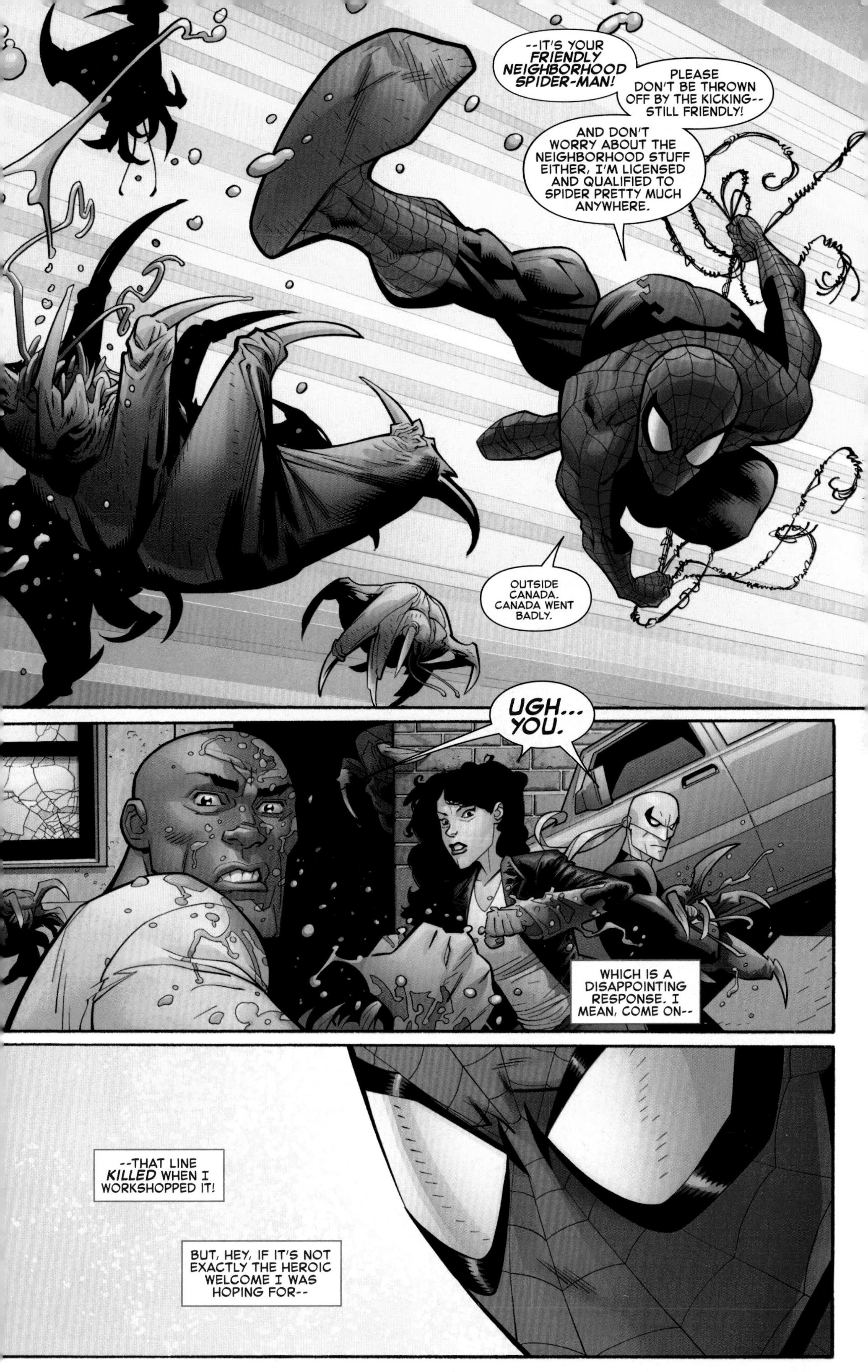
--IT'S YOUR *FRIENDLY NEIGHBORHOOD SPIDER-MAN!*
PLEASE DON'T BE THROWN OFF BY THE KICKING-- STILL FRIENDLY!
AND DON'T WORRY ABOUT THE NEIGHBORHOOD STUFF EITHER, I'M LICENSED AND QUALIFIED TO SPIDER PRETTY MUCH ANYWHERE.
OUTSIDE CANADA. CANADA WENT BADLY.
UGH... YOU.
WHICH IS A DISAPPOINTING RESPONSE. I MEAN, COME ON--
--THAT LINE *KILLED* WHEN I WORKSHOPPED IT!
BUT, HEY, IF IT'S NOT EXACTLY THE HEROIC WELCOME I WAS HOPING FOR--

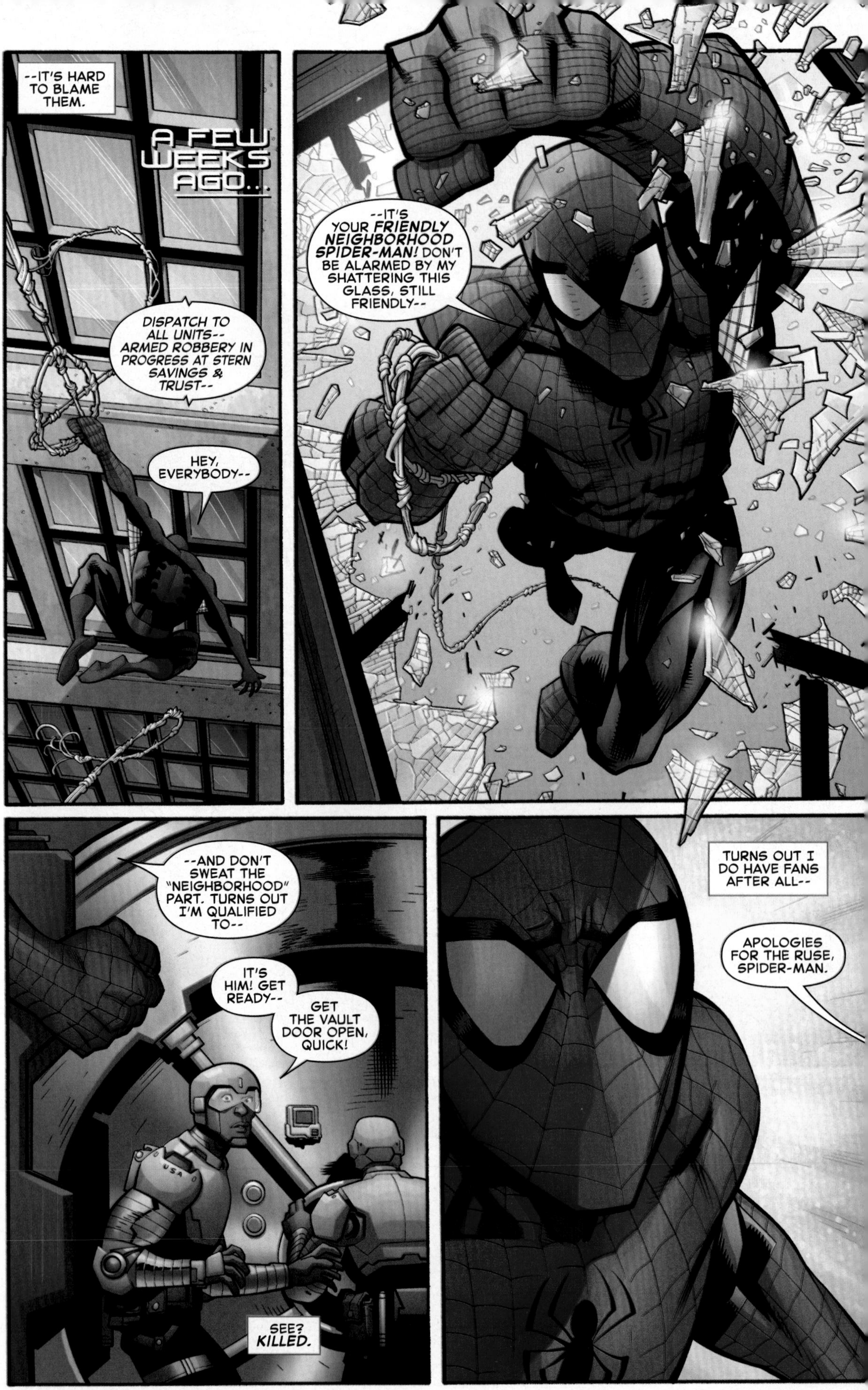
--IT'S HARD TO BLAME THEM.
A FEW WEEKS AGO...
DISPATCH TO ALL UNITS-- ARMED ROBBERY IN PROGRESS AT STERN SAVINGS & TRUST--
HEY, EVERYBODY--
--IT'S YOUR FRIENDLY NEIGHBORHOOD SPIDER-MAN! DON'T BE ALARMED BY MY SHATTERING THIS GLASS, STILL FRIENDLY--
--AND DON'T SWEAT THE "NEIGHBORHOOD" PART. TURNS OUT I'M QUALIFIED TO--
IT'S HIM! GET READY--
GET THE VAULT DOOR OPEN, QUICK!
SEE? KILLED.
TURNS OUT I DO HAVE FANS AFTER ALL--
APOLOGIES FOR THE RUSE, SPIDER-MAN.

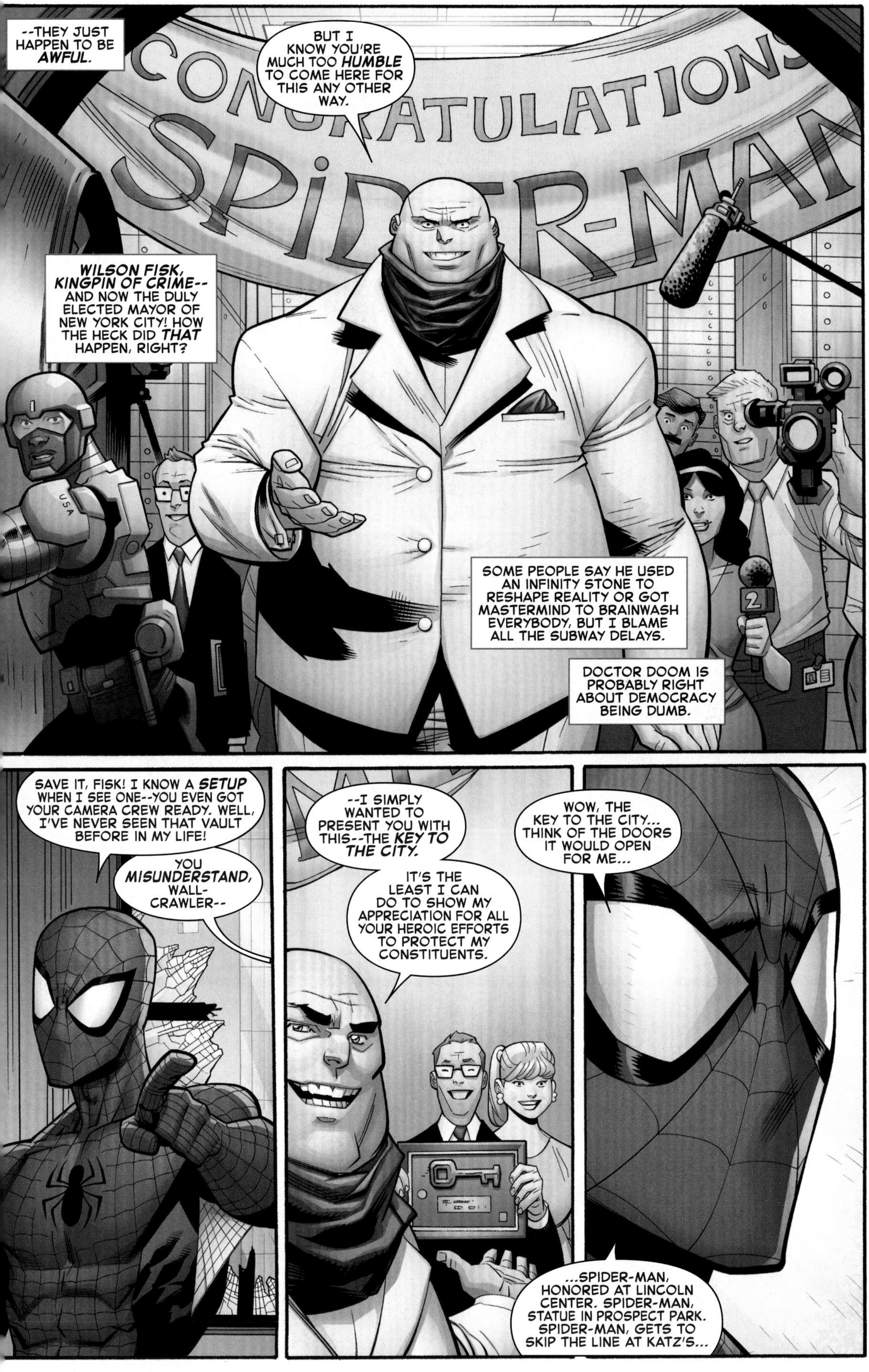
--THEY JUST HAPPEN TO BE AWFUL.
BUT I KNOW YOU'RE MUCH TOO HUMBLE TO COME HERE FOR THIS ANY OTHER WAY.
CONGRATULATIONS SPIDER-MAN
WILSON FISK, KINGPIN OF CRIME--AND NOW THE DULY ELECTED MAYOR OF NEW YORK CITY! HOW THE HECK DID THAT HAPPEN, RIGHT?
SOME PEOPLE SAY HE USED AN INFINITY STONE TO RESHAPE REALITY OR GOT MASTERMIND TO BRAINWASH EVERYBODY, BUT I BLAME ALL THE SUBWAY DELAYS.
DOCTOR DOOM IS PROBABLY RIGHT ABOUT DEMOCRACY BEING DUMB.
SAVE IT, FISK! I KNOW A SETUP WHEN I SEE ONE--YOU EVEN GOT YOUR CAMERA CREW READY. WELL, I'VE NEVER SEEN THAT VAULT BEFORE IN MY LIFE!
YOU MISUNDERSTAND, WALL-CRAWLER--
--I SIMPLY WANTED TO PRESENT YOU WITH THIS--THE KEY TO THE CITY.
IT'S THE LEAST I CAN DO TO SHOW MY APPRECIATION FOR ALL YOUR HEROIC EFFORTS TO PROTECT MY CONSTITUENTS.
WOW, THE KEY TO THE CITY... THINK OF THE DOORS IT WOULD OPEN FOR ME...
...SPIDER-MAN, HONORED AT LINCOLN CENTER. SPIDER-MAN, STATUE IN PROSPECT PARK. SPIDER-MAN, GETS TO SKIP THE LINE AT KATZ'S...

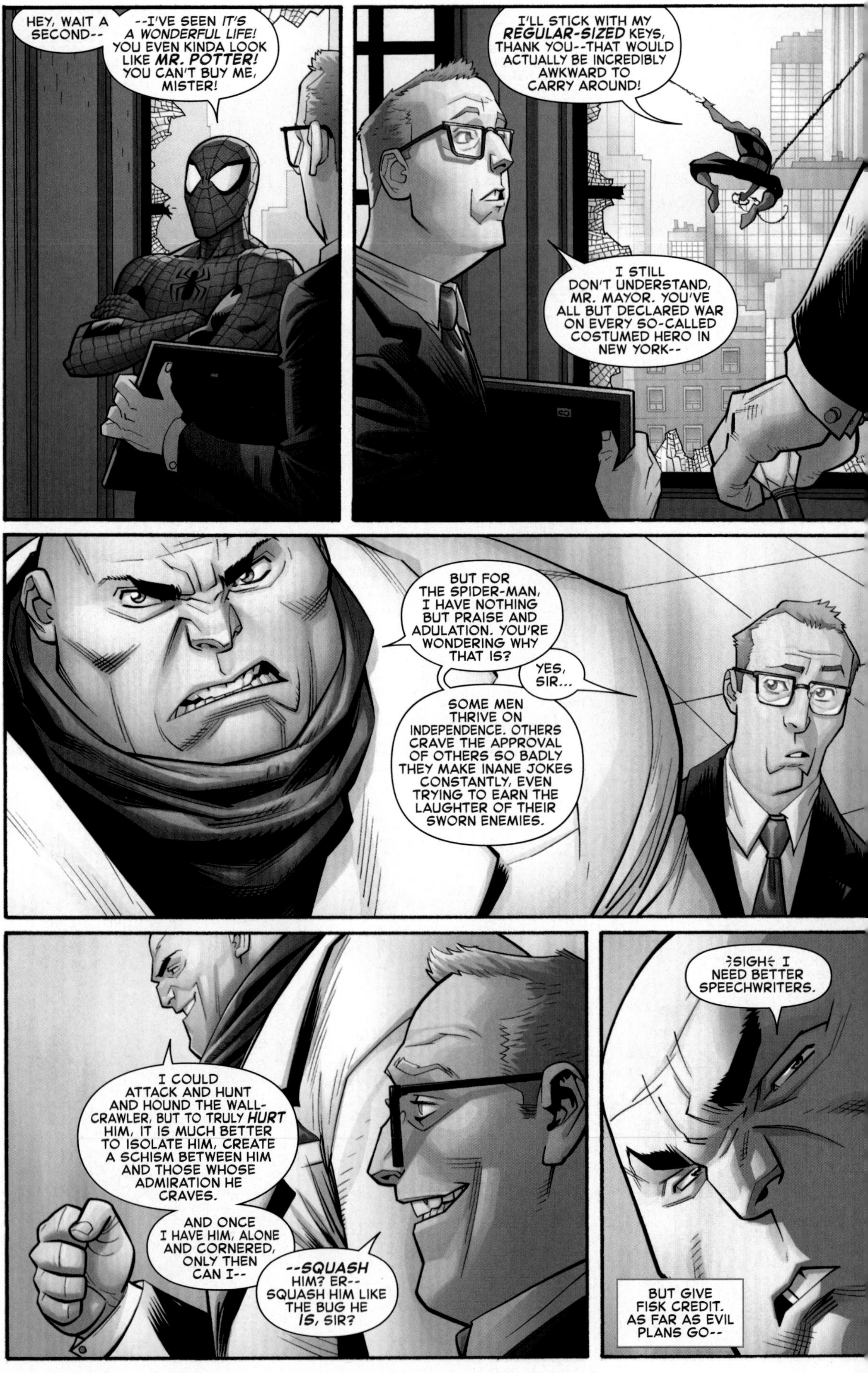

HEY, WAIT A SECOND--
--I'VE SEEN *IT'S A WONDERFUL LIFE!* YOU EVEN KINDA LOOK LIKE **MR. POTTER!** YOU CAN'T BUY ME, MISTER!
I'LL STICK WITH MY **REGULAR-SIZED** KEYS, THANK YOU--THAT WOULD ACTUALLY BE INCREDIBLY AWKWARD TO CARRY AROUND!
I STILL DON'T UNDERSTAND, MR. MAYOR. YOU'VE ALL BUT DECLARED WAR ON EVERY SO-CALLED COSTUMED HERO IN NEW YORK--
BUT FOR THE SPIDER-MAN, I HAVE NOTHING BUT PRAISE AND ADULATION. YOU'RE WONDERING WHY THAT IS?
YES, SIR...
SOME MEN THRIVE ON INDEPENDENCE. OTHERS CRAVE THE APPROVAL OF OTHERS SO BADLY THEY MAKE INANE JOKES CONSTANTLY, EVEN TRYING TO EARN THE LAUGHTER OF THEIR SWORN ENEMIES.
I COULD ATTACK AND HUNT AND HOUND THE WALL-CRAWLER, BUT TO TRULY **HURT** HIM, IT IS MUCH BETTER TO ISOLATE HIM, CREATE A SCHISM BETWEEN HIM AND THOSE WHOSE ADMIRATION HE CRAVES.
AND ONCE I HAVE HIM, ALONE AND CORNERED, ONLY THEN CAN I--
--SQUASH HIM? ER--SQUASH HIM LIKE THE BUG HE ***IS,*** SIR?
⸗SIGH⸗ I NEED BETTER SPEECHWRITERS.
BUT GIVE FISK CREDIT. AS FAR AS EVIL PLANS GO--

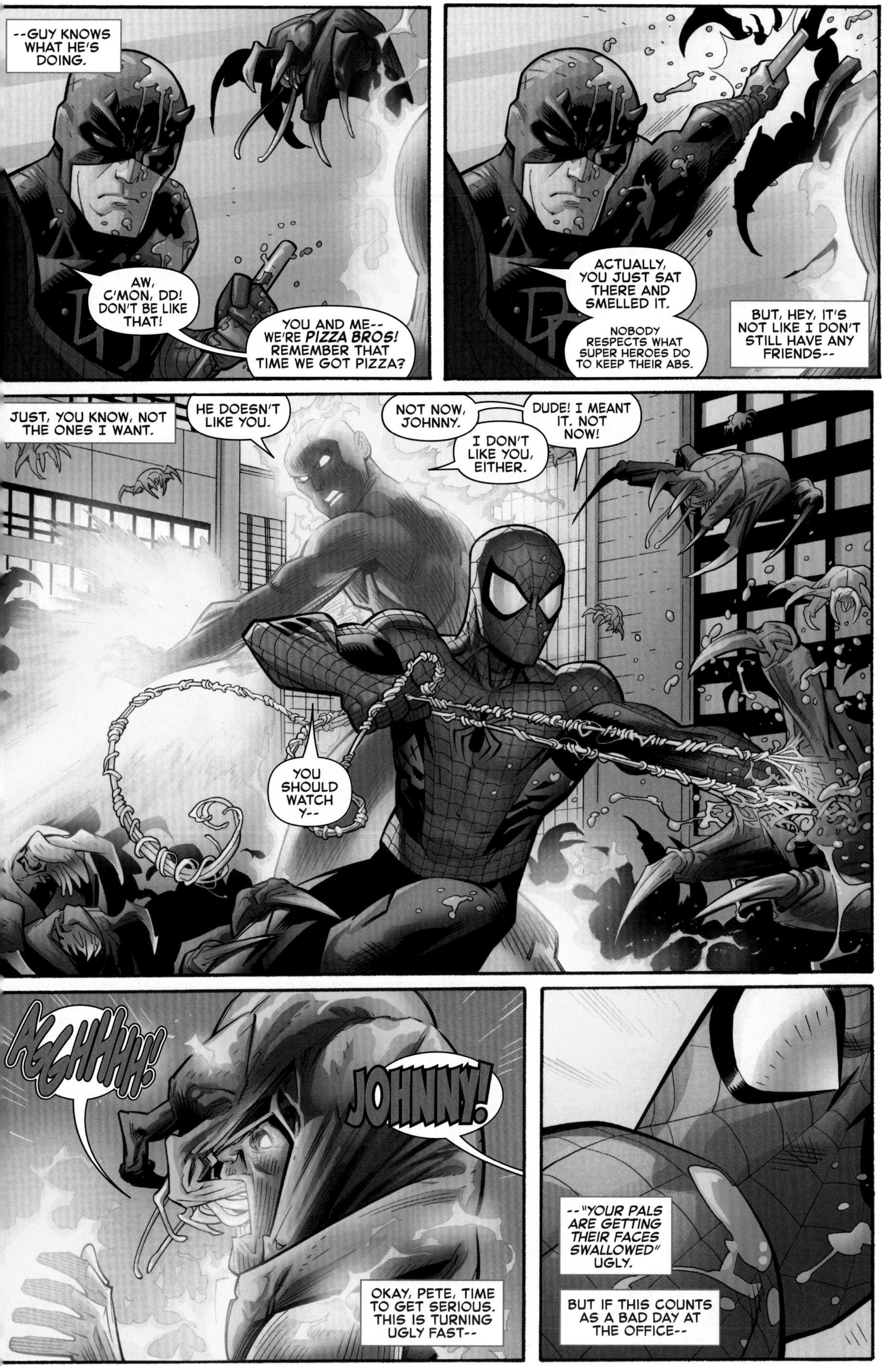
--GUY KNOWS WHAT HE'S DOING.
AW, C'MON, DD! DON'T BE LIKE THAT!
YOU AND ME--WE'RE *PIZZA BROS!* REMEMBER THAT TIME WE GOT PIZZA?
ACTUALLY, YOU JUST SAT THERE AND SMELLED IT.
NOBODY RESPECTS WHAT SUPER HEROES DO TO KEEP THEIR ABS.
BUT, HEY, IT'S NOT LIKE I DON'T STILL HAVE ANY FRIENDS--
JUST, YOU KNOW, NOT THE ONES I WANT.
HE DOESN'T LIKE YOU.
NOT NOW, JOHNNY.
I DON'T LIKE YOU, EITHER.
DUDE! I MEANT IT. NOT NOW!
YOU SHOULD WATCH Y--
AGGHHHH!
JOHNNY!
OKAY, PETE, TIME TO GET SERIOUS. THIS IS TURNING UGLY FAST--
--*"YOUR PALS ARE GETTING THEIR FACES SWALLOWED"* UGLY.
BUT IF THIS COUNTS AS A BAD DAY AT THE OFFICE--

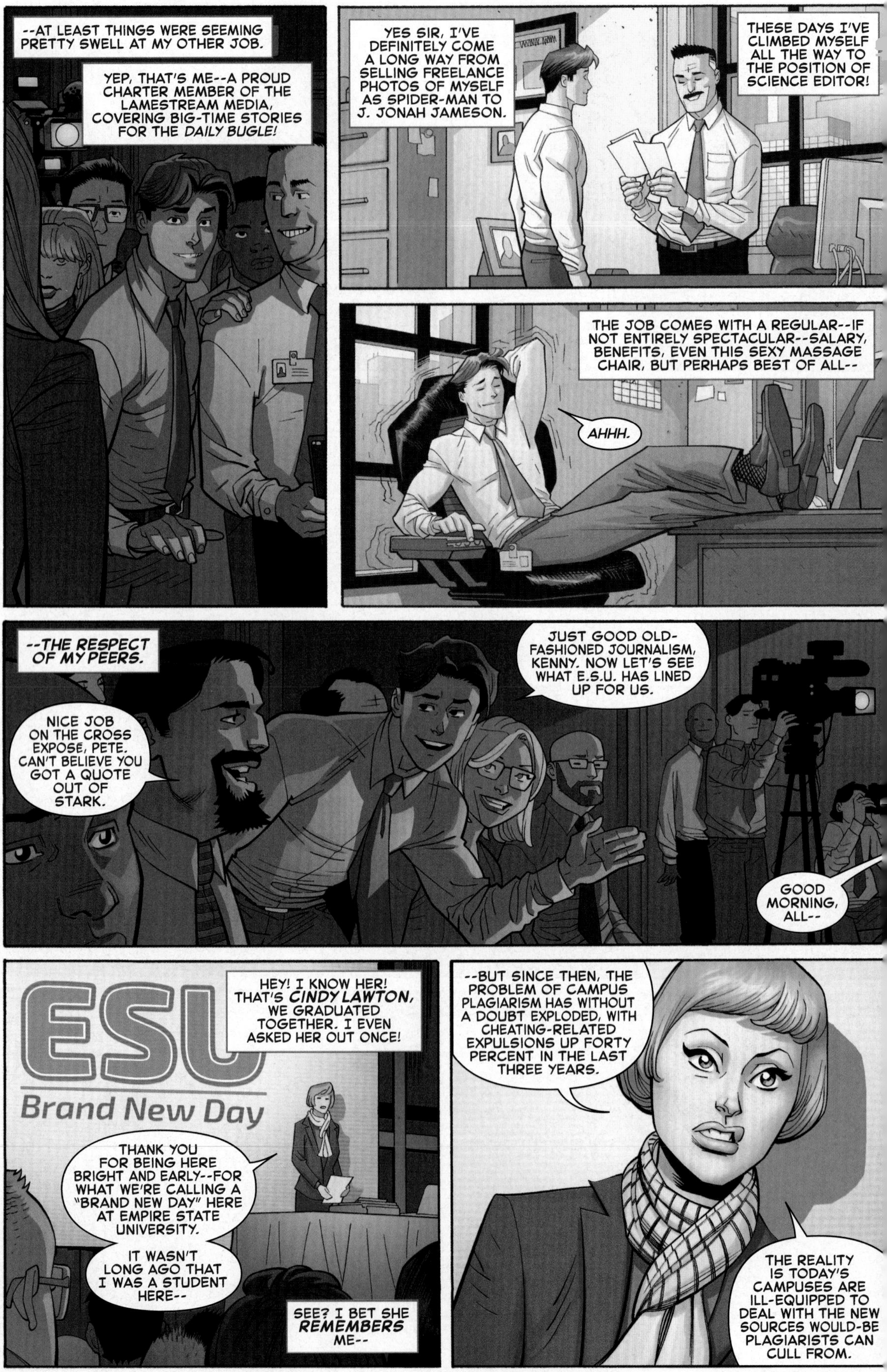
--AT LEAST THINGS WERE SEEMING PRETTY SWELL AT MY OTHER JOB.
YEP, THAT'S ME--A PROUD CHARTER MEMBER OF THE LAMESTREAM MEDIA, COVERING BIG-TIME STORIES FOR THE *DAILY BUGLE!*
YES SIR, I'VE DEFINITELY COME A LONG WAY FROM SELLING FREELANCE PHOTOS OF MYSELF AS SPIDER-MAN TO J. JONAH JAMESON.
THESE DAYS I'VE CLIMBED MYSELF ALL THE WAY TO THE POSITION OF SCIENCE EDITOR!
THE JOB COMES WITH A REGULAR--IF NOT ENTIRELY SPECTACULAR--SALARY, BENEFITS, EVEN THIS SEXY MASSAGE CHAIR, BUT PERHAPS BEST OF ALL--
AHHH.
--THE RESPECT OF MY PEERS.
NICE JOB ON THE CROSS EXPOSE, PETE. CAN'T BELIEVE YOU GOT A QUOTE OUT OF STARK.
JUST GOOD OLD-FASHIONED JOURNALISM, KENNY. NOW LET'S SEE WHAT E.S.U. HAS LINED UP FOR US.
GOOD MORNING, ALL--
ESU
Brand New Day
HEY! I KNOW HER! THAT'S *CINDY LAWTON,* WE GRADUATED TOGETHER. I EVEN ASKED HER OUT ONCE!
THANK YOU FOR BEING HERE BRIGHT AND EARLY--FOR WHAT WE'RE CALLING A "BRAND NEW DAY" HERE AT EMPIRE STATE UNIVERSITY.
IT WASN'T LONG AGO THAT I WAS A STUDENT HERE--
SEE? I BET SHE *REMEMBERS* ME--
--BUT SINCE THEN, THE PROBLEM OF CAMPUS PLAGIARISM HAS WITHOUT A DOUBT EXPLODED, WITH CHEATING-RELATED EXPULSIONS UP FORTY PERCENT IN THE LAST THREE YEARS.
THE REALITY IS TODAY'S CAMPUSES ARE ILL-EQUIPPED TO DEAL WITH THE NEW SOURCES WOULD-BE PLAGIARISTS CAN CULL FROM.

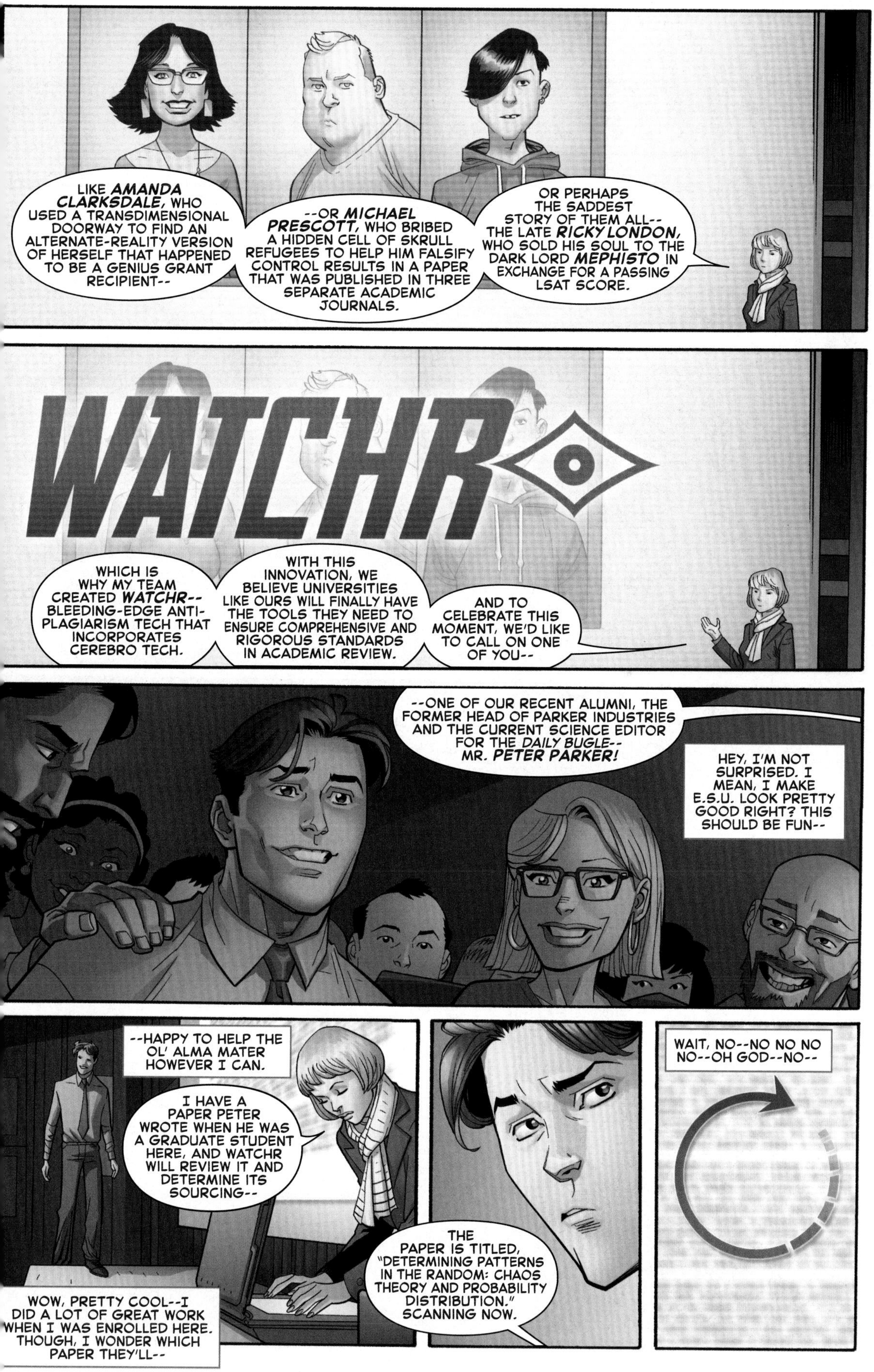
LIKE AMANDA CLARKSDALE, WHO USED A TRANSDIMENSIONAL DOORWAY TO FIND AN ALTERNATE-REALITY VERSION OF HERSELF THAT HAPPENED TO BE A GENIUS GRANT RECIPIENT--
--OR MICHAEL PRESCOTT, WHO BRIBED A HIDDEN CELL OF SKRULL REFUGEES TO HELP HIM FALSIFY CONTROL RESULTS IN A PAPER THAT WAS PUBLISHED IN THREE SEPARATE ACADEMIC JOURNALS.
OR PERHAPS THE SADDEST STORY OF THEM ALL--THE LATE RICKY LONDON, WHO SOLD HIS SOUL TO THE DARK LORD MEPHISTO IN EXCHANGE FOR A PASSING LSAT SCORE.
WATCHR
WHICH IS WHY MY TEAM CREATED WATCHR--BLEEDING-EDGE ANTI-PLAGIARISM TECH THAT INCORPORATES CEREBRO TECH.
WITH THIS INNOVATION, WE BELIEVE UNIVERSITIES LIKE OURS WILL FINALLY HAVE THE TOOLS THEY NEED TO ENSURE COMPREHENSIVE AND RIGOROUS STANDARDS IN ACADEMIC REVIEW.
AND TO CELEBRATE THIS MOMENT, WE'D LIKE TO CALL ON ONE OF YOU--
--ONE OF OUR RECENT ALUMNI, THE FORMER HEAD OF PARKER INDUSTRIES AND THE CURRENT SCIENCE EDITOR FOR THE DAILY BUGLE--MR. PETER PARKER!
HEY, I'M NOT SURPRISED. I MEAN, I MAKE E.S.U. LOOK PRETTY GOOD RIGHT? THIS SHOULD BE FUN--
--HAPPY TO HELP THE OL' ALMA MATER HOWEVER I CAN.
I HAVE A PAPER PETER WROTE WHEN HE WAS A GRADUATE STUDENT HERE, AND WATCHR WILL REVIEW IT AND DETERMINE ITS SOURCING--
WOW, PRETTY COOL--I DID A LOT OF GREAT WORK WHEN I WAS ENROLLED HERE. THOUGH, I WONDER WHICH PAPER THEY'LL--
THE PAPER IS TITLED, "DETERMINING PATTERNS IN THE RANDOM: CHAOS THEORY AND PROBABILITY DISTRIBUTION." SCANNING NOW.
WAIT, NO--NO NO NO NO--OH GOD--NO--

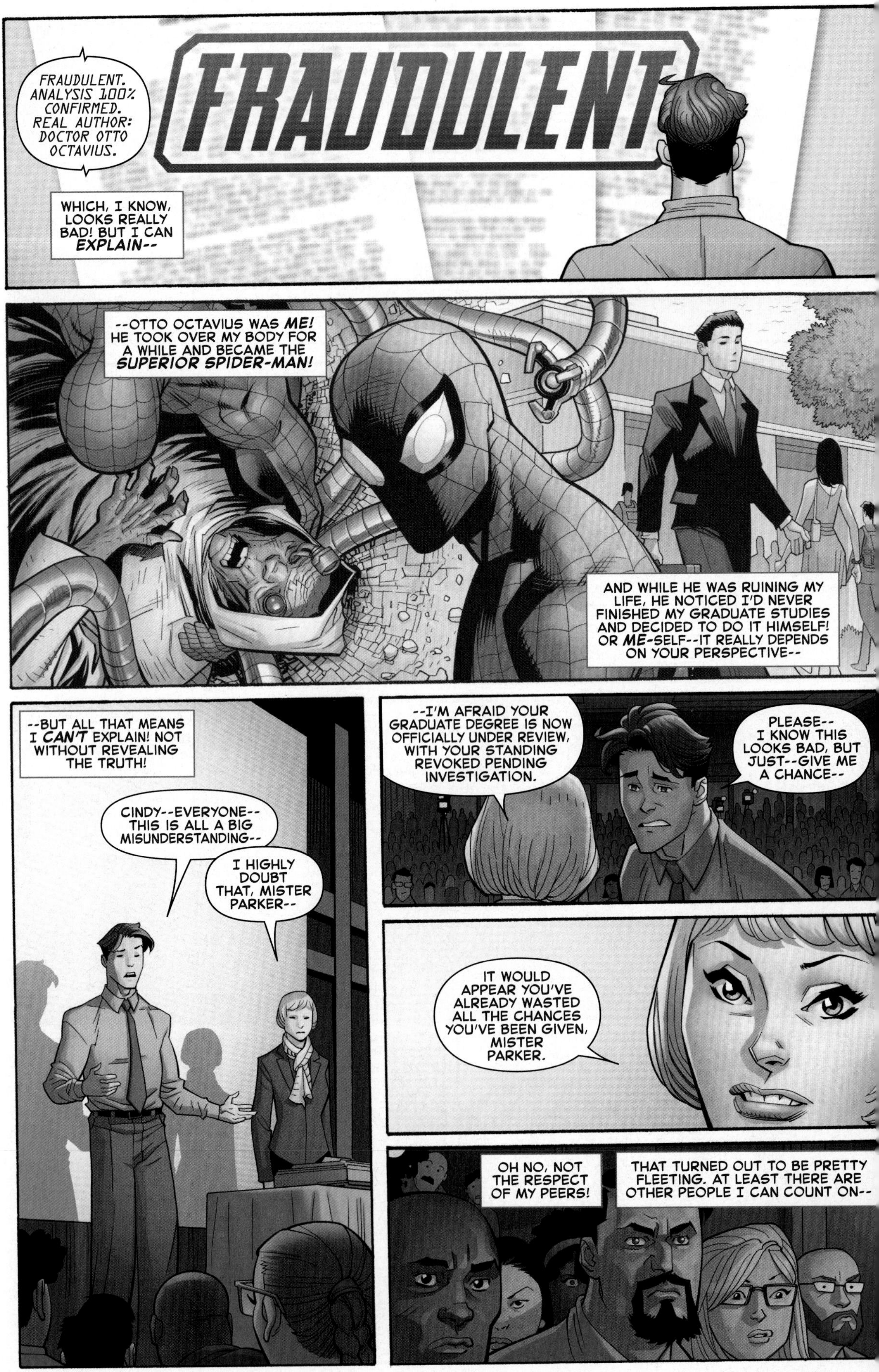
FRAUDULENT. ANALYSIS 100% CONFIRMED. REAL AUTHOR: DOCTOR OTTO OCTAVIUS.
FRAUDULENT
WHICH, I KNOW, LOOKS REALLY BAD! BUT I CAN EXPLAIN--
--OTTO OCTAVIUS WAS ME! HE TOOK OVER MY BODY FOR A WHILE AND BECAME THE SUPERIOR SPIDER-MAN!
AND WHILE HE WAS RUINING MY LIFE, HE NOTICED I'D NEVER FINISHED MY GRADUATE STUDIES AND DECIDED TO DO IT HIMSELF! OR ME-SELF--IT REALLY DEPENDS ON YOUR PERSPECTIVE--
--BUT ALL THAT MEANS I CAN'T EXPLAIN! NOT WITHOUT REVEALING THE TRUTH!
CINDY--EVERYONE-- THIS IS ALL A BIG MISUNDERSTANDING--
I HIGHLY DOUBT THAT, MISTER PARKER--
--I'M AFRAID YOUR GRADUATE DEGREE IS NOW OFFICIALLY UNDER REVIEW, WITH YOUR STANDING REVOKED PENDING INVESTIGATION.
PLEASE-- I KNOW THIS LOOKS BAD, BUT JUST--GIVE ME A CHANCE--
IT WOULD APPEAR YOU'VE ALREADY WASTED ALL THE CHANCES YOU'VE BEEN GIVEN, MISTER PARKER.
OH NO, NOT THE RESPECT OF MY PEERS!
THAT TURNED OUT TO BE PRETTY FLEETING. AT LEAST THERE ARE OTHER PEOPLE I CAN COUNT ON--

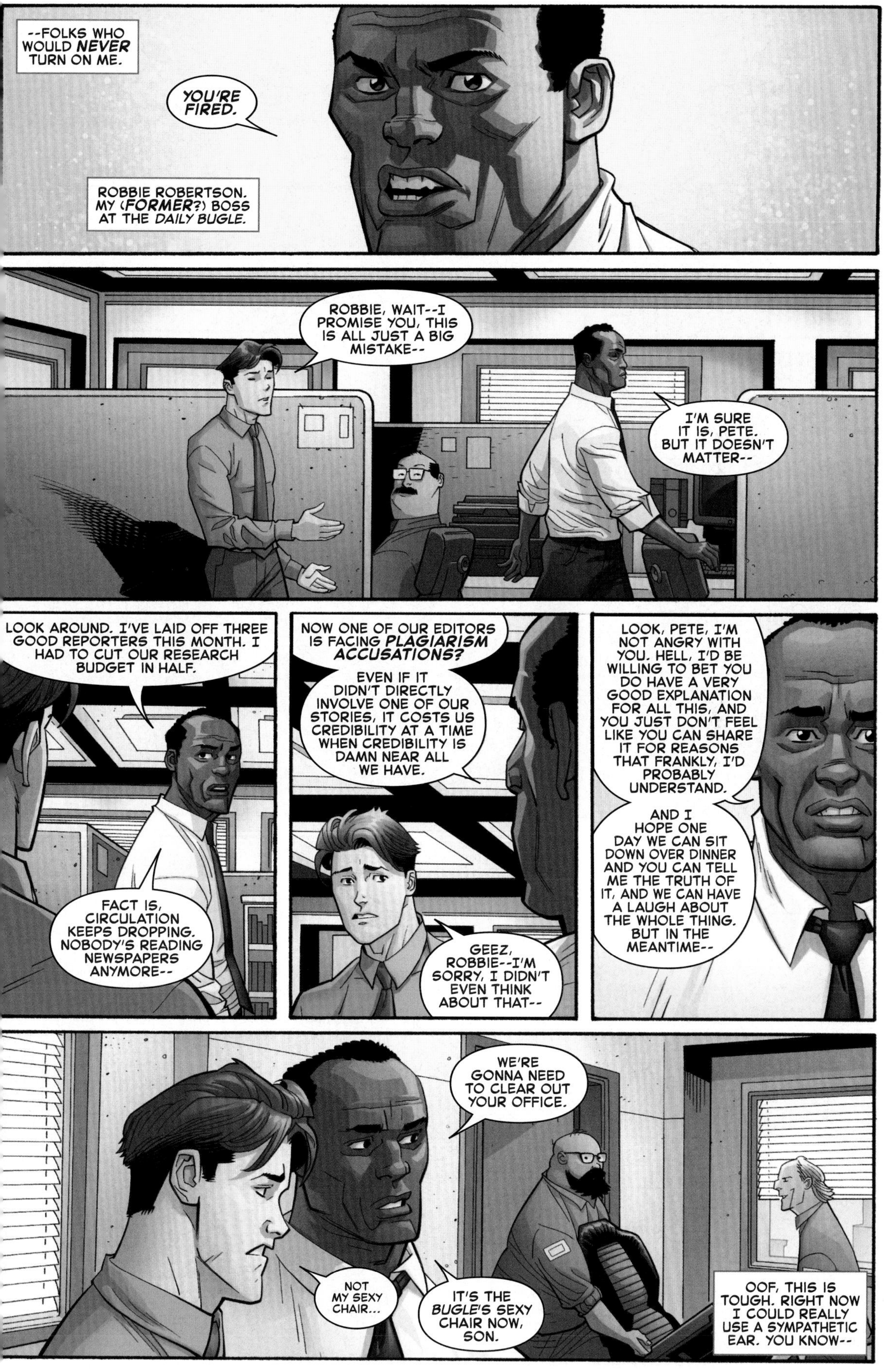
--FOLKS WHO WOULD *NEVER* TURN ON ME.
YOU'RE FIRED.
ROBBIE ROBERTSON. MY (*FORMER?*) BOSS AT THE *DAILY BUGLE.*
ROBBIE, WAIT--I PROMISE YOU, THIS IS ALL JUST A BIG MISTAKE--
I'M SURE IT IS, PETE. BUT IT DOESN'T MATTER--
LOOK AROUND. I'VE LAID OFF THREE GOOD REPORTERS THIS MONTH. I HAD TO CUT OUR RESEARCH BUDGET IN HALF.
FACT IS, CIRCULATION KEEPS DROPPING. NOBODY'S READING NEWSPAPERS ANYMORE--
NOW ONE OF OUR EDITORS IS FACING *PLAGIARISM ACCUSATIONS?*
EVEN IF IT DIDN'T DIRECTLY INVOLVE ONE OF OUR STORIES, IT COSTS US CREDIBILITY AT A TIME WHEN CREDIBILITY IS DAMN NEAR ALL WE HAVE.
GEEZ, ROBBIE--I'M SORRY, I DIDN'T EVEN THINK ABOUT THAT--
LOOK, PETE, I'M NOT ANGRY WITH YOU. HELL, I'D BE WILLING TO BET YOU DO HAVE A VERY GOOD EXPLANATION FOR ALL THIS, AND YOU JUST DON'T FEEL LIKE YOU CAN SHARE IT FOR REASONS THAT FRANKLY, I'D PROBABLY UNDERSTAND.
AND I HOPE ONE DAY WE CAN SIT DOWN OVER DINNER AND YOU CAN TELL ME THE TRUTH OF IT, AND WE CAN HAVE A LAUGH ABOUT THE WHOLE THING. BUT IN THE MEANTIME--
WE'RE GONNA NEED TO CLEAR OUT YOUR OFFICE.
NOT MY SEXY CHAIR...
IT'S THE *BUGLE'S* SEXY CHAIR NOW, SON.
OOF, THIS IS TOUGH. RIGHT NOW I COULD REALLY USE A SYMPATHETIC EAR. YOU KNOW--

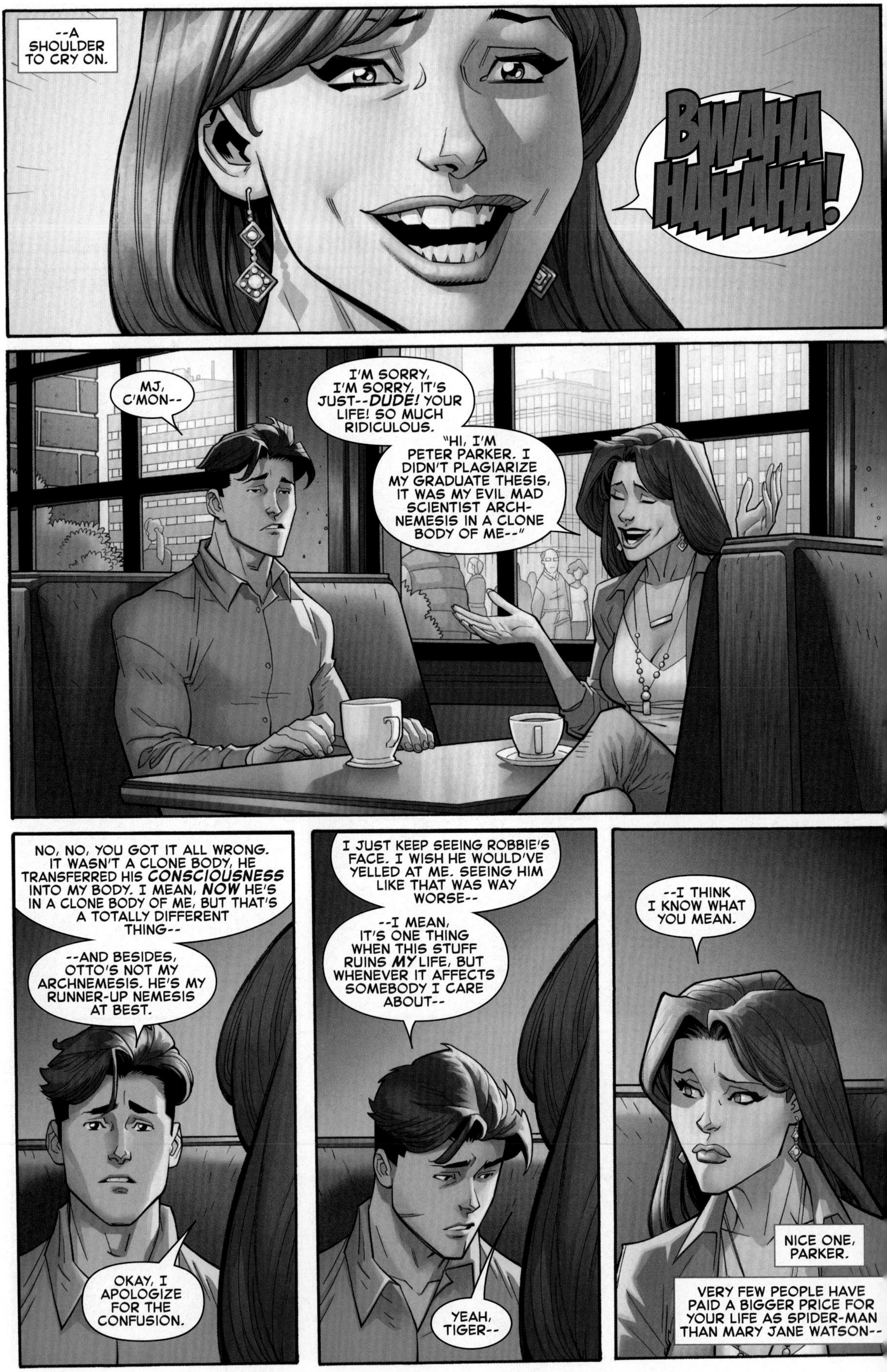
--A SHOULDER TO CRY ON.
BWAHA HAHAHA!
MJ, C'MON--
I'M SORRY, I'M SORRY, IT'S JUST--DUDE! YOUR LIFE! SO MUCH RIDICULOUS.
"HI, I'M PETER PARKER. I DIDN'T PLAGIARIZE MY GRADUATE THESIS, IT WAS MY EVIL MAD SCIENTIST ARCH-NEMESIS IN A CLONE BODY OF ME--"
NO, NO, YOU GOT IT ALL WRONG. IT WASN'T A CLONE BODY, HE TRANSFERRED HIS CONSCIOUSNESS INTO MY BODY. I MEAN, NOW HE'S IN A CLONE BODY OF ME, BUT THAT'S A TOTALLY DIFFERENT THING--
--AND BESIDES, OTTO'S NOT MY ARCHNEMESIS. HE'S MY RUNNER-UP NEMESIS AT BEST.
OKAY, I APOLOGIZE FOR THE CONFUSION.
I JUST KEEP SEEING ROBBIE'S FACE. I WISH HE WOULD'VE YELLED AT ME. SEEING HIM LIKE THAT WAS WAY WORSE--
--I MEAN, IT'S ONE THING WHEN THIS STUFF RUINS MY LIFE, BUT WHENEVER IT AFFECTS SOMEBODY I CARE ABOUT--
YEAH, TIGER--
--I THINK I KNOW WHAT YOU MEAN.
NICE ONE, PARKER.
VERY FEW PEOPLE HAVE PAID A BIGGER PRICE FOR YOUR LIFE AS SPIDER-MAN THAN MARY JANE WATSON--

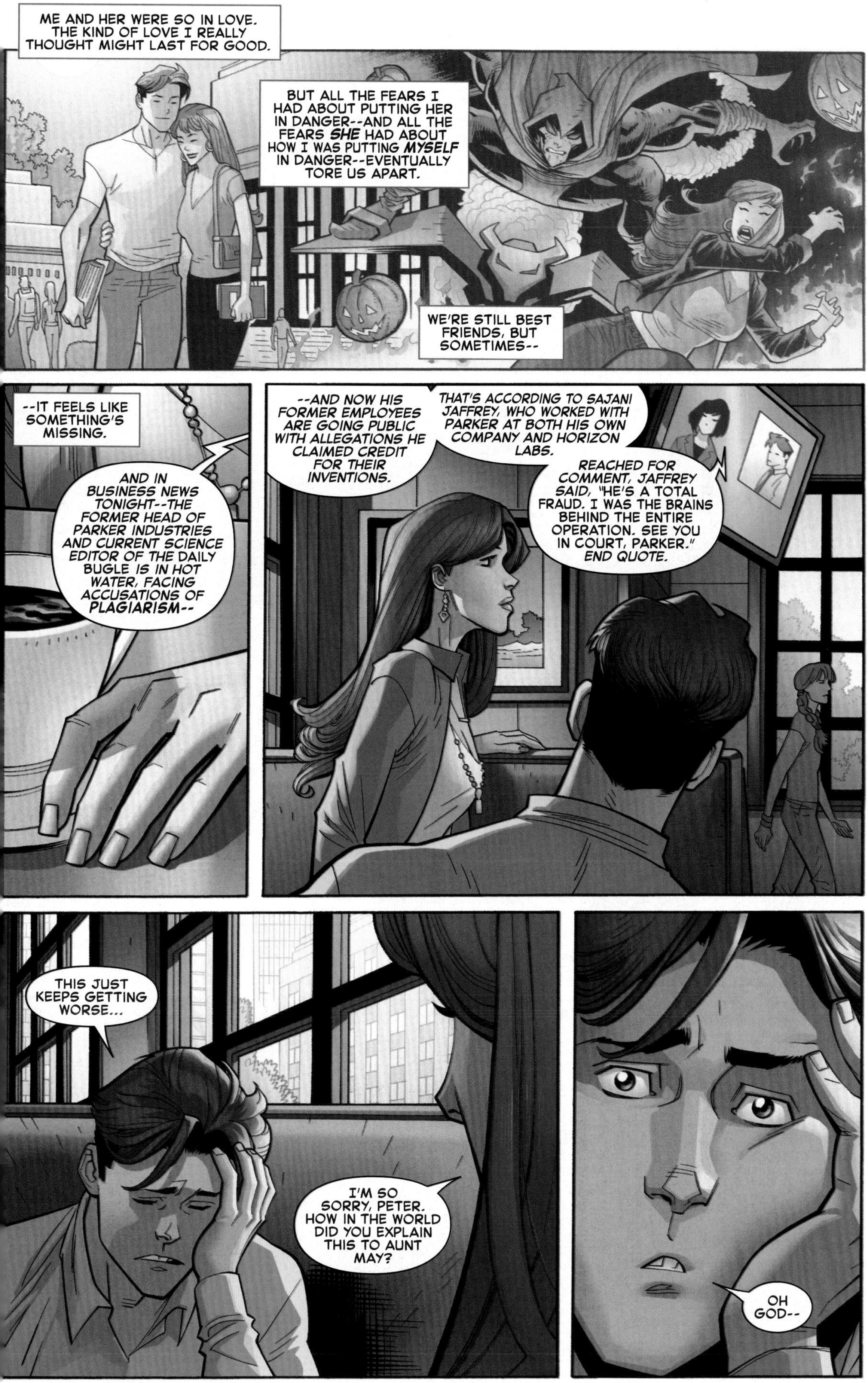
ME AND HER WERE SO IN LOVE. THE KIND OF LOVE I REALLY THOUGHT MIGHT LAST FOR GOOD.
BUT ALL THE FEARS I HAD ABOUT PUTTING HER IN DANGER--AND ALL THE FEARS SHE HAD ABOUT HOW I WAS PUTTING MYSELF IN DANGER--EVENTUALLY TORE US APART.
WE'RE STILL BEST FRIENDS, BUT SOMETIMES--
--IT FEELS LIKE SOMETHING'S MISSING.
AND IN BUSINESS NEWS TONIGHT--THE FORMER HEAD OF PARKER INDUSTRIES AND CURRENT SCIENCE EDITOR OF THE DAILY BUGLE IS IN HOT WATER, FACING ACCUSATIONS OF PLAGIARISM--
--AND NOW HIS FORMER EMPLOYEES ARE GOING PUBLIC WITH ALLEGATIONS HE CLAIMED CREDIT FOR THEIR INVENTIONS.
THAT'S ACCORDING TO SAJANI JAFFREY, WHO WORKED WITH PARKER AT BOTH HIS OWN COMPANY AND HORIZON LABS.
REACHED FOR COMMENT, JAFFREY SAID, "HE'S A TOTAL FRAUD. I WAS THE BRAINS BEHIND THE ENTIRE OPERATION. SEE YOU IN COURT, PARKER." END QUOTE.
THIS JUST KEEPS GETTING WORSE...
I'M SO SORRY, PETER. HOW IN THE WORLD DID YOU EXPLAIN THIS TO AUNT MAY?
OH GOD--

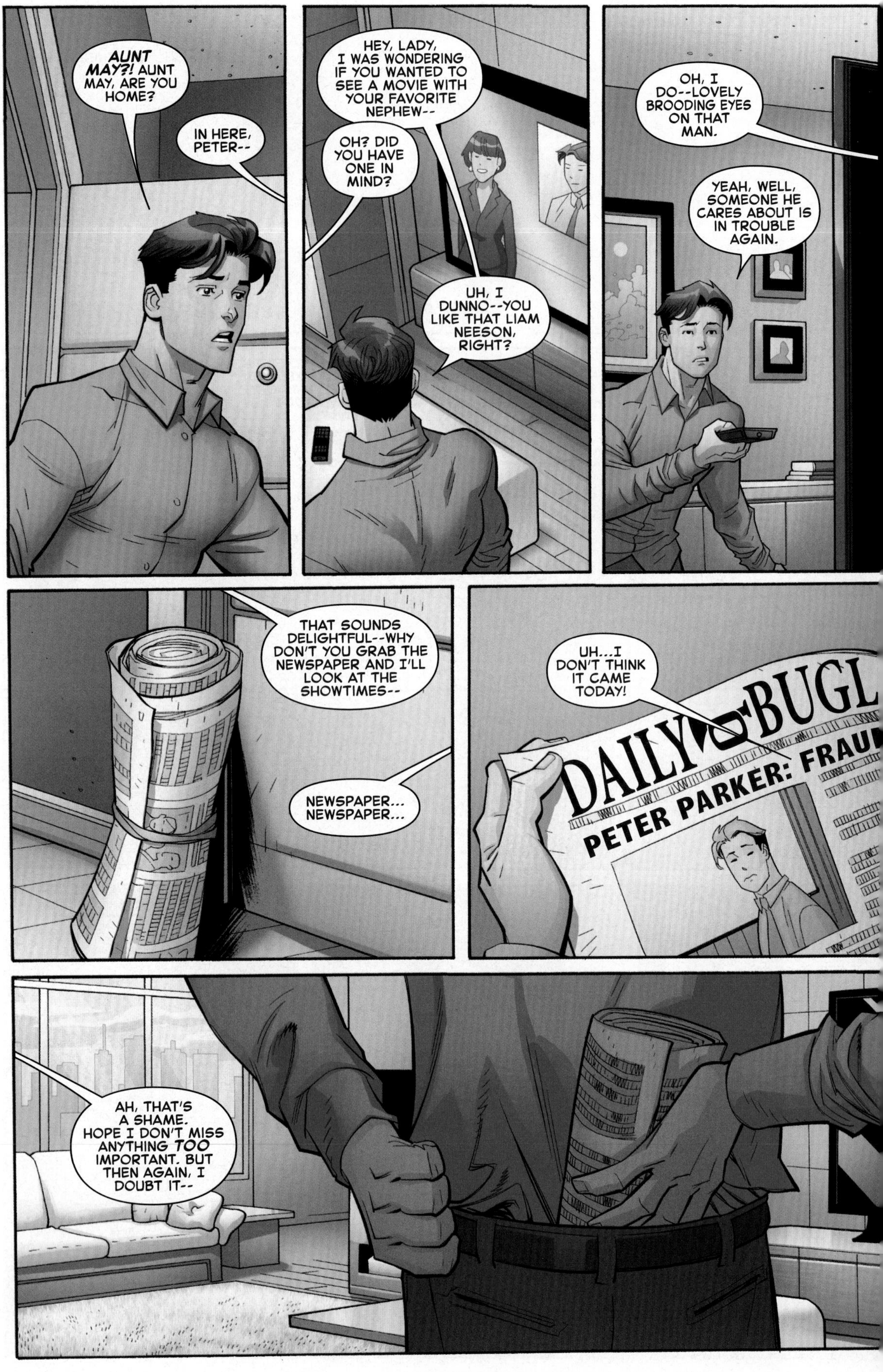
AUNT MAY?! AUNT MAY, ARE YOU HOME?
IN HERE, PETER--
HEY, LADY, I WAS WONDERING IF YOU WANTED TO SEE A MOVIE WITH YOUR FAVORITE NEPHEW--
OH? DID YOU HAVE ONE IN MIND?
UH, I DUNNO--YOU LIKE THAT LIAM NEESON, RIGHT?
OH, I DO--LOVELY BROODING EYES ON THAT MAN.
YEAH, WELL, SOMEONE HE CARES ABOUT IS IN TROUBLE AGAIN.
THAT SOUNDS DELIGHTFUL--WHY DON'T YOU GRAB THE NEWSPAPER AND I'LL LOOK AT THE SHOWTIMES--
NEWSPAPER... NEWSPAPER...
UH...I DON'T THINK IT CAME TODAY!
DAILY BUGL
PETER PARKER: FRAU
AH, THAT'S A SHAME. HOPE I DON'T MISS ANYTHING TOO IMPORTANT. BUT THEN AGAIN, I DOUBT IT--

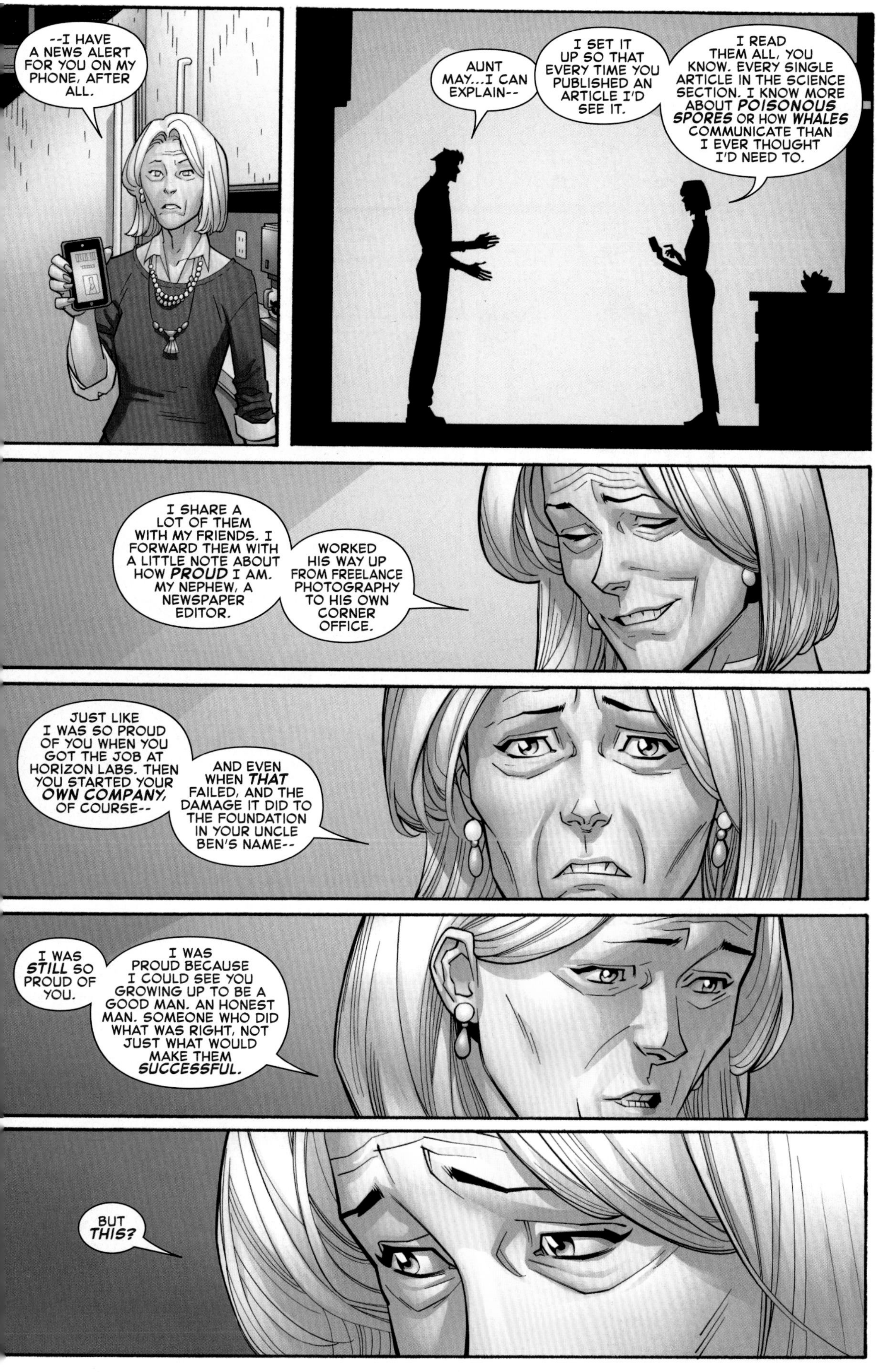
--I HAVE A NEWS ALERT FOR YOU ON MY PHONE, AFTER ALL.
AUNT MAY...I CAN EXPLAIN--
I SET IT UP SO THAT EVERY TIME YOU PUBLISHED AN ARTICLE I'D SEE IT.
I READ THEM ALL, YOU KNOW. EVERY SINGLE ARTICLE IN THE SCIENCE SECTION. I KNOW MORE ABOUT POISONOUS SPORES OR HOW WHALES COMMUNICATE THAN I EVER THOUGHT I'D NEED TO.
I SHARE A LOT OF THEM WITH MY FRIENDS. I FORWARD THEM WITH A LITTLE NOTE ABOUT HOW PROUD I AM. MY NEPHEW, A NEWSPAPER EDITOR.
WORKED HIS WAY UP FROM FREELANCE PHOTOGRAPHY TO HIS OWN CORNER OFFICE.
JUST LIKE I WAS SO PROUD OF YOU WHEN YOU GOT THE JOB AT HORIZON LABS. THEN YOU STARTED YOUR OWN COMPANY, OF COURSE--
AND EVEN WHEN THAT FAILED, AND THE DAMAGE IT DID TO THE FOUNDATION IN YOUR UNCLE BEN'S NAME--
I WAS STILL SO PROUD OF YOU.
I WAS PROUD BECAUSE I COULD SEE YOU GROWING UP TO BE A GOOD MAN. AN HONEST MAN. SOMEONE WHO DID WHAT WAS RIGHT, NOT JUST WHAT WOULD MAKE THEM SUCCESSFUL.
BUT THIS?

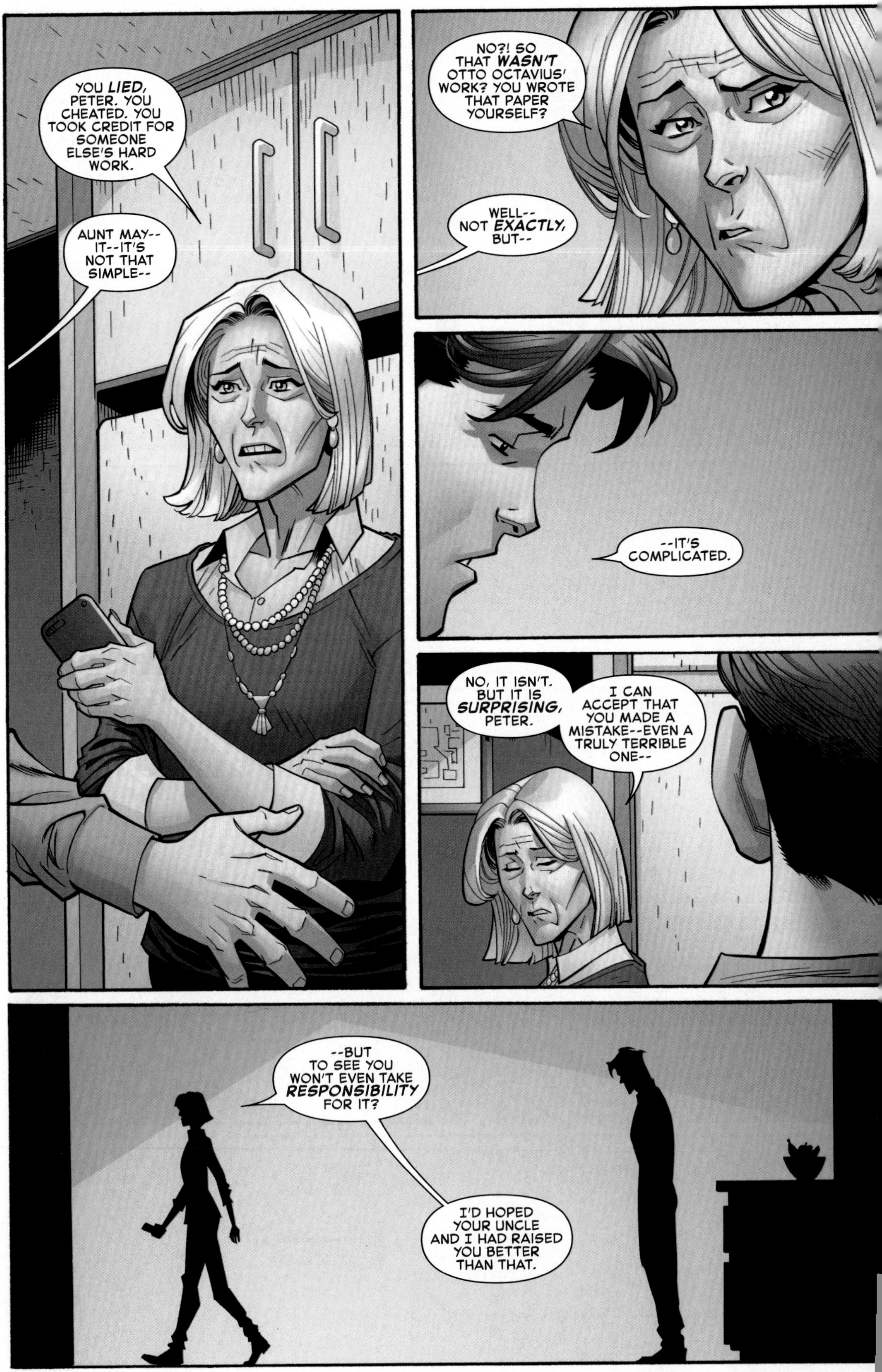
YOU LIED, PETER. YOU CHEATED. YOU TOOK CREDIT FOR SOMEONE ELSE'S HARD WORK.
AUNT MAY-- IT--IT'S NOT THAT SIMPLE--
NO?! SO THAT WASN'T OTTO OCTAVIUS' WORK? YOU WROTE THAT PAPER YOURSELF?
WELL-- NOT EXACTLY, BUT--
--IT'S COMPLICATED.
NO, IT ISN'T. BUT IT IS SURPRISING, PETER.
I CAN ACCEPT THAT YOU MADE A MISTAKE--EVEN A TRULY TERRIBLE ONE--
--BUT TO SEE YOU WON'T EVEN TAKE RESPONSIBILITY FOR IT?
I'D HOPED YOUR UNCLE AND I HAD RAISED YOU BETTER THAN THAT.

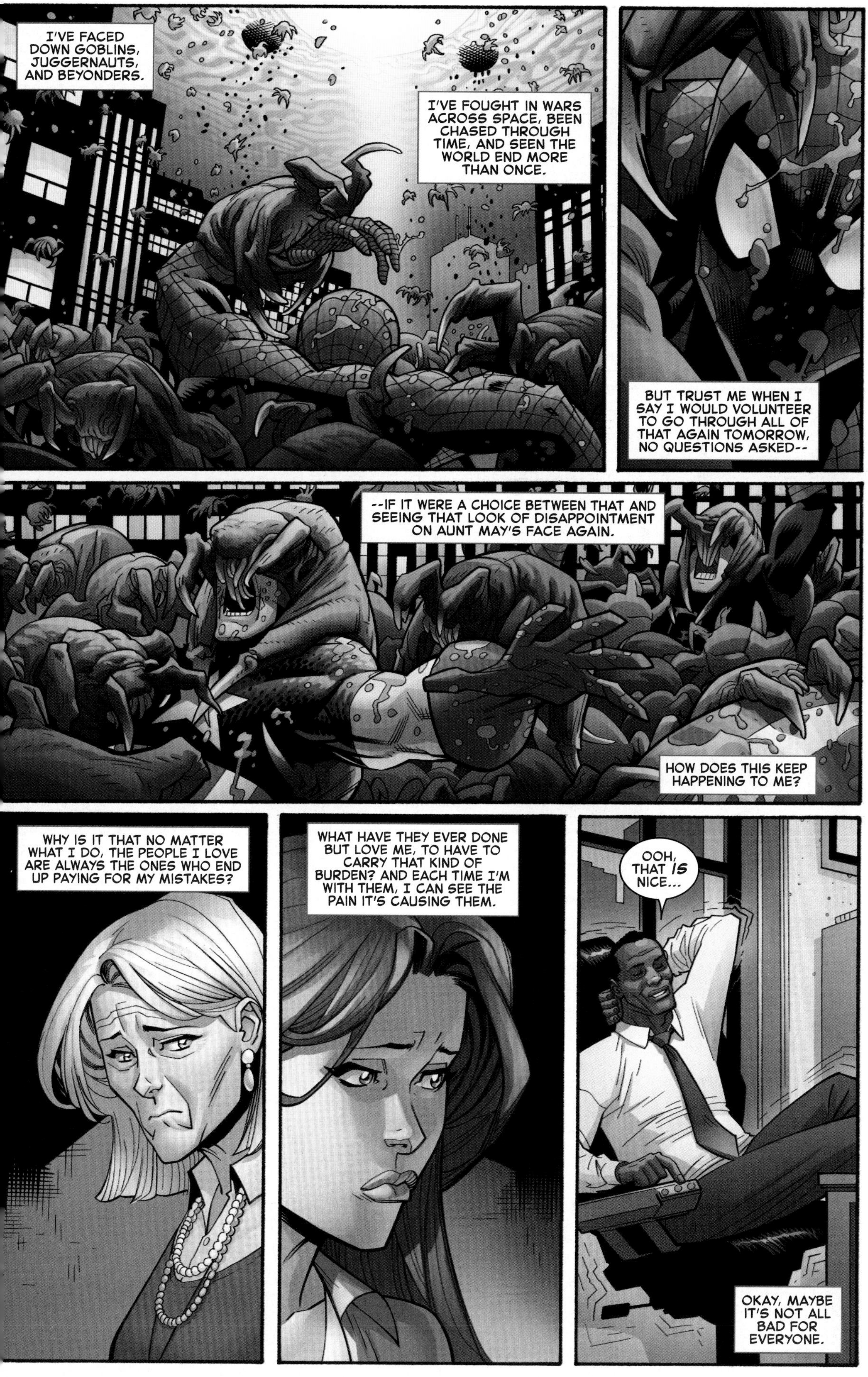
I'VE FACED DOWN GOBLINS, JUGGERNAUTS, AND BEYONDERS.
I'VE FOUGHT IN WARS ACROSS SPACE, BEEN CHASED THROUGH TIME, AND SEEN THE WORLD END MORE THAN ONCE.
BUT TRUST ME WHEN I SAY I WOULD VOLUNTEER TO GO THROUGH ALL OF THAT AGAIN TOMORROW, NO QUESTIONS ASKED--
--IF IT WERE A CHOICE BETWEEN THAT AND SEEING THAT LOOK OF DISAPPOINTMENT ON AUNT MAY'S FACE AGAIN.
HOW DOES THIS KEEP HAPPENING TO ME?
WHY IS IT THAT NO MATTER WHAT I DO, THE PEOPLE I LOVE ARE ALWAYS THE ONES WHO END UP PAYING FOR MY MISTAKES?
WHAT HAVE THEY EVER DONE BUT LOVE ME, TO HAVE TO CARRY THAT KIND OF BURDEN? AND EACH TIME I'M WITH THEM, I CAN SEE THE PAIN IT'S CAUSING THEM.
OOH, THAT *IS* NICE...
OKAY, MAYBE IT'S NOT ALL BAD FOR EVERYONE.

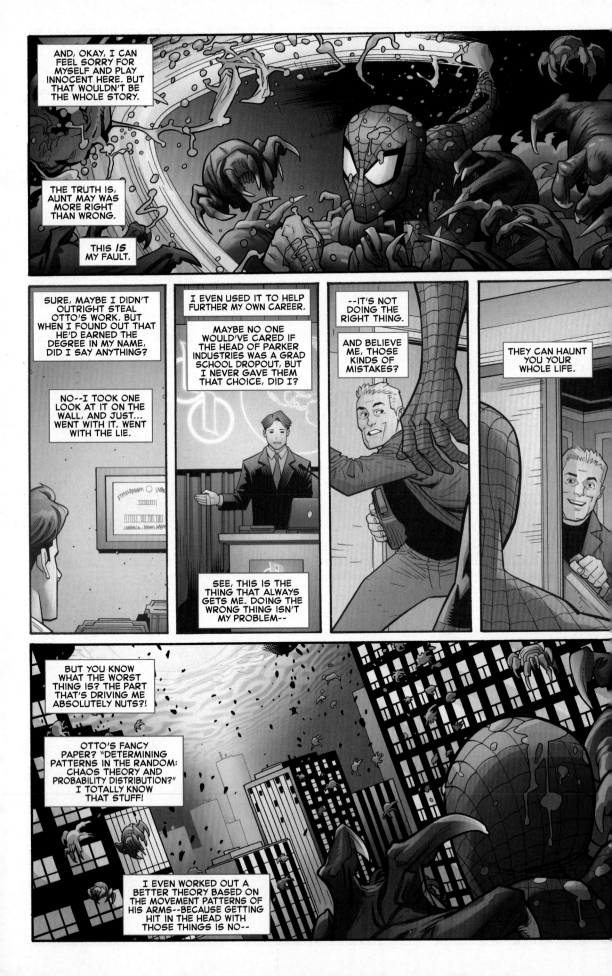

AND, OKAY, I CAN FEEL SORRY FOR MYSELF AND PLAY INNOCENT HERE. BUT THAT WOULDN'T BE THE WHOLE STORY.

THE TRUTH IS, AUNT MAY WAS MORE RIGHT THAN WRONG.

THIS *IS* MY FAULT.

SURE, MAYBE I DIDN'T OUTRIGHT STEAL OTTO'S WORK. BUT WHEN I FOUND OUT THAT HE'D EARNED THE DEGREE IN MY NAME, DID I SAY ANYTHING?

NO--I TOOK ONE LOOK AT IT ON THE WALL, AND JUST... WENT WITH IT. WENT WITH THE LIE.

I EVEN USED IT TO HELP FURTHER MY OWN CAREER.

MAYBE NO ONE WOULD'VE CARED IF THE HEAD OF PARKER INDUSTRIES WAS A GRAD SCHOOL DROPOUT, BUT I NEVER GAVE THEM THAT CHOICE, DID I?

SEE, THIS IS THE THING THAT ALWAYS GETS ME. DOING THE WRONG THING ISN'T MY PROBLEM--

--IT'S NOT DOING THE RIGHT THING.

AND BELIEVE ME, THOSE KINDS OF MISTAKES?

THEY CAN HAUNT YOU YOUR WHOLE LIFE.

BUT YOU KNOW WHAT THE WORST THING IS? THE PART THAT'S DRIVING ME ABSOLUTELY NUTS?!

OTTO'S FANCY PAPER? "DETERMINING PATTERNS IN THE RANDOM: CHAOS THEORY AND PROBABILITY DISTRIBUTION?" I TOTALLY KNOW THAT STUFF!

I EVEN WORKED OUT A BETTER THEORY BASED ON THE MOVEMENT PATTERNS OF HIS ARMS--BECAUSE GETTING HIT IN THE HEAD WITH THOSE THINGS IS NO--

WAIT, THAT'S IT!

THERE'S A PATTERN TO THESE PORTAL OPENINGS, IT'S NOT RANDOM AT ALL-- THEY'RE INTERCONNECTED!

AND IF I CAN FORMULATE WHICH ONE IS AT THE CENTER OF IT, I MIGHT BE ABLE TO SHUT IT DOWN--

--AND ALL OF THE OTHERS WITH IT!

OF COURSE, BETTER THAN DECENT ODDS THAT WOULD BE A ONE-WAY TRIP. TOO BAD I CAN'T FIND ANY HEAVY HITTERS SUBSUMED IN THE PILES AND PILES OF ALIENS. I MEAN, THOR EVEN *LIKES* SPACE!

AH, WELL--

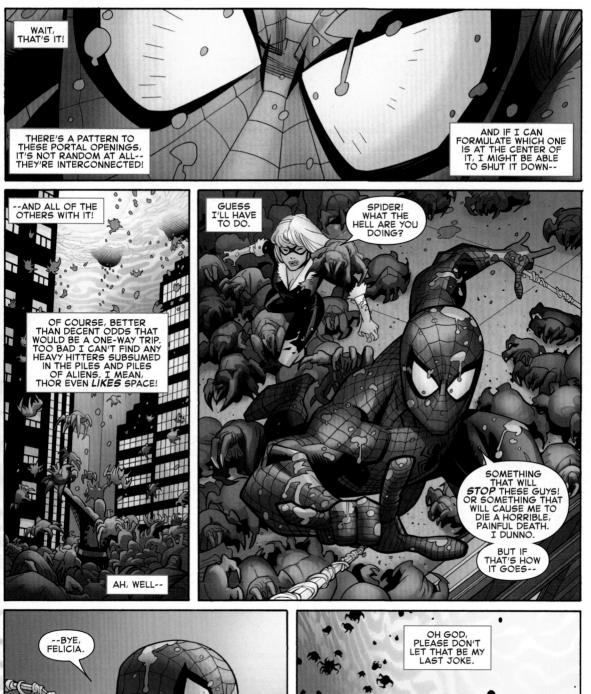

GUESS I'LL HAVE TO DO.

SPIDER! WHAT THE HELL ARE YOU DOING?

SOMETHING THAT WILL *STOP* THESE GUYS! OR SOMETHING THAT WILL CAUSE ME TO DIE A HORRIBLE, PAINFUL DEATH. I DUNNO.

BUT IF THAT'S HOW IT GOES--

--BYE, FELICIA.

OH GOD, PLEASE DON'T LET THAT BE MY LAST JOKE.

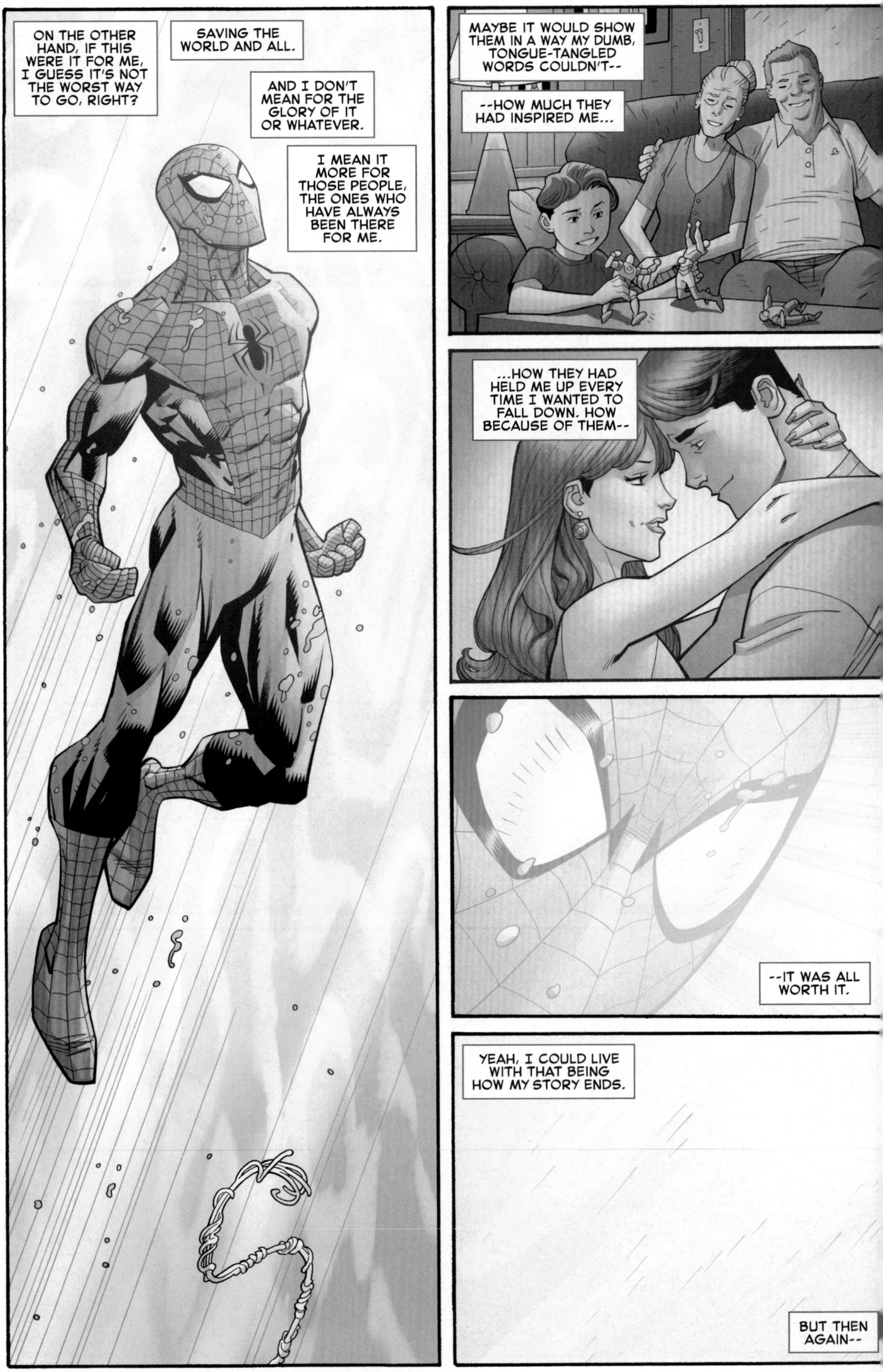
ON THE OTHER HAND, IF THIS WERE IT FOR ME, I GUESS IT'S NOT THE WORST WAY TO GO, RIGHT?
SAVING THE WORLD AND ALL.
AND I DON'T MEAN FOR THE GLORY OF IT OR WHATEVER.
I MEAN IT MORE FOR THOSE PEOPLE, THE ONES WHO HAVE ALWAYS BEEN THERE FOR ME.
MAYBE IT WOULD SHOW THEM IN A WAY MY DUMB, TONGUE-TANGLED WORDS COULDN'T--
--HOW MUCH THEY HAD INSPIRED ME...
...HOW THEY HAD HELD ME UP EVERY TIME I WANTED TO FALL DOWN. HOW BECAUSE OF THEM--
--IT WAS ALL WORTH IT.
YEAH, I COULD LIVE WITH THAT BEING HOW MY STORY ENDS.
BUT THEN AGAIN--

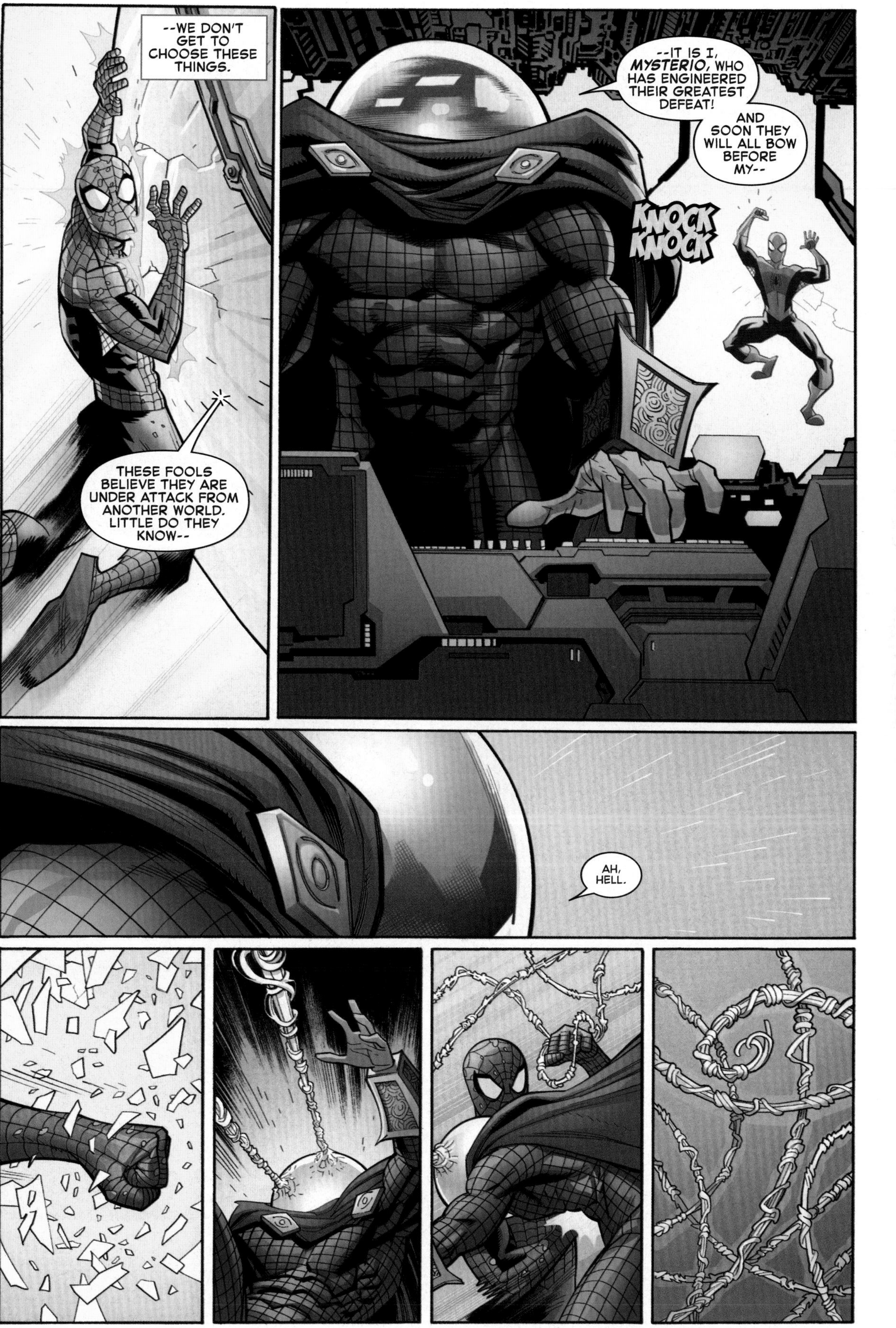
--WE DON'T GET TO CHOOSE THESE THINGS.
THESE FOOLS BELIEVE THEY ARE UNDER ATTACK FROM ANOTHER WORLD. LITTLE DO THEY KNOW--
--IT IS I, MYSTERIO, WHO HAS ENGINEERED THEIR GREATEST DEFEAT!
AND SOON THEY WILL ALL BOW BEFORE MY--
KNOCK KNOCK
AH, HELL.

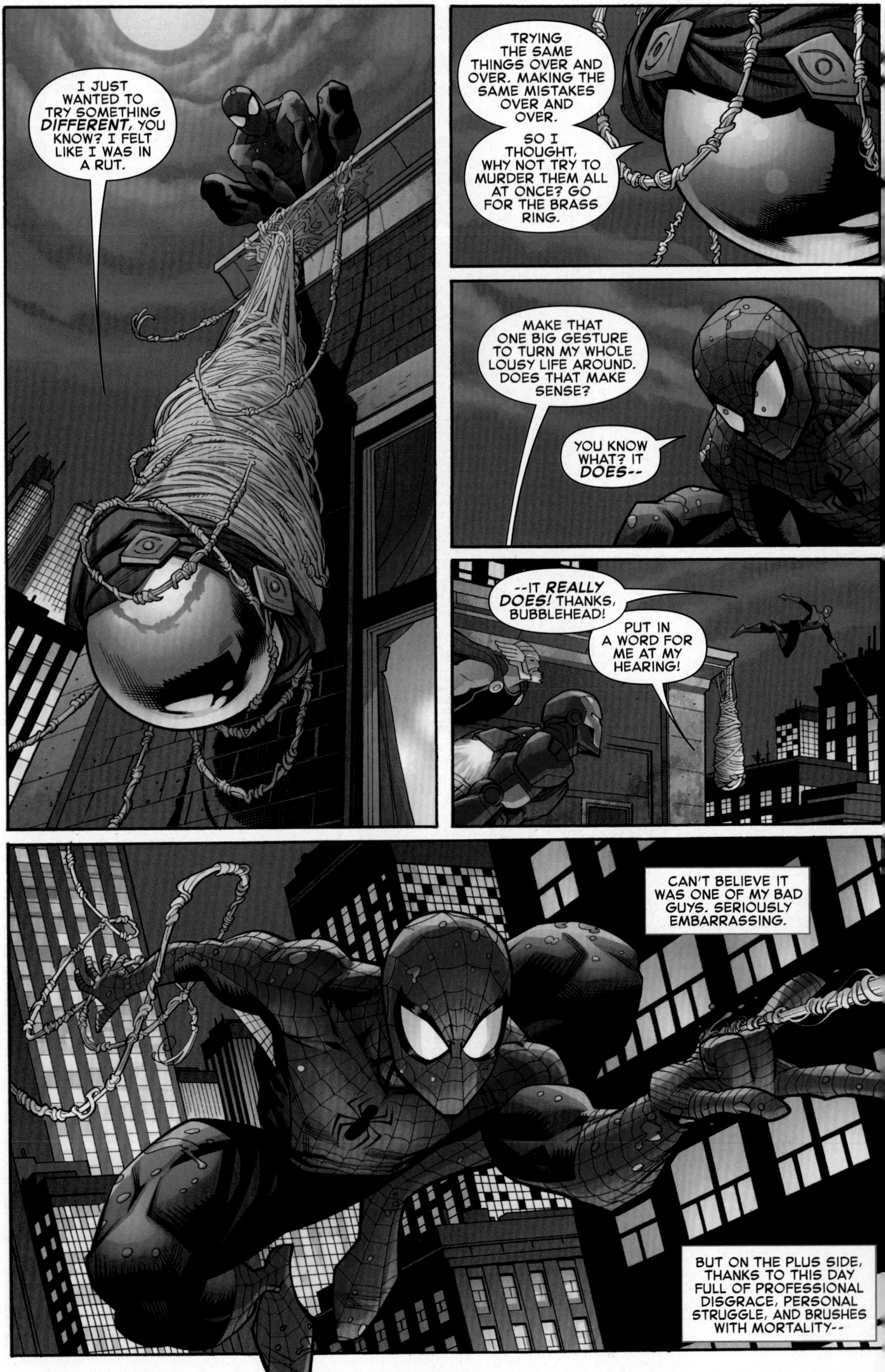
I JUST WANTED TO TRY SOMETHING *DIFFERENT*, YOU KNOW? I FELT LIKE I WAS IN A RUT.
TRYING THE SAME THINGS OVER AND OVER. MAKING THE SAME MISTAKES OVER AND OVER.
SO I THOUGHT, WHY NOT TRY TO MURDER THEM ALL AT ONCE? GO FOR THE BRASS RING.
MAKE THAT ONE BIG GESTURE TO TURN MY WHOLE LOUSY LIFE AROUND. DOES THAT MAKE SENSE?
YOU KNOW WHAT? IT *DOES--*
--IT *REALLY DOES!* THANKS, BUBBLEHEAD!
PUT IN A WORD FOR ME AT MY HEARING!
CAN'T BELIEVE IT WAS ONE OF MY BAD GUYS. SERIOUSLY EMBARRASSING.
BUT ON THE PLUS SIDE, THANKS TO THIS DAY FULL OF PROFESSIONAL DISGRACE, PERSONAL STRUGGLE, AND BRUSHES WITH MORTALITY--

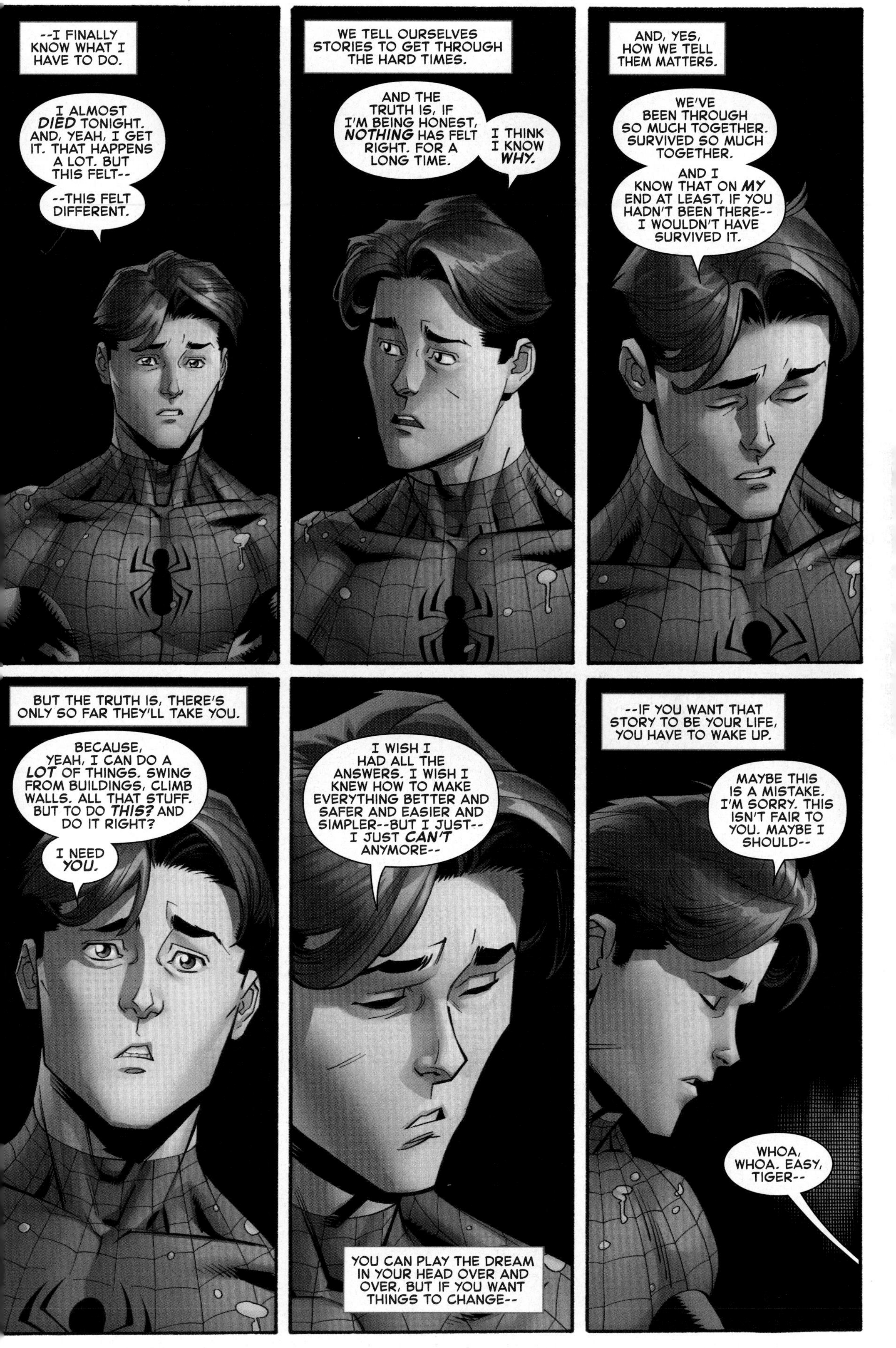
--I FINALLY KNOW WHAT I HAVE TO DO.
I ALMOST *DIED* TONIGHT. AND, YEAH, I GET IT. THAT HAPPENS A LOT. BUT THIS FELT--
--THIS FELT DIFFERENT.
WE TELL OURSELVES STORIES TO GET THROUGH THE HARD TIMES.
AND THE TRUTH IS, IF I'M BEING HONEST, *NOTHING* HAS FELT RIGHT. FOR A LONG TIME.
I THINK I KNOW *WHY.*
AND, YES, HOW WE TELL THEM MATTERS.
WE'VE BEEN THROUGH SO MUCH TOGETHER. SURVIVED SO MUCH TOGETHER.
AND I KNOW THAT ON *MY* END AT LEAST, IF YOU HADN'T BEEN THERE-- I WOULDN'T HAVE SURVIVED IT.
BUT THE TRUTH IS, THERE'S ONLY SO FAR THEY'LL TAKE YOU.
BECAUSE, YEAH, I CAN DO A *LOT* OF THINGS. SWING FROM BUILDINGS, CLIMB WALLS. ALL THAT STUFF. BUT TO DO *THIS?* AND DO IT RIGHT?
I NEED *YOU.*
I WISH I HAD ALL THE ANSWERS. I WISH I KNEW HOW TO MAKE EVERYTHING BETTER AND SAFER AND EASIER AND SIMPLER--BUT I JUST-- I JUST *CAN'T* ANYMORE--
YOU CAN PLAY THE DREAM IN YOUR HEAD OVER AND OVER, BUT IF YOU WANT THINGS TO CHANGE--
--IF YOU WANT THAT STORY TO BE YOUR LIFE, YOU HAVE TO WAKE UP.
MAYBE THIS IS A MISTAKE. I'M SORRY. THIS ISN'T FAIR TO YOU. MAYBE I SHOULD--
WHOA, WHOA. EASY, TIGER--

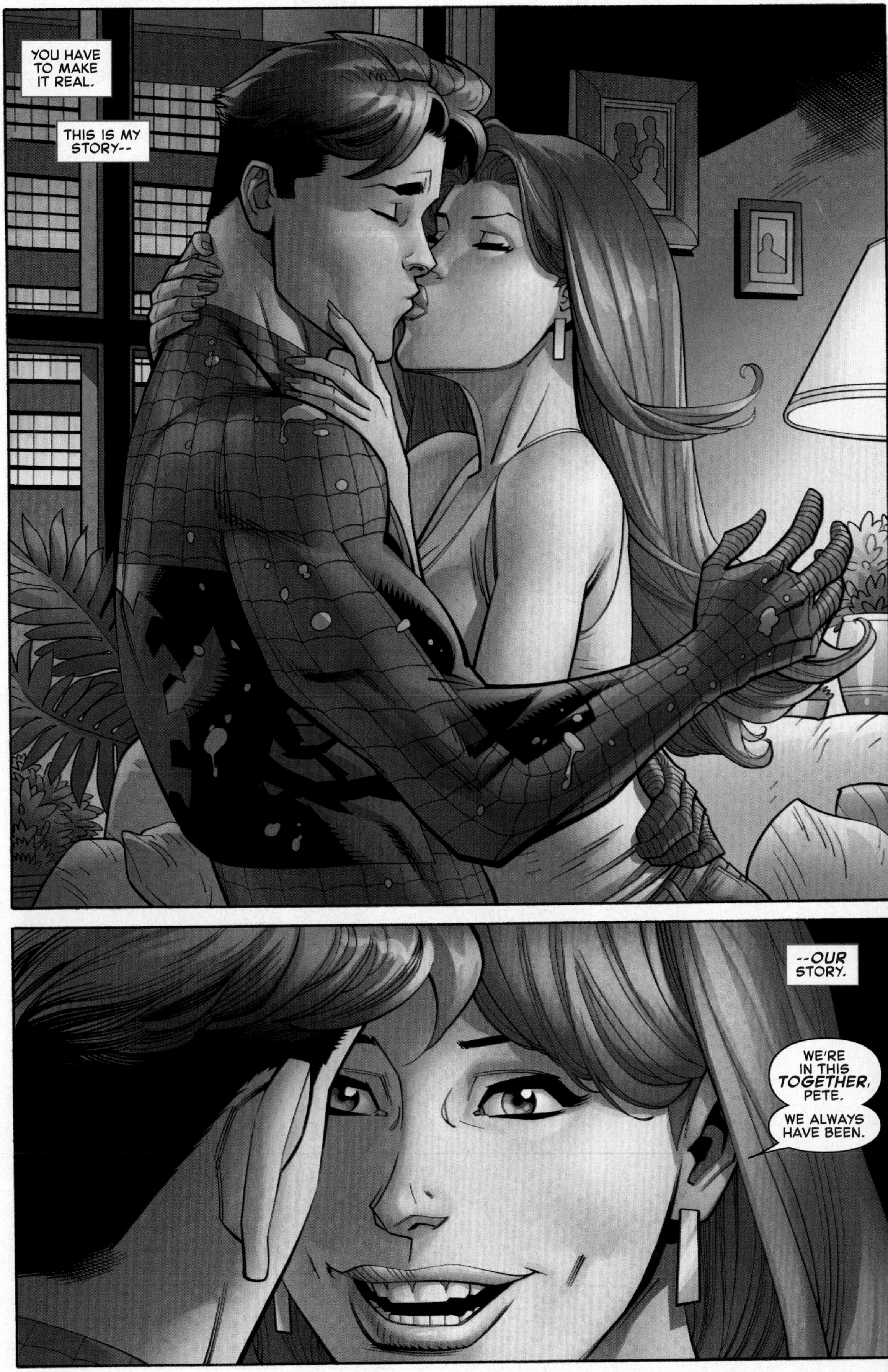
YOU HAVE TO MAKE IT REAL.
THIS IS MY STORY--
--OUR STORY.
WE'RE IN THIS TOGETHER, PETE.
WE ALWAYS HAVE BEEN.

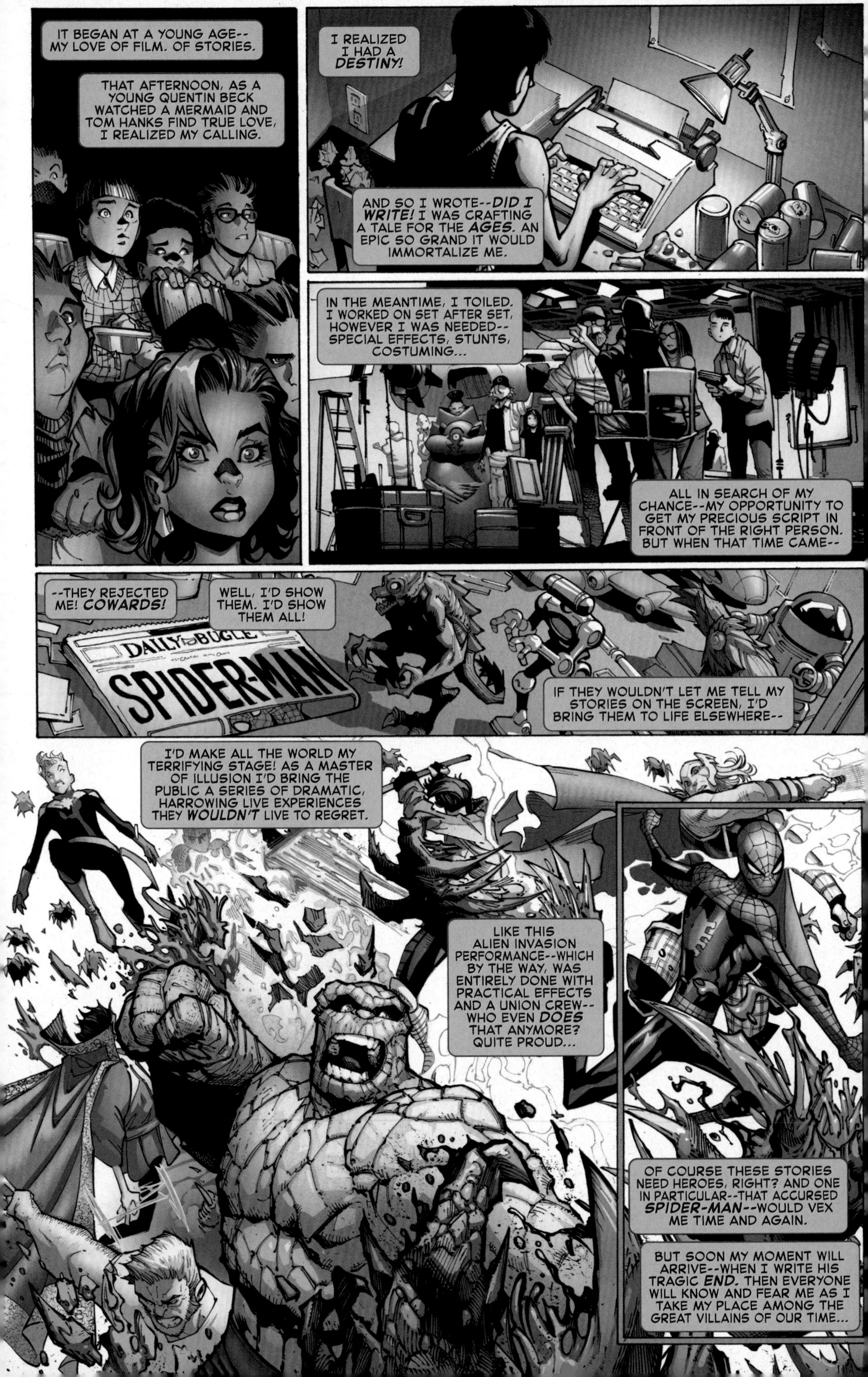
IT BEGAN AT A YOUNG AGE--MY LOVE OF FILM. OF STORIES.
THAT AFTERNOON, AS A YOUNG QUENTIN BECK WATCHED A MERMAID AND TOM HANKS FIND TRUE LOVE, I REALIZED MY CALLING.
I REALIZED I HAD A DESTINY!
AND SO I WROTE--DID I WRITE! I WAS CRAFTING A TALE FOR THE AGES. AN EPIC SO GRAND IT WOULD IMMORTALIZE ME.
IN THE MEANTIME, I TOILED. I WORKED ON SET AFTER SET, HOWEVER I WAS NEEDED--SPECIAL EFFECTS, STUNTS, COSTUMING...
ALL IN SEARCH OF MY CHANCE--MY OPPORTUNITY TO GET MY PRECIOUS SCRIPT IN FRONT OF THE RIGHT PERSON. BUT WHEN THAT TIME CAME--
--THEY REJECTED ME! COWARDS!
WELL, I'D SHOW THEM. I'D SHOW THEM ALL!
DAILY BUGLE
SPIDER-MAN
IF THEY WOULDN'T LET ME TELL MY STORIES ON THE SCREEN, I'D BRING THEM TO LIFE ELSEWHERE--
I'D MAKE ALL THE WORLD MY TERRIFYING STAGE! AS A MASTER OF ILLUSION I'D BRING THE PUBLIC A SERIES OF DRAMATIC, HARROWING LIVE EXPERIENCES THEY WOULDN'T LIVE TO REGRET.
LIKE THIS ALIEN INVASION PERFORMANCE--WHICH BY THE WAY, WAS ENTIRELY DONE WITH PRACTICAL EFFECTS AND A UNION CREW--WHO EVEN DOES THAT ANYMORE? QUITE PROUD...
OF COURSE THESE STORIES NEED HEROES, RIGHT? AND ONE IN PARTICULAR--THAT ACCURSED SPIDER-MAN--WOULD VEX ME TIME AND AGAIN.
BUT SOON MY MOMENT WILL ARRIVE--WHEN I WRITE HIS TRAGIC END. THEN EVERYONE WILL KNOW AND FEAR ME AS I TAKE MY PLACE AMONG THE GREAT VILLAINS OF OUR TIME...

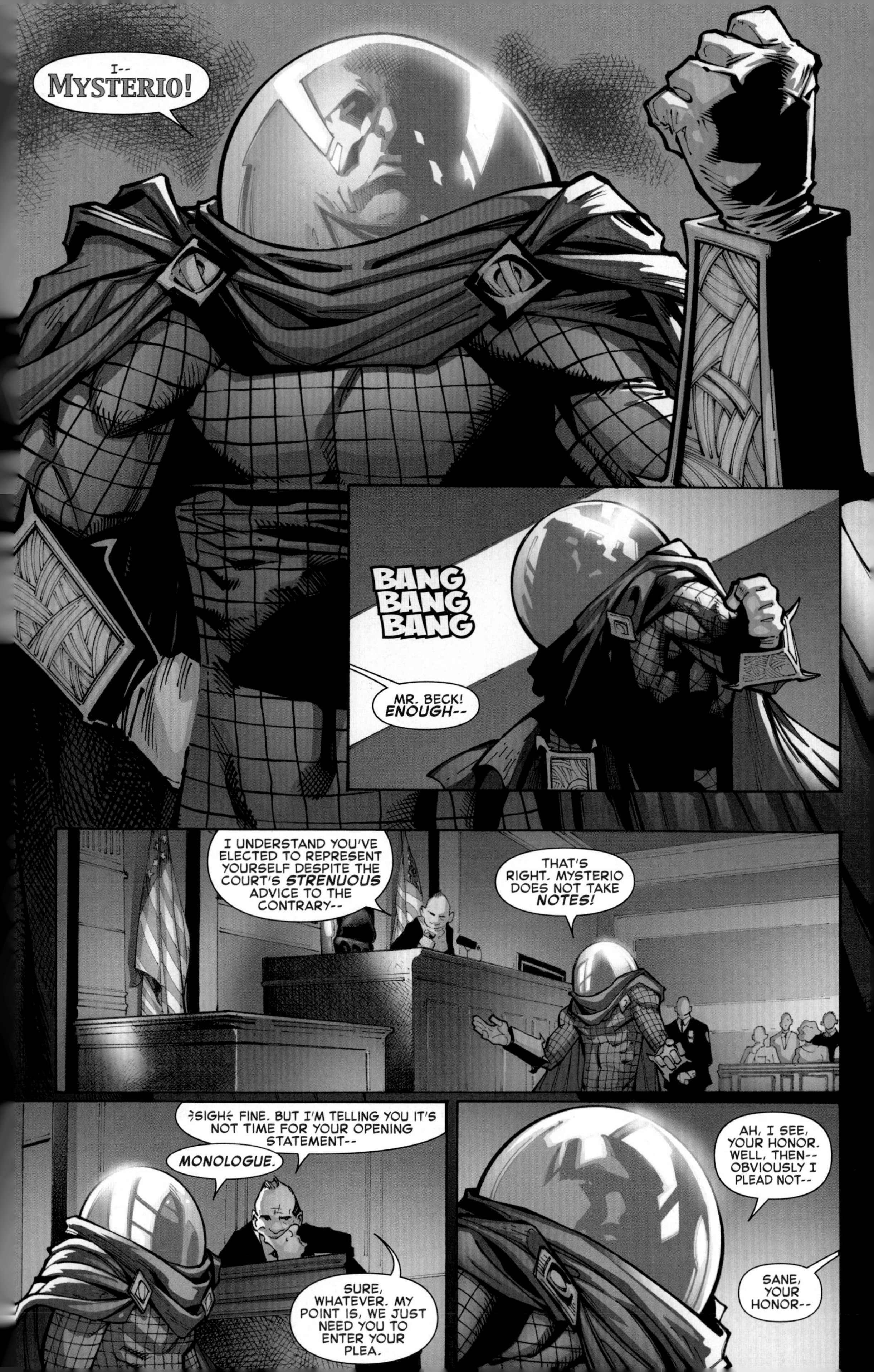
I-- MYSTERIO!
BANG BANG BANG
MR. BECK! ENOUGH--
I UNDERSTAND YOU'VE ELECTED TO REPRESENT YOURSELF DESPITE THE COURT'S STRENUOUS ADVICE TO THE CONTRARY--
THAT'S RIGHT. MYSTERIO DOES NOT TAKE NOTES!
SIGH FINE. BUT I'M TELLING YOU IT'S NOT TIME FOR YOUR OPENING STATEMENT--
MONOLOGUE.
SURE, WHATEVER. MY POINT IS, WE JUST NEED YOU TO ENTER YOUR PLEA.
AH, I SEE, YOUR HONOR. WELL, THEN-- OBVIOUSLY I PLEAD NOT--
SANE, YOUR HONOR--

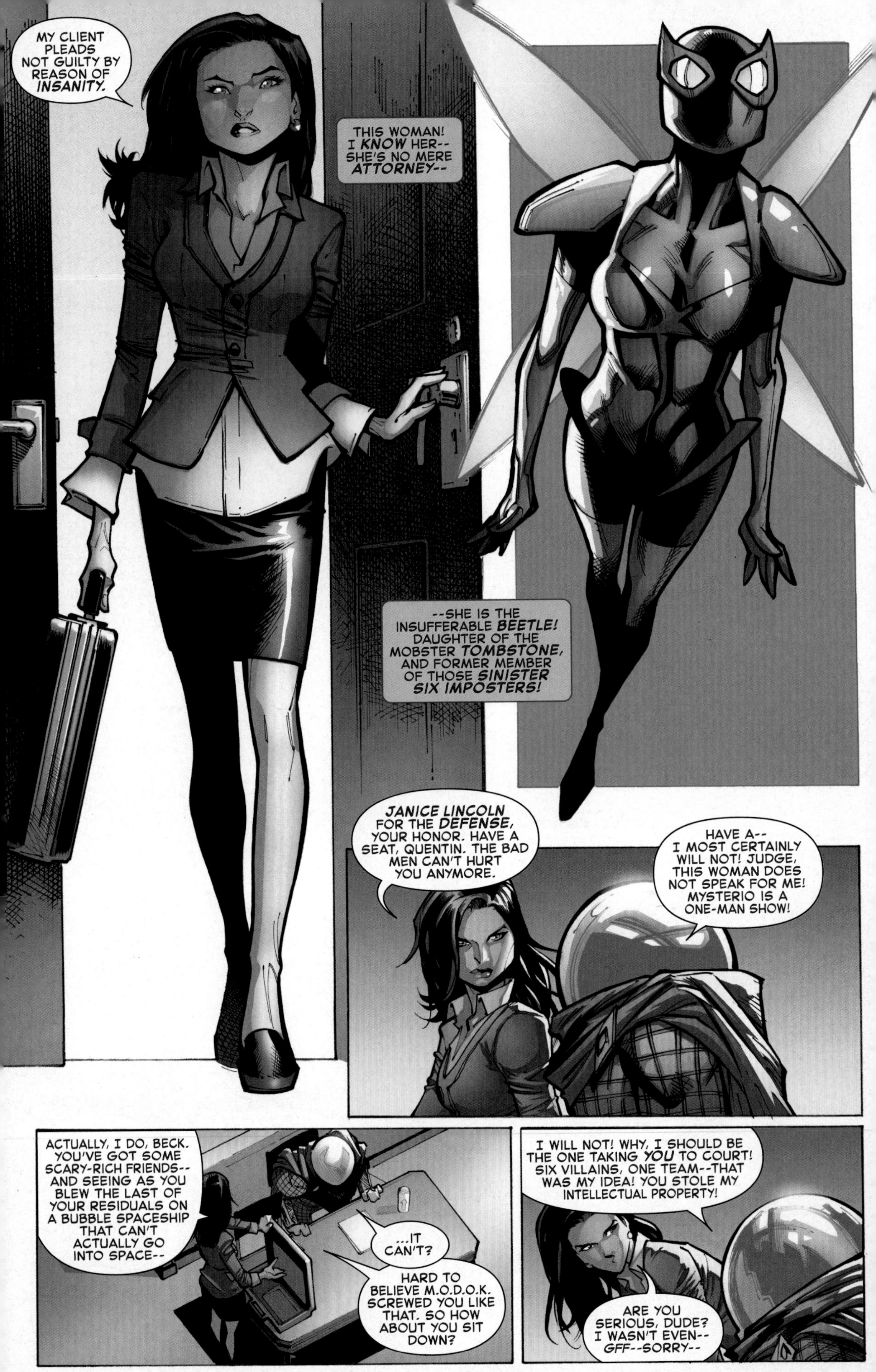
MY CLIENT PLEADS NOT GUILTY BY REASON OF INSANITY.
THIS WOMAN! I KNOW HER--SHE'S NO MERE ATTORNEY--
--SHE IS THE INSUFFERABLE BEETLE! DAUGHTER OF THE MOBSTER TOMBSTONE, AND FORMER MEMBER OF THOSE SINISTER SIX IMPOSTERS!
JANICE LINCOLN FOR THE DEFENSE, YOUR HONOR. HAVE A SEAT, QUENTIN. THE BAD MEN CAN'T HURT YOU ANYMORE.
HAVE A-- I MOST CERTAINLY WILL NOT! JUDGE, THIS WOMAN DOES NOT SPEAK FOR ME! MYSTERIO IS A ONE-MAN SHOW!
ACTUALLY, I DO, BECK. YOU'VE GOT SOME SCARY-RICH FRIENDS--AND SEEING AS YOU BLEW THE LAST OF YOUR RESIDUALS ON A BUBBLE SPACESHIP THAT CAN'T ACTUALLY GO INTO SPACE--
...IT CAN'T?
HARD TO BELIEVE M.O.D.O.K. SCREWED YOU LIKE THAT. SO HOW ABOUT YOU SIT DOWN?
I WILL NOT! WHY, I SHOULD BE THE ONE TAKING YOU TO COURT! SIX VILLAINS, ONE TEAM--THAT WAS MY IDEA! YOU STOLE MY INTELLECTUAL PROPERTY!
ARE YOU SERIOUS, DUDE? I WASN'T EVEN--GFF--SORRY--

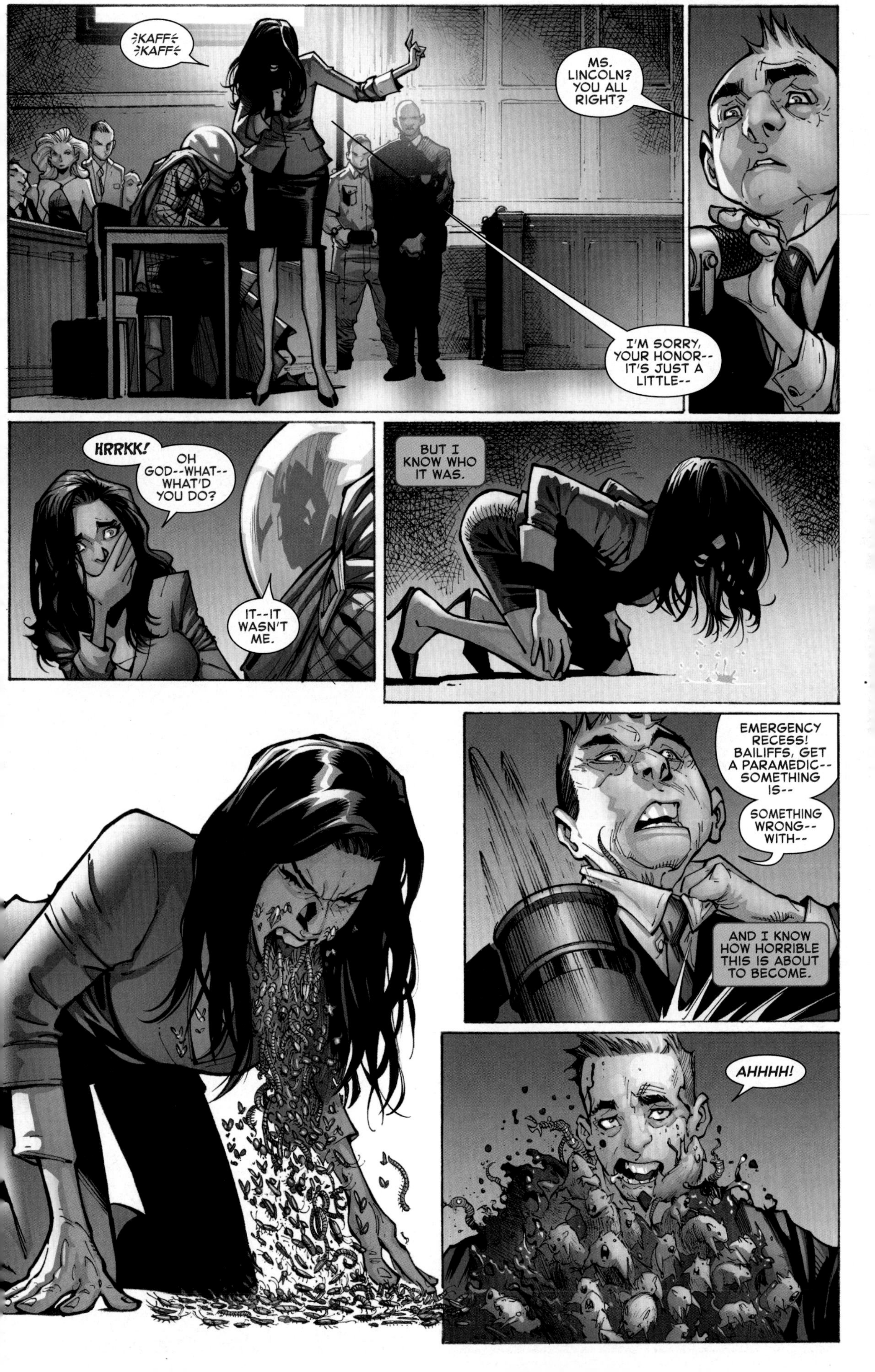

KAFF KAFF
MS. LINCOLN? YOU ALL RIGHT?
I'M SORRY, YOUR HONOR-- IT'S JUST A LITTLE--
HRRKK!
OH GOD--WHAT-- WHAT'D YOU DO?
IT--IT WASN'T ME.
BUT I KNOW WHO IT WAS.
EMERGENCY RECESS! BAILIFFS, GET A PARAMEDIC-- SOMETHING IS--
SOMETHING WRONG-- WITH--
AND I KNOW HOW HORRIBLE THIS IS ABOUT TO BECOME.
AHHHH!

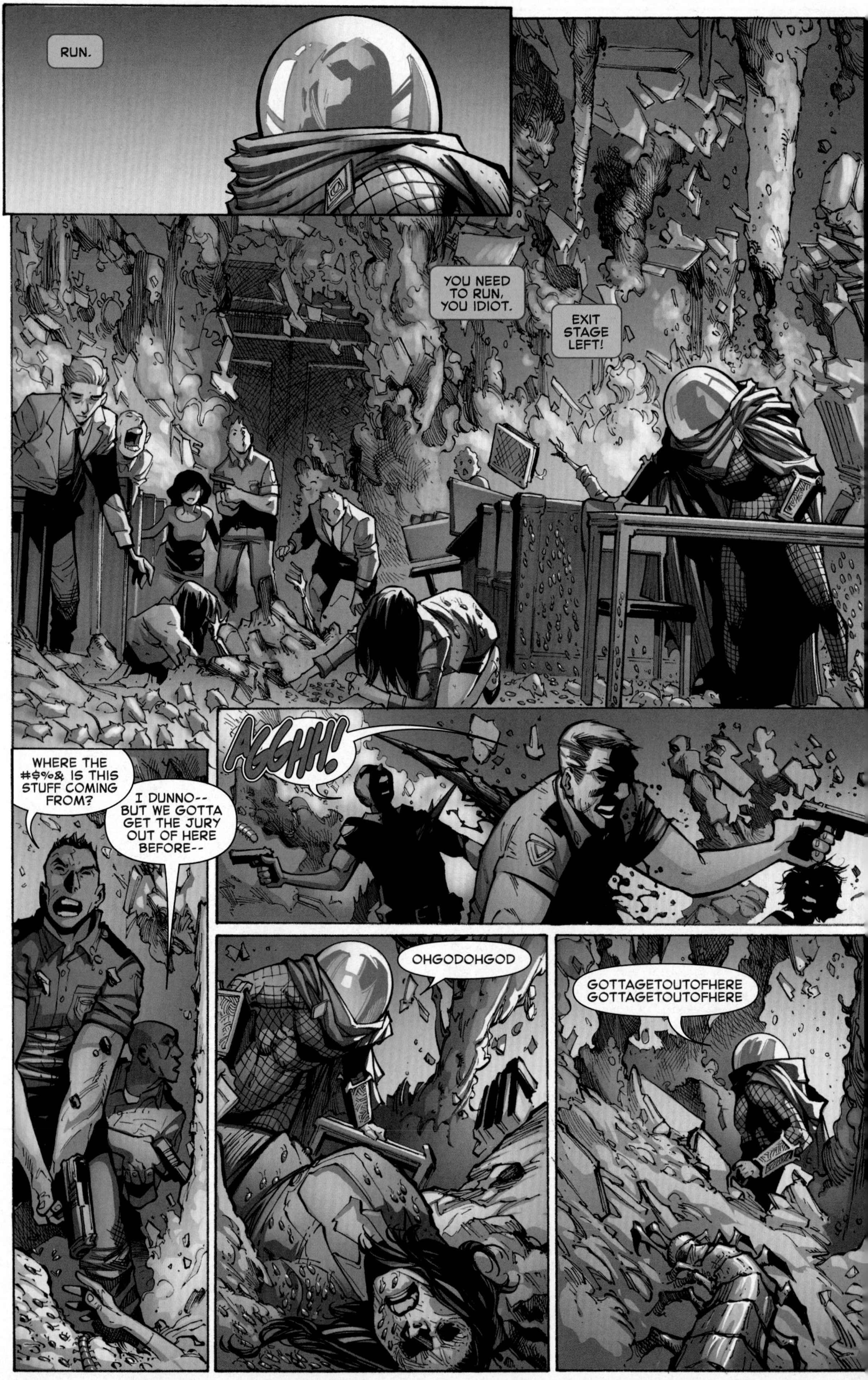
RUN.
YOU NEED TO RUN, YOU IDIOT.
EXIT STAGE LEFT!
WHERE THE #$%& IS THIS STUFF COMING FROM?
I DUNNO-- BUT WE GOTTA GET THE JURY OUT OF HERE BEFORE--
AGGHH!
OHGODOHGOD
GOTTAGETOUTOFHERE GOTTAGETOUTOFHERE

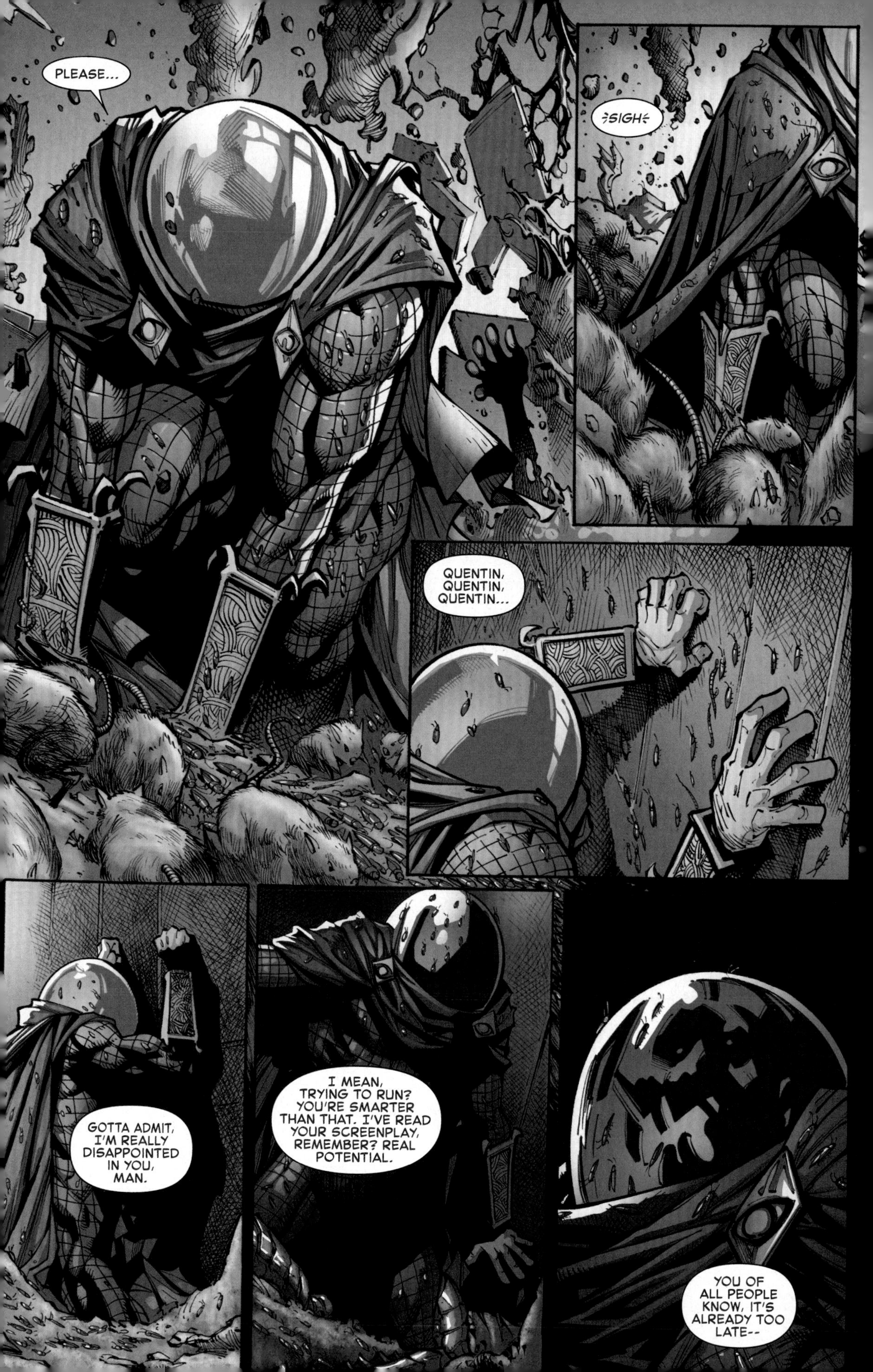
PLEASE...
⁓SIGH⁓
QUENTIN, QUENTIN, QUENTIN...
GOTTA ADMIT, I'M REALLY DISAPPOINTED IN YOU, MAN.
I MEAN, TRYING TO RUN? YOU'RE SMARTER THAN THAT. I'VE READ YOUR SCREENPLAY, REMEMBER? REAL POTENTIAL.
YOU OF ALL PEOPLE KNOW, IT'S ALREADY TOO LATE--

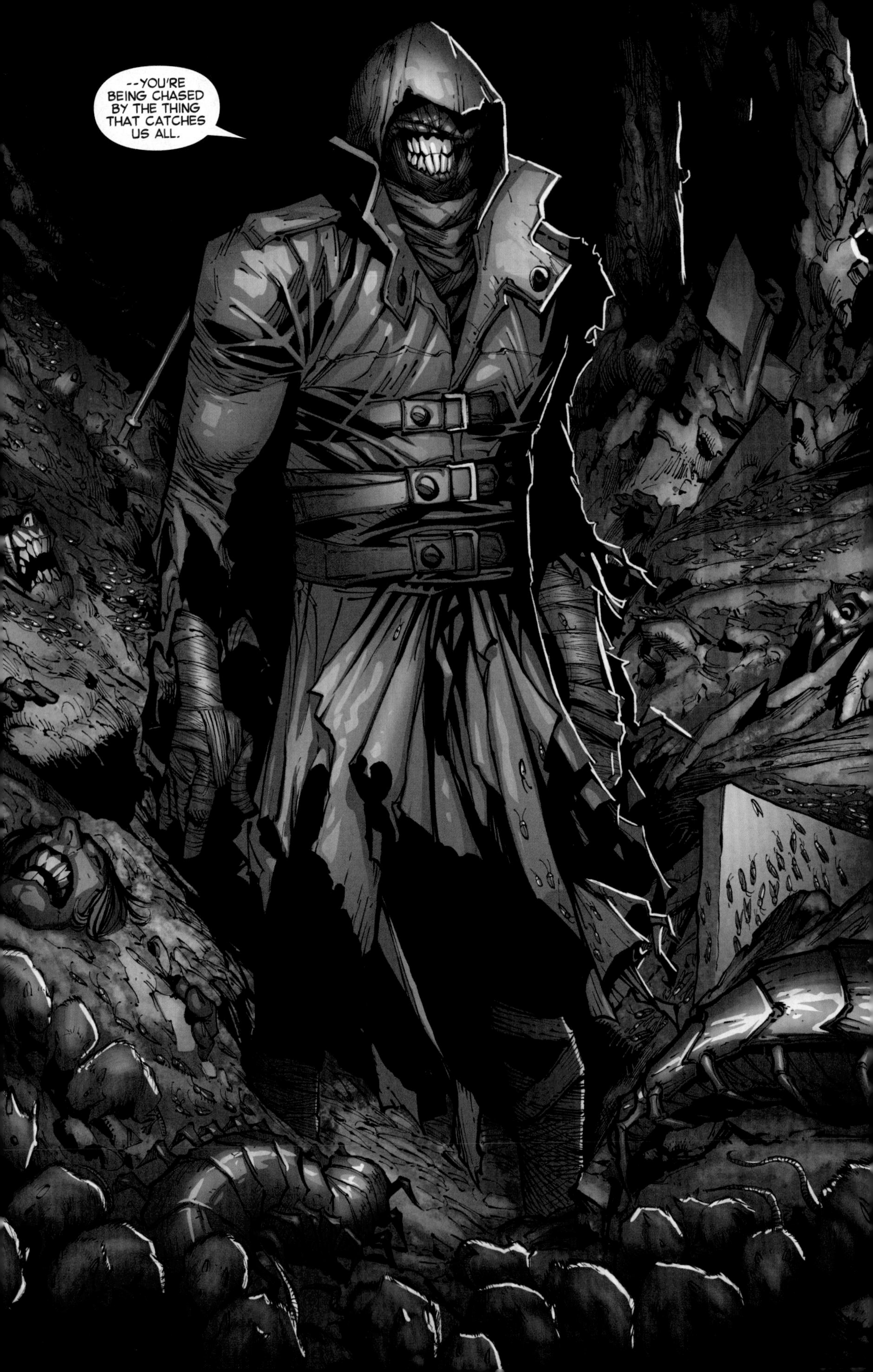
--YOU'RE BEING CHASED BY THE THING THAT CATCHES US ALL.

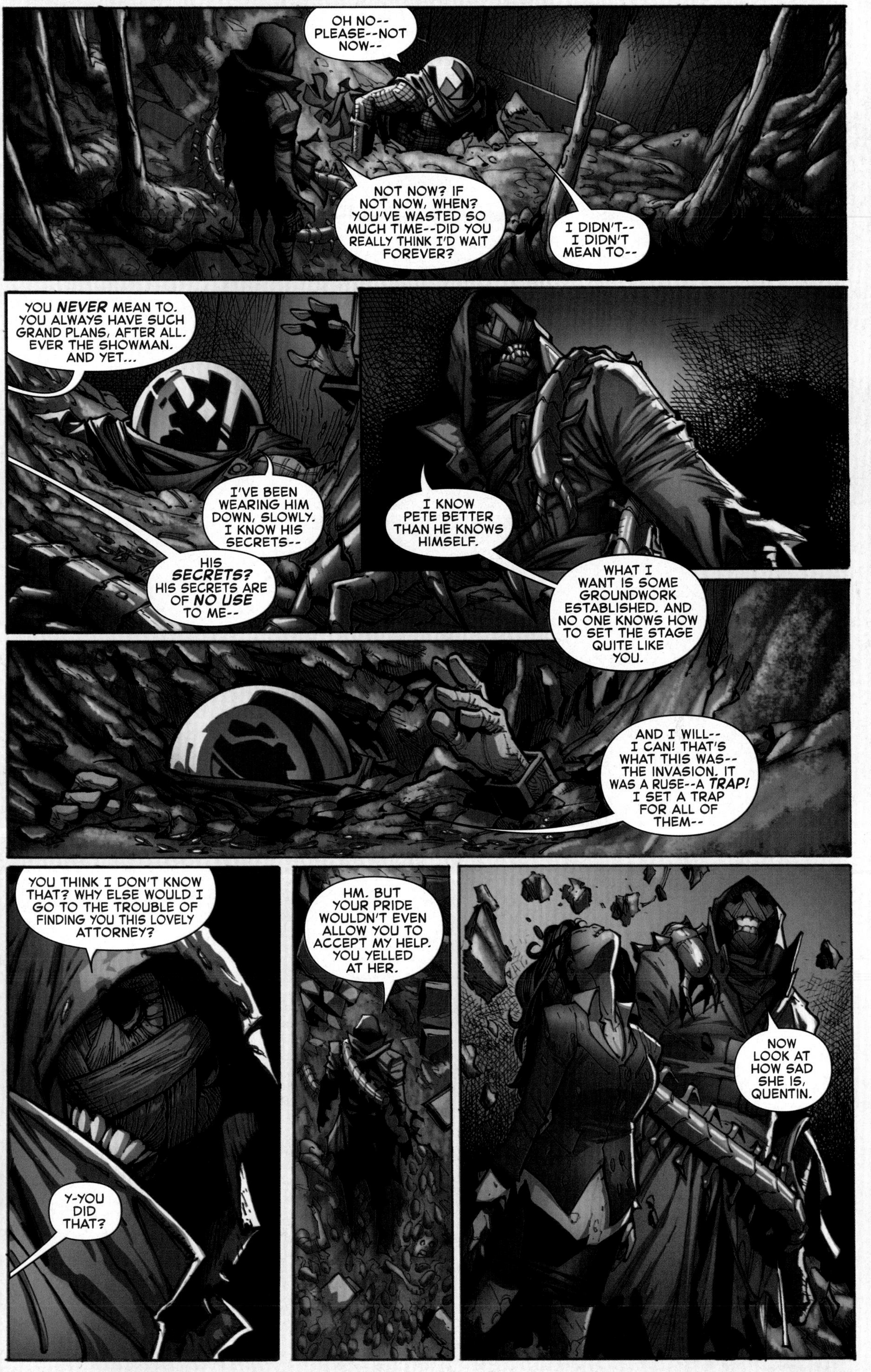
OH NO-- PLEASE--NOT NOW--
NOT NOW? IF NOT NOW, WHEN? YOU'VE WASTED SO MUCH TIME--DID YOU REALLY THINK I'D WAIT FOREVER?
I DIDN'T-- I DIDN'T MEAN TO--
YOU **NEVER** MEAN TO. YOU ALWAYS HAVE SUCH GRAND PLANS, AFTER ALL. EVER THE SHOWMAN. AND YET...
I'VE BEEN WEARING HIM DOWN, SLOWLY. I KNOW HIS SECRETS--
HIS ***SECRETS?*** HIS SECRETS ARE OF ***NO USE*** TO ME--
I KNOW PETE BETTER THAN HE KNOWS HIMSELF.
WHAT I WANT IS SOME GROUNDWORK ESTABLISHED. AND NO ONE KNOWS HOW TO SET THE STAGE QUITE LIKE YOU.
AND I WILL-- I CAN! THAT'S WHAT THIS WAS-- THE INVASION. IT WAS A RUSE--A ***TRAP!*** I SET A TRAP FOR ALL OF THEM--
YOU THINK I DON'T KNOW THAT? WHY ELSE WOULD I GO TO THE TROUBLE OF FINDING YOU THIS LOVELY ATTORNEY?
Y-YOU DID THAT?
HM. BUT YOUR PRIDE WOULDN'T EVEN ALLOW YOU TO ACCEPT MY HELP. YOU YELLED AT HER.
NOW LOOK AT HOW SAD SHE IS, QUENTIN.

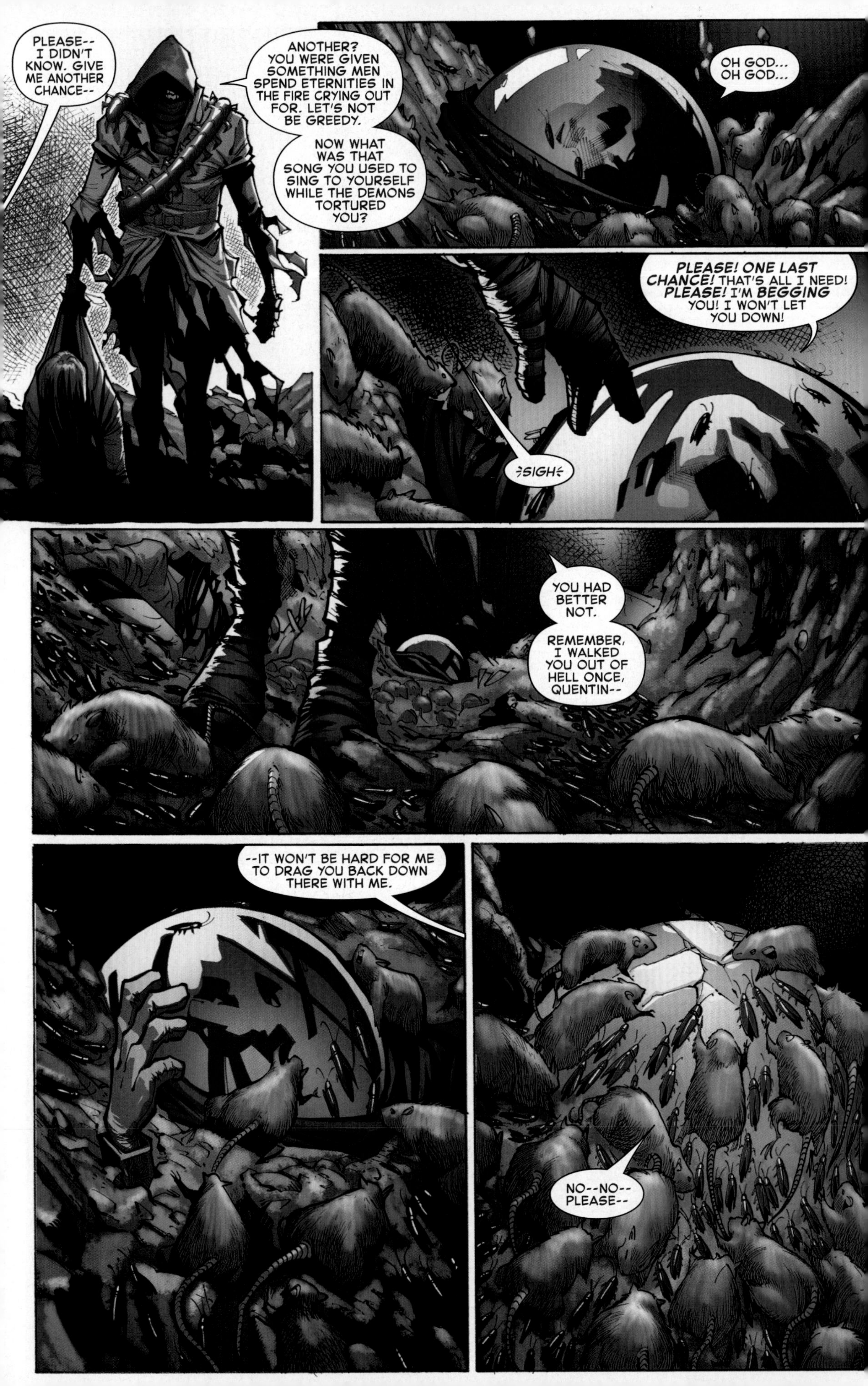
PLEASE-- I DIDN'T KNOW. GIVE ME ANOTHER CHANCE--
ANOTHER? YOU WERE GIVEN SOMETHING MEN SPEND ETERNITIES IN THE FIRE CRYING OUT FOR. LET'S NOT BE GREEDY.
NOW WHAT WAS THAT SONG YOU USED TO SING TO YOURSELF WHILE THE DEMONS TORTURED YOU?
OH GOD... OH GOD...
PLEASE! ONE LAST CHANCE! THAT'S ALL I NEED! PLEASE! I'M BEGGING YOU! I WON'T LET YOU DOWN!
SIGH
YOU HAD BETTER NOT.
REMEMBER, I WALKED YOU OUT OF HELL ONCE, QUENTIN--
--IT WON'T BE HARD FOR ME TO DRAG YOU BACK DOWN THERE WITH ME.
NO--NO-- PLEASE--

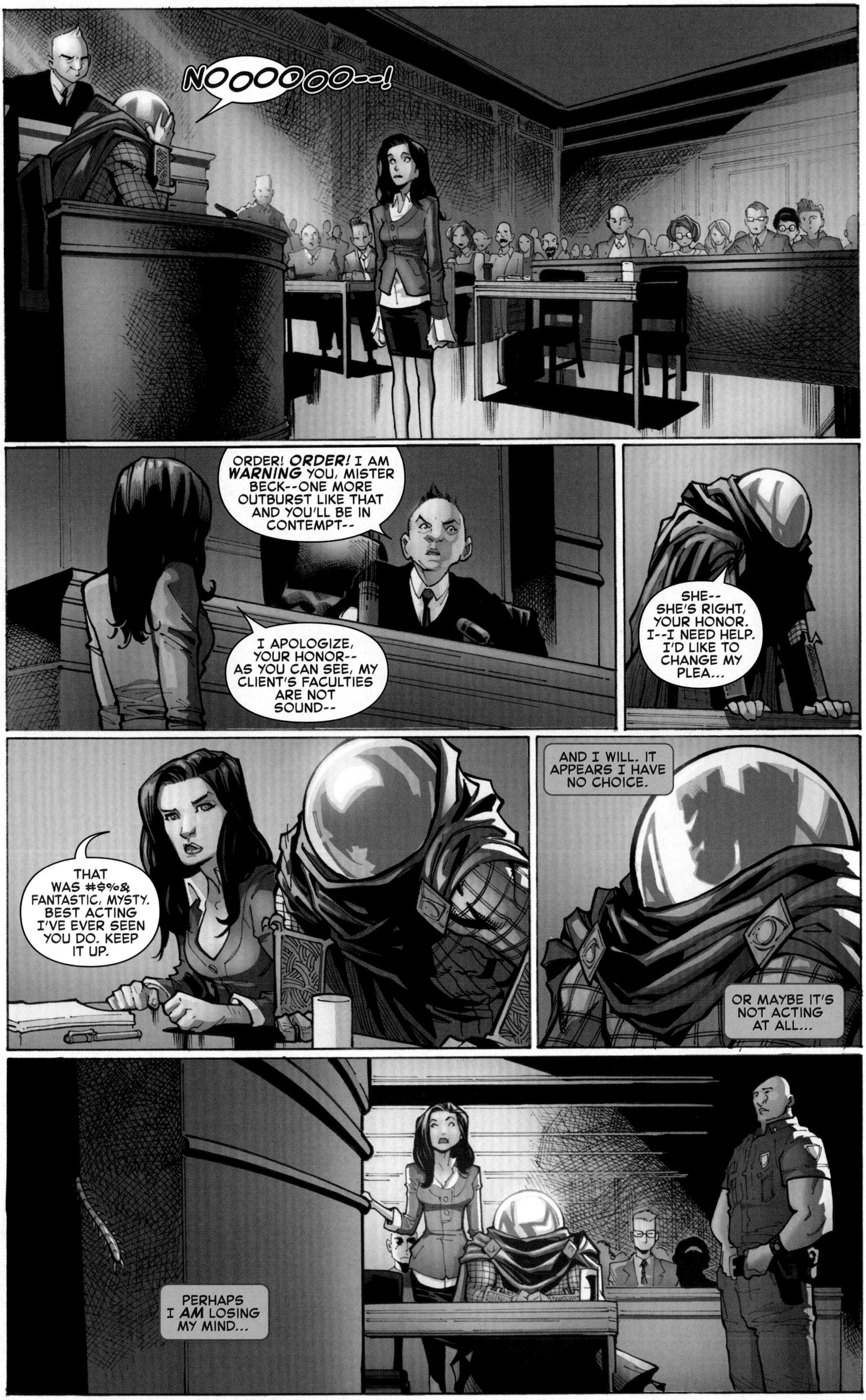
NOOOOOOO--!
ORDER! ORDER! I AM WARNING YOU, MISTER BECK--ONE MORE OUTBURST LIKE THAT AND YOU'LL BE IN CONTEMPT--
I APOLOGIZE, YOUR HONOR--AS YOU CAN SEE, MY CLIENT'S FACULTIES ARE NOT SOUND--
SHE--SHE'S RIGHT, YOUR HONOR. I--I NEED HELP. I'D LIKE TO CHANGE MY PLEA...
THAT WAS #$%& FANTASTIC, MYSTY. BEST ACTING I'VE EVER SEEN YOU DO. KEEP IT UP.
AND I WILL. IT APPEARS I HAVE NO CHOICE.
OR MAYBE IT'S NOT ACTING AT ALL...
PERHAPS I AM LOSING MY MIND...

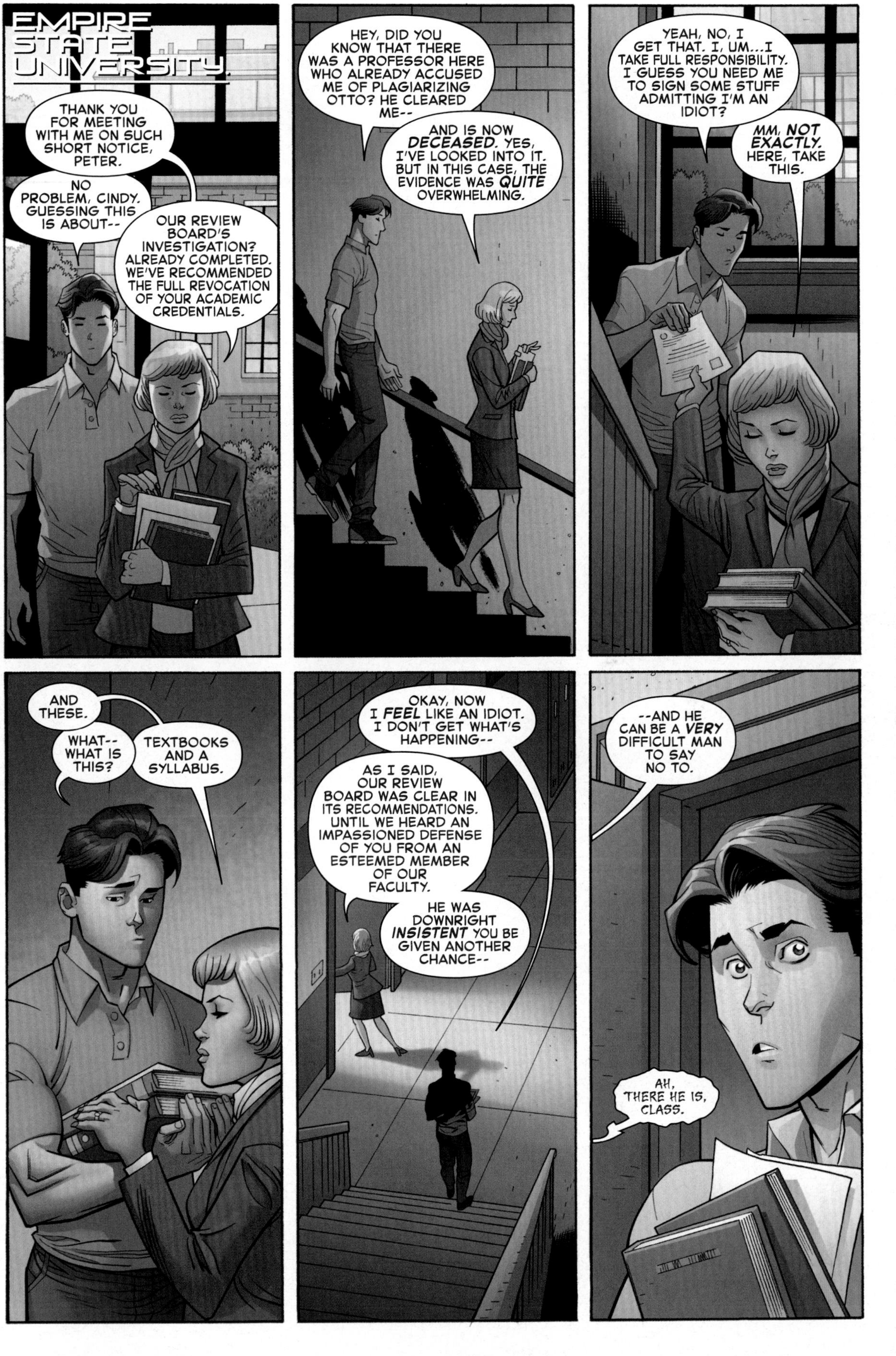
EMPIRE STATE UNIVERSITY.
THANK YOU FOR MEETING WITH ME ON SUCH SHORT NOTICE, PETER.
NO PROBLEM, CINDY. GUESSING THIS IS ABOUT--
OUR REVIEW BOARD'S INVESTIGATION? ALREADY COMPLETED. WE'VE RECOMMENDED THE FULL REVOCATION OF YOUR ACADEMIC CREDENTIALS.
HEY, DID YOU KNOW THAT THERE WAS A PROFESSOR HERE WHO ALREADY ACCUSED ME OF PLAGIARIZING OTTO? HE CLEARED ME--
AND IS NOW DECEASED. YES, I'VE LOOKED INTO IT. BUT IN THIS CASE, THE EVIDENCE WAS QUITE OVERWHELMING.
YEAH, NO, I GET THAT. I, UM...I TAKE FULL RESPONSIBILITY. I GUESS YOU NEED ME TO SIGN SOME STUFF ADMITTING I'M AN IDIOT?
MM, NOT EXACTLY. HERE, TAKE THIS.
AND THESE.
WHAT-- WHAT IS THIS?
TEXTBOOKS AND A SYLLABUS.
OKAY, NOW I FEEL LIKE AN IDIOT. I DON'T GET WHAT'S HAPPENING--
AS I SAID, OUR REVIEW BOARD WAS CLEAR IN ITS RECOMMENDATIONS. UNTIL WE HEARD AN IMPASSIONED DEFENSE OF YOU FROM AN ESTEEMED MEMBER OF OUR FACULTY.
HE WAS DOWNRIGHT INSISTENT YOU BE GIVEN ANOTHER CHANCE--
--AND HE CAN BE A VERY DIFFICULT MAN TO SAY NO TO.
AH, THERE HE IS, CLASS.

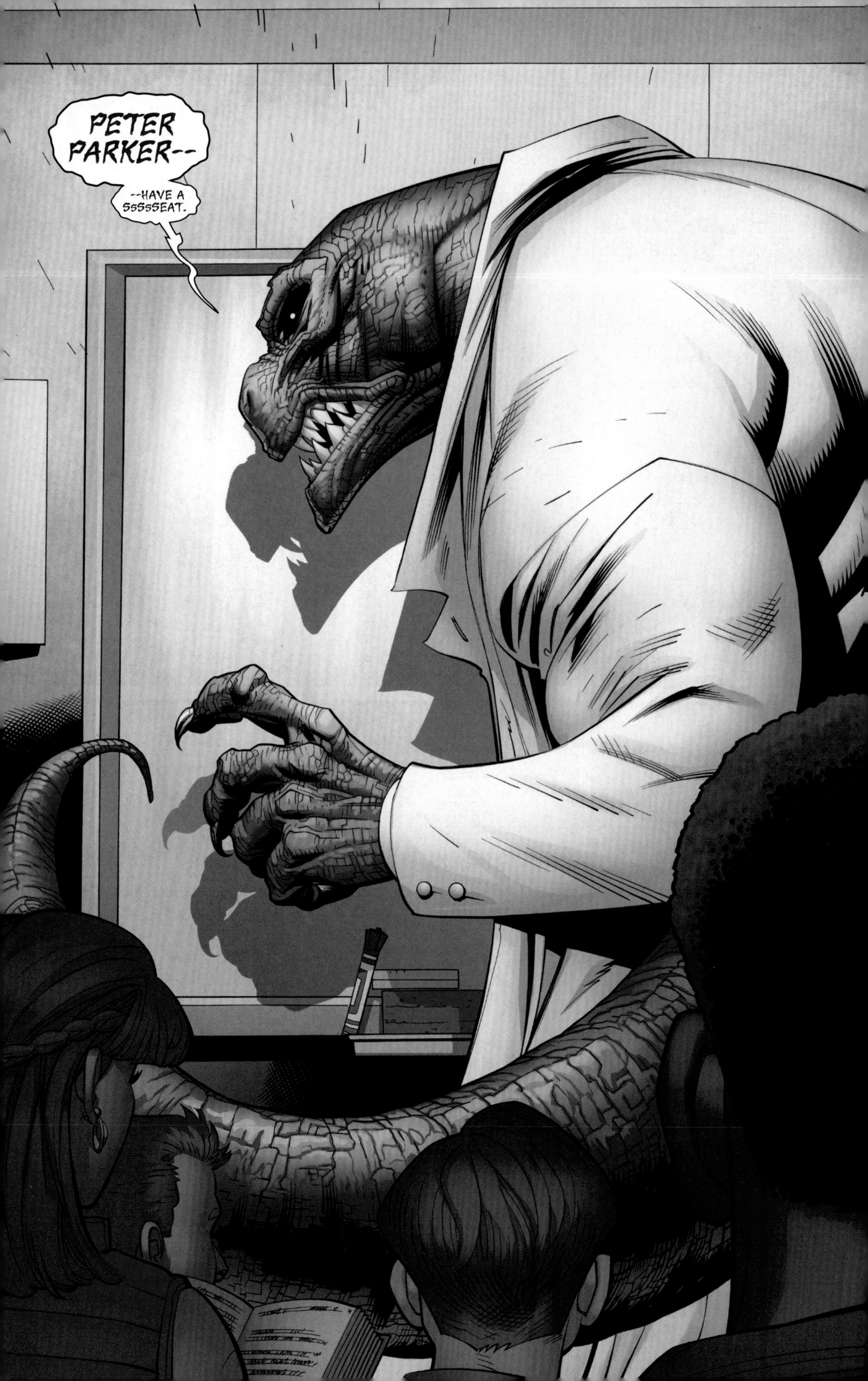
PETER PARKER--
--HAVE A SSSSSEAT.

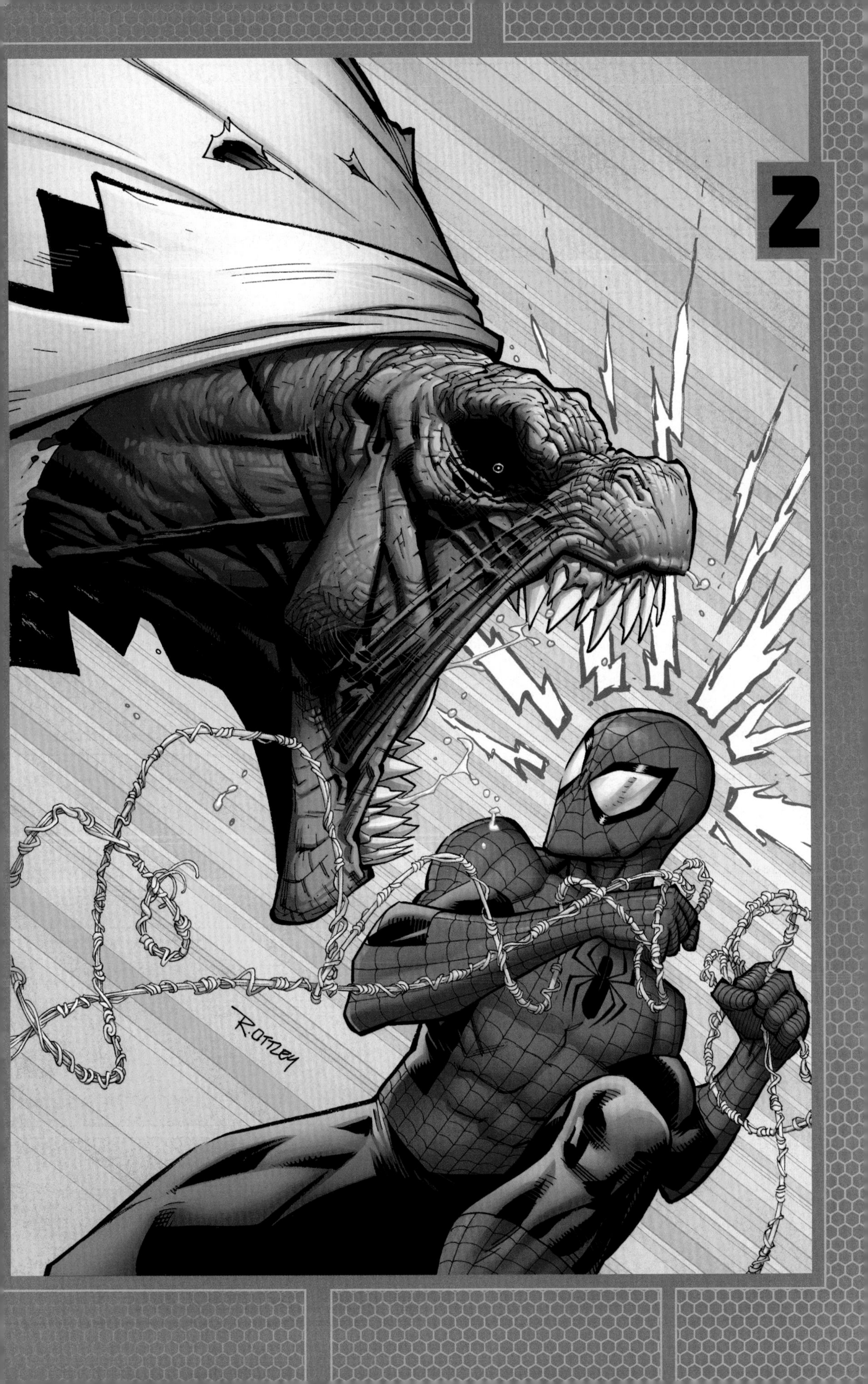
2
R.OTTLEY

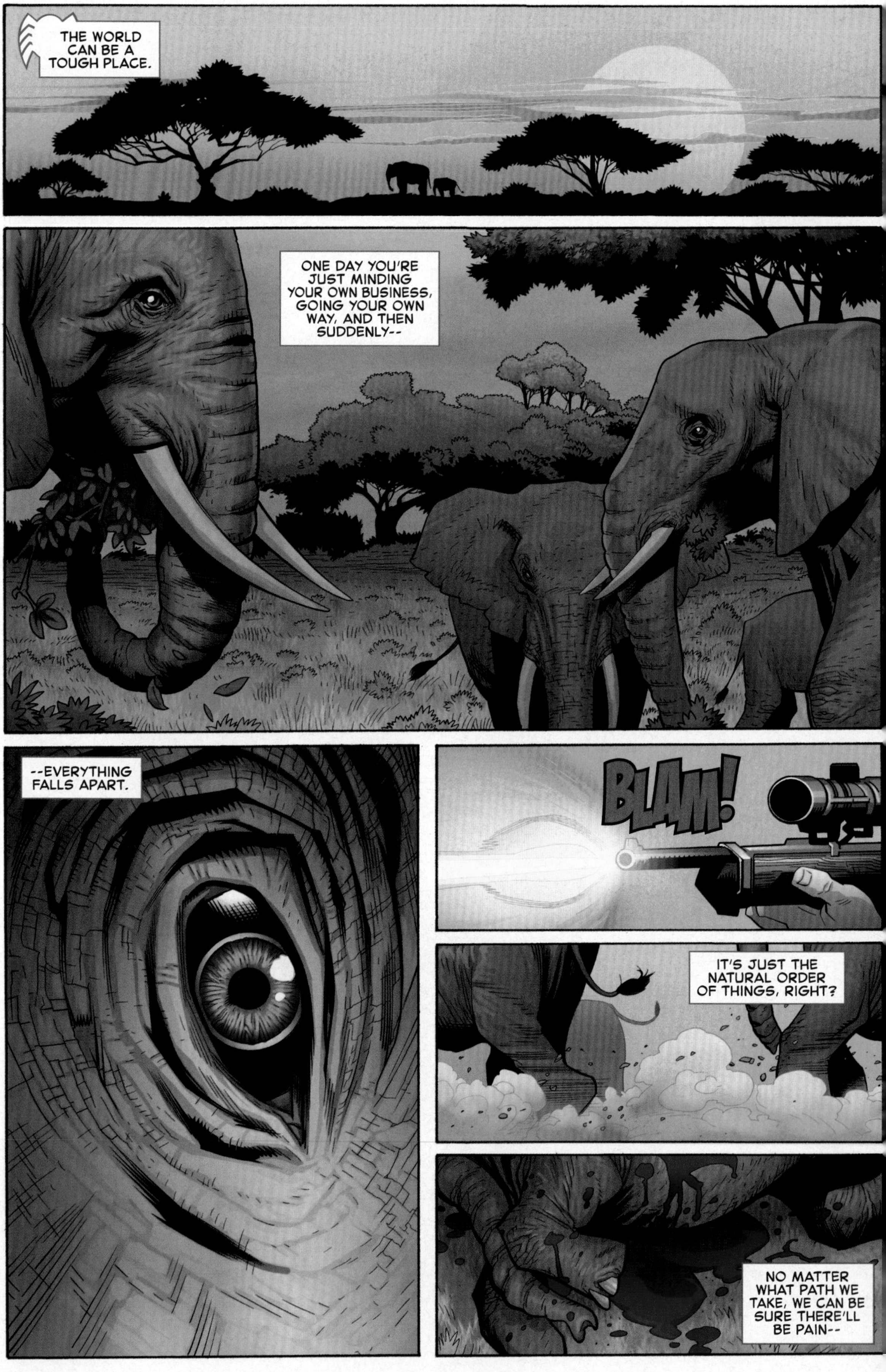
THE WORLD CAN BE A TOUGH PLACE.
ONE DAY YOU'RE JUST MINDING YOUR OWN BUSINESS, GOING YOUR OWN WAY, AND THEN SUDDENLY--
--EVERYTHING FALLS APART.
BLAM!
IT'S JUST THE NATURAL ORDER OF THINGS, RIGHT?
NO MATTER WHAT PATH WE TAKE, WE CAN BE SURE THERE'LL BE PAIN--

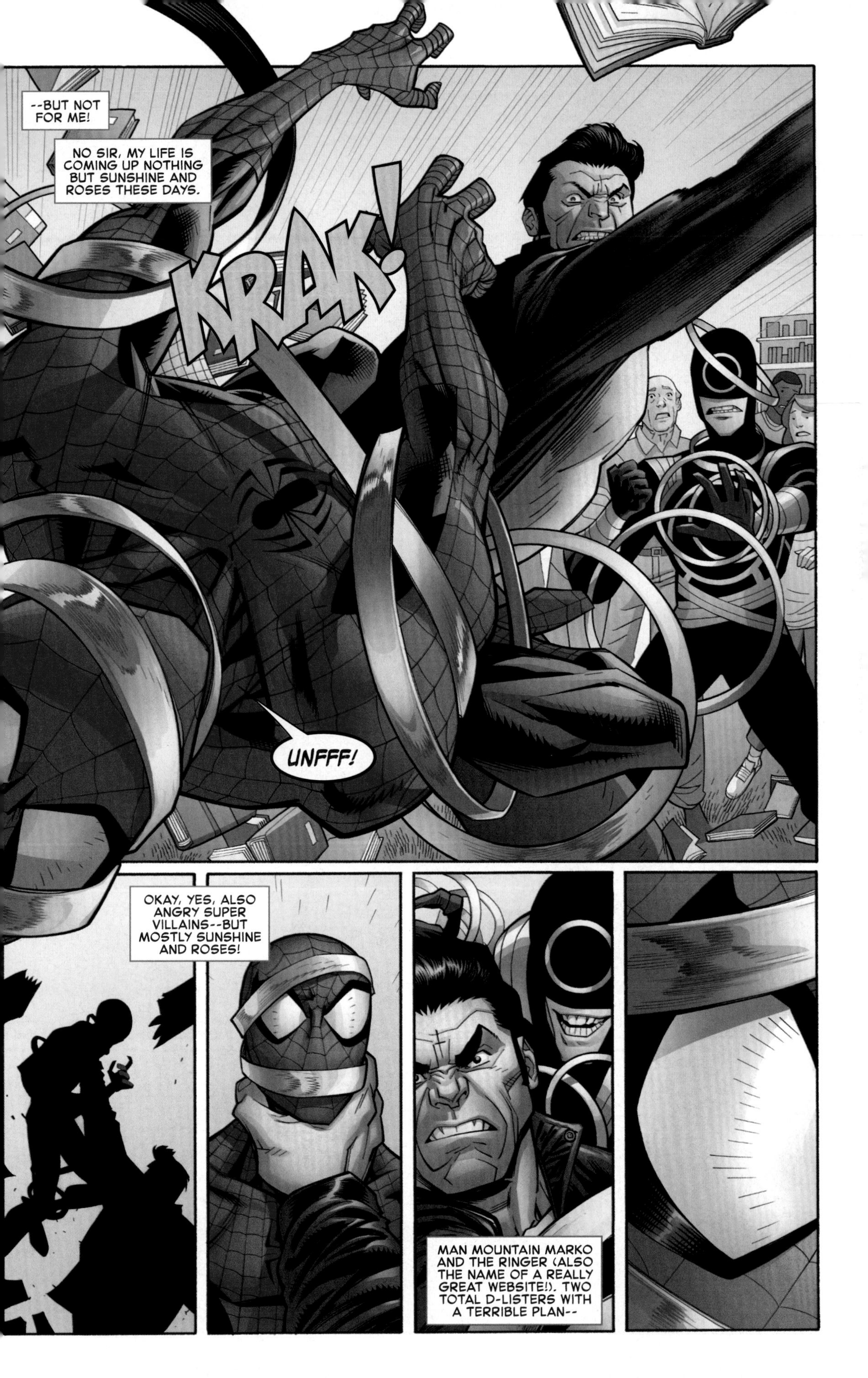
--BUT NOT FOR ME!
NO SIR, MY LIFE IS COMING UP NOTHING BUT SUNSHINE AND ROSES THESE DAYS.
KRAK!
UNFFF!
OKAY, YES, ALSO ANGRY SUPER VILLAINS--BUT MOSTLY SUNSHINE AND ROSES!
MAN MOUNTAIN MARKO AND THE RINGER (ALSO THE NAME OF A REALLY GREAT WEBSITE!). TWO TOTAL D-LISTERS WITH A TERRIBLE PLAN--

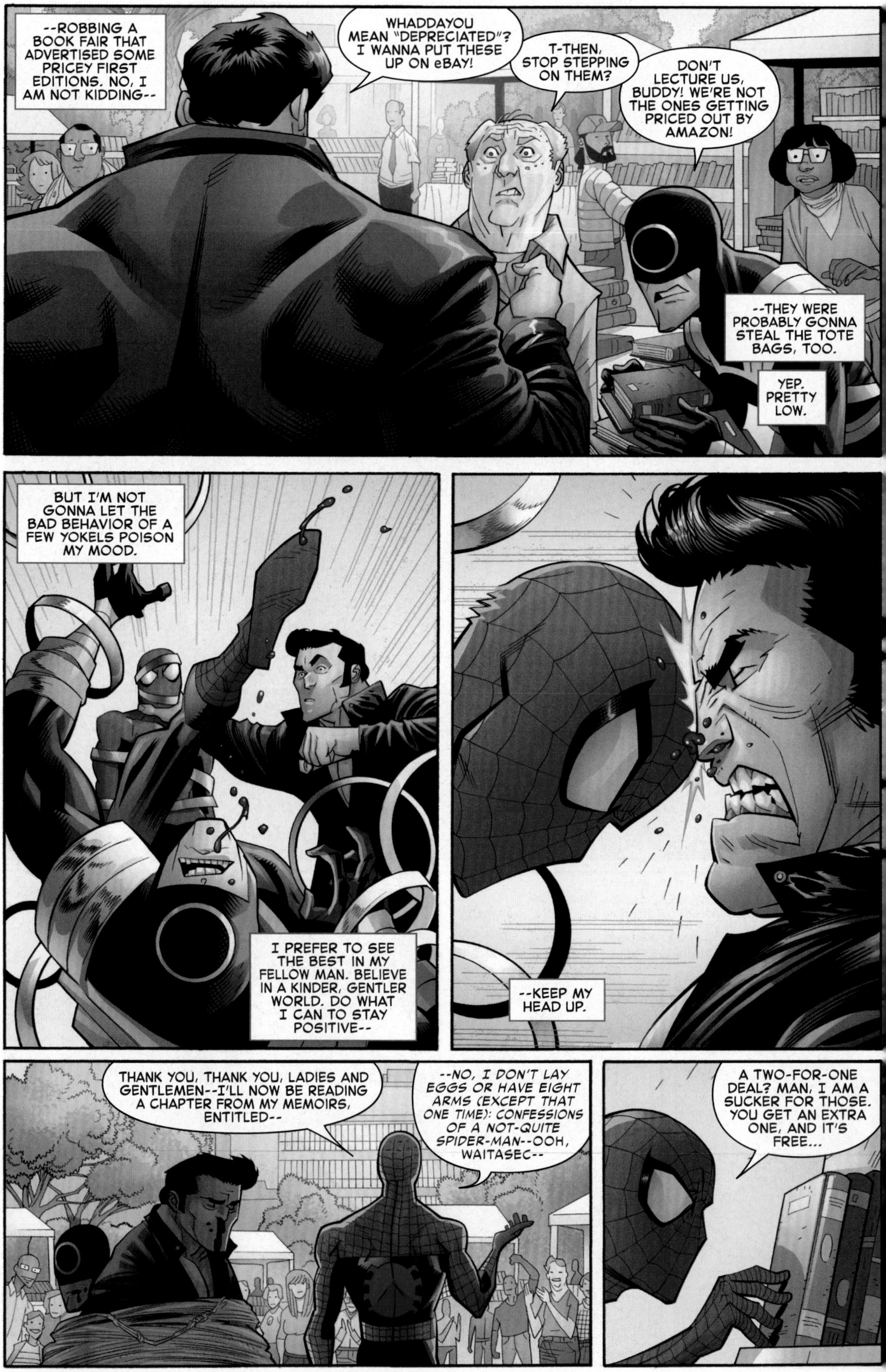
--ROBBING A BOOK FAIR THAT ADVERTISED SOME PRICEY FIRST EDITIONS. NO, I AM NOT KIDDING--
WHADDAYOU MEAN "DEPRECIATED"? I WANNA PUT THESE UP ON eBAY!
T-THEN, STOP STEPPING ON THEM?
DON'T LECTURE US, BUDDY! WE'RE NOT THE ONES GETTING PRICED OUT BY AMAZON!
--THEY WERE PROBABLY GONNA STEAL THE TOTE BAGS, TOO.
YEP. PRETTY LOW.
BUT I'M NOT GONNA LET THE BAD BEHAVIOR OF A FEW YOKELS POISON MY MOOD.
I PREFER TO SEE THE BEST IN MY FELLOW MAN. BELIEVE IN A KINDER, GENTLER WORLD. DO WHAT I CAN TO STAY POSITIVE--
--KEEP MY HEAD UP.
THANK YOU, THANK YOU, LADIES AND GENTLEMEN--I'LL NOW BE READING A CHAPTER FROM MY MEMOIRS, ENTITLED--
--NO, I DON'T LAY EGGS OR HAVE EIGHT ARMS (EXCEPT THAT ONE TIME): CONFESSIONS OF A NOT-QUITE SPIDER-MAN--OOH, WAITASEC--
A TWO-FOR-ONE DEAL? MAN, I AM A SUCKER FOR THOSE. YOU GET AN EXTRA ONE, AND IT'S FREE...

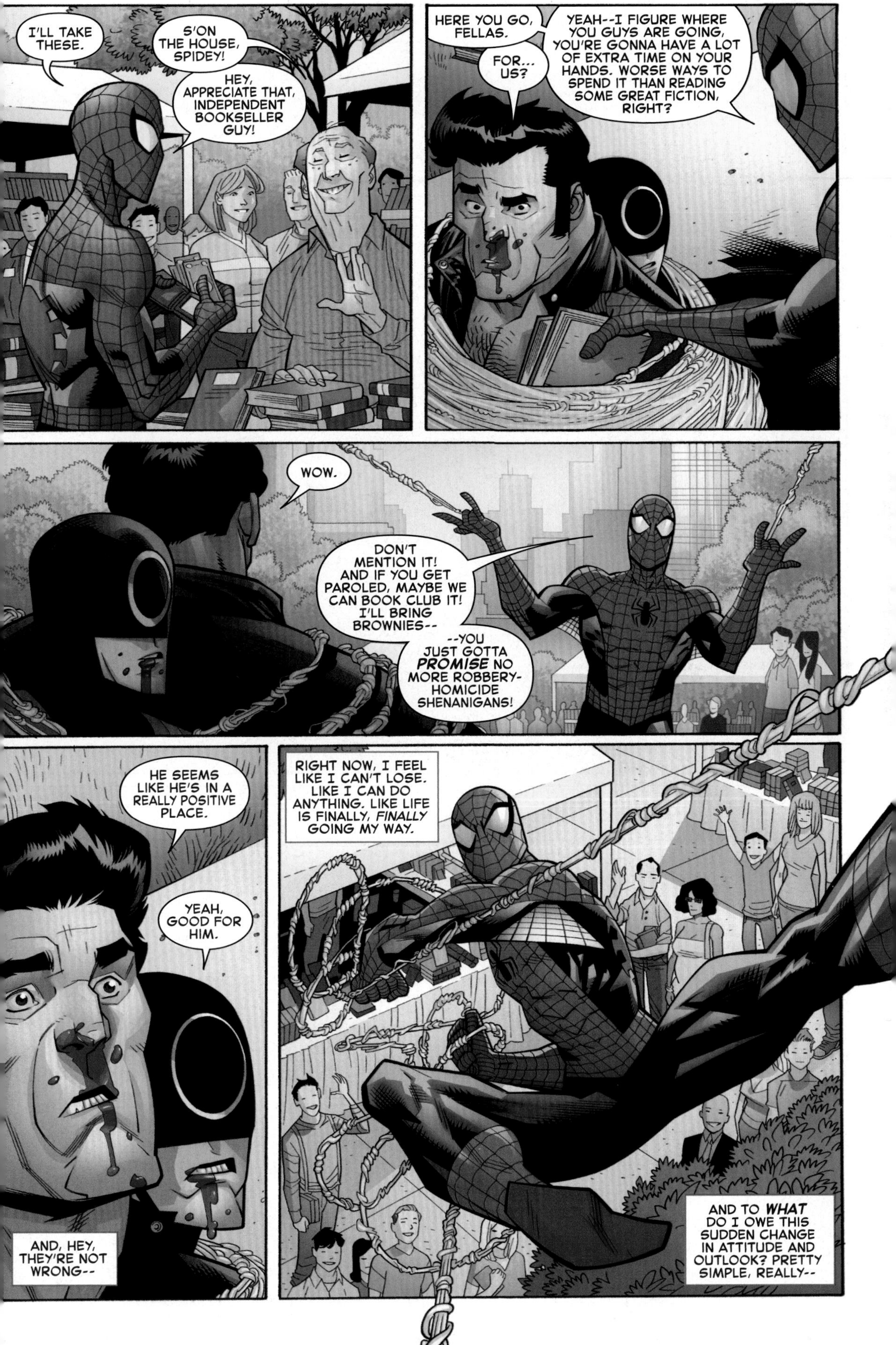
I'LL TAKE THESE.
S'ON THE HOUSE, SPIDEY!
HEY, APPRECIATE THAT, INDEPENDENT BOOKSELLER GUY!
HERE YOU GO, FELLAS.
FOR... US?
YEAH--I FIGURE WHERE YOU GUYS ARE GOING, YOU'RE GONNA HAVE A LOT OF EXTRA TIME ON YOUR HANDS. WORSE WAYS TO SPEND IT THAN READING SOME GREAT FICTION, RIGHT?
WOW.
DON'T MENTION IT! AND IF YOU GET PAROLED, MAYBE WE CAN BOOK CLUB IT! I'LL BRING BROWNIES--
--YOU JUST GOTTA PROMISE NO MORE ROBBERY-HOMICIDE SHENANIGANS!
HE SEEMS LIKE HE'S IN A REALLY POSITIVE PLACE.
YEAH, GOOD FOR HIM.
AND, HEY, THEY'RE NOT WRONG--
RIGHT NOW, I FEEL LIKE I CAN'T LOSE. LIKE I CAN DO ANYTHING. LIKE LIFE IS FINALLY, FINALLY GOING MY WAY.
AND TO WHAT DO I OWE THIS SUDDEN CHANGE IN ATTITUDE AND OUTLOOK? PRETTY SIMPLE, REALLY--

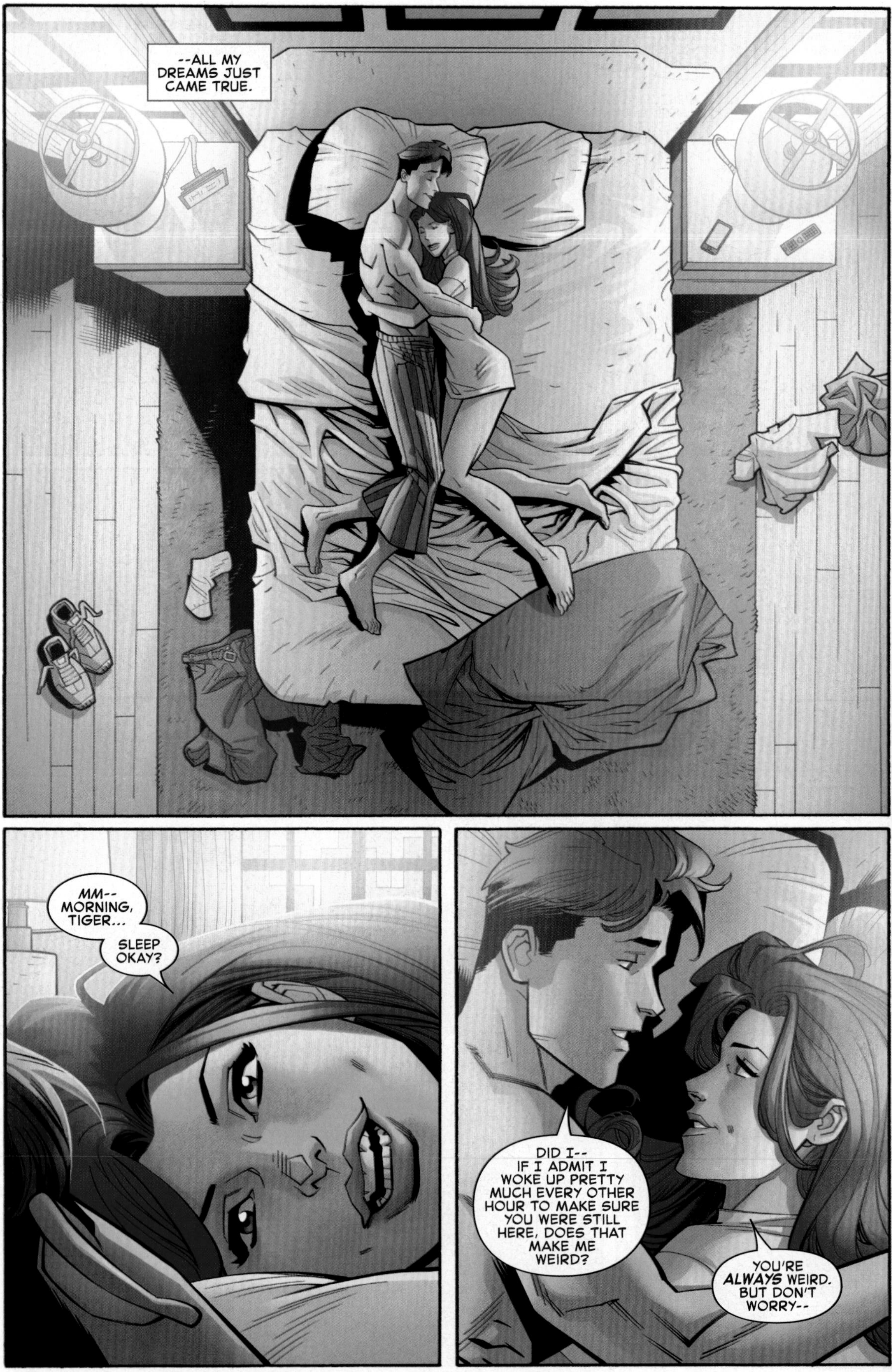
--ALL MY DREAMS JUST CAME TRUE.
MM--MORNING, TIGER...
SLEEP OKAY?
DID I--IF I ADMIT I WOKE UP PRETTY MUCH EVERY OTHER HOUR TO MAKE SURE YOU WERE STILL HERE, DOES THAT MAKE ME WEIRD?
YOU'RE ALWAYS WEIRD. BUT DON'T WORRY--

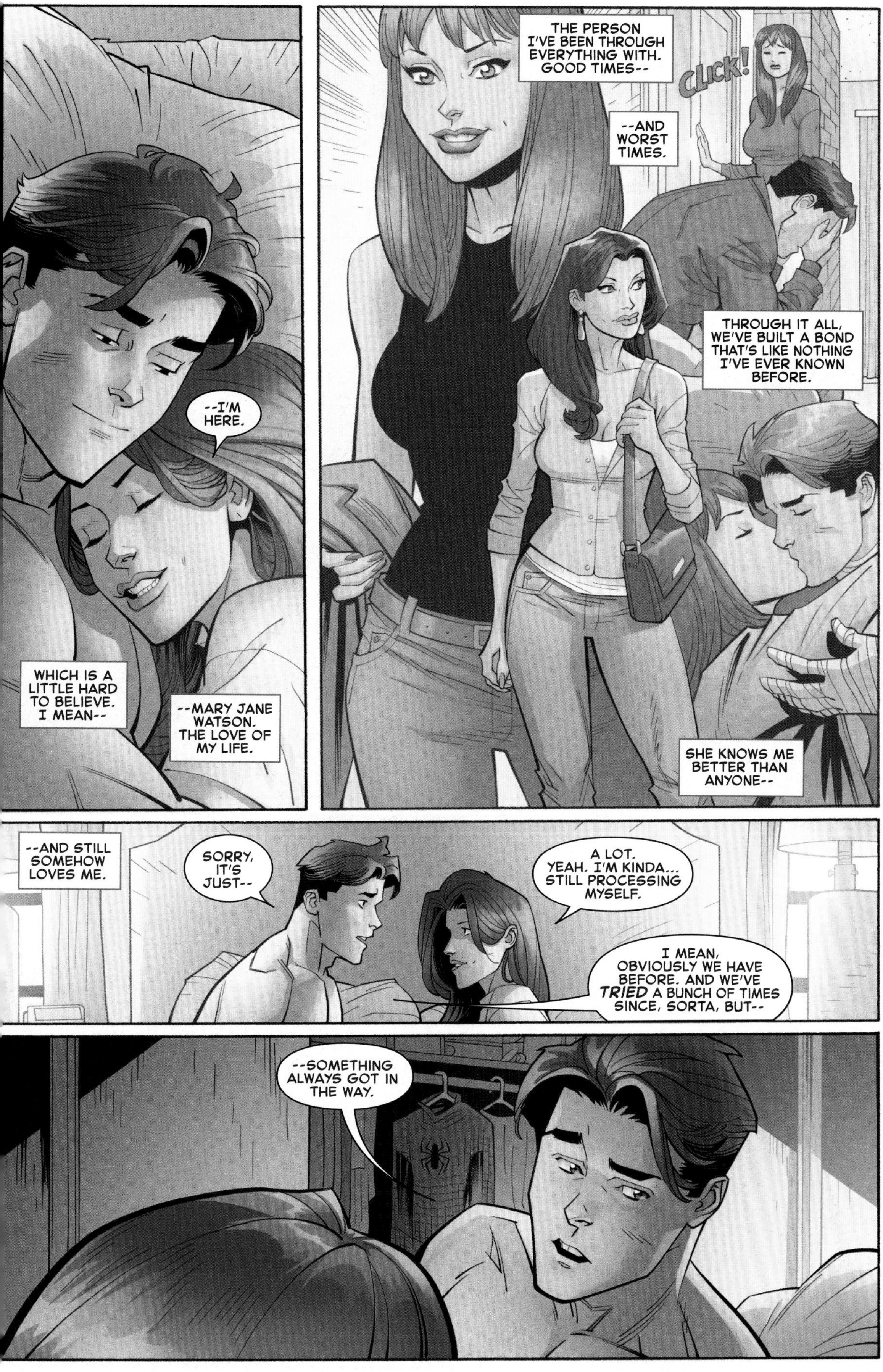
--I'M HERE.
WHICH IS A LITTLE HARD TO BELIEVE. I MEAN--
--MARY JANE WATSON. THE LOVE OF MY LIFE.
THE PERSON I'VE BEEN THROUGH EVERYTHING WITH. GOOD TIMES--
CLICK!
--AND WORST TIMES.
THROUGH IT ALL, WE'VE BUILT A BOND THAT'S LIKE NOTHING I'VE EVER KNOWN BEFORE.
SHE KNOWS ME BETTER THAN ANYONE--
--AND STILL SOMEHOW LOVES ME.
SORRY, IT'S JUST--
A LOT. YEAH. I'M KINDA... STILL PROCESSING MYSELF.
I MEAN, OBVIOUSLY WE HAVE BEFORE. AND WE'VE TRIED A BUNCH OF TIMES SINCE, SORTA, BUT--
--SOMETHING ALWAYS GOT IN THE WAY.

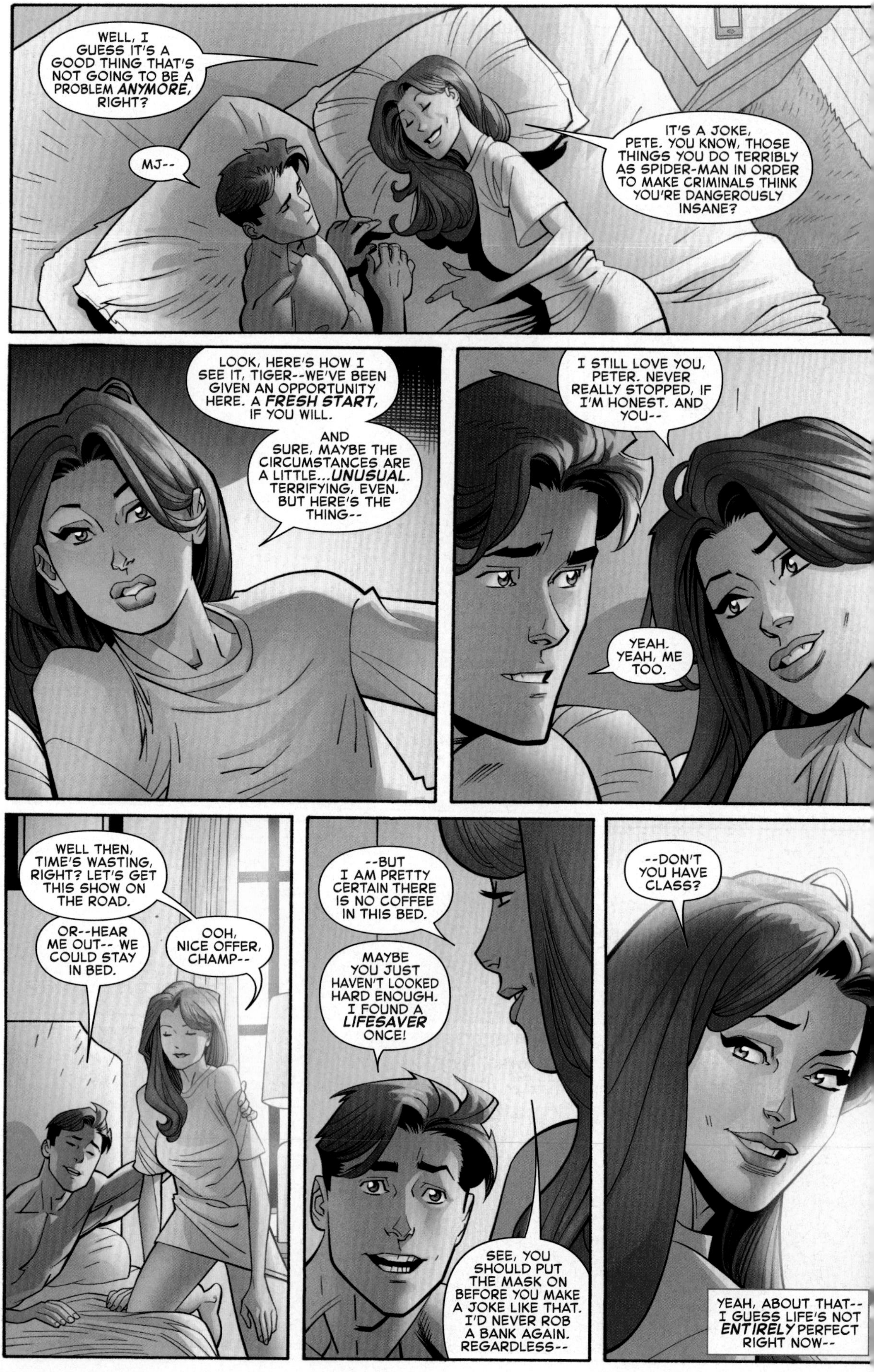
WELL, I GUESS IT'S A GOOD THING THAT'S NOT GOING TO BE A PROBLEM ANYMORE, RIGHT?
MJ--
IT'S A JOKE, PETE. YOU KNOW, THOSE THINGS YOU DO TERRIBLY AS SPIDER-MAN IN ORDER TO MAKE CRIMINALS THINK YOU'RE DANGEROUSLY INSANE?
LOOK, HERE'S HOW I SEE IT, TIGER--WE'VE BEEN GIVEN AN OPPORTUNITY HERE. A FRESH START, IF YOU WILL.
AND SURE, MAYBE THE CIRCUMSTANCES ARE A LITTLE...UNUSUAL. TERRIFYING, EVEN. BUT HERE'S THE THING--
I STILL LOVE YOU, PETER. NEVER REALLY STOPPED, IF I'M HONEST. AND YOU--
YEAH. YEAH, ME TOO.
WELL THEN, TIME'S WASTING, RIGHT? LET'S GET THIS SHOW ON THE ROAD.
OR--HEAR ME OUT-- WE COULD STAY IN BED.
OOH, NICE OFFER, CHAMP--
--BUT I AM PRETTY CERTAIN THERE IS NO COFFEE IN THIS BED.
MAYBE YOU JUST HAVEN'T LOOKED HARD ENOUGH. I FOUND A LIFESAVER ONCE!
SEE, YOU SHOULD PUT THE MASK ON BEFORE YOU MAKE A JOKE LIKE THAT. I'D NEVER ROB A BANK AGAIN. REGARDLESS--
--DON'T YOU HAVE CLASS?
YEAH, ABOUT THAT-- I GUESS LIFE'S NOT ENTIRELY PERFECT RIGHT NOW--

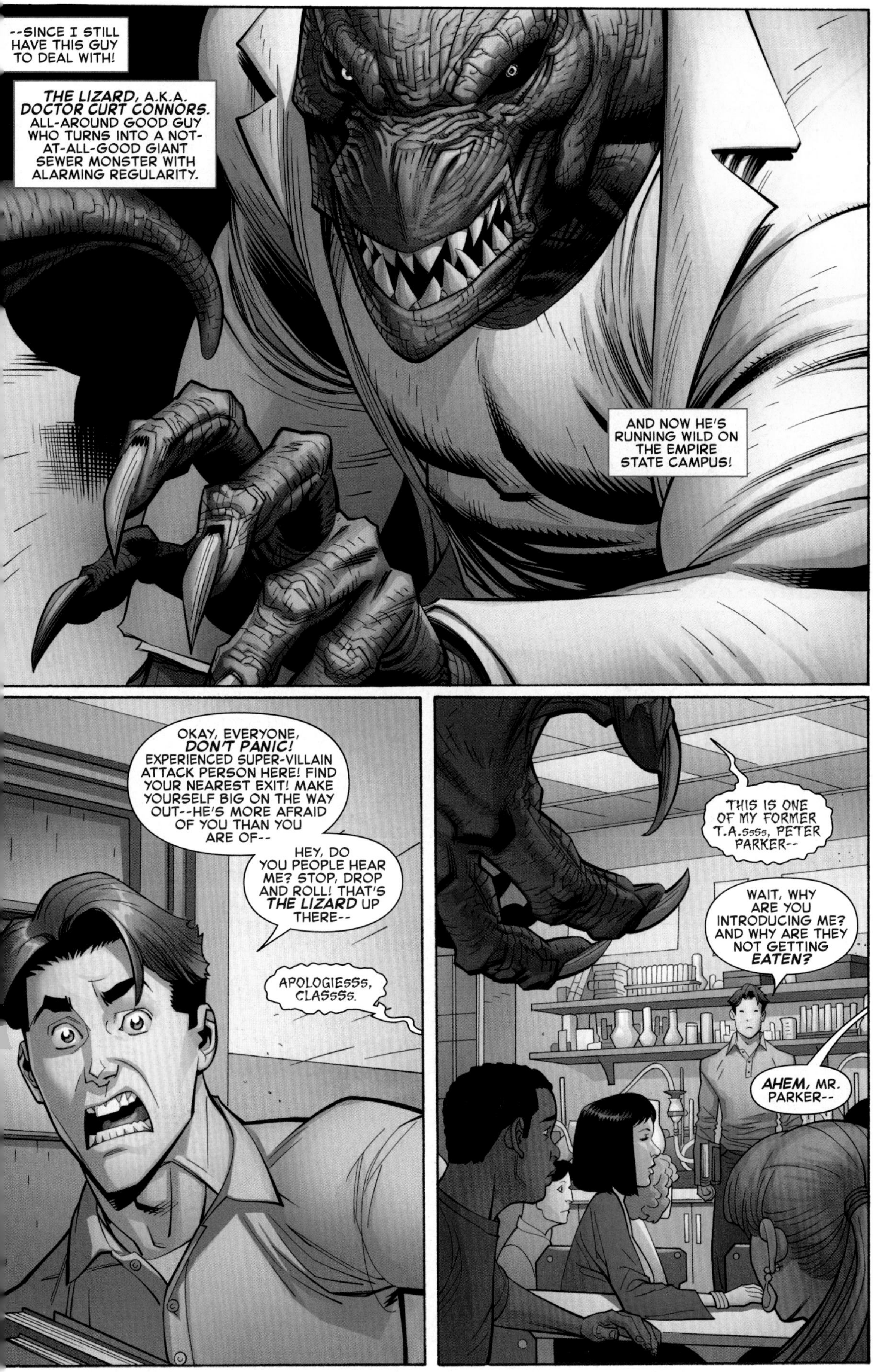
--SINCE I STILL HAVE THIS GUY TO DEAL WITH!
THE LIZARD, A.K.A. DOCTOR CURT CONNORS. ALL-AROUND GOOD GUY WHO TURNS INTO A NOT-AT-ALL-GOOD GIANT SEWER MONSTER WITH ALARMING REGULARITY.
AND NOW HE'S RUNNING WILD ON THE EMPIRE STATE CAMPUS!
OKAY, EVERYONE, DON'T PANIC! EXPERIENCED SUPER-VILLAIN ATTACK PERSON HERE! FIND YOUR NEAREST EXIT! MAKE YOURSELF BIG ON THE WAY OUT--HE'S MORE AFRAID OF YOU THAN YOU ARE OF--
HEY, DO YOU PEOPLE HEAR ME? STOP, DROP AND ROLL! THAT'S THE LIZARD UP THERE--
APOLOGIESSS, CLASSSS.
THIS IS ONE OF MY FORMER T.A.ssss, PETER PARKER--
WAIT, WHY ARE YOU INTRODUCING ME? AND WHY ARE THEY NOT GETTING EATEN?
AHEM, MR. PARKER--

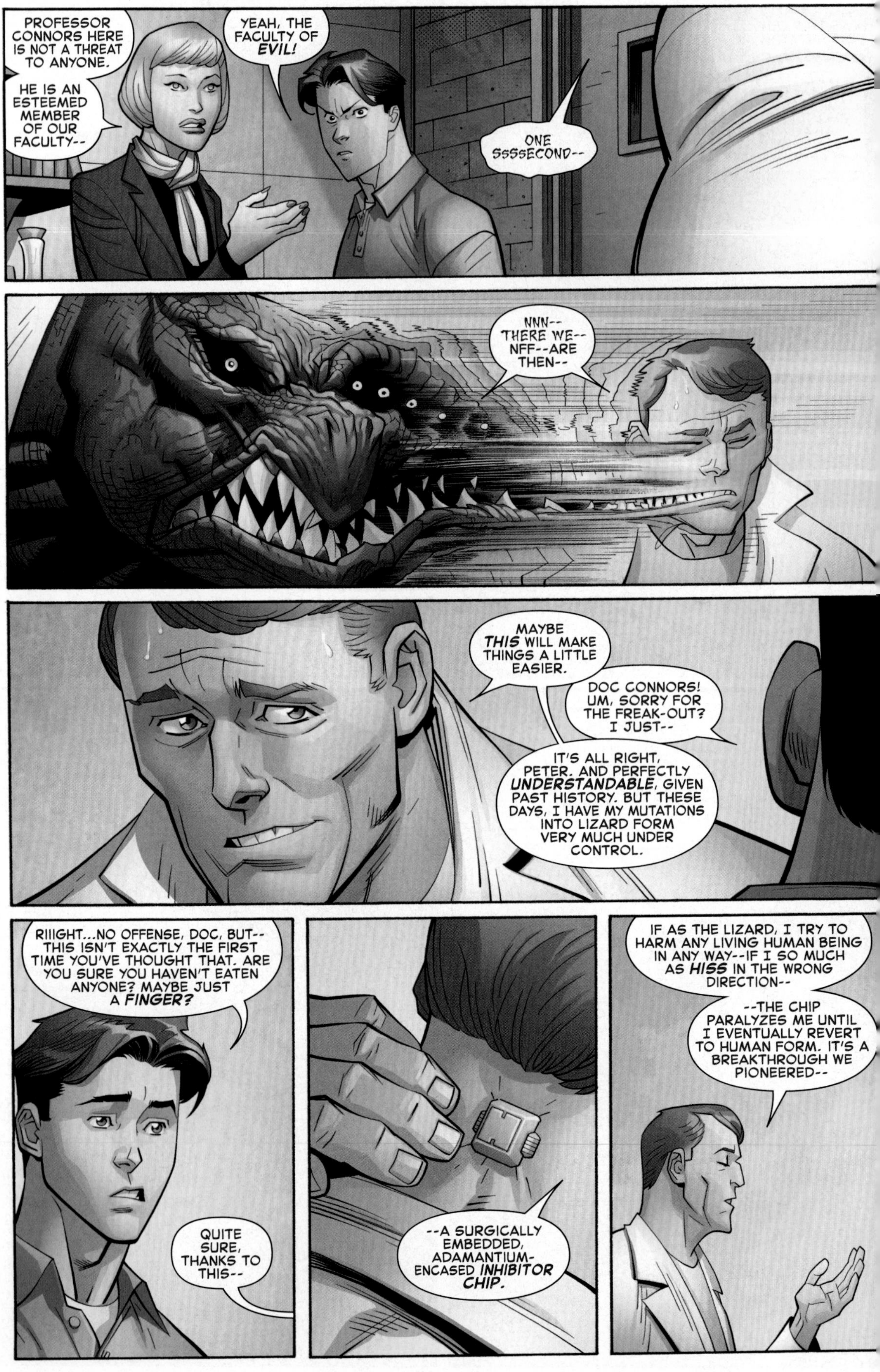
PROFESSOR CONNORS HERE IS NOT A THREAT TO ANYONE.
HE IS AN ESTEEMED MEMBER OF OUR FACULTY--
YEAH, THE FACULTY OF EVIL!
ONE SSSSECOND--
NNN-- THERE WE-- NFF--ARE THEN--
MAYBE THIS WILL MAKE THINGS A LITTLE EASIER.
DOC CONNORS! UM, SORRY FOR THE FREAK-OUT? I JUST--
IT'S ALL RIGHT, PETER. AND PERFECTLY UNDERSTANDABLE, GIVEN PAST HISTORY. BUT THESE DAYS, I HAVE MY MUTATIONS INTO LIZARD FORM VERY MUCH UNDER CONTROL.
RIIIGHT...NO OFFENSE, DOC, BUT-- THIS ISN'T EXACTLY THE FIRST TIME YOU'VE THOUGHT THAT. ARE YOU SURE YOU HAVEN'T EATEN ANYONE? MAYBE JUST A FINGER?
QUITE SURE, THANKS TO THIS--
--A SURGICALLY EMBEDDED, ADAMANTIUM-ENCASED INHIBITOR CHIP.
IF AS THE LIZARD, I TRY TO HARM ANY LIVING HUMAN BEING IN ANY WAY--IF I SO MUCH AS HISS IN THE WRONG DIRECTION--
--THE CHIP PARALYZES ME UNTIL I EVENTUALLY REVERT TO HUMAN FORM. IT'S A BREAKTHROUGH WE PIONEERED--

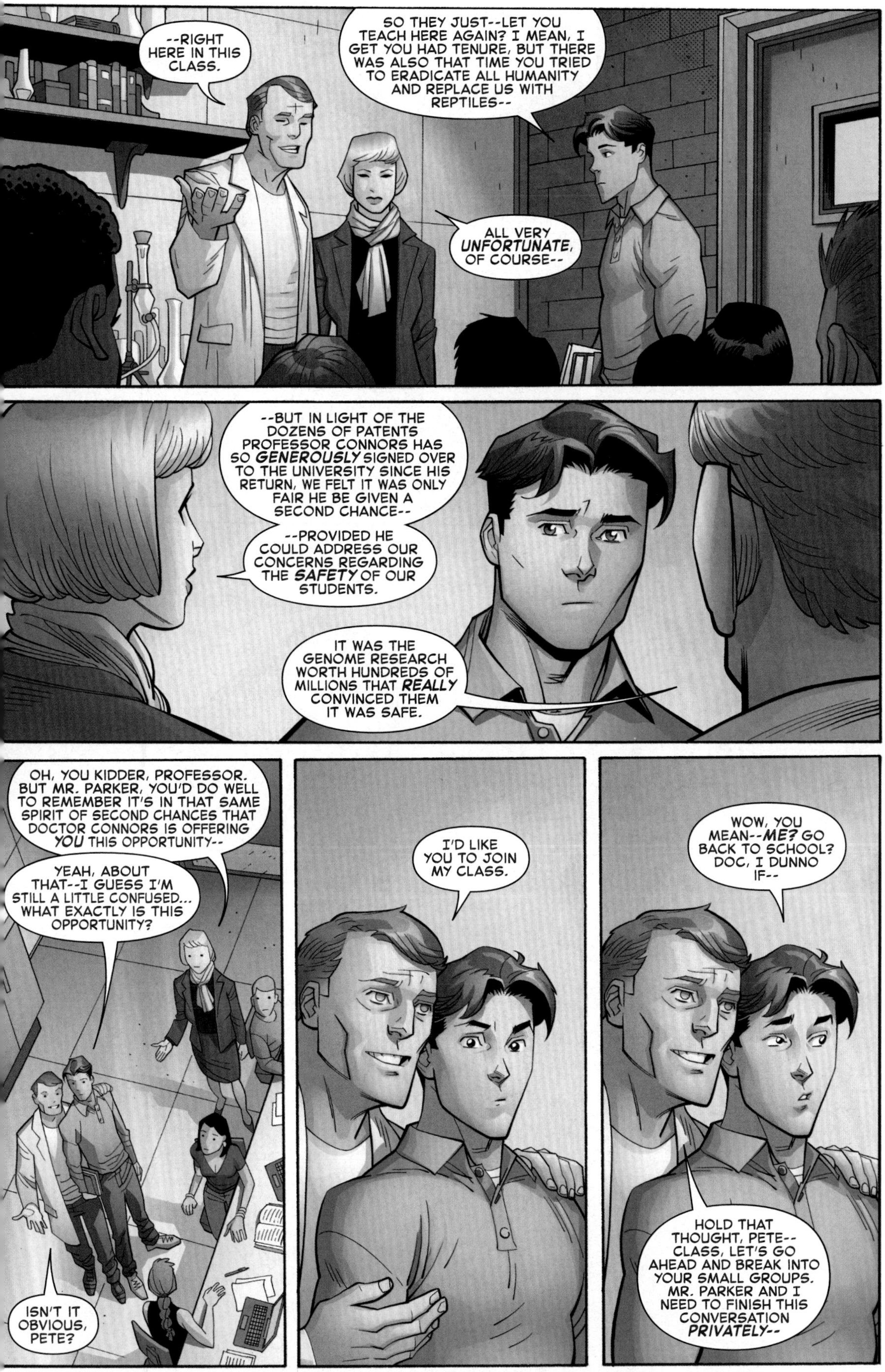
--RIGHT HERE IN THIS CLASS.
SO THEY JUST--LET YOU TEACH HERE AGAIN? I MEAN, I GET YOU HAD TENURE, BUT THERE WAS ALSO THAT TIME YOU TRIED TO ERADICATE ALL HUMANITY AND REPLACE US WITH REPTILES--
ALL VERY UNFORTUNATE, OF COURSE--
--BUT IN LIGHT OF THE DOZENS OF PATENTS PROFESSOR CONNORS HAS SO GENEROUSLY SIGNED OVER TO THE UNIVERSITY SINCE HIS RETURN, WE FELT IT WAS ONLY FAIR HE BE GIVEN A SECOND CHANCE--
--PROVIDED HE COULD ADDRESS OUR CONCERNS REGARDING THE SAFETY OF OUR STUDENTS.
IT WAS THE GENOME RESEARCH WORTH HUNDREDS OF MILLIONS THAT REALLY CONVINCED THEM IT WAS SAFE.
OH, YOU KIDDER, PROFESSOR. BUT MR. PARKER, YOU'D DO WELL TO REMEMBER IT'S IN THAT SAME SPIRIT OF SECOND CHANCES THAT DOCTOR CONNORS IS OFFERING YOU THIS OPPORTUNITY--
YEAH, ABOUT THAT--I GUESS I'M STILL A LITTLE CONFUSED... WHAT EXACTLY IS THIS OPPORTUNITY?
ISN'T IT OBVIOUS, PETE?
I'D LIKE YOU TO JOIN MY CLASS.
WOW, YOU MEAN--ME? GO BACK TO SCHOOL? DOC, I DUNNO IF--
HOLD THAT THOUGHT, PETE--CLASS, LET'S GO AHEAD AND BREAK INTO YOUR SMALL GROUPS. MR. PARKER AND I NEED TO FINISH THIS CONVERSATION PRIVATELY--

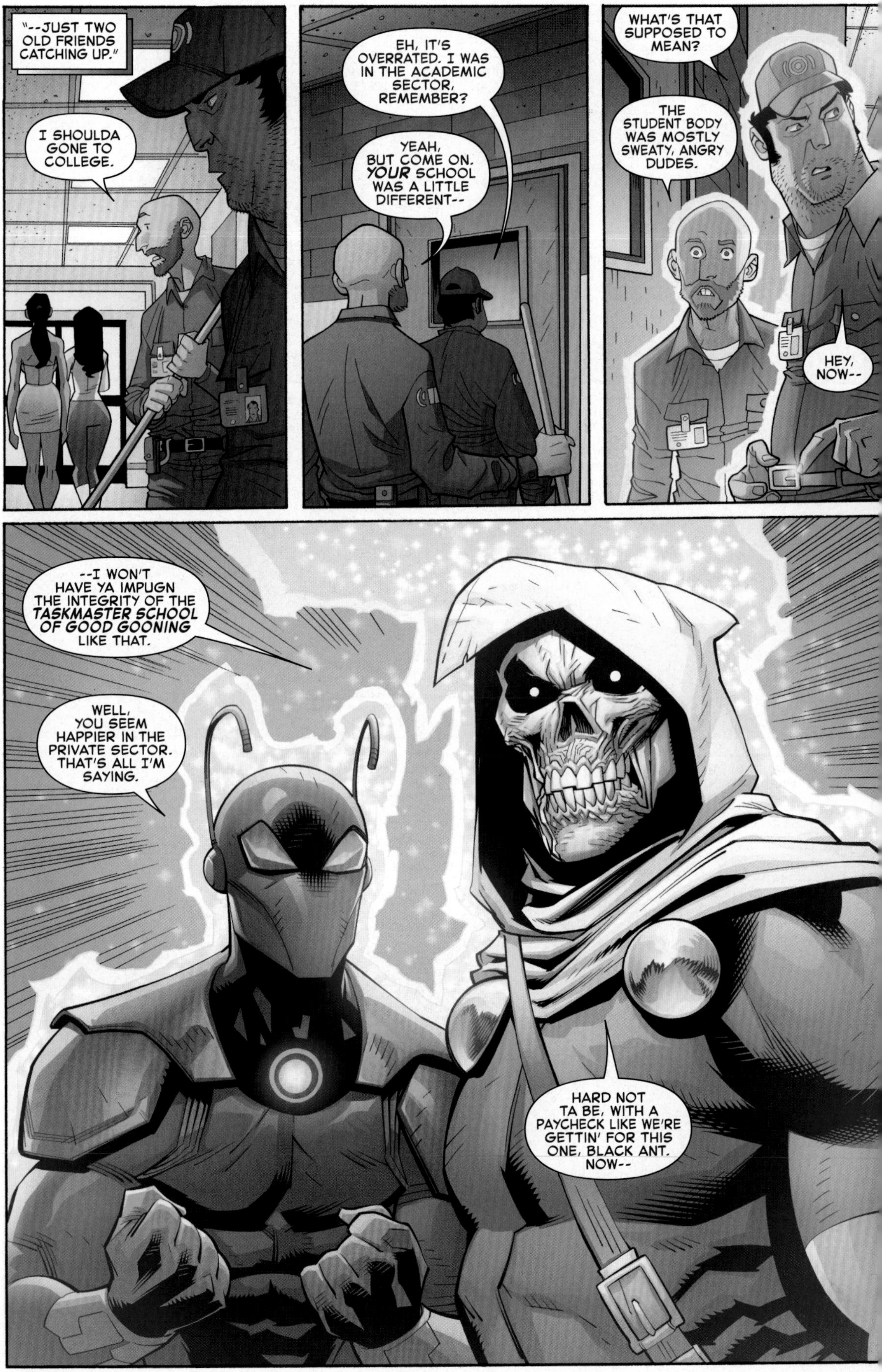
"--JUST TWO OLD FRIENDS CATCHING UP."
I SHOULDA GONE TO COLLEGE.
EH, IT'S OVERRATED. I WAS IN THE ACADEMIC SECTOR, REMEMBER?
YEAH, BUT COME ON. YOUR SCHOOL WAS A LITTLE DIFFERENT--
WHAT'S THAT SUPPOSED TO MEAN?
THE STUDENT BODY WAS MOSTLY SWEATY, ANGRY DUDES.
HEY, NOW--
--I WON'T HAVE YA IMPUGN THE INTEGRITY OF THE TASKMASTER SCHOOL OF GOOD GOONING LIKE THAT.
WELL, YOU SEEM HAPPIER IN THE PRIVATE SECTOR. THAT'S ALL I'M SAYING.
HARD NOT TA BE, WITH A PAYCHECK LIKE WE'RE GETTIN' FOR THIS ONE, BLACK ANT. NOW--

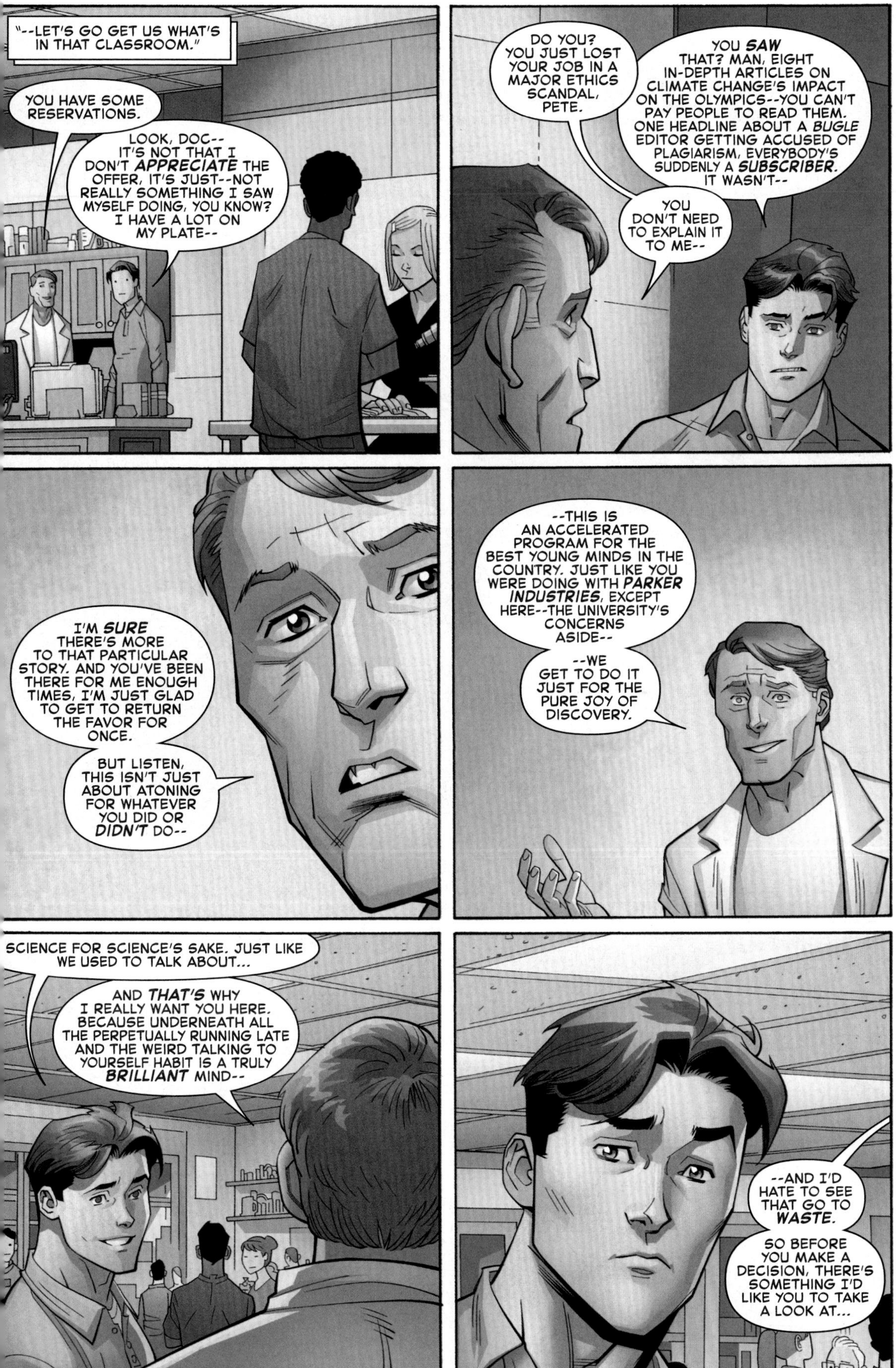
"--LET'S GO GET US WHAT'S IN THAT CLASSROOM."
YOU HAVE SOME RESERVATIONS.
LOOK, DOC-- IT'S NOT THAT I DON'T APPRECIATE THE OFFER, IT'S JUST--NOT REALLY SOMETHING I SAW MYSELF DOING, YOU KNOW? I HAVE A LOT ON MY PLATE--
YOU SAW THAT? MAN, EIGHT IN-DEPTH ARTICLES ON CLIMATE CHANGE'S IMPACT ON THE OLYMPICS--YOU CAN'T PAY PEOPLE TO READ THEM. ONE HEADLINE ABOUT A BUGLE EDITOR GETTING ACCUSED OF PLAGIARISM, EVERYBODY'S SUDDENLY A SUBSCRIBER. IT WASN'T--
DO YOU? YOU JUST LOST YOUR JOB IN A MAJOR ETHICS SCANDAL, PETE.
YOU DON'T NEED TO EXPLAIN IT TO ME--
I'M SURE THERE'S MORE TO THAT PARTICULAR STORY. AND YOU'VE BEEN THERE FOR ME ENOUGH TIMES, I'M JUST GLAD TO GET TO RETURN THE FAVOR FOR ONCE.
BUT LISTEN, THIS ISN'T JUST ABOUT ATONING FOR WHATEVER YOU DID OR DIDN'T DO--
--THIS IS AN ACCELERATED PROGRAM FOR THE BEST YOUNG MINDS IN THE COUNTRY. JUST LIKE YOU WERE DOING WITH PARKER INDUSTRIES, EXCEPT HERE--THE UNIVERSITY'S CONCERNS ASIDE--
--WE GET TO DO IT JUST FOR THE PURE JOY OF DISCOVERY.
SCIENCE FOR SCIENCE'S SAKE. JUST LIKE WE USED TO TALK ABOUT...
AND THAT'S WHY I REALLY WANT YOU HERE. BECAUSE UNDERNEATH ALL THE PERPETUALLY RUNNING LATE AND THE WEIRD TALKING TO YOURSELF HABIT IS A TRULY BRILLIANT MIND--
--AND I'D HATE TO SEE THAT GO TO WASTE.
SO BEFORE YOU MAKE A DECISION, THERE'S SOMETHING I'D LIKE YOU TO TAKE A LOOK AT...

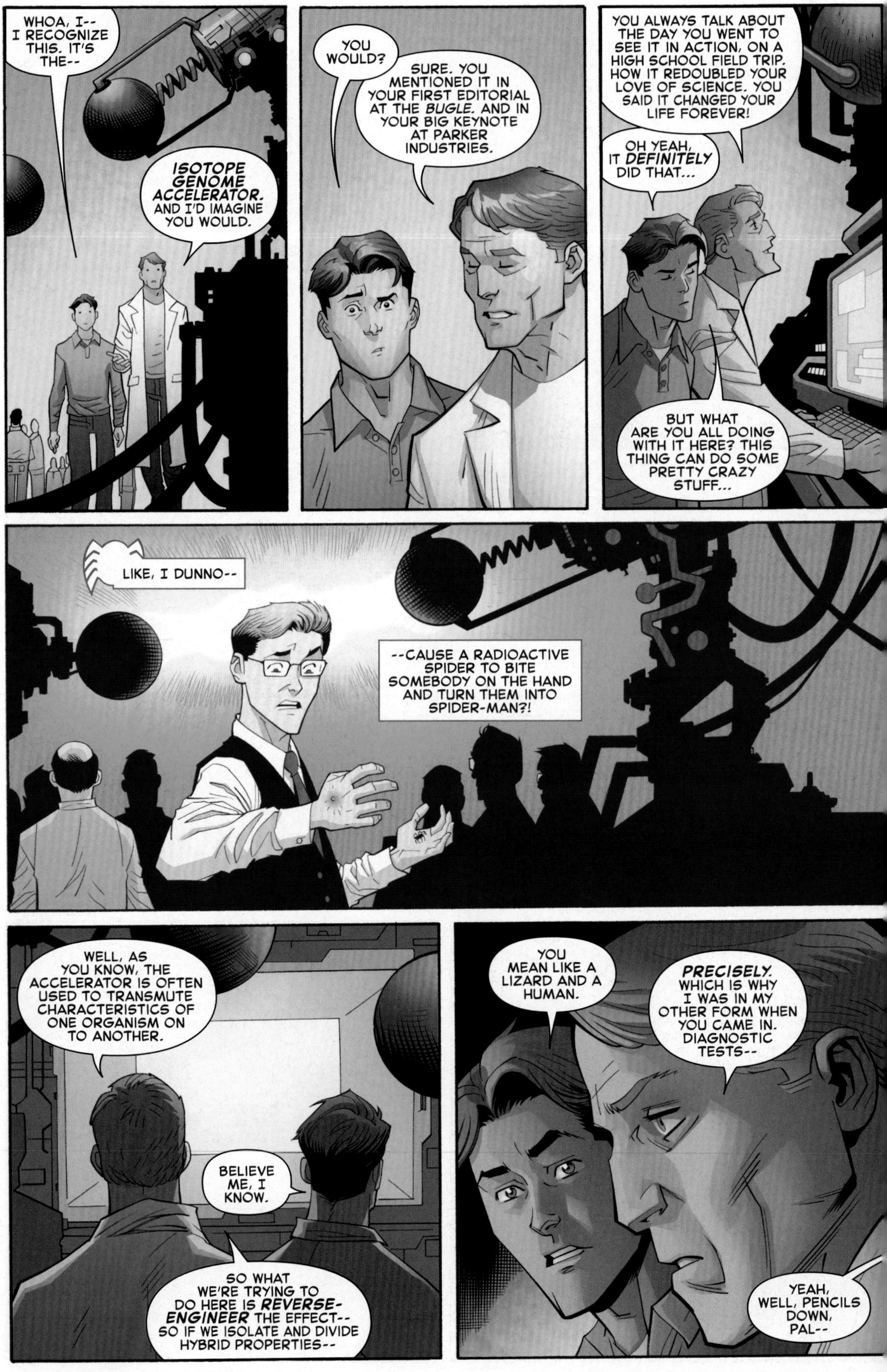
WHOA, I-- I RECOGNIZE THIS. IT'S THE--
ISOTOPE GENOME ACCELERATOR. AND I'D IMAGINE YOU WOULD.
YOU WOULD?
SURE. YOU MENTIONED IT IN YOUR FIRST EDITORIAL AT THE BUGLE. AND IN YOUR BIG KEYNOTE AT PARKER INDUSTRIES.
YOU ALWAYS TALK ABOUT THE DAY YOU WENT TO SEE IT IN ACTION, ON A HIGH SCHOOL FIELD TRIP. HOW IT REDOUBLED YOUR LOVE OF SCIENCE. YOU SAID IT CHANGED YOUR LIFE FOREVER!
OH YEAH, IT DEFINITELY DID THAT...
BUT WHAT ARE YOU ALL DOING WITH IT HERE? THIS THING CAN DO SOME PRETTY CRAZY STUFF...
LIKE, I DUNNO--
--CAUSE A RADIOACTIVE SPIDER TO BITE SOMEBODY ON THE HAND AND TURN THEM INTO SPIDER-MAN?!
WELL, AS YOU KNOW, THE ACCELERATOR IS OFTEN USED TO TRANSMUTE CHARACTERISTICS OF ONE ORGANISM ON TO ANOTHER.
BELIEVE ME, I KNOW.
SO WHAT WE'RE TRYING TO DO HERE IS REVERSE-ENGINEER THE EFFECT-- SO IF WE ISOLATE AND DIVIDE HYBRID PROPERTIES--
YOU MEAN LIKE A LIZARD AND A HUMAN.
PRECISELY. WHICH IS WHY I WAS IN MY OTHER FORM WHEN YOU CAME IN. DIAGNOSTIC TESTS--
YEAH, WELL, PENCILS DOWN, PAL--

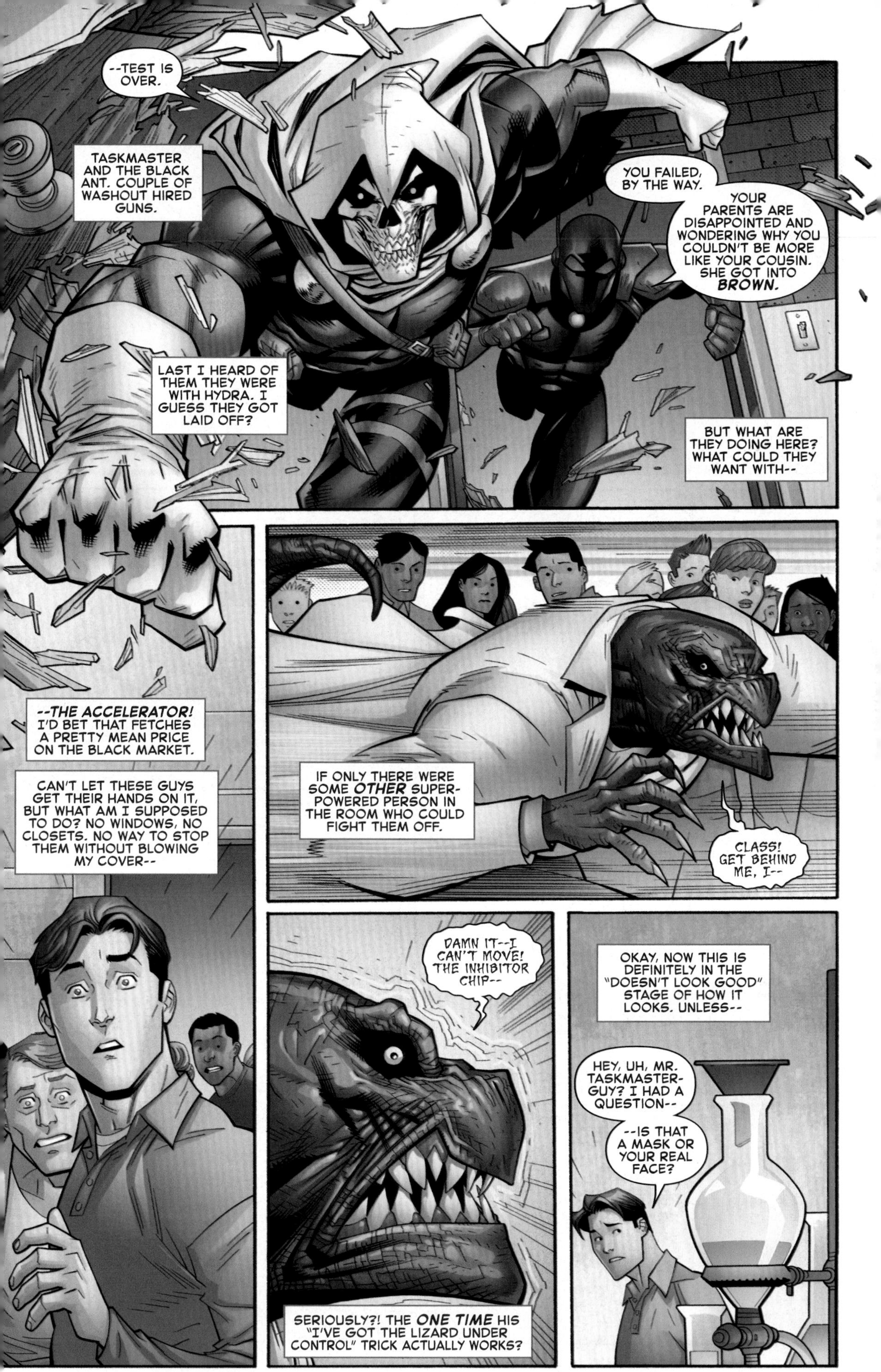
--TEST IS OVER.
TASKMASTER AND THE BLACK ANT. COUPLE OF WASHOUT HIRED GUNS.
YOU FAILED, BY THE WAY.
YOUR PARENTS ARE DISAPPOINTED AND WONDERING WHY YOU COULDN'T BE MORE LIKE YOUR COUSIN. SHE GOT INTO BROWN.
LAST I HEARD OF THEM THEY WERE WITH HYDRA. I GUESS THEY GOT LAID OFF?
BUT WHAT ARE THEY DOING HERE? WHAT COULD THEY WANT WITH--
--THE ACCELERATOR! I'D BET THAT FETCHES A PRETTY MEAN PRICE ON THE BLACK MARKET.
CAN'T LET THESE GUYS GET THEIR HANDS ON IT, BUT WHAT AM I SUPPOSED TO DO? NO WINDOWS, NO CLOSETS. NO WAY TO STOP THEM WITHOUT BLOWING MY COVER--
IF ONLY THERE WERE SOME OTHER SUPER-POWERED PERSON IN THE ROOM WHO COULD FIGHT THEM OFF.
CLASS! GET BEHIND ME, I--
DAMN IT--I CAN'T MOVE! THE INHIBITOR CHIP--
SERIOUSLY?! THE ONE TIME HIS "I'VE GOT THE LIZARD UNDER CONTROL" TRICK ACTUALLY WORKS?
OKAY, NOW THIS IS DEFINITELY IN THE "DOESN'T LOOK GOOD" STAGE OF HOW IT LOOKS. UNLESS--
HEY, UH, MR. TASKMASTER-GUY? I HAD A QUESTION--
--IS THAT A MASK OR YOUR REAL FACE?

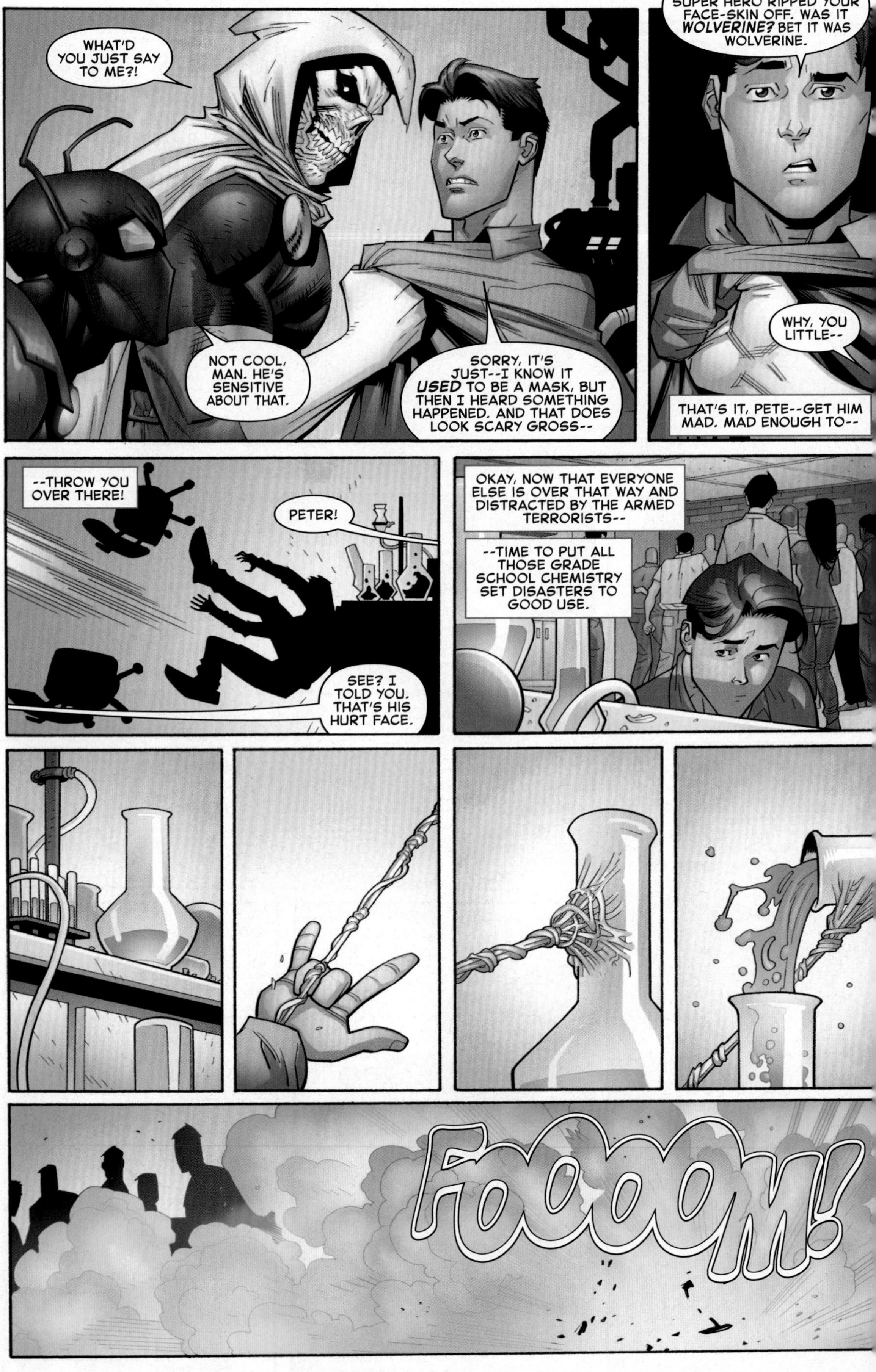
WHAT'D YOU JUST SAY TO ME?!
--SO, I WAS JUST CURIOUS WHICH SUPER HERO RIPPED YOUR FACE-SKIN OFF. WAS IT WOLVERINE? BET IT WAS WOLVERINE.
NOT COOL, MAN. HE'S SENSITIVE ABOUT THAT.
SORRY, IT'S JUST--I KNOW IT USED TO BE A MASK, BUT THEN I HEARD SOMETHING HAPPENED. AND THAT DOES LOOK SCARY GROSS--
WHY, YOU LITTLE--
THAT'S IT, PETE--GET HIM MAD. MAD ENOUGH TO--
--THROW YOU OVER THERE!
PETER!
SEE? I TOLD YOU. THAT'S HIS HURT FACE.
OKAY, NOW THAT EVERYONE ELSE IS OVER THAT WAY AND DISTRACTED BY THE ARMED TERRORISTS--
--TIME TO PUT ALL THOSE GRADE SCHOOL CHEMISTRY SET DISASTERS TO GOOD USE.
FOOOOM!

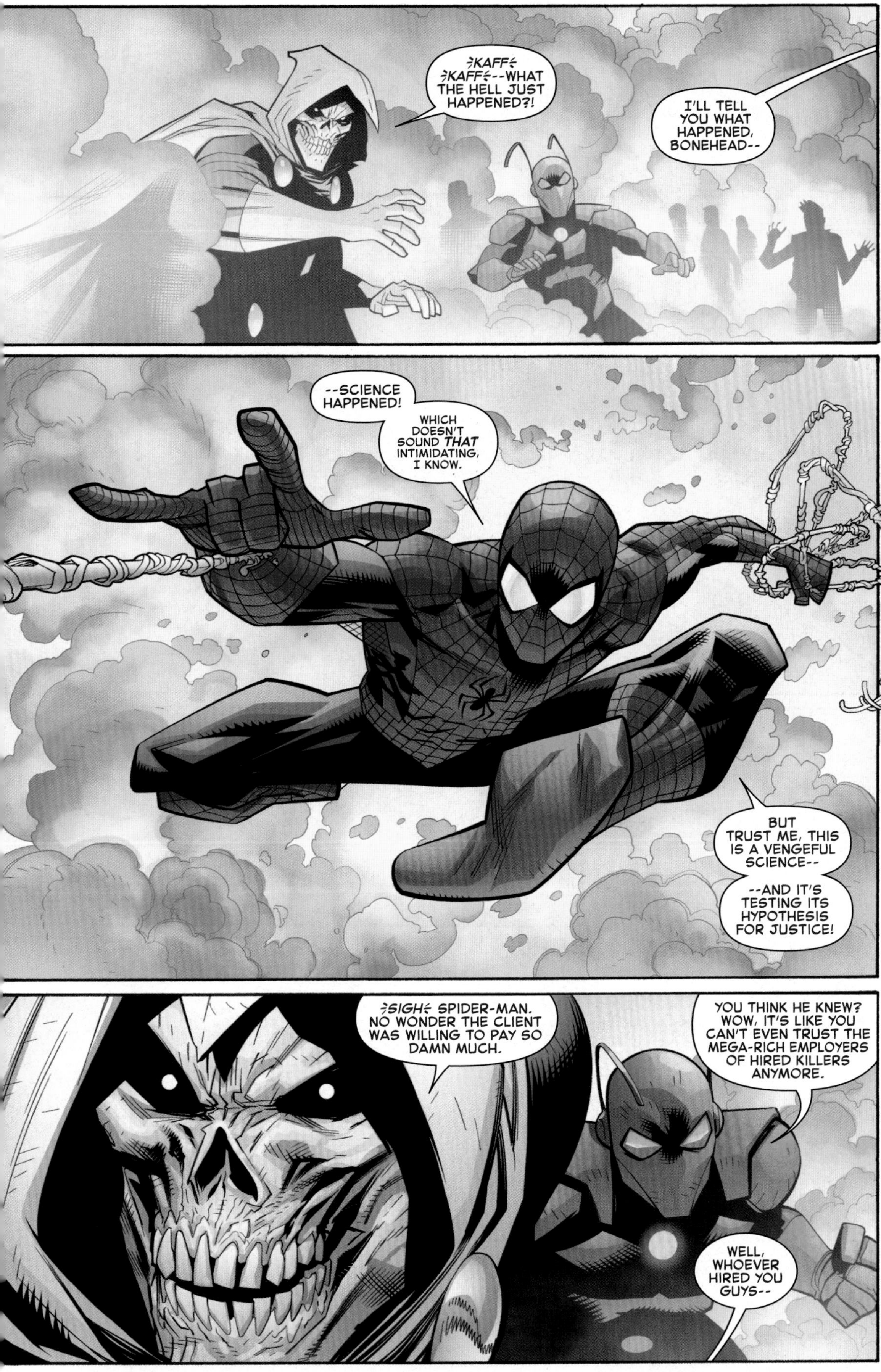

⚡KAFF⚡ ⚡KAFF⚡--WHAT THE HELL JUST HAPPENED?!
I'LL TELL YOU WHAT HAPPENED, BONEHEAD--
--SCIENCE HAPPENED!
WHICH DOESN'T SOUND *THAT* INTIMIDATING, I KNOW.
BUT TRUST ME, THIS IS A VENGEFUL SCIENCE--
--AND IT'S TESTING ITS HYPOTHESIS FOR JUSTICE!
⚡SIGH⚡ SPIDER-MAN. NO WONDER THE CLIENT WAS WILLING TO PAY SO DAMN MUCH.
YOU THINK HE KNEW? WOW, IT'S LIKE YOU CAN'T EVEN TRUST THE MEGA-RICH EMPLOYERS OF HIRED KILLERS ANYMORE.
WELL, WHOEVER HIRED YOU GUYS--

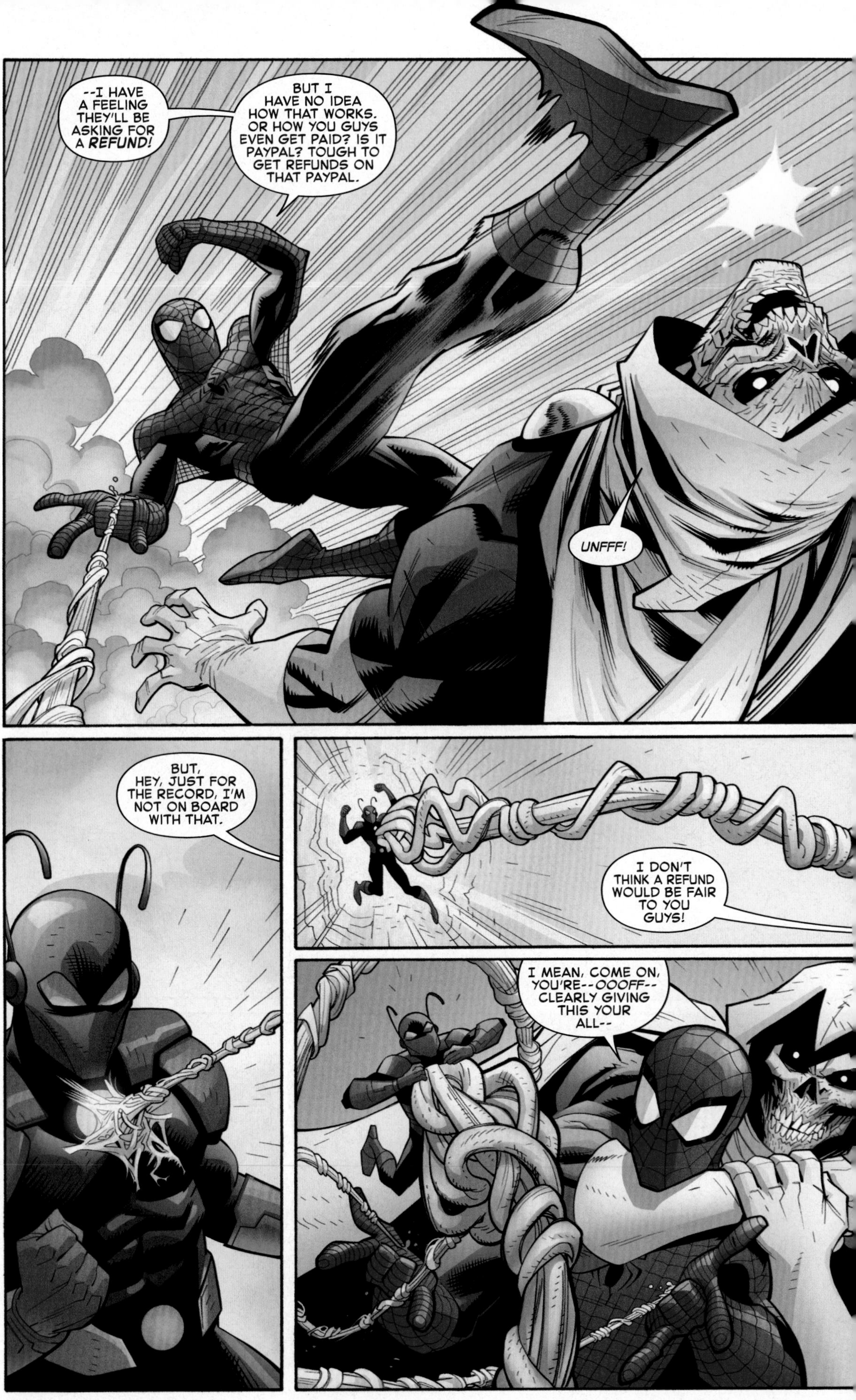
--I HAVE A FEELING THEY'LL BE ASKING FOR A *REFUND*!
BUT I HAVE NO IDEA HOW THAT WORKS. OR HOW YOU GUYS EVEN GET PAID? IS IT PAYPAL? TOUGH TO GET REFUNDS ON THAT PAYPAL.
UNFFF!
BUT, HEY, JUST FOR THE RECORD, I'M NOT ON BOARD WITH THAT.
I DON'T THINK A REFUND WOULD BE FAIR TO YOU GUYS!
I MEAN, COME ON, YOU'RE--*OOOFF*--CLEARLY GIVING THIS YOUR ALL--

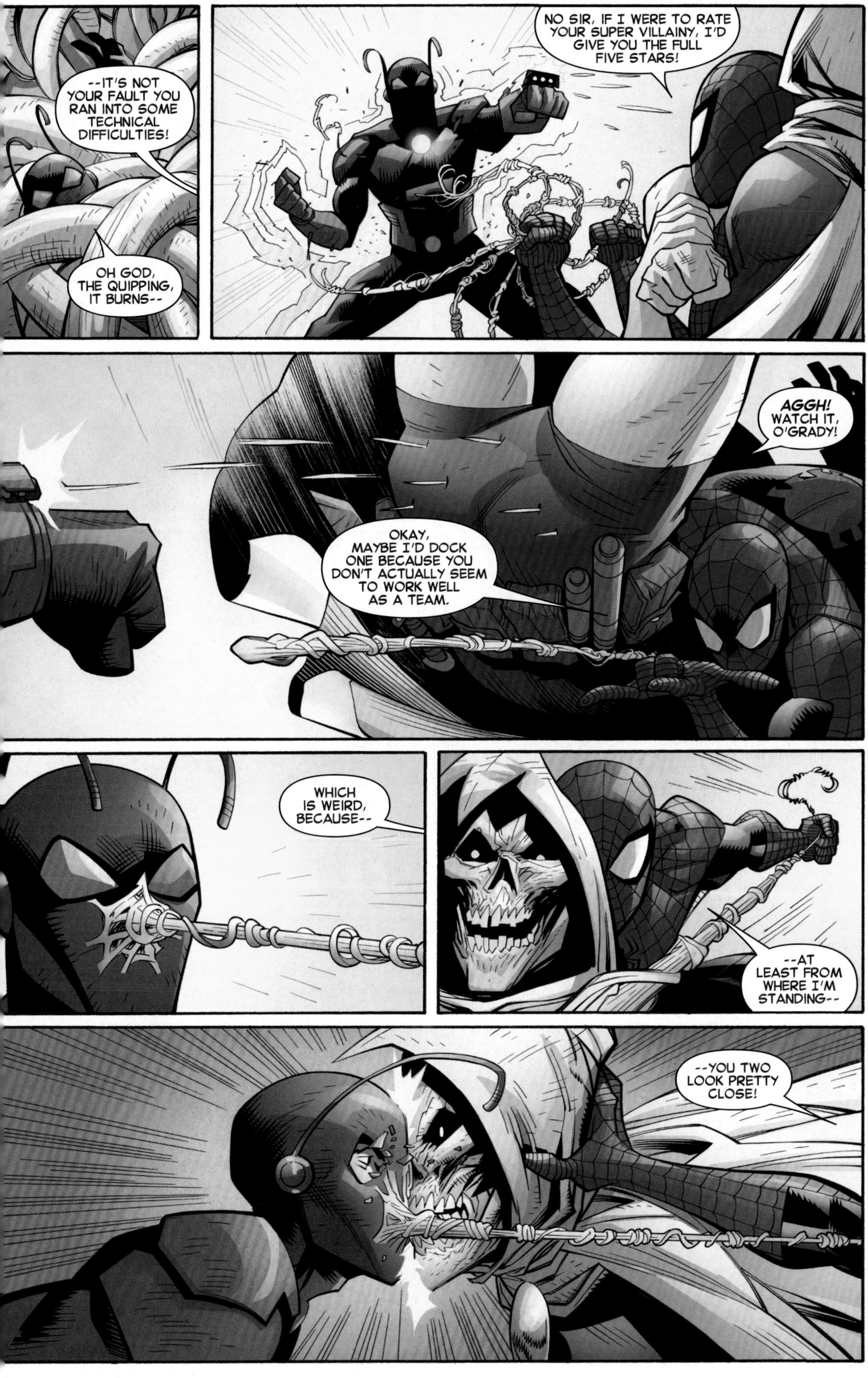
--IT'S NOT YOUR FAULT YOU RAN INTO SOME TECHNICAL DIFFICULTIES!
OH GOD, THE QUIPPING, IT BURNS--
NO SIR, IF I WERE TO RATE YOUR SUPER VILLAINY, I'D GIVE YOU THE FULL FIVE STARS!
AGGH! WATCH IT, O'GRADY!
OKAY, MAYBE I'D DOCK ONE BECAUSE YOU DON'T ACTUALLY SEEM TO WORK WELL AS A TEAM.
WHICH IS WEIRD, BECAUSE--
--AT LEAST FROM WHERE I'M STANDING--
--YOU TWO LOOK PRETTY CLOSE!

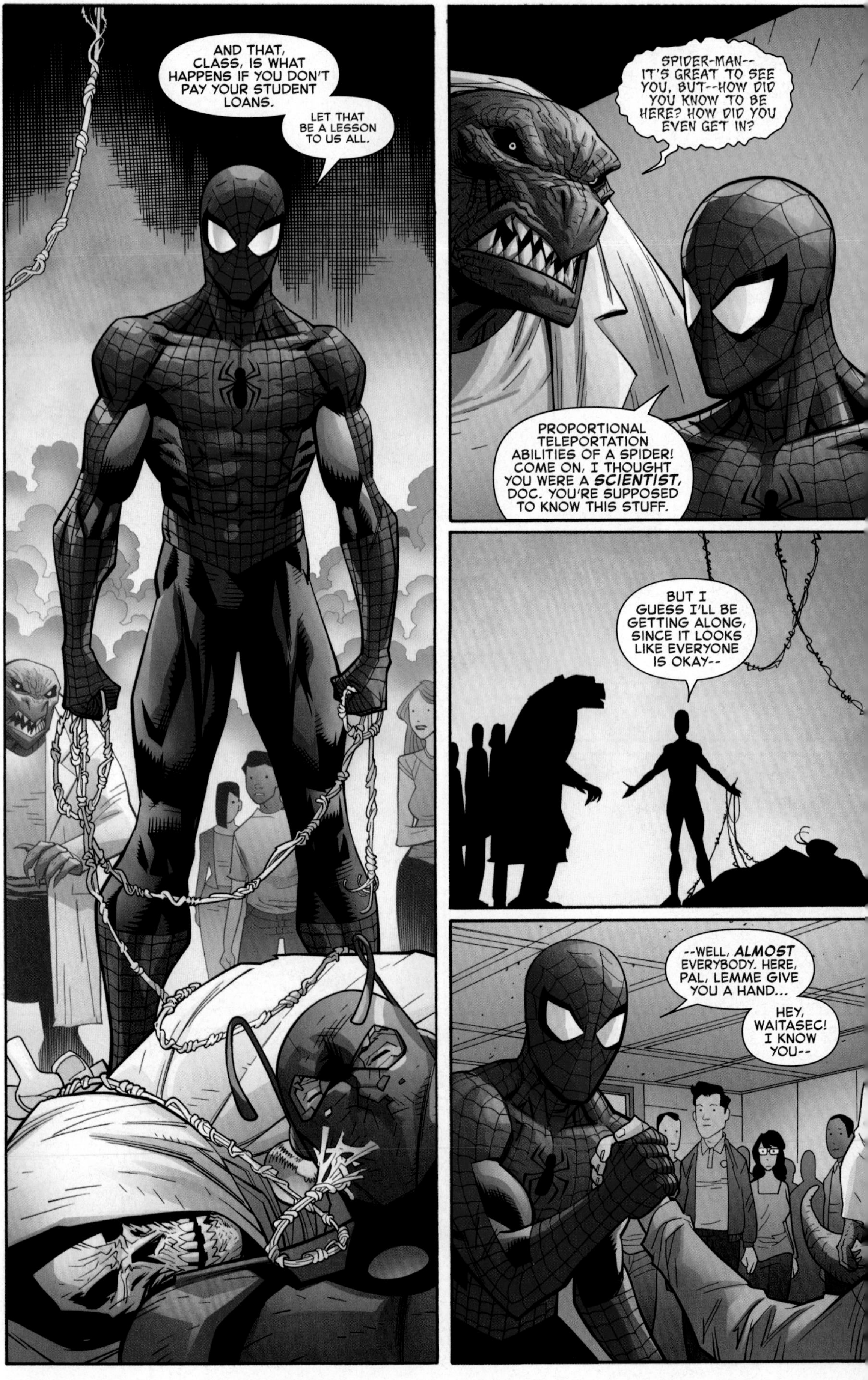
AND THAT, CLASS, IS WHAT HAPPENS IF YOU DON'T PAY YOUR STUDENT LOANS.
LET THAT BE A LESSON TO US ALL.
SPIDER-MAN-- IT'S GREAT TO SEE YOU, BUT--HOW DID YOU KNOW TO BE HERE? HOW DID YOU EVEN GET IN?
PROPORTIONAL TELEPORTATION ABILITIES OF A SPIDER! COME ON, I THOUGHT YOU WERE A ***SCIENTIST***, DOC. YOU'RE SUPPOSED TO KNOW THIS STUFF.
BUT I GUESS I'LL BE GETTING ALONG, SINCE IT LOOKS LIKE EVERYONE IS OKAY--
--WELL, ***ALMOST*** EVERYBODY. HERE, PAL, LEMME GIVE YOU A HAND...
HEY, WAITASEC! I KNOW YOU--

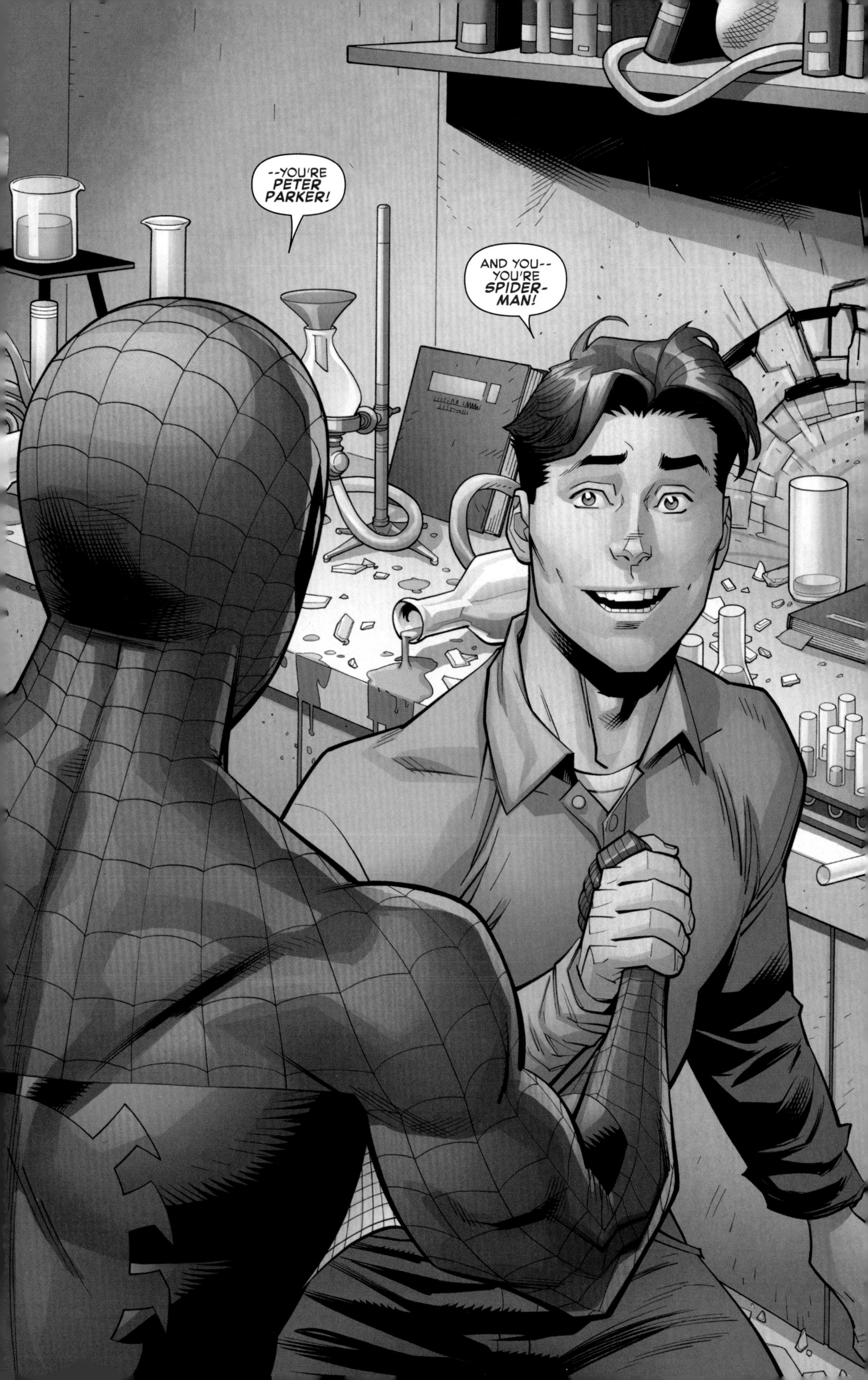
--YOU'RE PETER PARKER!
AND YOU--YOU'RE SPIDER-MAN!

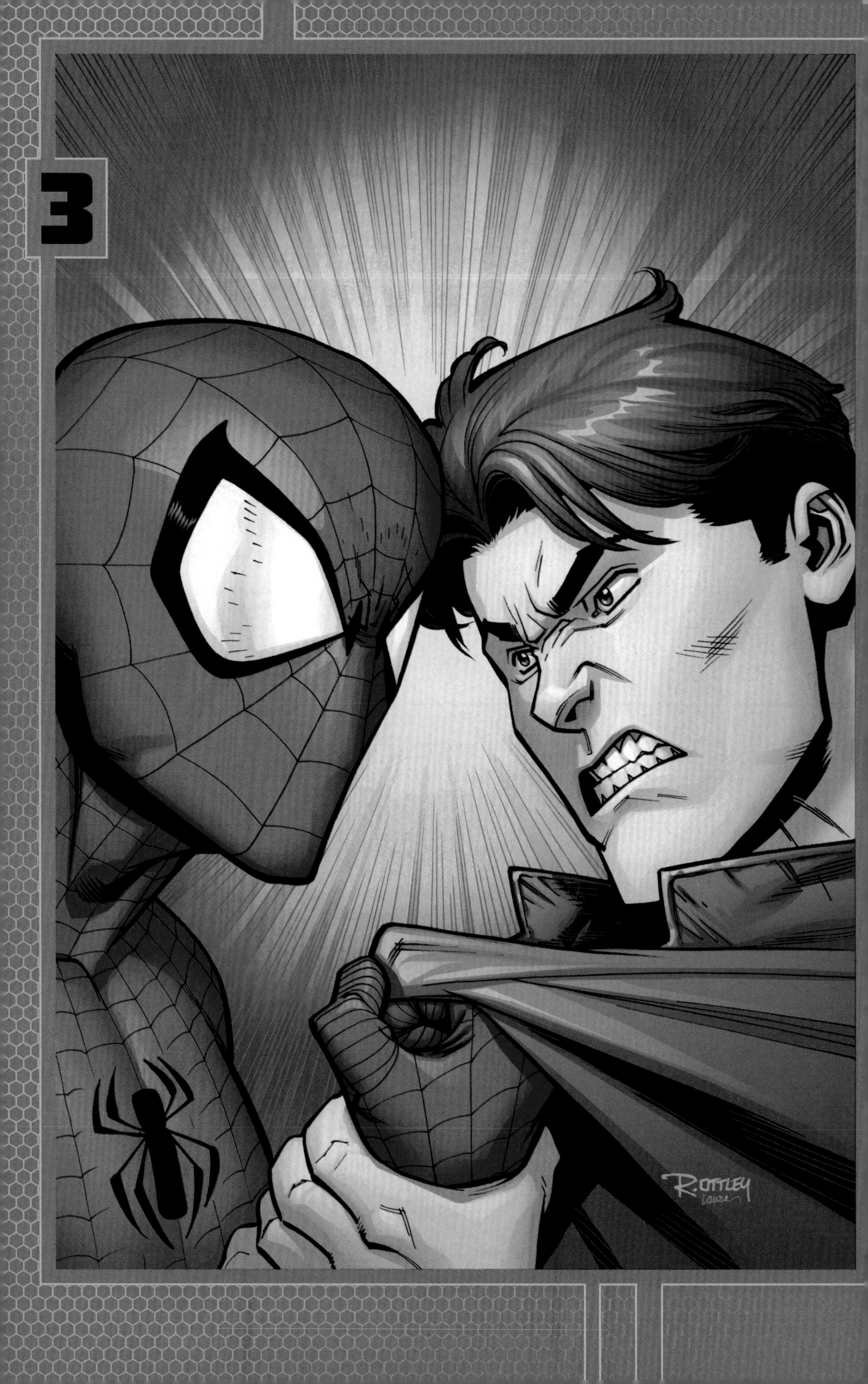
3
R. OTTLEY

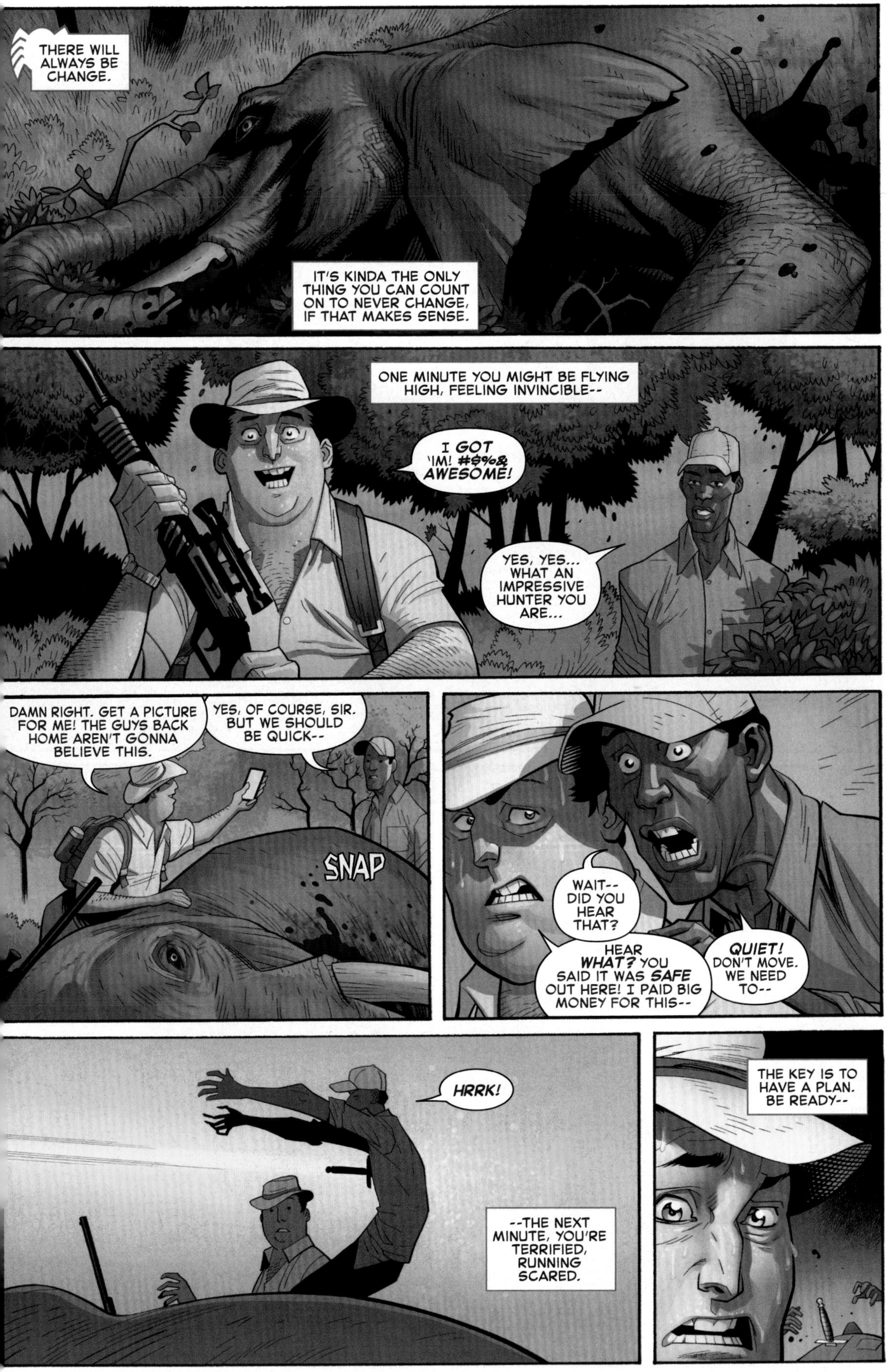
THERE WILL ALWAYS BE CHANGE.
IT'S KINDA THE ONLY THING YOU CAN COUNT ON TO NEVER CHANGE, IF THAT MAKES SENSE.
ONE MINUTE YOU MIGHT BE FLYING HIGH, FEELING INVINCIBLE--
I GOT 'IM! #$%& AWESOME!
YES, YES... WHAT AN IMPRESSIVE HUNTER YOU ARE...
DAMN RIGHT. GET A PICTURE FOR ME! THE GUYS BACK HOME AREN'T GONNA BELIEVE THIS.
YES, OF COURSE, SIR. BUT WE SHOULD BE QUICK--
SNAP
WAIT-- DID YOU HEAR THAT?
HEAR WHAT? YOU SAID IT WAS SAFE OUT HERE! I PAID BIG MONEY FOR THIS--
QUIET! DON'T MOVE. WE NEED TO--
HRRK!
--THE NEXT MINUTE, YOU'RE TERRIFIED, RUNNING SCARED.
THE KEY IS TO HAVE A PLAN. BE READY--

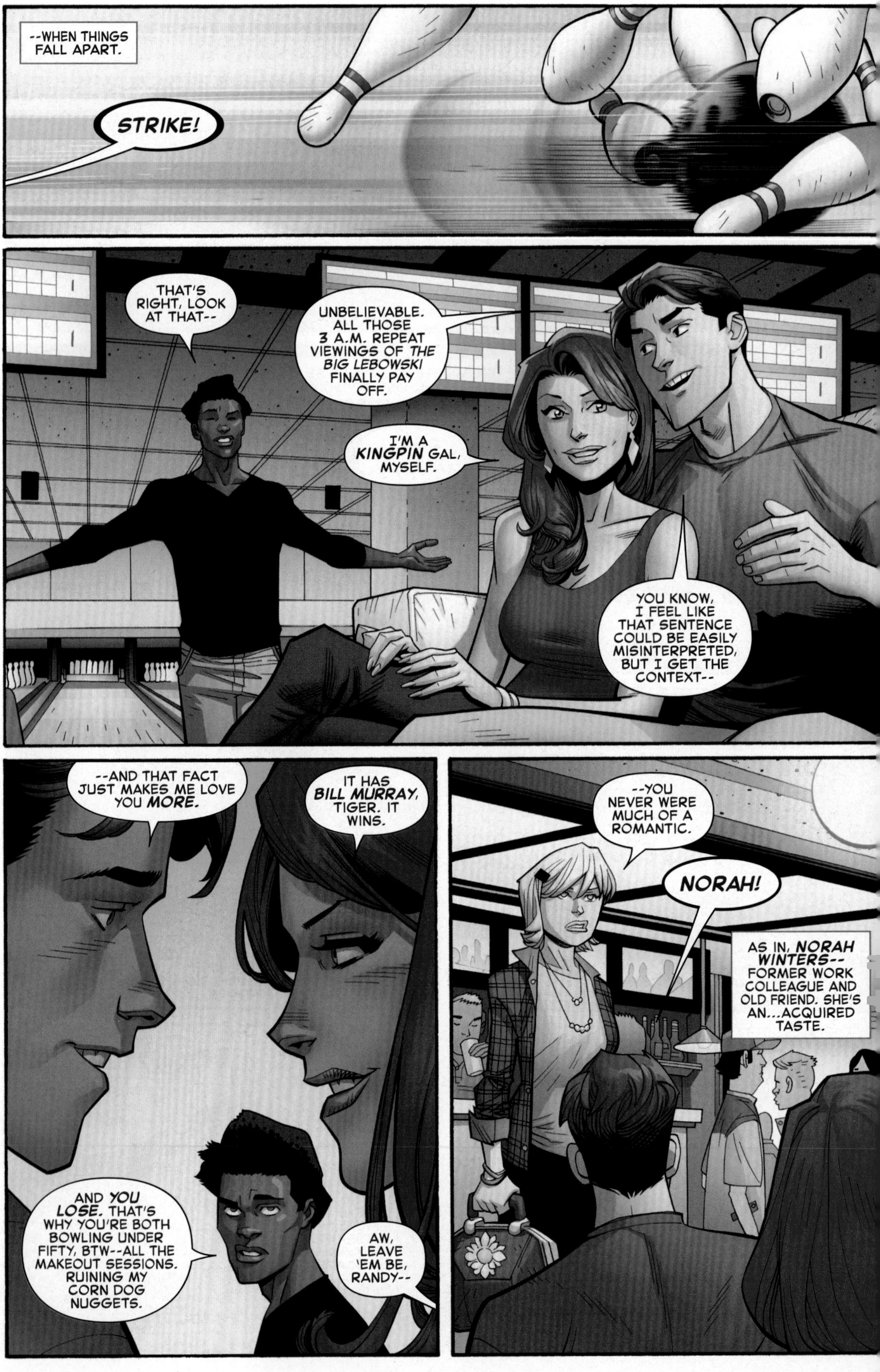
--WHEN THINGS FALL APART.
STRIKE!
THAT'S RIGHT, LOOK AT THAT--
UNBELIEVABLE. ALL THOSE 3 A.M. REPEAT VIEWINGS OF THE BIG LEBOWSKI FINALLY PAY OFF.
I'M A KINGPIN GAL, MYSELF.
YOU KNOW, I FEEL LIKE THAT SENTENCE COULD BE EASILY MISINTERPRETED, BUT I GET THE CONTEXT--
--AND THAT FACT JUST MAKES ME LOVE YOU MORE.
IT HAS BILL MURRAY, TIGER. IT WINS.
AND YOU LOSE. THAT'S WHY YOU'RE BOTH BOWLING UNDER FIFTY, BTW--ALL THE MAKEOUT SESSIONS. RUINING MY CORN DOG NUGGETS.
AW, LEAVE 'EM BE, RANDY--
--YOU NEVER WERE MUCH OF A ROMANTIC.
NORAH!
AS IN, NORAH WINTERS--FORMER WORK COLLEAGUE AND OLD FRIEND. SHE'S AN...ACQUIRED TASTE.

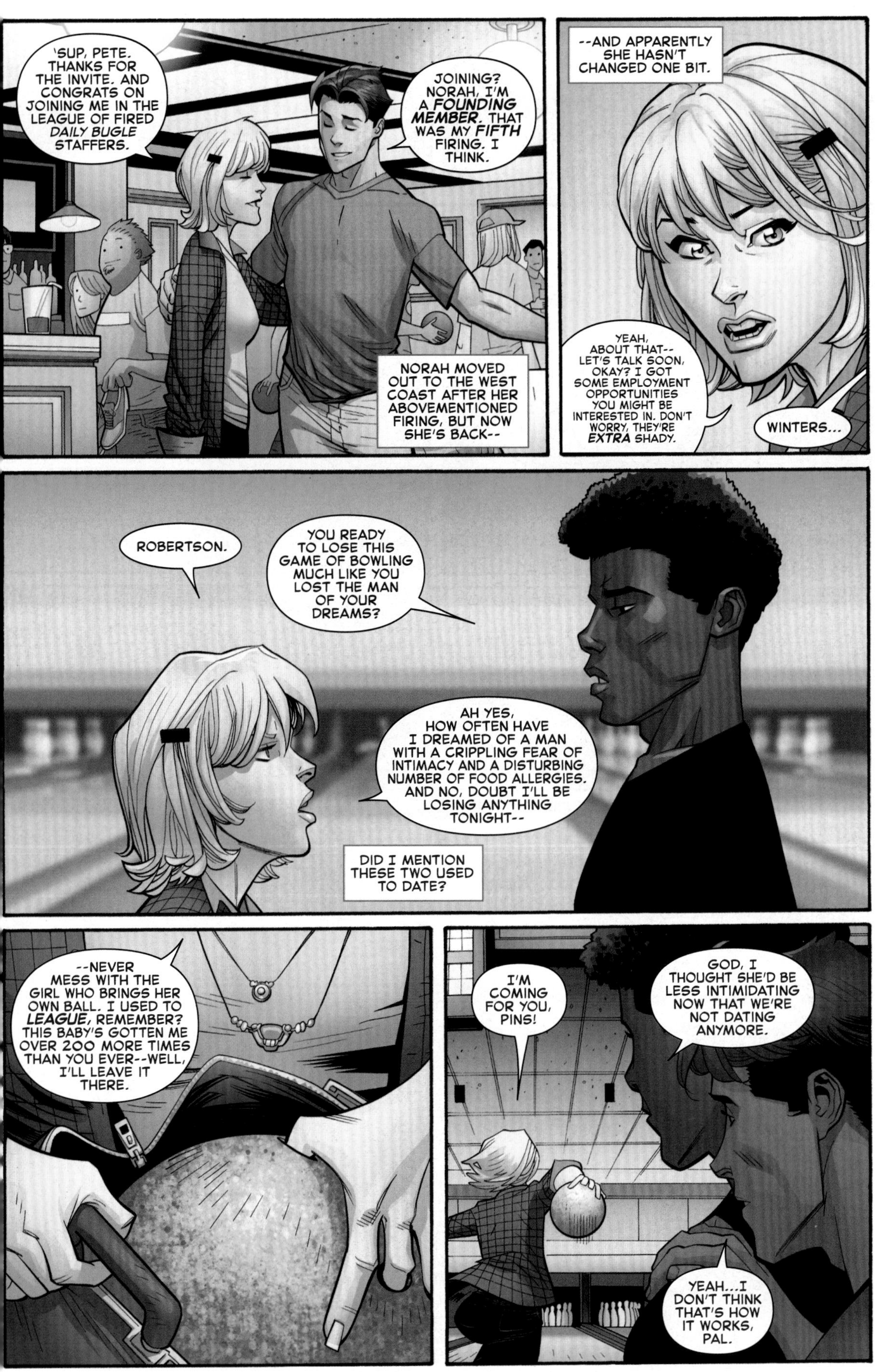
'SUP, PETE. THANKS FOR THE INVITE. AND CONGRATS ON JOINING ME IN THE LEAGUE OF FIRED *DAILY BUGLE* STAFFERS.
JOINING? NORAH, I'M A ***FOUNDING MEMBER.*** THAT WAS MY ***FIFTH*** FIRING. I THINK.
NORAH MOVED OUT TO THE WEST COAST AFTER HER ABOVEMENTIONED FIRING, BUT NOW SHE'S BACK--
--AND APPARENTLY SHE HASN'T CHANGED ONE BIT.
YEAH, ABOUT THAT-- LET'S TALK SOON, OKAY? I GOT SOME EMPLOYMENT OPPORTUNITIES YOU MIGHT BE INTERESTED IN. DON'T WORRY, THEY'RE ***EXTRA*** SHADY.
WINTERS...
ROBERTSON.
YOU READY TO LOSE THIS GAME OF BOWLING MUCH LIKE YOU LOST THE MAN OF YOUR DREAMS?
AH YES, HOW OFTEN HAVE I DREAMED OF A MAN WITH A CRIPPLING FEAR OF INTIMACY AND A DISTURBING NUMBER OF FOOD ALLERGIES. AND NO, DOUBT I'LL BE LOSING ANYTHING TONIGHT--
DID I MENTION THESE TWO USED TO DATE?
--NEVER MESS WITH THE GIRL WHO BRINGS HER OWN BALL. I USED TO ***LEAGUE,*** REMEMBER? THIS BABY'S GOTTEN ME OVER 200 MORE TIMES THAN YOU EVER--WELL, I'LL LEAVE IT THERE.
I'M COMING FOR YOU, PINS!
GOD, I THOUGHT SHE'D BE LESS INTIMIDATING NOW THAT WE'RE NOT DATING ANYMORE.
YEAH...I DON'T THINK THAT'S HOW IT WORKS, PAL.

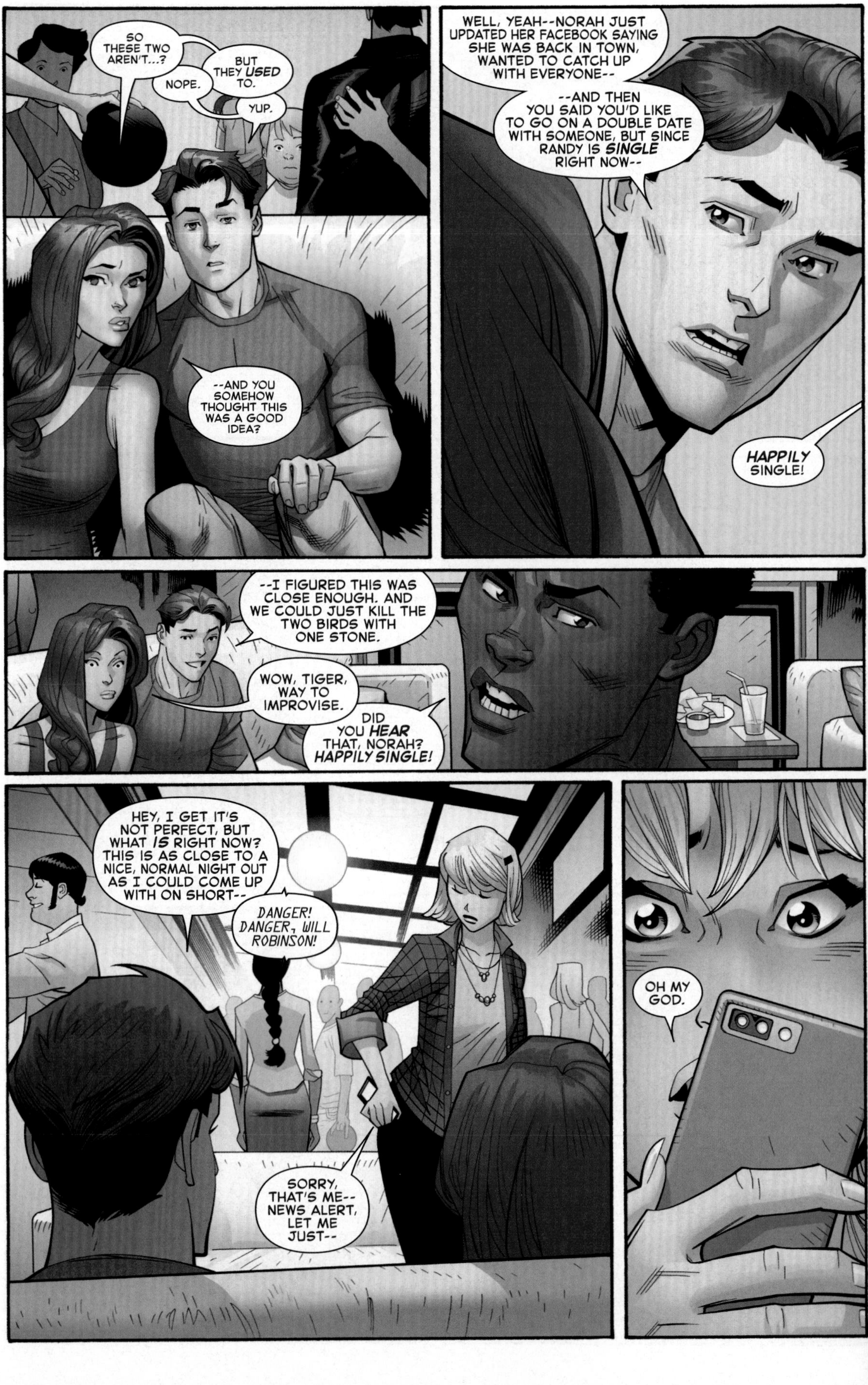
SO THESE TWO AREN'T...?
NOPE.
BUT THEY USED TO.
YUP.
--AND YOU SOMEHOW THOUGHT THIS WAS A GOOD IDEA?
WELL, YEAH--NORAH JUST UPDATED HER FACEBOOK SAYING SHE WAS BACK IN TOWN, WANTED TO CATCH UP WITH EVERYONE--
--AND THEN YOU SAID YOU'D LIKE TO GO ON A DOUBLE DATE WITH SOMEONE, BUT SINCE RANDY IS SINGLE RIGHT NOW--
HAPPILY SINGLE!
--I FIGURED THIS WAS CLOSE ENOUGH. AND WE COULD JUST KILL THE TWO BIRDS WITH ONE STONE.
WOW, TIGER, WAY TO IMPROVISE.
DID YOU HEAR THAT, NORAH? HAPPILY SINGLE!
HEY, I GET IT'S NOT PERFECT, BUT WHAT IS RIGHT NOW? THIS IS AS CLOSE TO A NICE, NORMAL NIGHT OUT AS I COULD COME UP WITH ON SHORT--
DANGER! DANGER, WILL ROBINSON!
SORRY, THAT'S ME-- NEWS ALERT, LET ME JUST--
OH MY GOD.

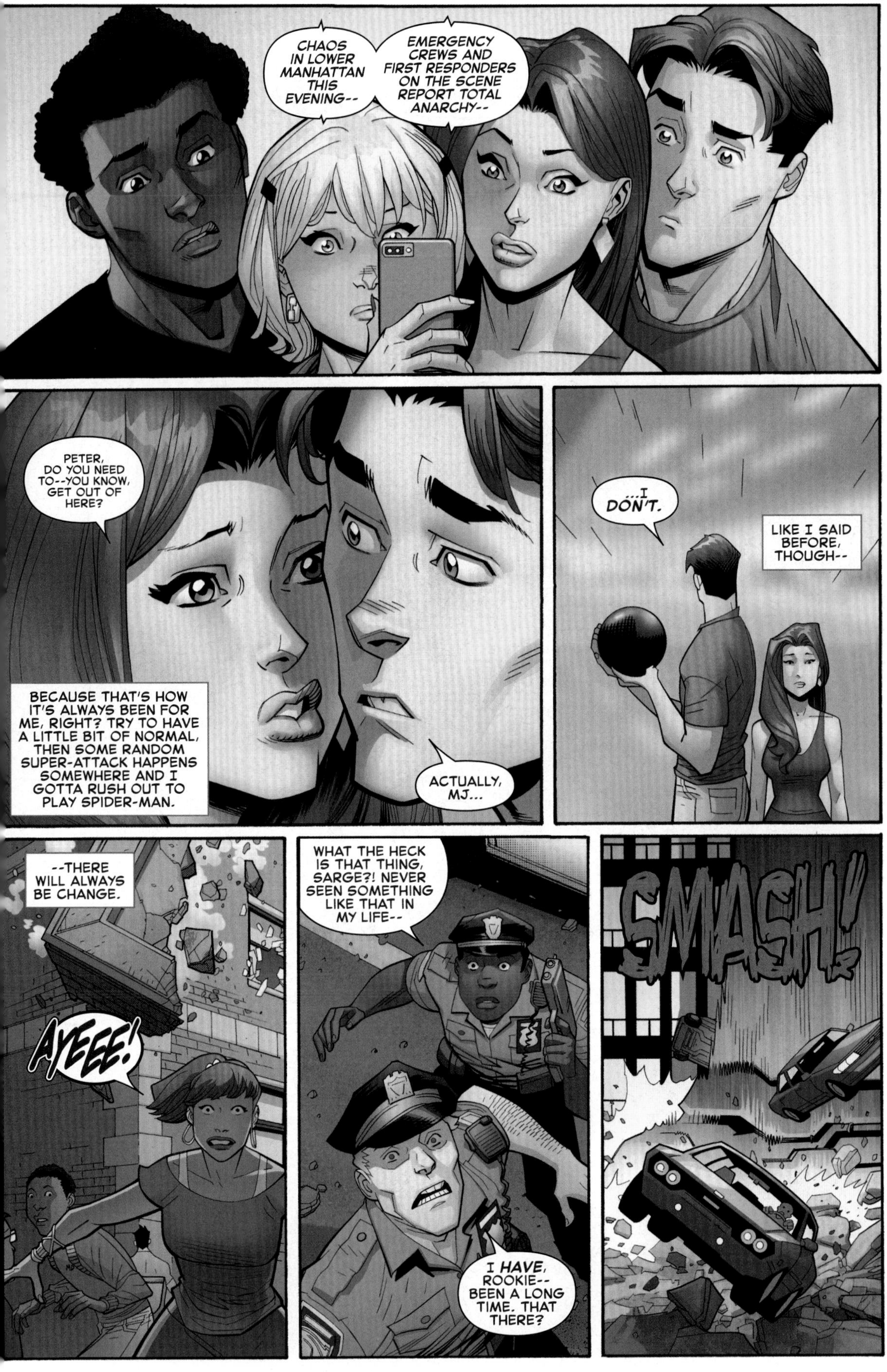
CHAOS IN LOWER MANHATTAN THIS EVENING--
EMERGENCY CREWS AND FIRST RESPONDERS ON THE SCENE REPORT TOTAL ANARCHY--
PETER, DO YOU NEED TO--YOU KNOW, GET OUT OF HERE?
BECAUSE THAT'S HOW IT'S ALWAYS BEEN FOR ME, RIGHT? TRY TO HAVE A LITTLE BIT OF NORMAL, THEN SOME RANDOM SUPER-ATTACK HAPPENS SOMEWHERE AND I GOTTA RUSH OUT TO PLAY SPIDER-MAN.
ACTUALLY, MJ...
...I DON'T.
LIKE I SAID BEFORE, THOUGH--
--THERE WILL ALWAYS BE CHANGE.
AYEEE!
WHAT THE HECK IS THAT THING, SARGE?! NEVER SEEN SOMETHING LIKE THAT IN MY LIFE--
I HAVE, ROOKIE-- BEEN A LONG TIME. THAT THERE?
SMASH!

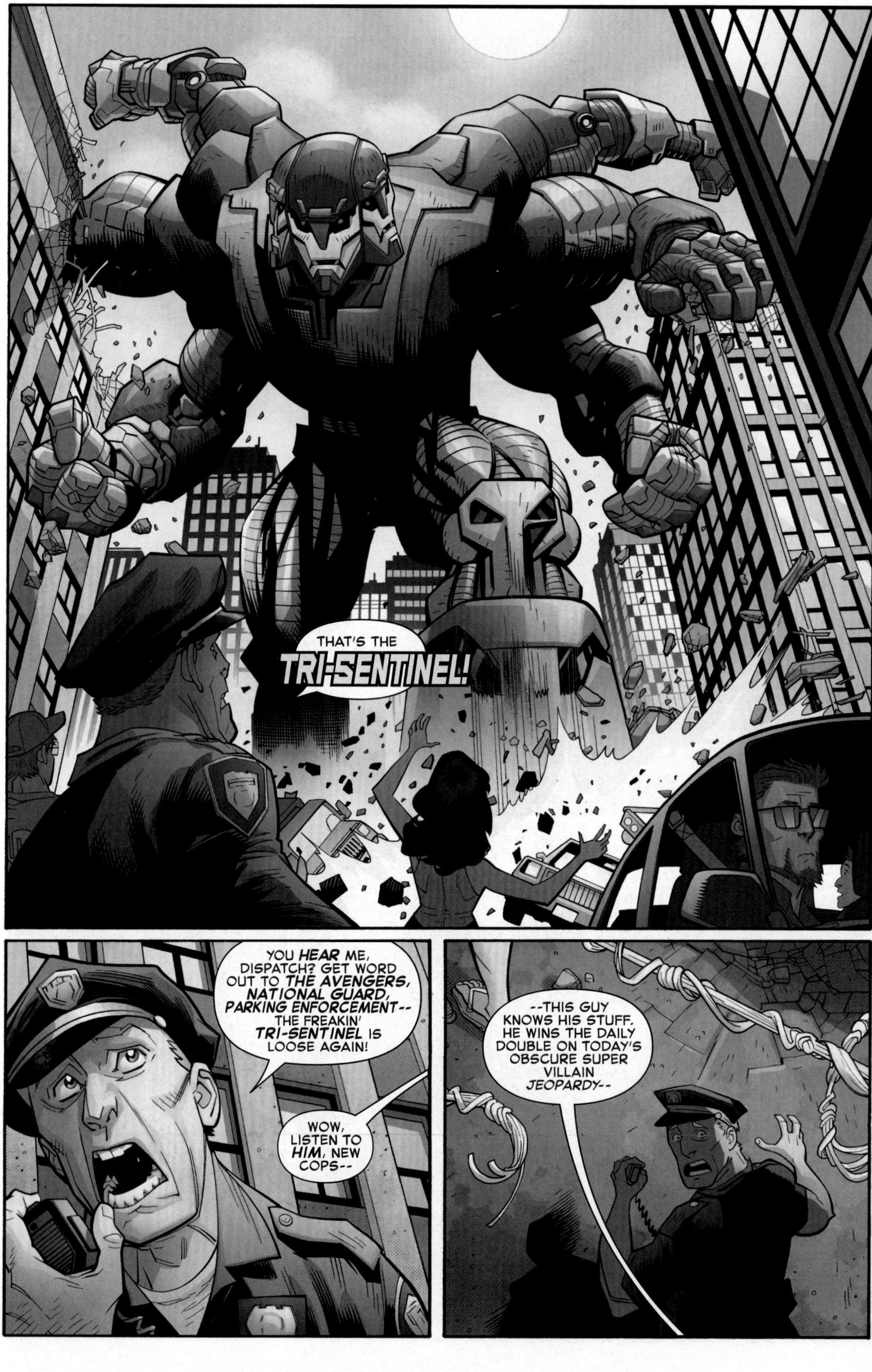
THAT'S THE TRI-SENTINEL!
YOU HEAR ME, DISPATCH? GET WORD OUT TO THE AVENGERS, NATIONAL GUARD, PARKING ENFORCEMENT-- THE FREAKIN' TRI-SENTINEL IS LOOSE AGAIN!
WOW, LISTEN TO HIM, NEW COPS--
--THIS GUY KNOWS HIS STUFF. HE WINS THE DAILY DOUBLE ON TODAY'S OBSCURE SUPER VILLAIN JEOPARDY--

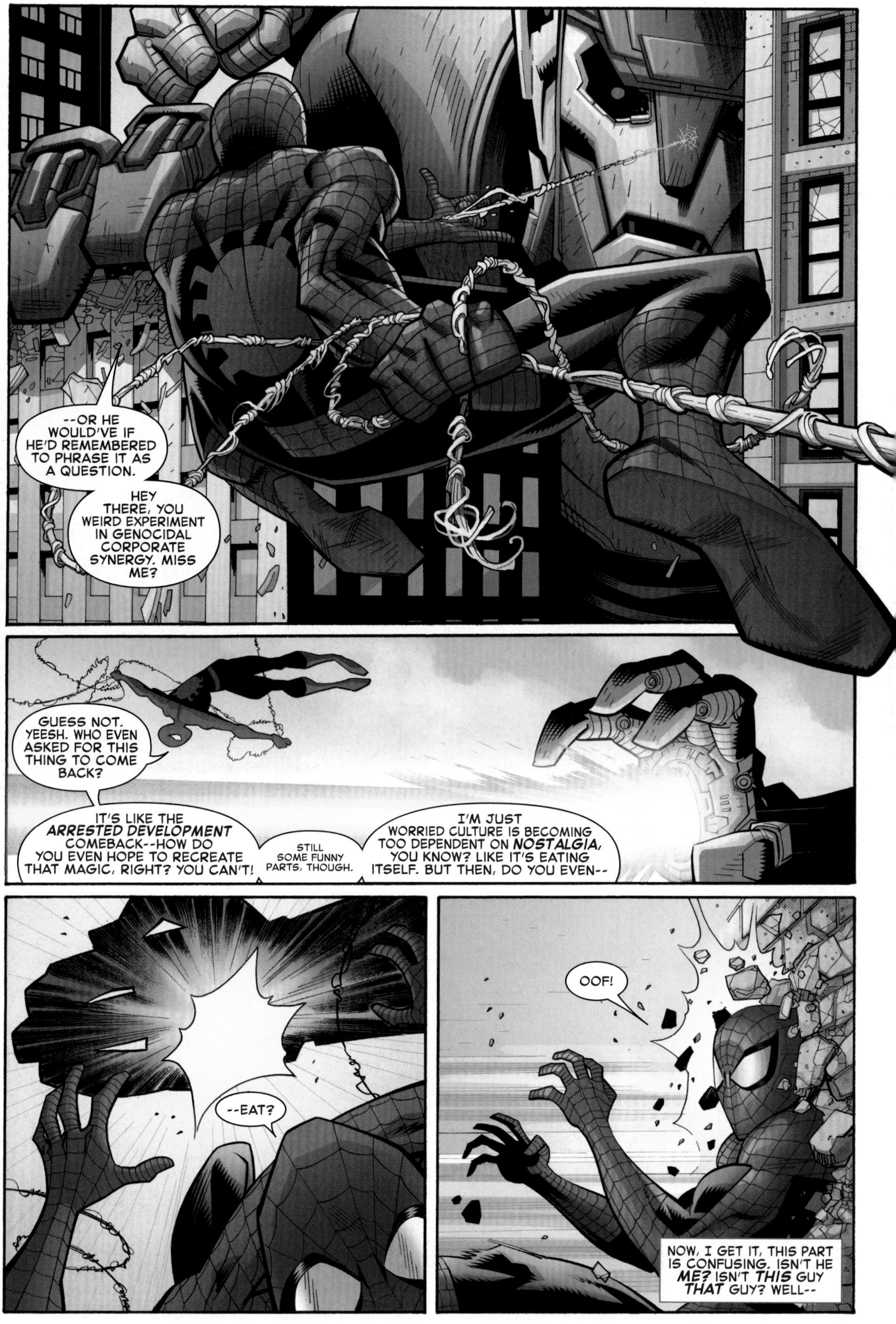
--OR HE WOULD'VE IF HE'D REMEMBERED TO PHRASE IT AS A QUESTION.
HEY THERE, YOU WEIRD EXPERIMENT IN GENOCIDAL CORPORATE SYNERGY. MISS ME?
GUESS NOT. YEESH. WHO EVEN ASKED FOR THIS THING TO COME BACK?
IT'S LIKE THE ARRESTED DEVELOPMENT COMEBACK--HOW DO YOU EVEN HOPE TO RECREATE THAT MAGIC, RIGHT? YOU CAN'T!
STILL SOME FUNNY PARTS, THOUGH.
I'M JUST WORRIED CULTURE IS BECOMING TOO DEPENDENT ON NOSTALGIA, YOU KNOW? LIKE IT'S EATING ITSELF. BUT THEN, DO YOU EVEN--
--EAT?
OOF!
NOW, I GET IT, THIS PART IS CONFUSING. ISN'T HE ME? ISN'T THIS GUY THAT GUY? WELL--

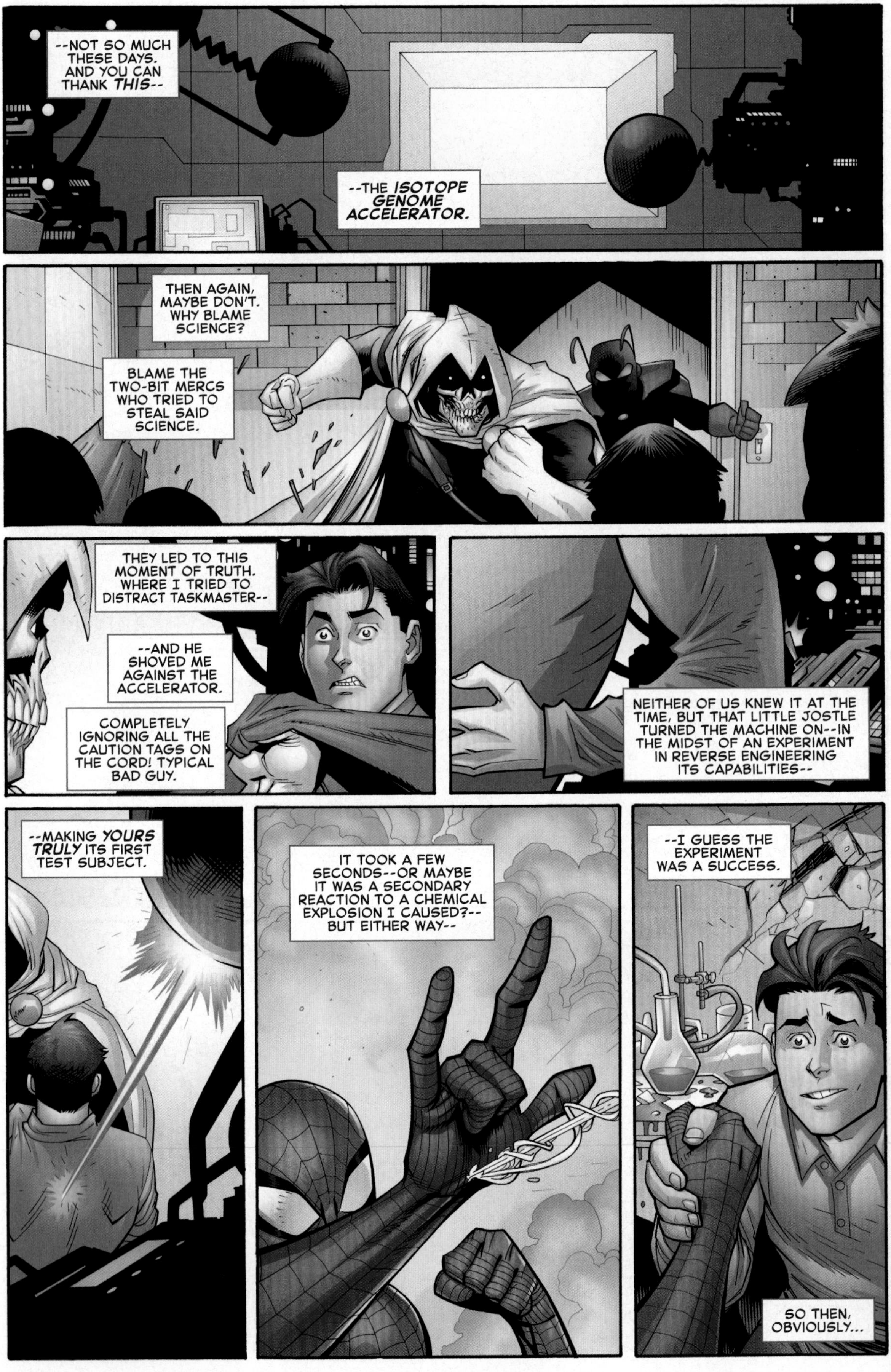
--NOT SO MUCH THESE DAYS. AND YOU CAN THANK THIS--
--THE ISOTOPE GENOME ACCELERATOR.
THEN AGAIN, MAYBE DON'T. WHY BLAME SCIENCE?
BLAME THE TWO-BIT MERCS WHO TRIED TO STEAL SAID SCIENCE.
THEY LED TO THIS MOMENT OF TRUTH. WHERE I TRIED TO DISTRACT TASKMASTER--
--AND HE SHOVED ME AGAINST THE ACCELERATOR.
COMPLETELY IGNORING ALL THE CAUTION TAGS ON THE CORD! TYPICAL BAD GUY.
NEITHER OF US KNEW IT AT THE TIME, BUT THAT LITTLE JOSTLE TURNED THE MACHINE ON--IN THE MIDST OF AN EXPERIMENT IN REVERSE ENGINEERING ITS CAPABILITIES--
--MAKING YOURS TRULY ITS FIRST TEST SUBJECT.
IT TOOK A FEW SECONDS--OR MAYBE IT WAS A SECONDARY REACTION TO A CHEMICAL EXPLOSION I CAUSED?--BUT EITHER WAY--
--I GUESS THE EXPERIMENT WAS A SUCCESS.
SO THEN, OBVIOUSLY...

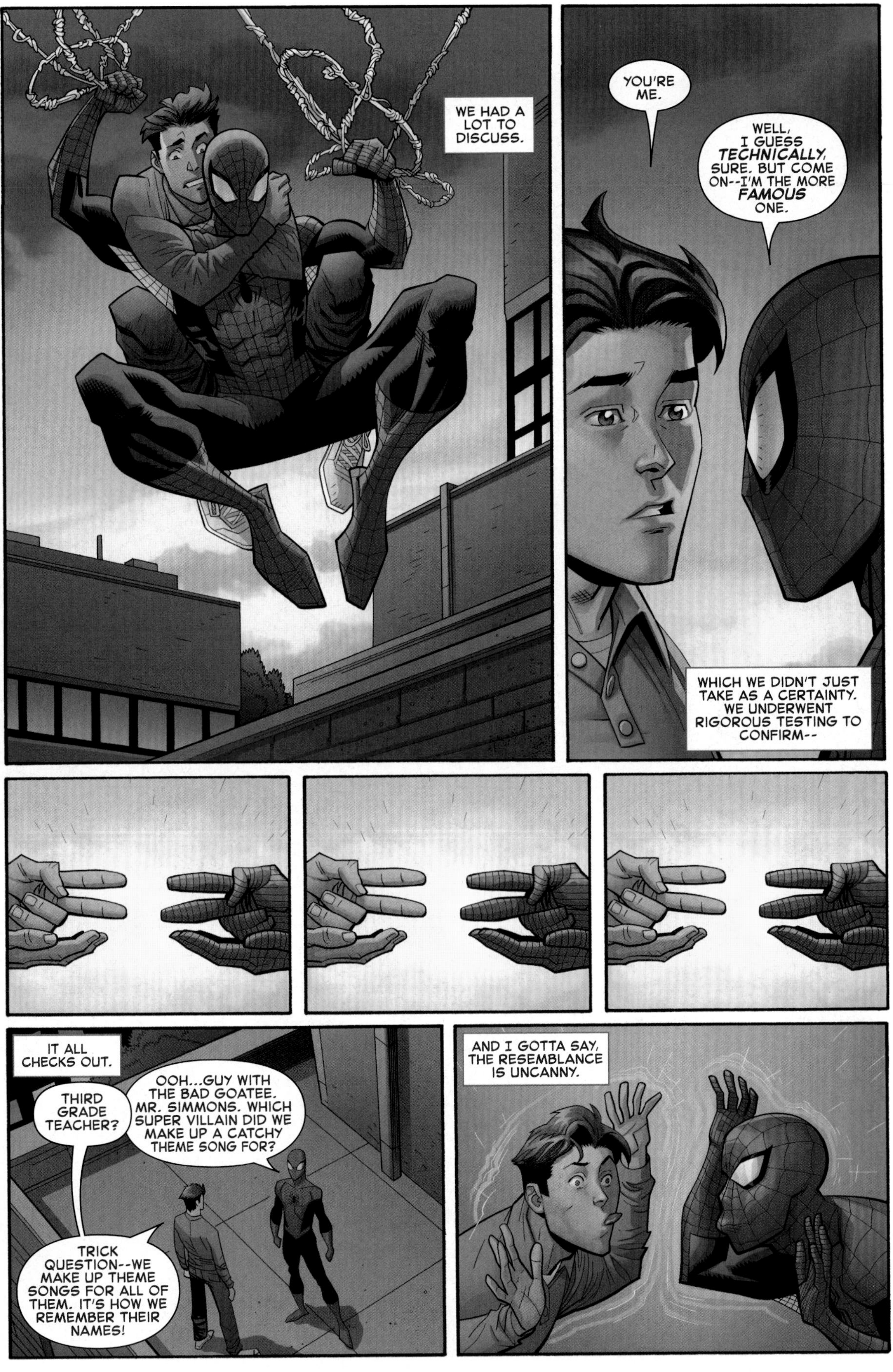
WE HAD A LOT TO DISCUSS.
YOU'RE ME.
WELL, I GUESS TECHNICALLY, SURE. BUT COME ON--I'M THE MORE FAMOUS ONE.
WHICH WE DIDN'T JUST TAKE AS A CERTAINTY. WE UNDERWENT RIGOROUS TESTING TO CONFIRM--
IT ALL CHECKS OUT.
THIRD GRADE TEACHER?
OOH...GUY WITH THE BAD GOATEE. MR. SIMMONS. WHICH SUPER VILLAIN DID WE MAKE UP A CATCHY THEME SONG FOR?
TRICK QUESTION--WE MAKE UP THEME SONGS FOR ALL OF THEM. IT'S HOW WE REMEMBER THEIR NAMES!
AND I GOTTA SAY, THE RESEMBLANCE IS UNCANNY.

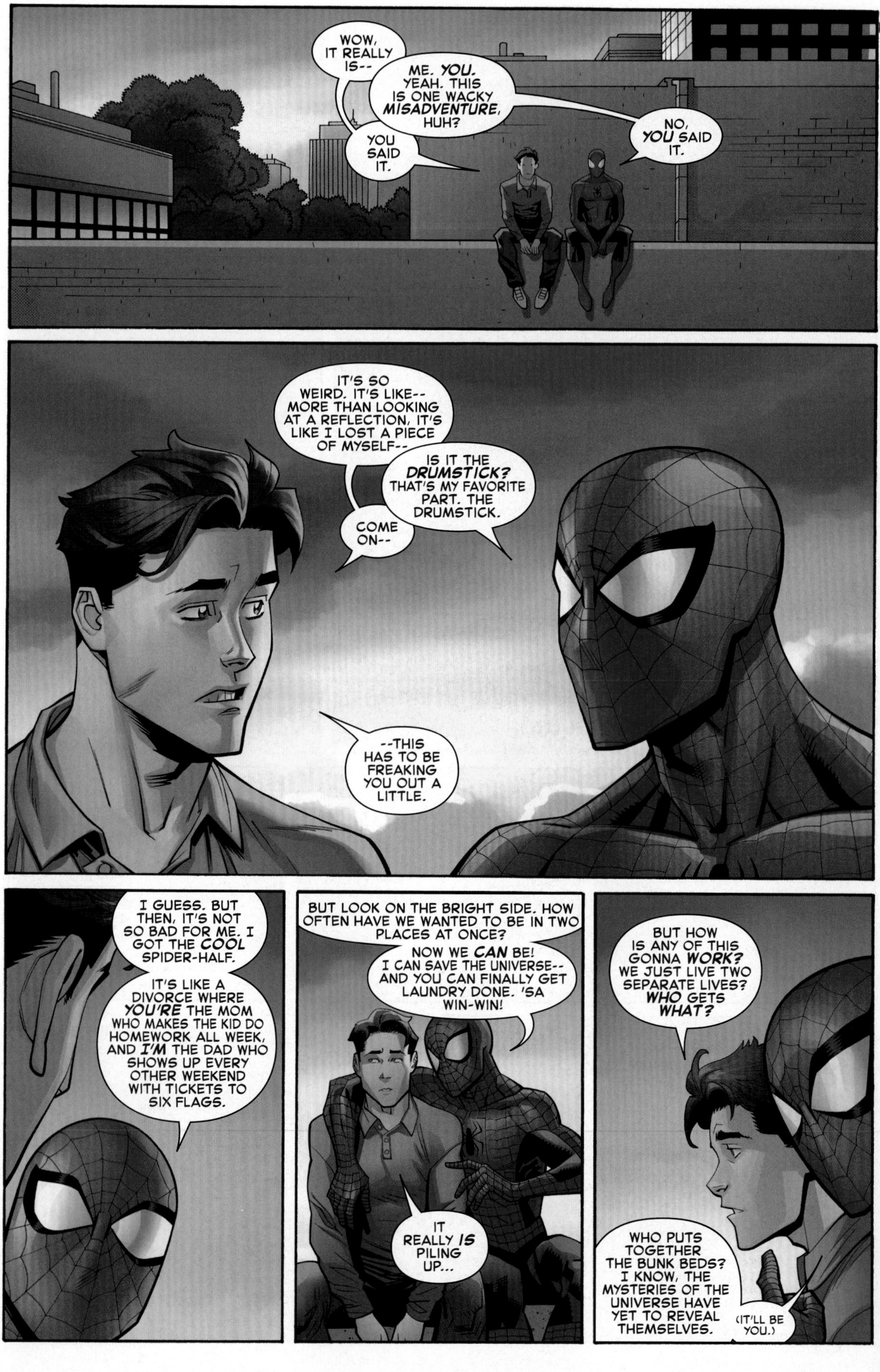
WOW, IT REALLY IS--
ME. YOU. YEAH. THIS IS ONE WACKY MISADVENTURE, HUH?
YOU SAID IT.
NO, YOU SAID IT.
IT'S SO WEIRD. IT'S LIKE-- MORE THAN LOOKING AT A REFLECTION, IT'S LIKE I LOST A PIECE OF MYSELF--
IS IT THE DRUMSTICK? THAT'S MY FAVORITE PART. THE DRUMSTICK.
COME ON--
--THIS HAS TO BE FREAKING YOU OUT A LITTLE.
I GUESS. BUT THEN, IT'S NOT SO BAD FOR ME. I GOT THE COOL SPIDER-HALF.
IT'S LIKE A DIVORCE WHERE YOU'RE THE MOM WHO MAKES THE KID DO HOMEWORK ALL WEEK, AND I'M THE DAD WHO SHOWS UP EVERY OTHER WEEKEND WITH TICKETS TO SIX FLAGS.
BUT LOOK ON THE BRIGHT SIDE. HOW OFTEN HAVE WE WANTED TO BE IN TWO PLACES AT ONCE?
NOW WE CAN BE! I CAN SAVE THE UNIVERSE-- AND YOU CAN FINALLY GET LAUNDRY DONE. 'SA WIN-WIN!
IT REALLY IS PILING UP...
BUT HOW IS ANY OF THIS GONNA WORK? WE JUST LIVE TWO SEPARATE LIVES? WHO GETS WHAT?
WHO PUTS TOGETHER THE BUNK BEDS? I KNOW, THE MYSTERIES OF THE UNIVERSE HAVE YET TO REVEAL THEMSELVES.
(IT'LL BE YOU.)

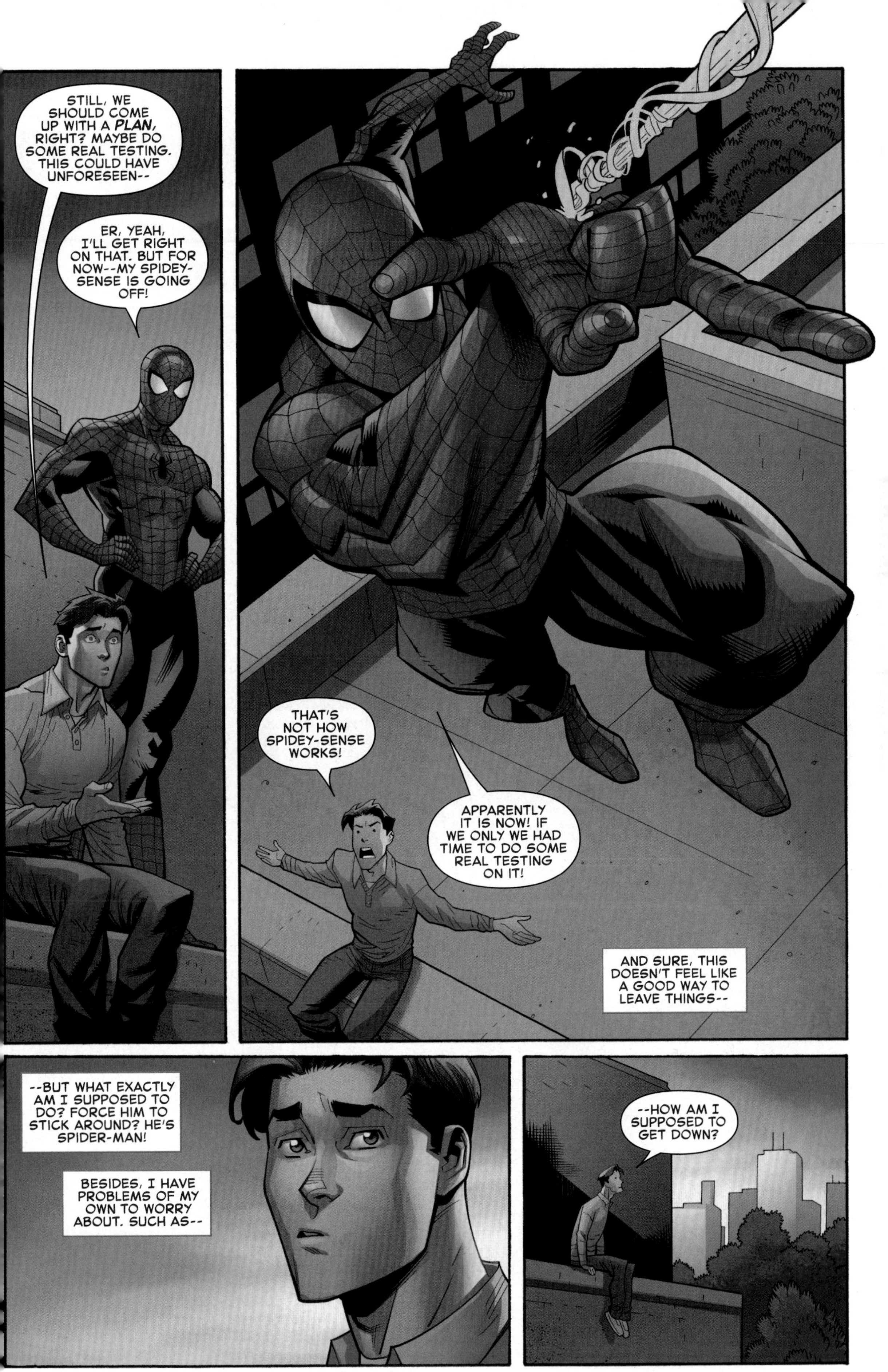
STILL, WE SHOULD COME UP WITH A *PLAN*, RIGHT? MAYBE DO SOME REAL TESTING. THIS COULD HAVE UNFORESEEN--
ER, YEAH, I'LL GET RIGHT ON THAT. BUT FOR NOW--MY SPIDEY-SENSE IS GOING OFF!
THAT'S NOT HOW SPIDEY-SENSE WORKS!
APPARENTLY IT IS NOW! IF WE ONLY WE HAD TIME TO DO SOME REAL TESTING ON IT!
AND SURE, THIS DOESN'T FEEL LIKE A GOOD WAY TO LEAVE THINGS--
--BUT WHAT EXACTLY AM I SUPPOSED TO DO? FORCE HIM TO STICK AROUND? HE'S SPIDER-MAN!
BESIDES, I HAVE PROBLEMS OF MY OWN TO WORRY ABOUT. SUCH AS--
--HOW AM I SUPPOSED TO GET DOWN?

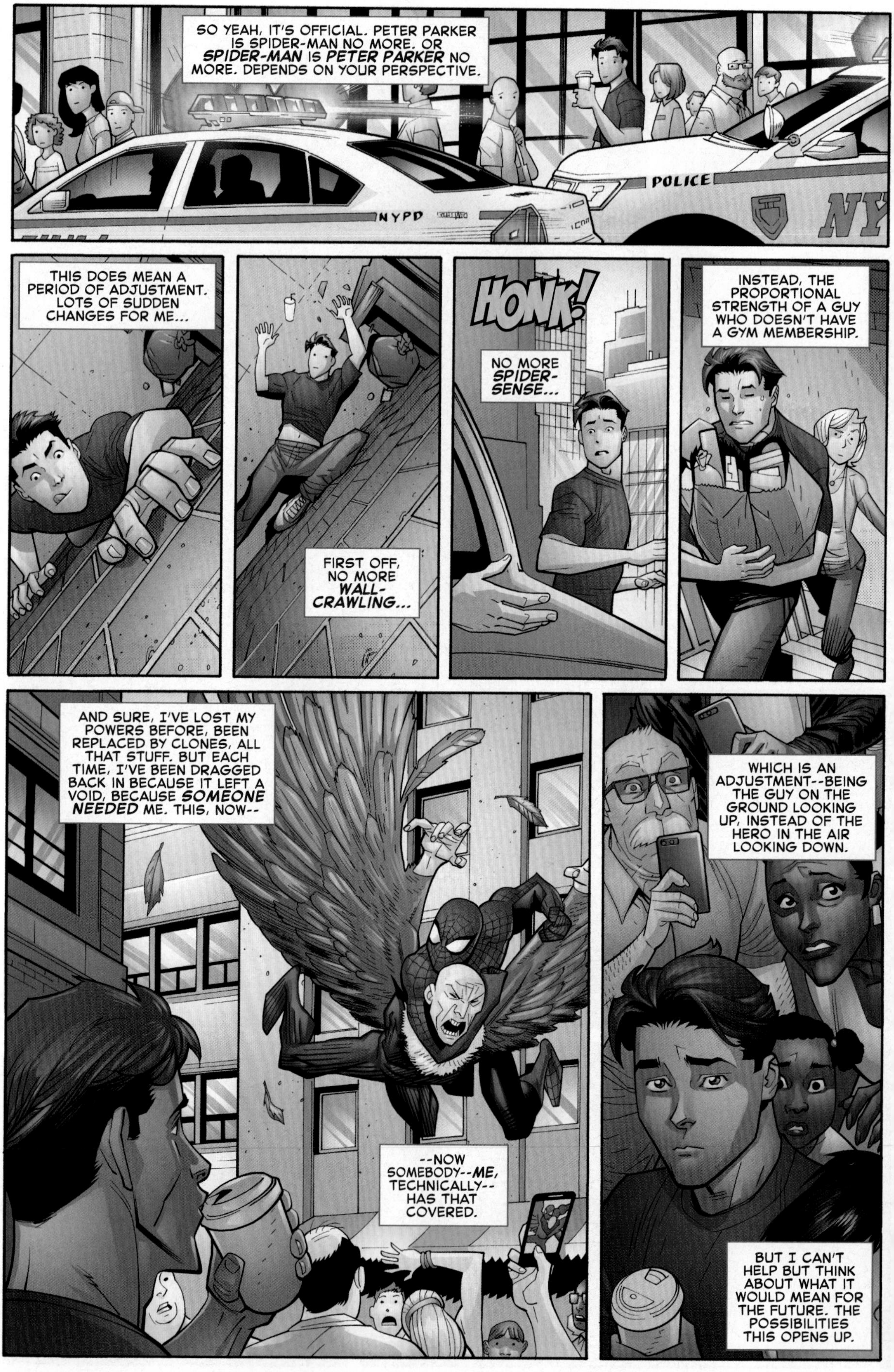
SO YEAH, IT'S OFFICIAL. PETER PARKER IS SPIDER-MAN NO MORE. OR SPIDER-MAN IS PETER PARKER NO MORE. DEPENDS ON YOUR PERSPECTIVE.
POLICE
NYPD
THIS DOES MEAN A PERIOD OF ADJUSTMENT. LOTS OF SUDDEN CHANGES FOR ME...
FIRST OFF, NO MORE WALL-CRAWLING...
HONK!
NO MORE SPIDER-SENSE...
INSTEAD, THE PROPORTIONAL STRENGTH OF A GUY WHO DOESN'T HAVE A GYM MEMBERSHIP.
AND SURE, I'VE LOST MY POWERS BEFORE, BEEN REPLACED BY CLONES, ALL THAT STUFF. BUT EACH TIME, I'VE BEEN DRAGGED BACK IN BECAUSE IT LEFT A VOID, BECAUSE SOMEONE NEEDED ME. THIS, NOW--
--NOW SOMEBODY--ME, TECHNICALLY--HAS THAT COVERED.
WHICH IS AN ADJUSTMENT--BEING THE GUY ON THE GROUND LOOKING UP, INSTEAD OF THE HERO IN THE AIR LOOKING DOWN.
BUT I CAN'T HELP BUT THINK ABOUT WHAT IT WOULD MEAN FOR THE FUTURE. THE POSSIBILITIES THIS OPENS UP.

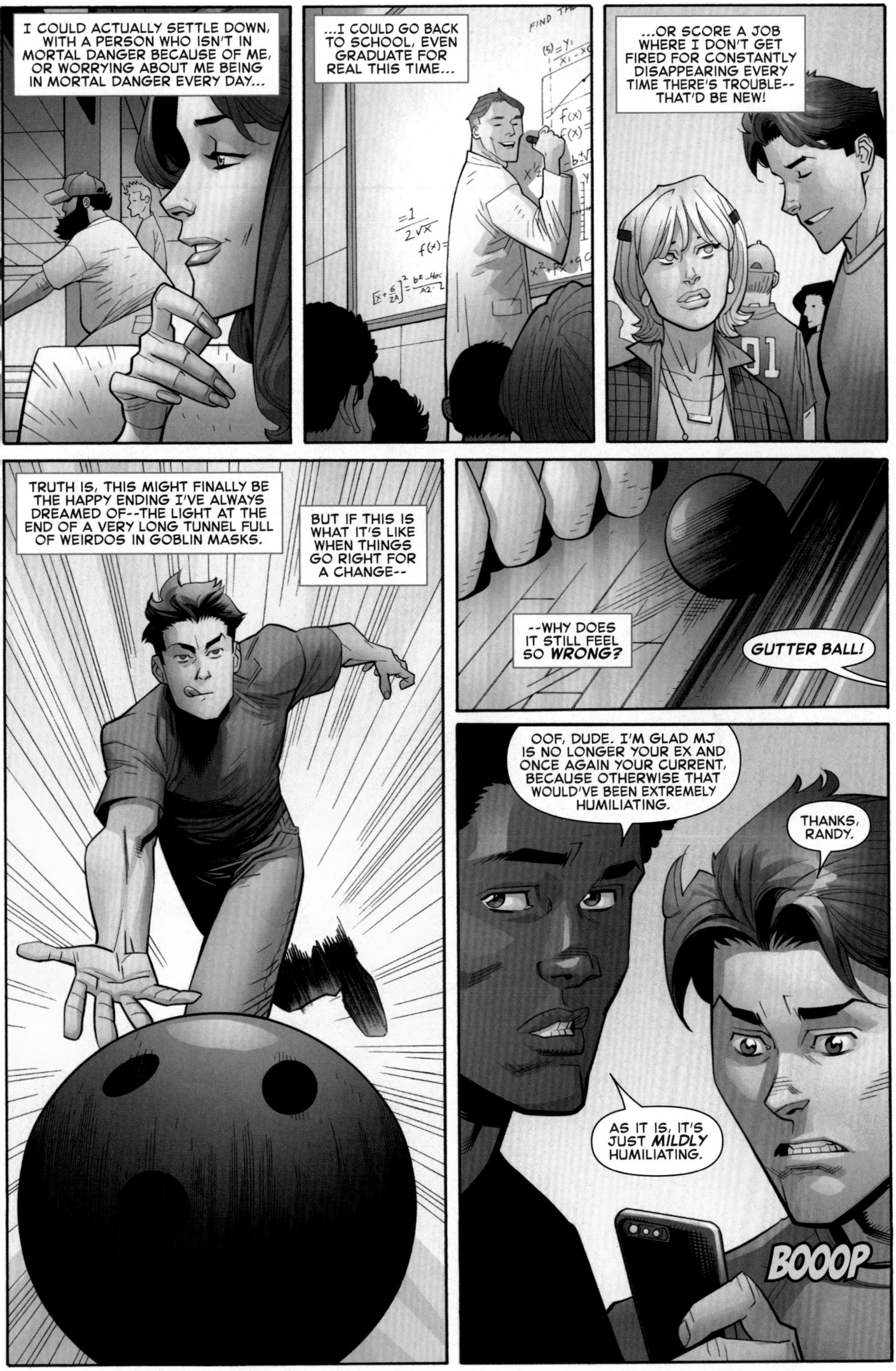
I COULD ACTUALLY SETTLE DOWN, WITH A PERSON WHO ISN'T IN MORTAL DANGER BECAUSE OF ME, OR WORRYING ABOUT ME BEING IN MORTAL DANGER EVERY DAY...
...I COULD GO BACK TO SCHOOL, EVEN GRADUATE FOR REAL THIS TIME...
...OR SCORE A JOB WHERE I DON'T GET FIRED FOR CONSTANTLY DISAPPEARING EVERY TIME THERE'S TROUBLE-- THAT'D BE NEW!
TRUTH IS, THIS MIGHT FINALLY BE THE HAPPY ENDING I'VE ALWAYS DREAMED OF--THE LIGHT AT THE END OF A VERY LONG TUNNEL FULL OF WEIRDOS IN GOBLIN MASKS.
BUT IF THIS IS WHAT IT'S LIKE WHEN THINGS GO RIGHT FOR A CHANGE--
--WHY DOES IT STILL FEEL SO WRONG?
GUTTER BALL!
OOF, DUDE. I'M GLAD MJ IS NO LONGER YOUR EX AND ONCE AGAIN YOUR CURRENT, BECAUSE OTHERWISE THAT WOULD'VE BEEN EXTREMELY HUMILIATING.
THANKS, RANDY.
AS IT IS, IT'S JUST MILDLY HUMILIATING.
BOOOP

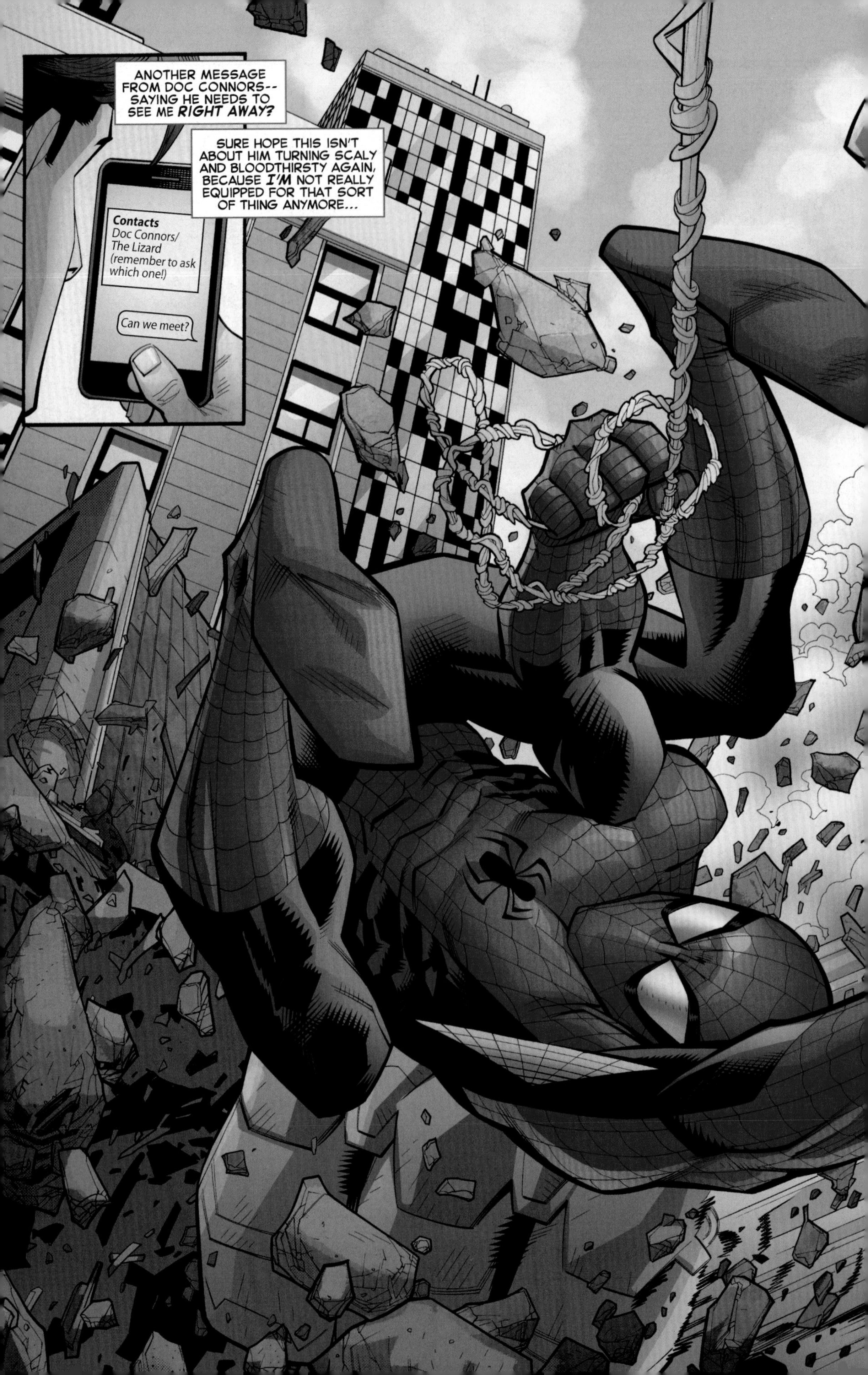
ANOTHER MESSAGE FROM DOC CONNORS-- SAYING HE NEEDS TO SEE ME RIGHT AWAY?
SURE HOPE THIS ISN'T ABOUT HIM TURNING SCALY AND BLOODTHIRSTY AGAIN, BECAUSE I'M NOT REALLY EQUIPPED FOR THAT SORT OF THING ANYMORE...
Contacts
Doc Connors/ The Lizard (remember to ask which one!)
Can we meet?

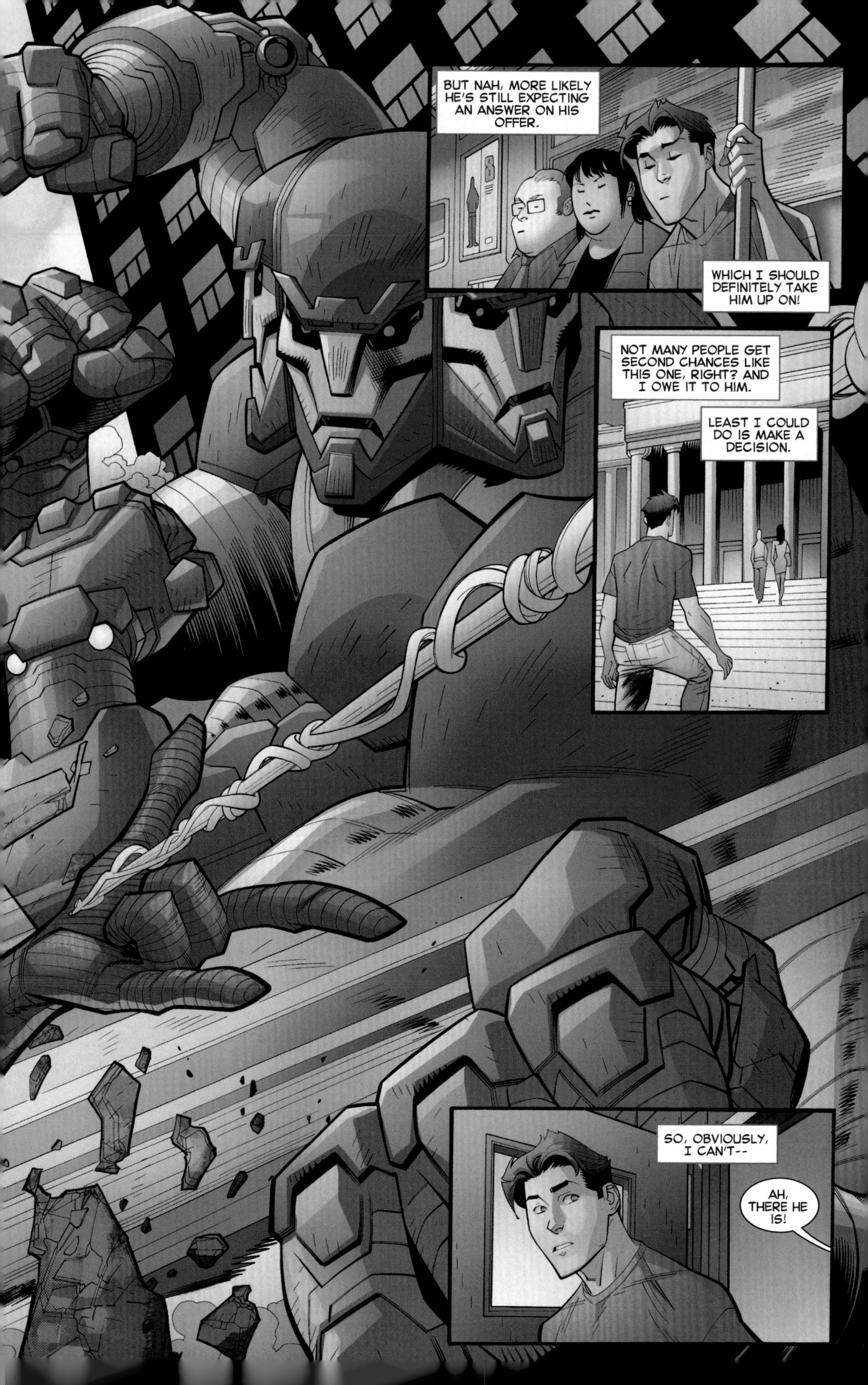
BUT NAH, MORE LIKELY HE'S STILL EXPECTING AN ANSWER ON HIS OFFER.
WHICH I SHOULD DEFINITELY TAKE HIM UP ON!
NOT MANY PEOPLE GET SECOND CHANCES LIKE THIS ONE, RIGHT? AND I OWE IT TO HIM.
LEAST I COULD DO IS MAKE A DECISION.
SO, OBVIOUSLY, I CAN'T--
AH, THERE HE IS!

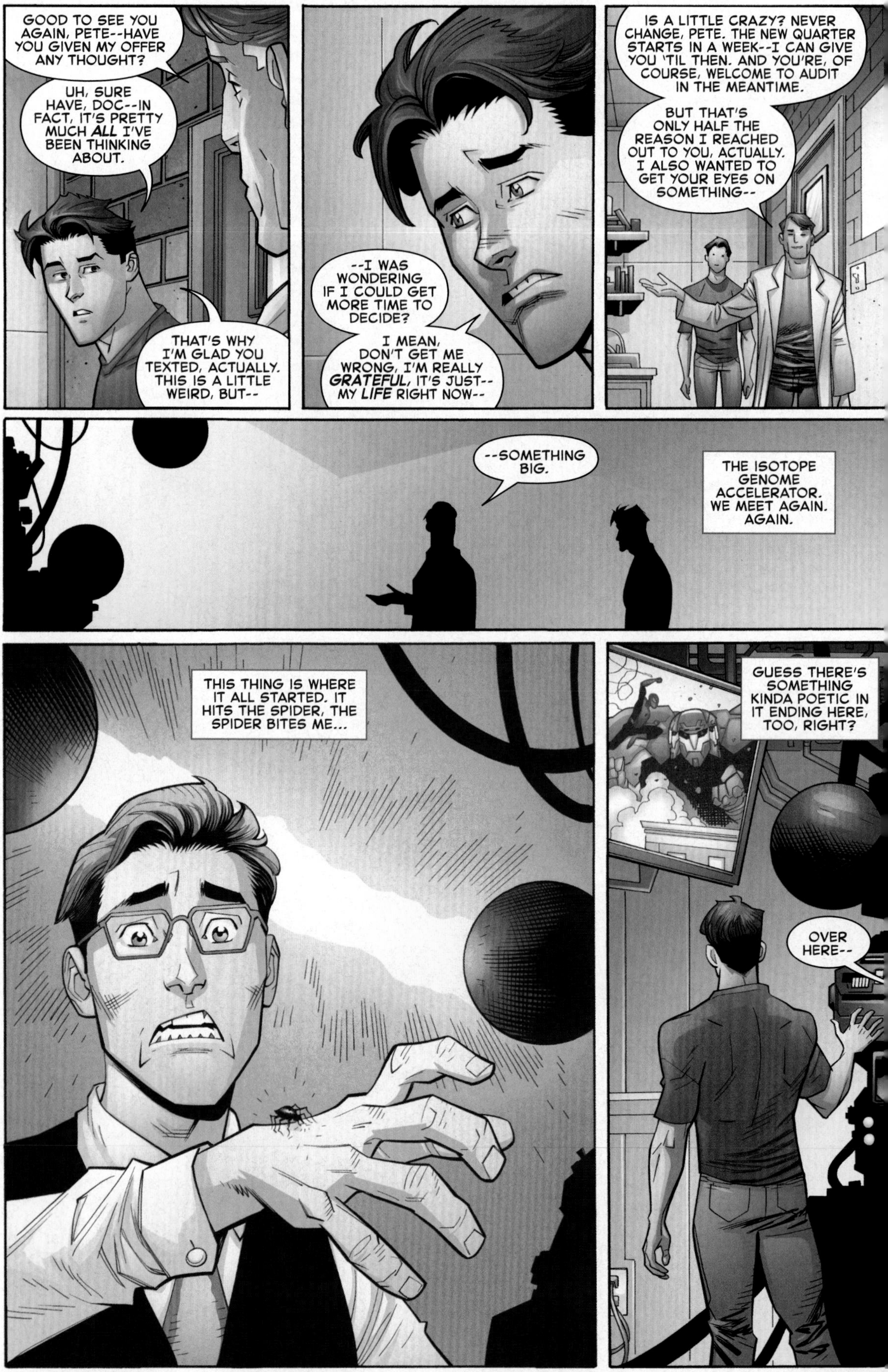
GOOD TO SEE YOU AGAIN, PETE--HAVE YOU GIVEN MY OFFER ANY THOUGHT?
UH, SURE HAVE, DOC--IN FACT, IT'S PRETTY MUCH ALL I'VE BEEN THINKING ABOUT.
THAT'S WHY I'M GLAD YOU TEXTED, ACTUALLY. THIS IS A LITTLE WEIRD, BUT--
--I WAS WONDERING IF I COULD GET MORE TIME TO DECIDE?
I MEAN, DON'T GET ME WRONG, I'M REALLY GRATEFUL, IT'S JUST--MY LIFE RIGHT NOW--
IS A LITTLE CRAZY? NEVER CHANGE, PETE. THE NEW QUARTER STARTS IN A WEEK--I CAN GIVE YOU 'TIL THEN. AND YOU'RE, OF COURSE, WELCOME TO AUDIT IN THE MEANTIME.
BUT THAT'S ONLY HALF THE REASON I REACHED OUT TO YOU, ACTUALLY. I ALSO WANTED TO GET YOUR EYES ON SOMETHING--
--SOMETHING BIG.
THE ISOTOPE GENOME ACCELERATOR. WE MEET AGAIN. AGAIN.
THIS THING IS WHERE IT ALL STARTED. IT HITS THE SPIDER, THE SPIDER BITES ME...
GUESS THERE'S SOMETHING KINDA POETIC IN IT ENDING HERE, TOO, RIGHT?
OVER HERE--

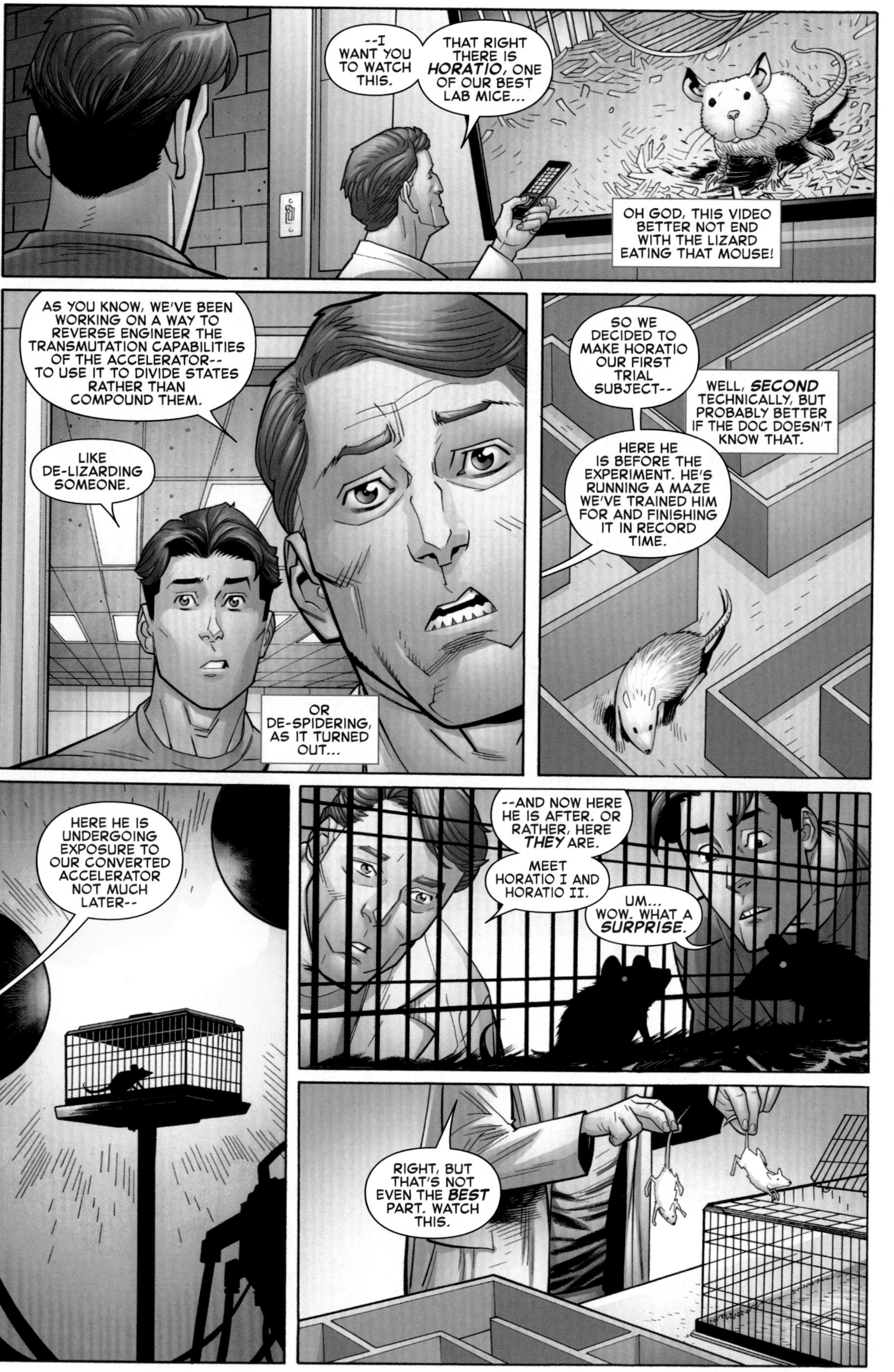
--I WANT YOU TO WATCH THIS.
THAT RIGHT THERE IS HORATIO, ONE OF OUR BEST LAB MICE...
OH GOD, THIS VIDEO BETTER NOT END WITH THE LIZARD EATING THAT MOUSE!
AS YOU KNOW, WE'VE BEEN WORKING ON A WAY TO REVERSE ENGINEER THE TRANSMUTATION CAPABILITIES OF THE ACCELERATOR--TO USE IT TO DIVIDE STATES RATHER THAN COMPOUND THEM.
LIKE DE-LIZARDING SOMEONE.
OR DE-SPIDERING, AS IT TURNED OUT...
SO WE DECIDED TO MAKE HORATIO OUR FIRST TRIAL SUBJECT--
WELL, SECOND TECHNICALLY, BUT PROBABLY BETTER IF THE DOC DOESN'T KNOW THAT.
HERE HE IS BEFORE THE EXPERIMENT. HE'S RUNNING A MAZE WE'VE TRAINED HIM FOR AND FINISHING IT IN RECORD TIME.
HERE HE IS UNDERGOING EXPOSURE TO OUR CONVERTED ACCELERATOR NOT MUCH LATER--
--AND NOW HERE HE IS AFTER. OR RATHER, HERE THEY ARE.
MEET HORATIO I AND HORATIO II.
UM... WOW. WHAT A SURPRISE.
RIGHT, BUT THAT'S NOT EVEN THE BEST PART. WATCH THIS.

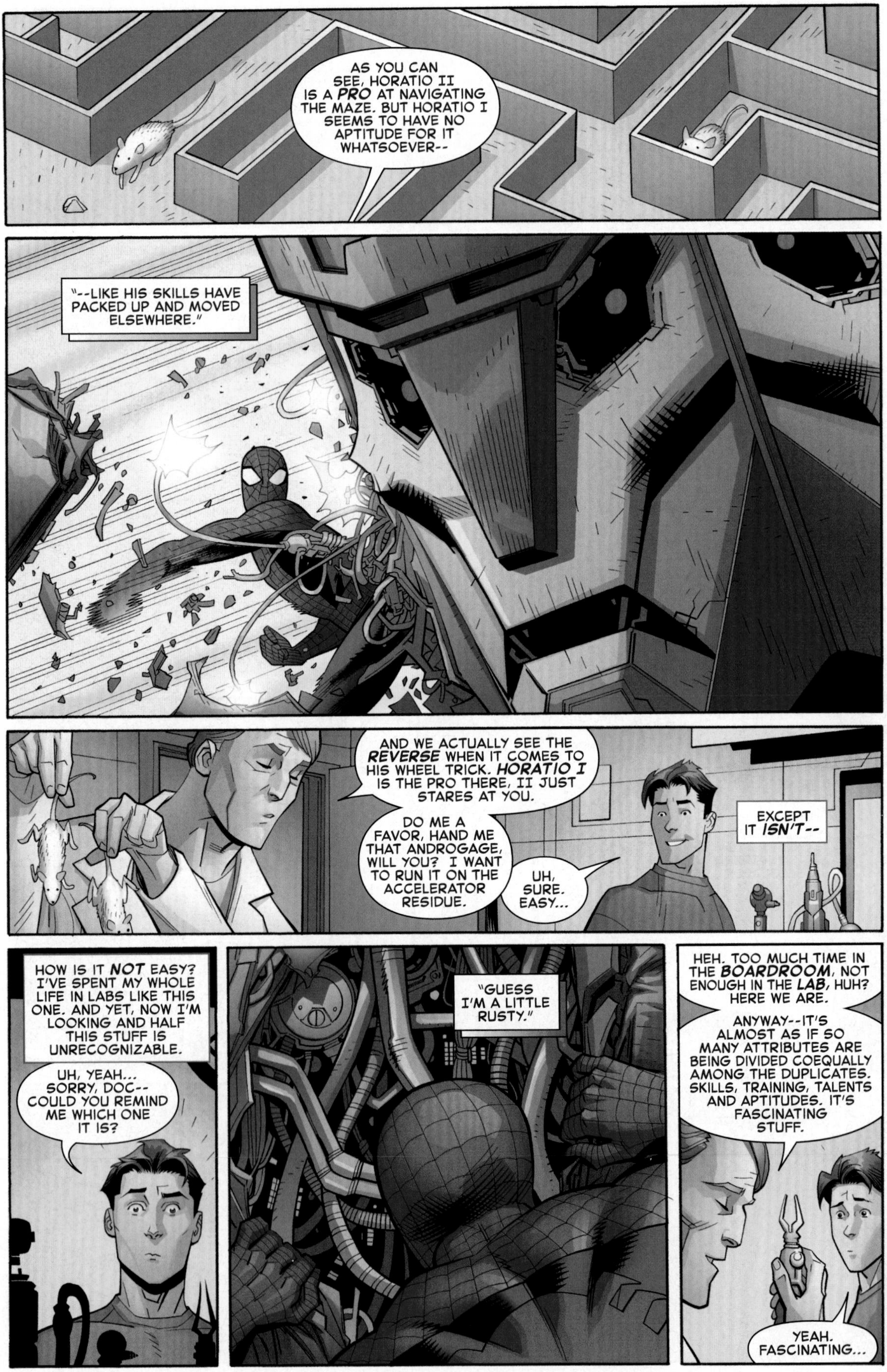

AS YOU CAN SEE, HORATIO II IS A PRO AT NAVIGATING THE MAZE. BUT HORATIO I SEEMS TO HAVE NO APTITUDE FOR IT WHATSOEVER--
"--LIKE HIS SKILLS HAVE PACKED UP AND MOVED ELSEWHERE."
AND WE ACTUALLY SEE THE REVERSE WHEN IT COMES TO HIS WHEEL TRICK. HORATIO I IS THE PRO THERE, II JUST STARES AT YOU.
DO ME A FAVOR, HAND ME THAT ANDROGAGE, WILL YOU? I WANT TO RUN IT ON THE ACCELERATOR RESIDUE.
UH, SURE. EASY...
EXCEPT IT ISN'T--
HOW IS IT NOT EASY? I'VE SPENT MY WHOLE LIFE IN LABS LIKE THIS ONE. AND YET, NOW I'M LOOKING AND HALF THIS STUFF IS UNRECOGNIZABLE.
UH, YEAH... SORRY, DOC-- COULD YOU REMIND ME WHICH ONE IT IS?
"GUESS I'M A LITTLE RUSTY."
HEH. TOO MUCH TIME IN THE BOARDROOM, NOT ENOUGH IN THE LAB, HUH? HERE WE ARE.
ANYWAY--IT'S ALMOST AS IF SO MANY ATTRIBUTES ARE BEING DIVIDED COEQUALLY AMONG THE DUPLICATES. SKILLS, TRAINING, TALENTS AND APTITUDES. IT'S FASCINATING STUFF.
YEAH. FASCINATING...

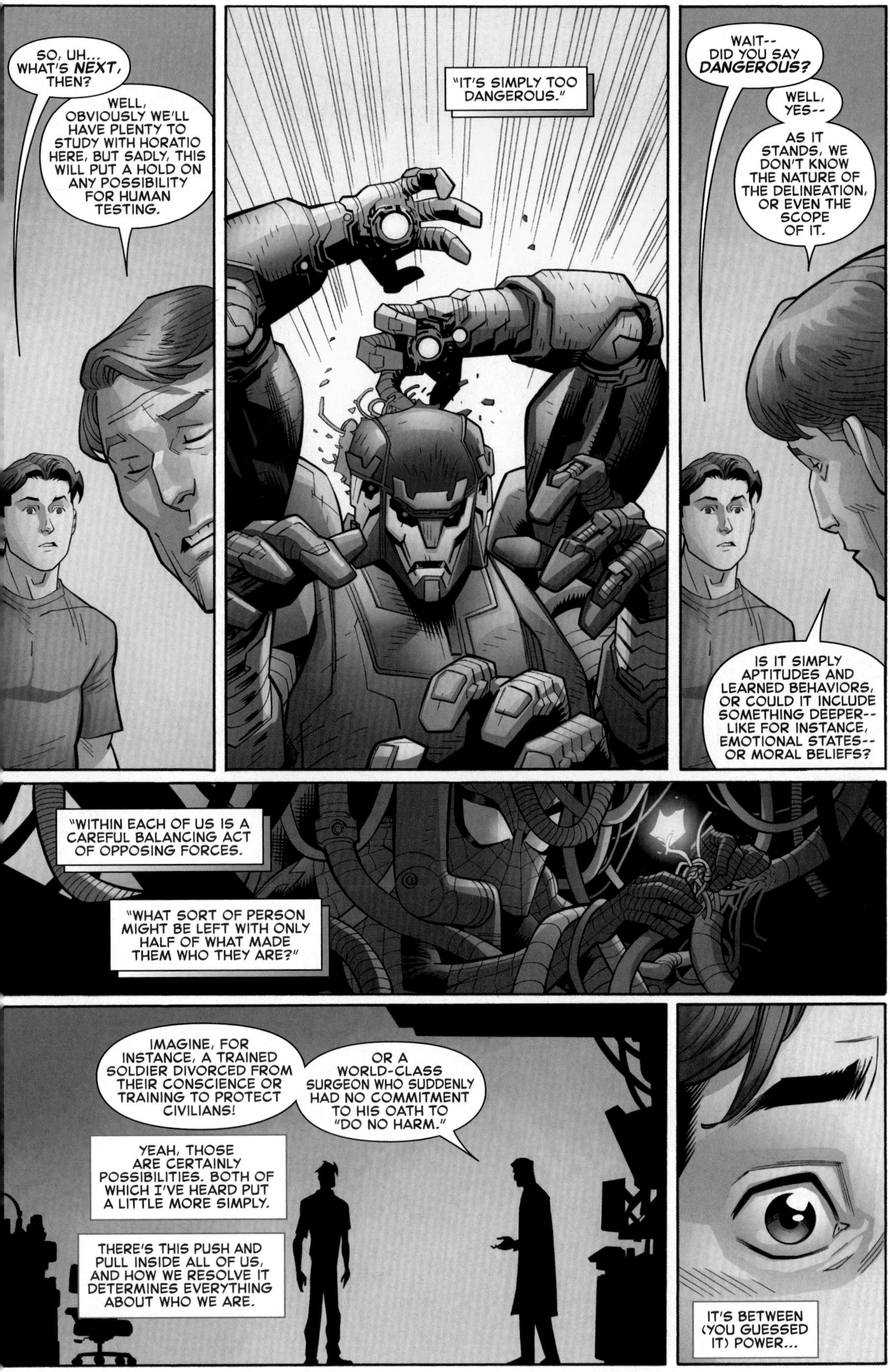
SO, UH... WHAT'S *NEXT*, THEN?
WELL, OBVIOUSLY WE'LL HAVE PLENTY TO STUDY WITH HORATIO HERE, BUT SADLY, THIS WILL PUT A HOLD ON ANY POSSIBILITY FOR HUMAN TESTING.
"IT'S SIMPLY TOO DANGEROUS."
WAIT-- DID YOU SAY *DANGEROUS?*
WELL, YES--
AS IT STANDS, WE DON'T KNOW THE NATURE OF THE DELINEATION, OR EVEN THE SCOPE OF IT.
IS IT SIMPLY APTITUDES AND LEARNED BEHAVIORS, OR COULD IT INCLUDE SOMETHING DEEPER-- LIKE FOR INSTANCE, EMOTIONAL STATES-- OR MORAL BELIEFS?
"WITHIN EACH OF US IS A CAREFUL BALANCING ACT OF OPPOSING FORCES.
"WHAT SORT OF PERSON MIGHT BE LEFT WITH ONLY HALF OF WHAT MADE THEM WHO THEY ARE?"
IMAGINE, FOR INSTANCE, A TRAINED SOLDIER DIVORCED FROM THEIR CONSCIENCE OR TRAINING TO PROTECT CIVILIANS!
OR A WORLD-CLASS SURGEON WHO SUDDENLY HAD NO COMMITMENT TO HIS OATH TO "DO NO HARM."
YEAH, THOSE ARE CERTAINLY POSSIBILITIES. BOTH OF WHICH I'VE HEARD PUT A LITTLE MORE SIMPLY.
THERE'S THIS PUSH AND PULL INSIDE ALL OF US, AND HOW WE RESOLVE IT DETERMINES EVERYTHING ABOUT WHO WE ARE.
IT'S BETWEEN (YOU GUESSED IT) POWER...

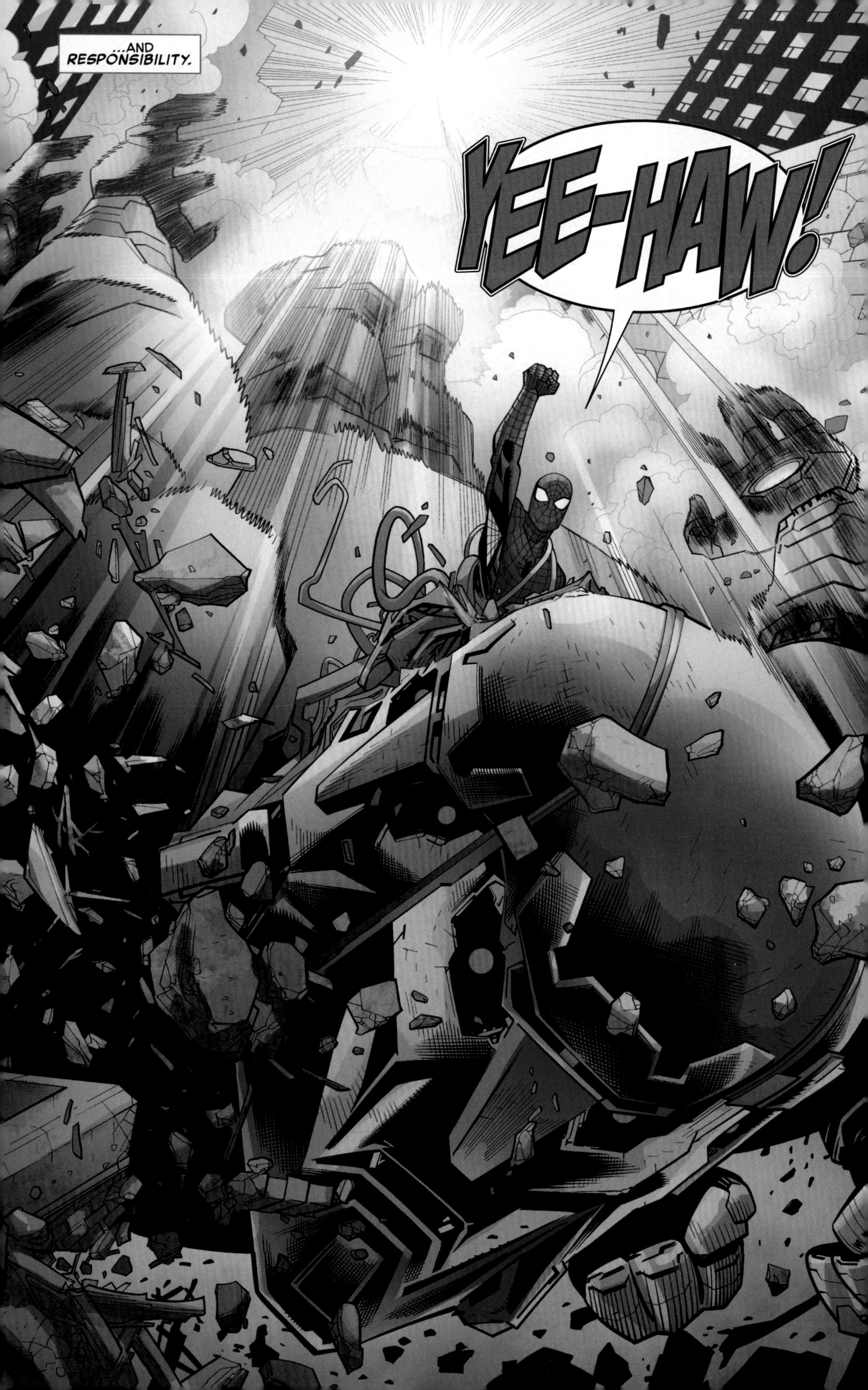
...AND RESPONSIBILITY.
YEE-HAW!

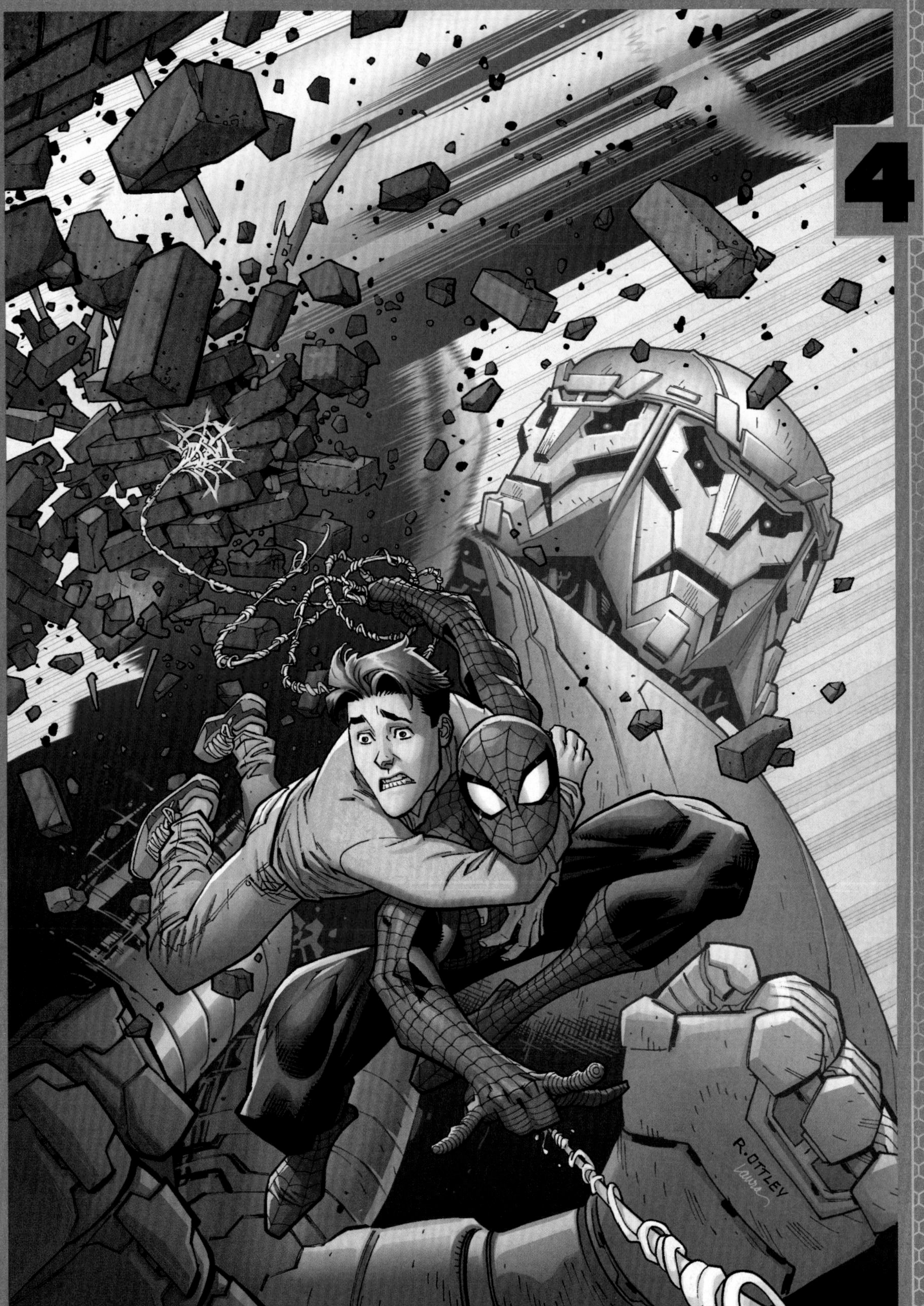

4
R. OTTLEY

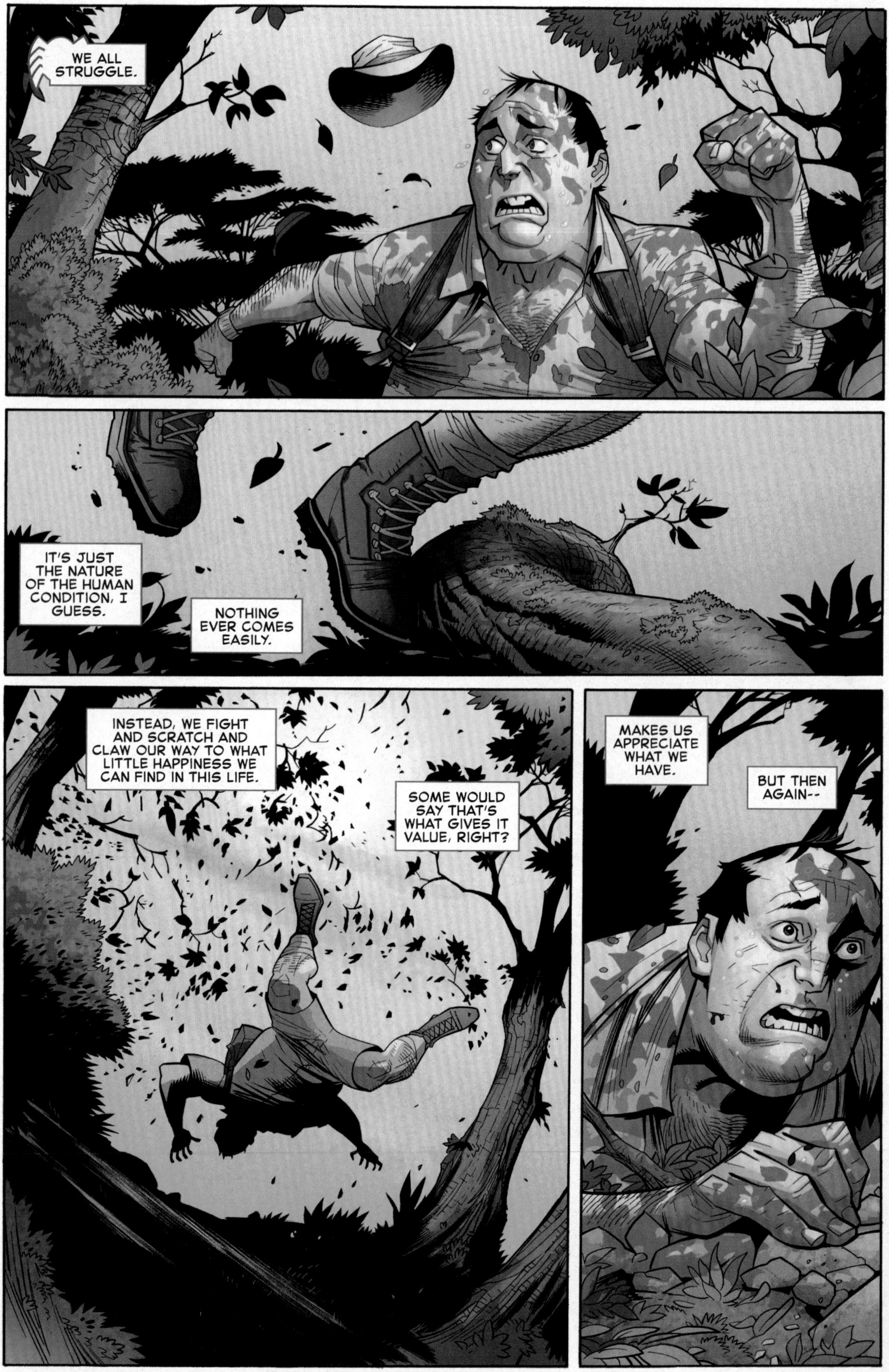
WE ALL STRUGGLE.
IT'S JUST THE NATURE OF THE HUMAN CONDITION, I GUESS.
NOTHING EVER COMES EASILY.
INSTEAD, WE FIGHT AND SCRATCH AND CLAW OUR WAY TO WHAT LITTLE HAPPINESS WE CAN FIND IN THIS LIFE.
SOME WOULD SAY THAT'S WHAT GIVES IT VALUE, RIGHT?
MAKES US APPRECIATE WHAT WE HAVE.
BUT THEN AGAIN--

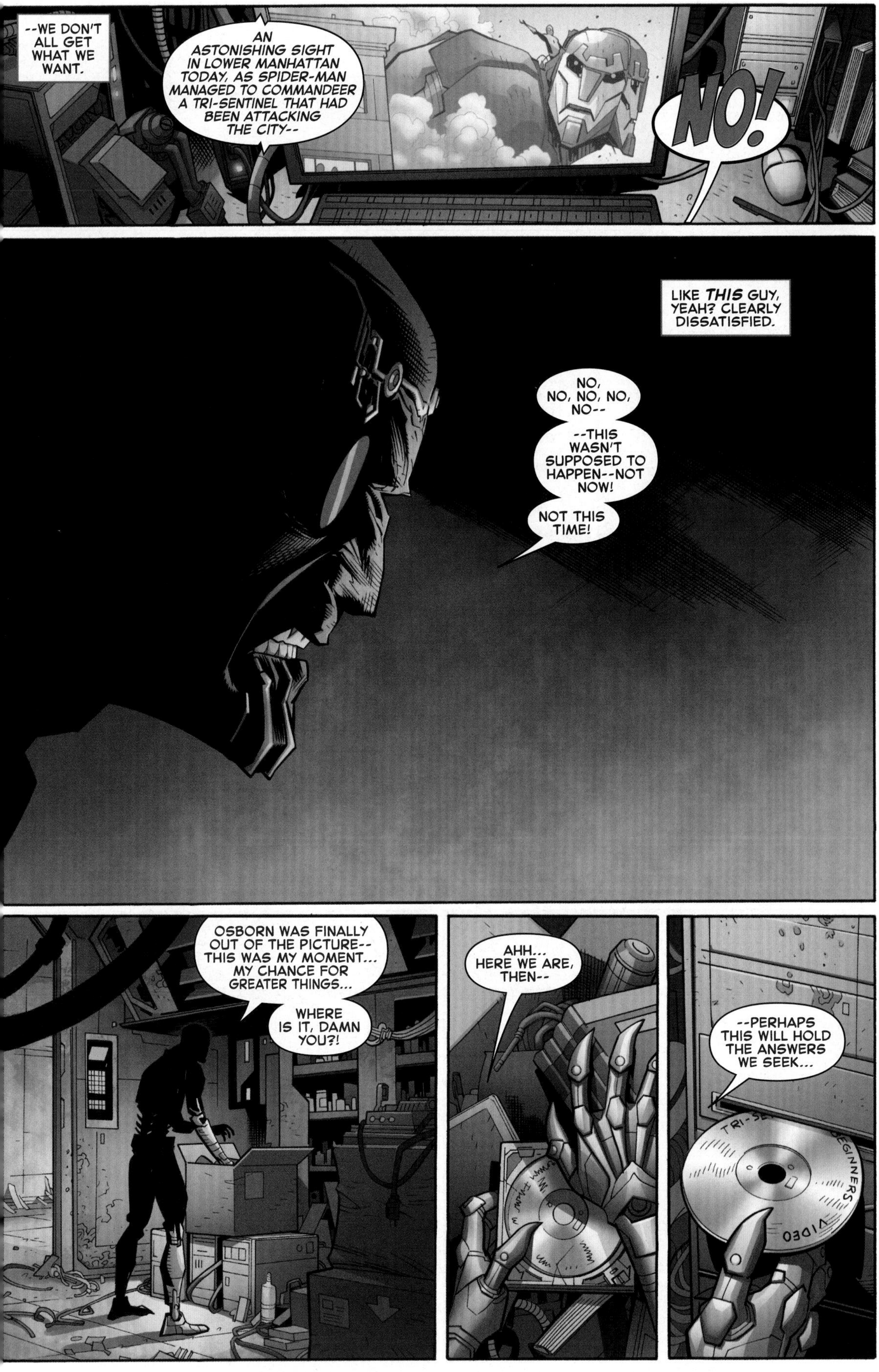
--WE DON'T ALL GET WHAT WE WANT.
AN ASTONISHING SIGHT IN LOWER MANHATTAN TODAY, AS SPIDER-MAN MANAGED TO COMMANDEER A TRI-SENTINEL THAT HAD BEEN ATTACKING THE CITY--
NO!
LIKE THIS GUY, YEAH? CLEARLY DISSATISFIED.
NO, NO, NO, NO, NO--
--THIS WASN'T SUPPOSED TO HAPPEN--NOT NOW!
NOT THIS TIME!
OSBORN WAS FINALLY OUT OF THE PICTURE-- THIS WAS MY MOMENT... MY CHANCE FOR GREATER THINGS...
WHERE IS IT, DAMN YOU?!
AHH... HERE WE ARE, THEN--
--PERHAPS THIS WILL HOLD THE ANSWERS WE SEEK...

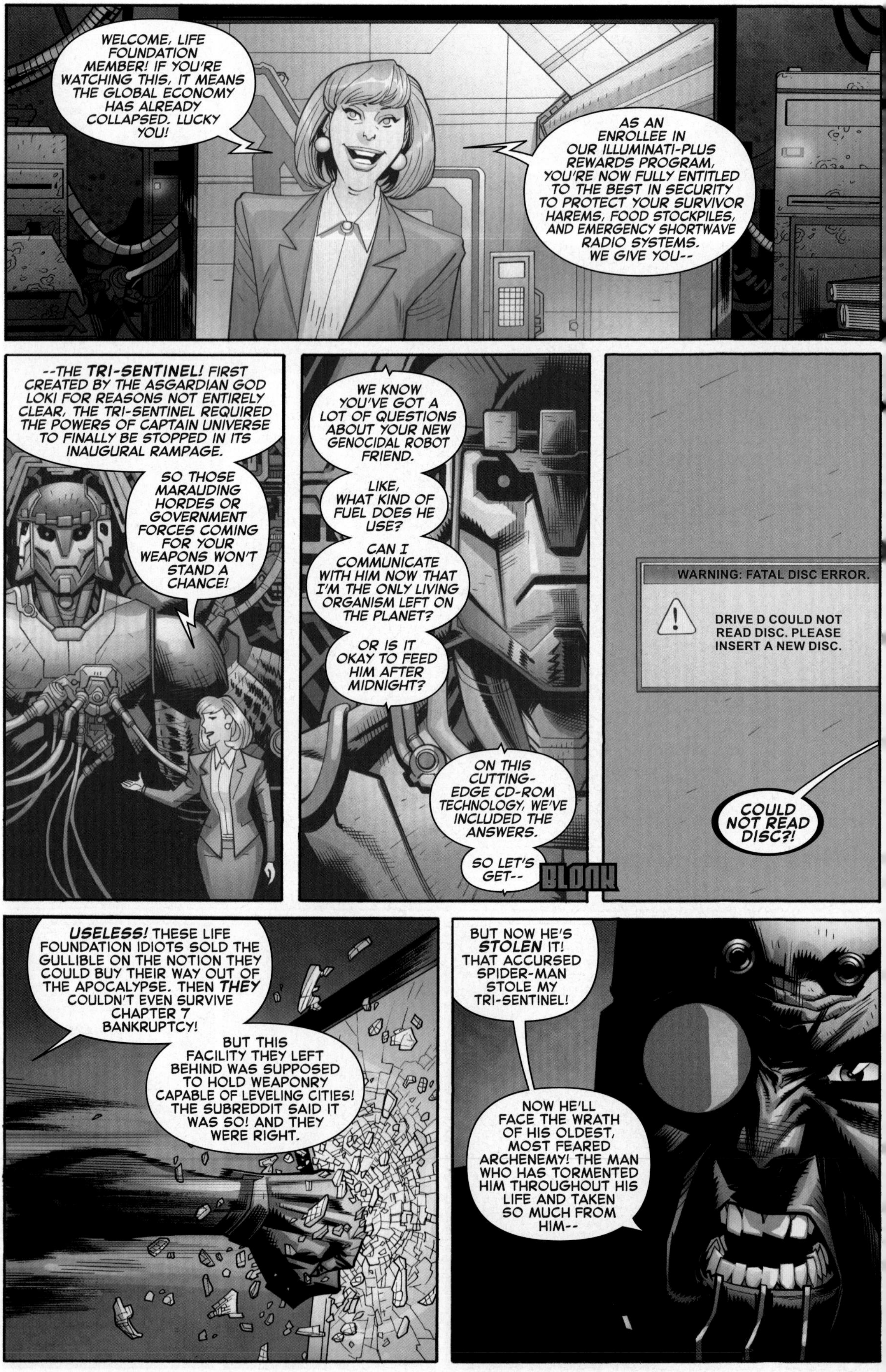
WELCOME, LIFE FOUNDATION MEMBER! IF YOU'RE WATCHING THIS, IT MEANS THE GLOBAL ECONOMY HAS ALREADY COLLAPSED. LUCKY YOU!
AS AN ENROLLEE IN OUR ILLUMINATI-PLUS REWARDS PROGRAM, YOU'RE NOW FULLY ENTITLED TO THE BEST IN SECURITY TO PROTECT YOUR SURVIVOR HAREMS, FOOD STOCKPILES, AND EMERGENCY SHORTWAVE RADIO SYSTEMS. WE GIVE YOU--
--THE TRI-SENTINEL! FIRST CREATED BY THE ASGARDIAN GOD LOKI FOR REASONS NOT ENTIRELY CLEAR, THE TRI-SENTINEL REQUIRED THE POWERS OF CAPTAIN UNIVERSE TO FINALLY BE STOPPED IN ITS INAUGURAL RAMPAGE.
SO THOSE MARAUDING HORDES OR GOVERNMENT FORCES COMING FOR YOUR WEAPONS WON'T STAND A CHANCE!
WE KNOW YOU'VE GOT A LOT OF QUESTIONS ABOUT YOUR NEW GENOCIDAL ROBOT FRIEND.
LIKE, WHAT KIND OF FUEL DOES HE USE?
CAN I COMMUNICATE WITH HIM NOW THAT I'M THE ONLY LIVING ORGANISM LEFT ON THE PLANET?
OR IS IT OKAY TO FEED HIM AFTER MIDNIGHT?
ON THIS CUTTING-EDGE CD-ROM TECHNOLOGY, WE'VE INCLUDED THE ANSWERS.
SO LET'S GET--
BLONK
WARNING: FATAL DISC ERROR.
DRIVE D COULD NOT READ DISC. PLEASE INSERT A NEW DISC.
COULD NOT READ DISC?!
USELESS! THESE LIFE FOUNDATION IDIOTS SOLD THE GULLIBLE ON THE NOTION THEY COULD BUY THEIR WAY OUT OF THE APOCALYPSE. THEN THEY COULDN'T EVEN SURVIVE CHAPTER 7 BANKRUPTCY!
BUT THIS FACILITY THEY LEFT BEHIND WAS SUPPOSED TO HOLD WEAPONRY CAPABLE OF LEVELING CITIES! THE SUBREDDIT SAID IT WAS SO! AND THEY WERE RIGHT.
BUT NOW HE'S STOLEN IT! THAT ACCURSED SPIDER-MAN STOLE MY TRI-SENTINEL!
NOW HE'LL FACE THE WRATH OF HIS OLDEST, MOST FEARED ARCHENEMY! THE MAN WHO HAS TORMENTED HIM THROUGHOUT HIS LIFE AND TAKEN SO MUCH FROM HIM--

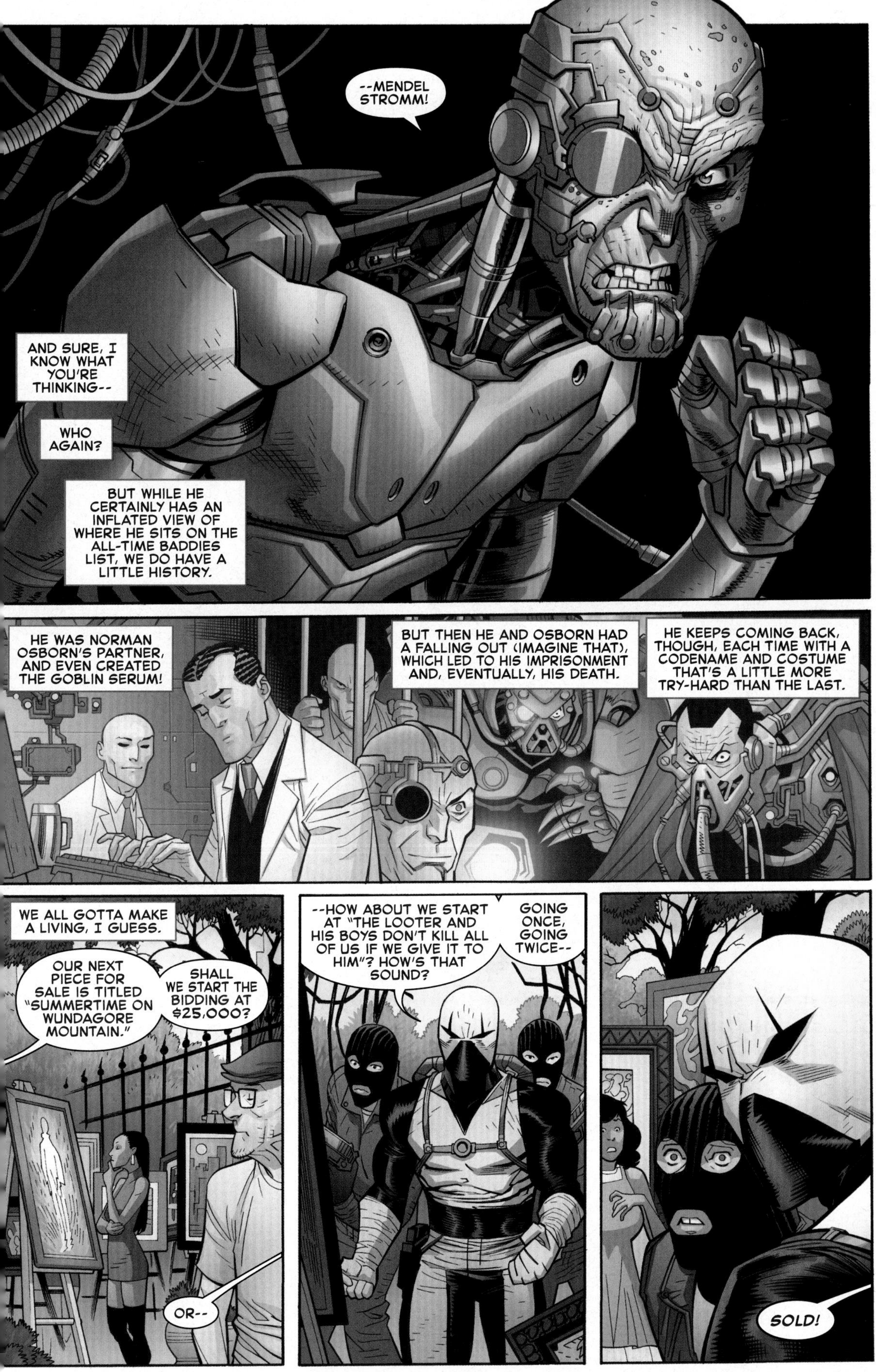
--MENDEL STROMM!
AND SURE, I KNOW WHAT YOU'RE THINKING--
WHO AGAIN?
BUT WHILE HE CERTAINLY HAS AN INFLATED VIEW OF WHERE HE SITS ON THE ALL-TIME BADDIES LIST, WE DO HAVE A LITTLE HISTORY.
HE WAS NORMAN OSBORN'S PARTNER, AND EVEN CREATED THE GOBLIN SERUM!
BUT THEN HE AND OSBORN HAD A FALLING OUT (IMAGINE THAT), WHICH LED TO HIS IMPRISONMENT AND, EVENTUALLY, HIS DEATH.
HE KEEPS COMING BACK, THOUGH, EACH TIME WITH A CODENAME AND COSTUME THAT'S A LITTLE MORE TRY-HARD THAN THE LAST.
WE ALL GOTTA MAKE A LIVING, I GUESS.
OUR NEXT PIECE FOR SALE IS TITLED "SUMMERTIME ON WUNDAGORE MOUNTAIN."
SHALL WE START THE BIDDING AT $25,000?
OR--
--HOW ABOUT WE START AT "THE LOOTER AND HIS BOYS DON'T KILL ALL OF US IF WE GIVE IT TO HIM"? HOW'S THAT SOUND?
GOING ONCE, GOING TWICE--
SOLD!

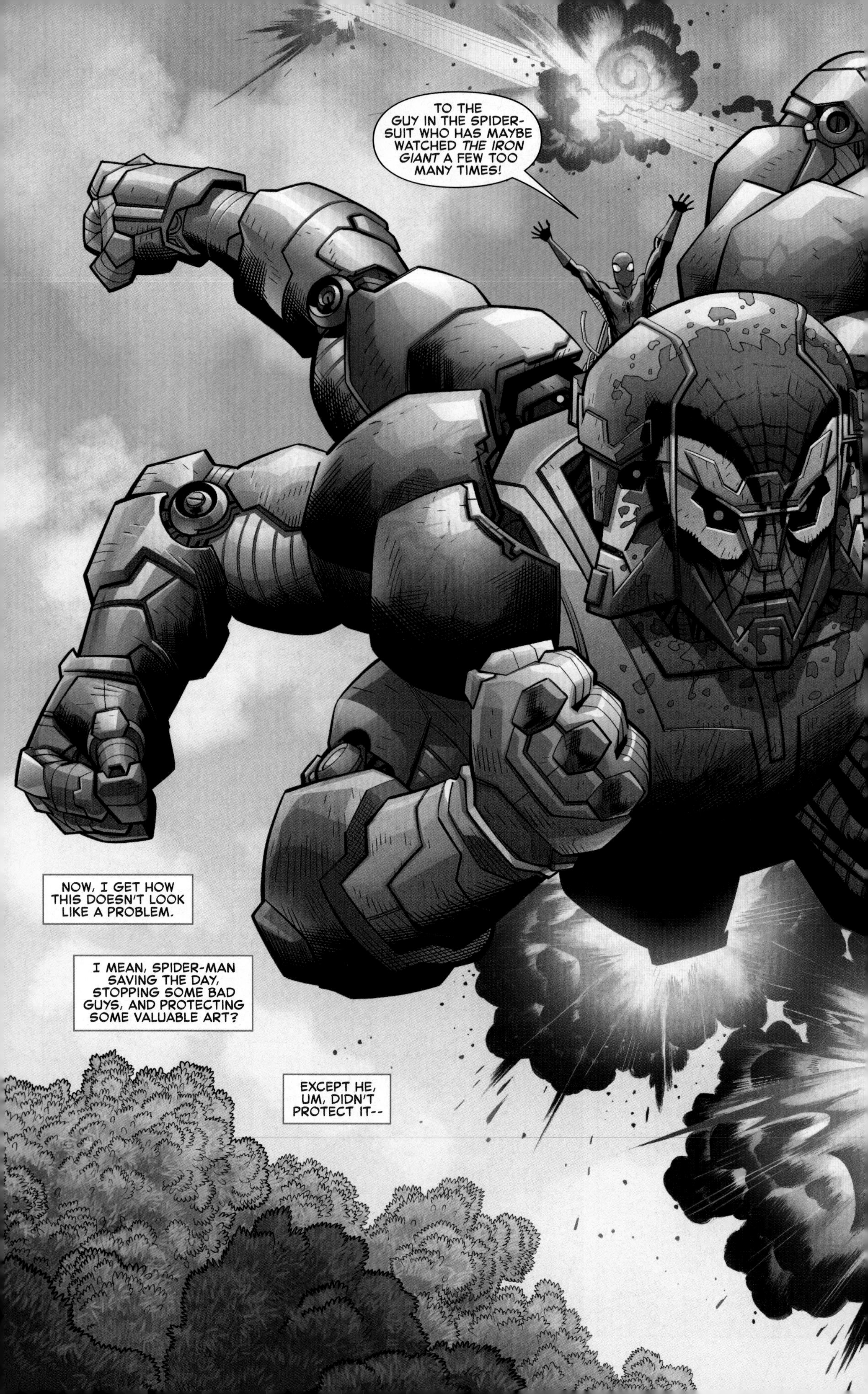
TO THE GUY IN THE SPIDER-SUIT WHO HAS MAYBE WATCHED *THE IRON GIANT* A FEW TOO MANY TIMES!
NOW, I GET HOW THIS DOESN'T LOOK LIKE A PROBLEM.
I MEAN, SPIDER-MAN SAVING THE DAY, STOPPING SOME BAD GUYS, AND PROTECTING SOME VALUABLE ART?
EXCEPT HE, UM, DIDN'T PROTECT IT--

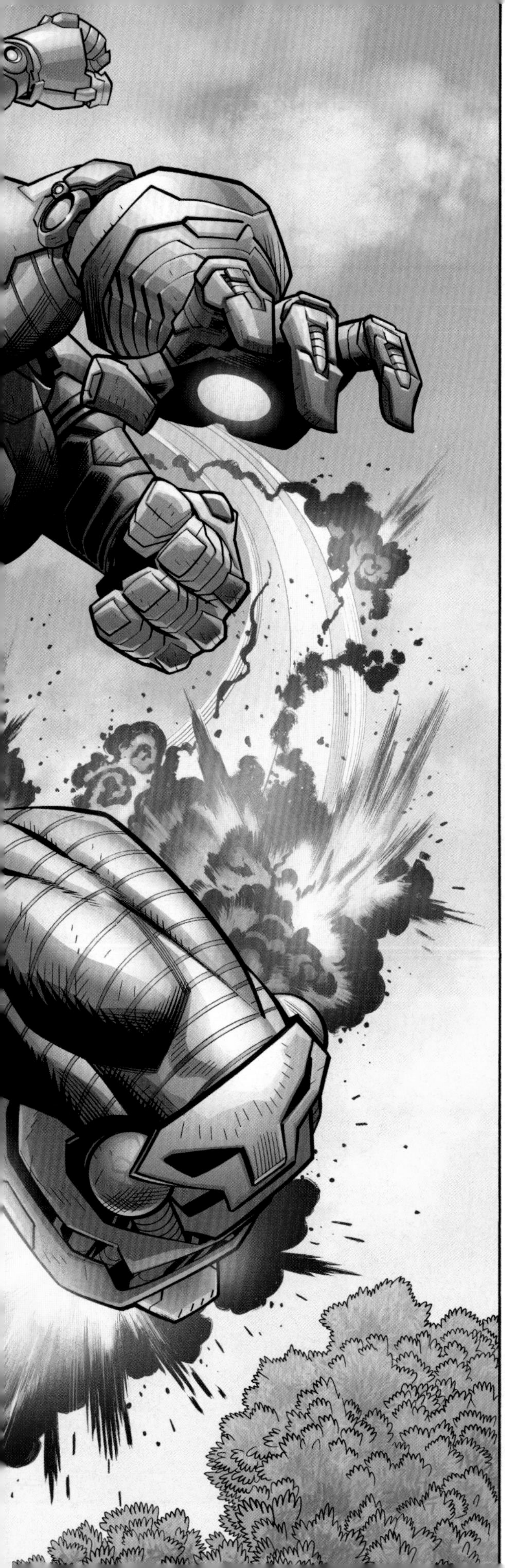

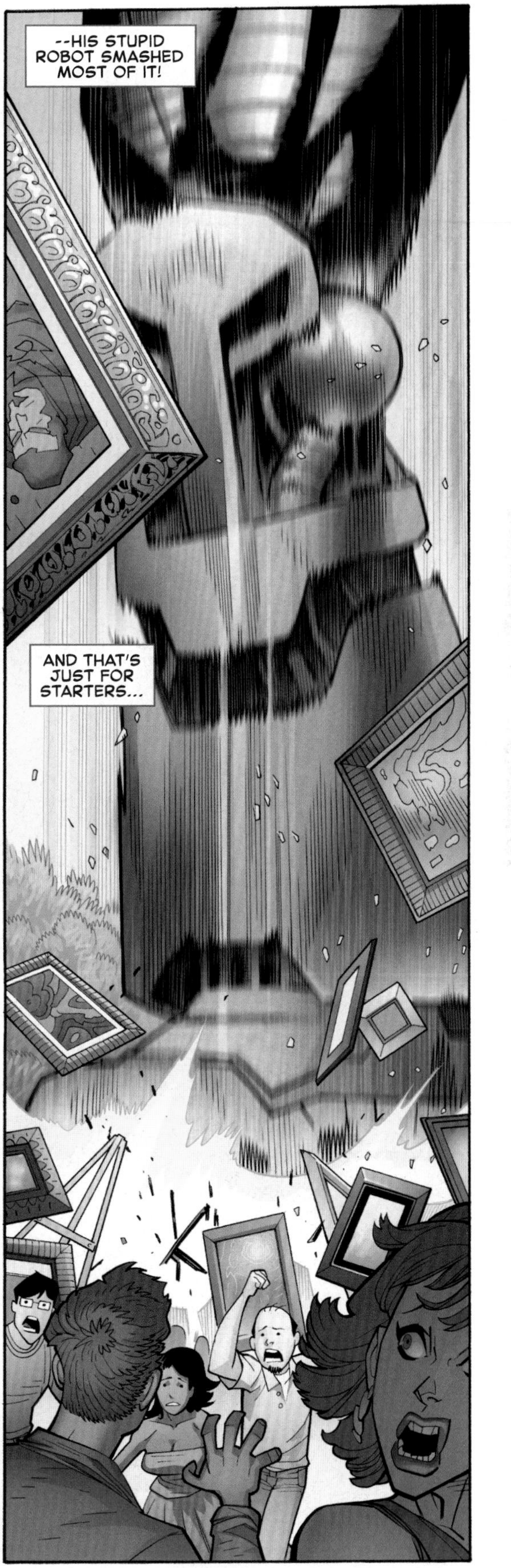
--HIS STUPID ROBOT SMASHED MOST OF IT!
AND THAT'S JUST FOR STARTERS...

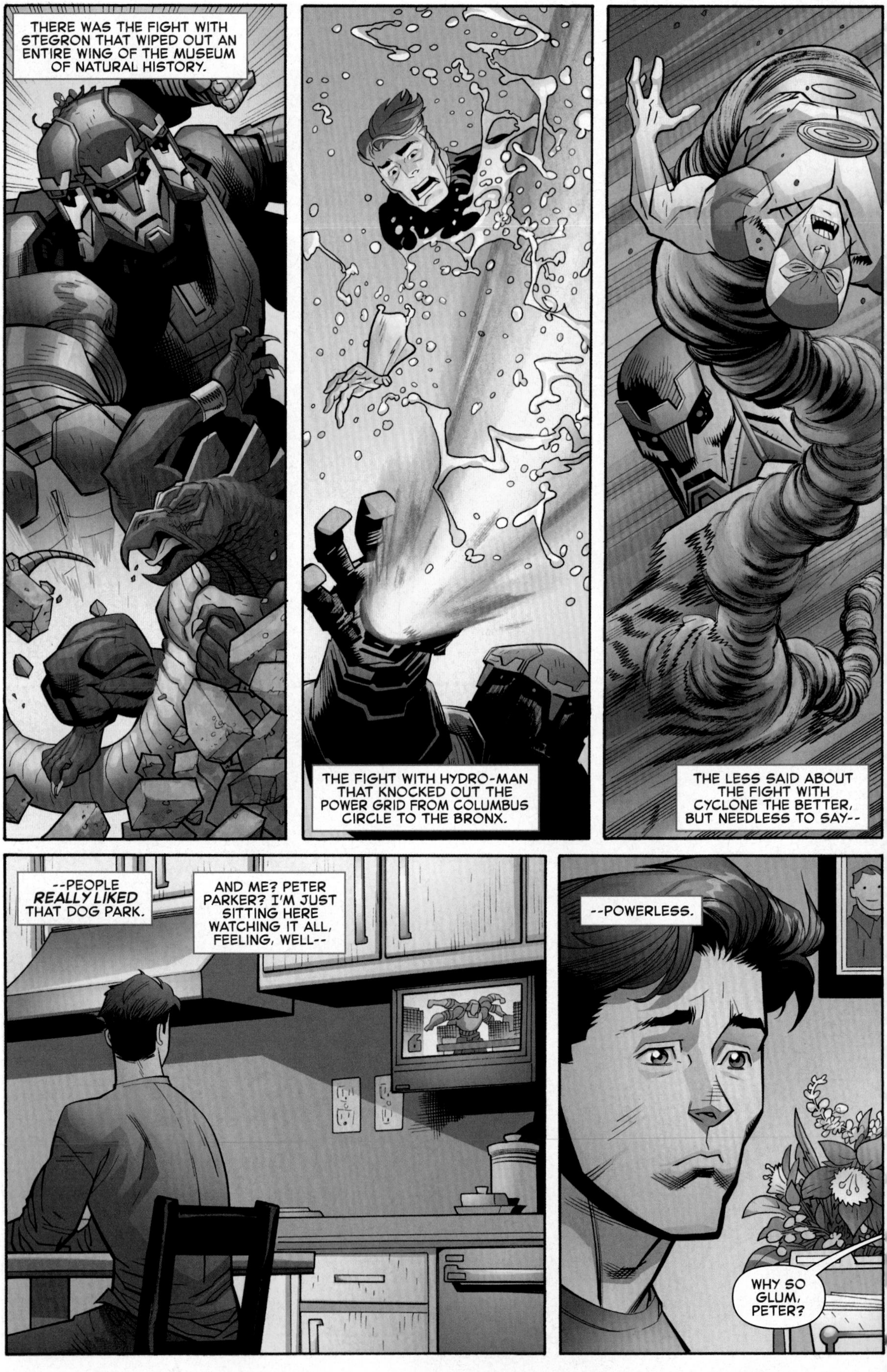
THERE WAS THE FIGHT WITH STEGRON THAT WIPED OUT AN ENTIRE WING OF THE MUSEUM OF NATURAL HISTORY.
THE FIGHT WITH HYDRO-MAN THAT KNOCKED OUT THE POWER GRID FROM COLUMBUS CIRCLE TO THE BRONX.
THE LESS SAID ABOUT THE FIGHT WITH CYCLONE THE BETTER, BUT NEEDLESS TO SAY--
--PEOPLE REALLY LIKED THAT DOG PARK.
AND ME? PETER PARKER? I'M JUST SITTING HERE WATCHING IT ALL, FEELING, WELL--
--POWERLESS.
WHY SO GLUM, PETER?

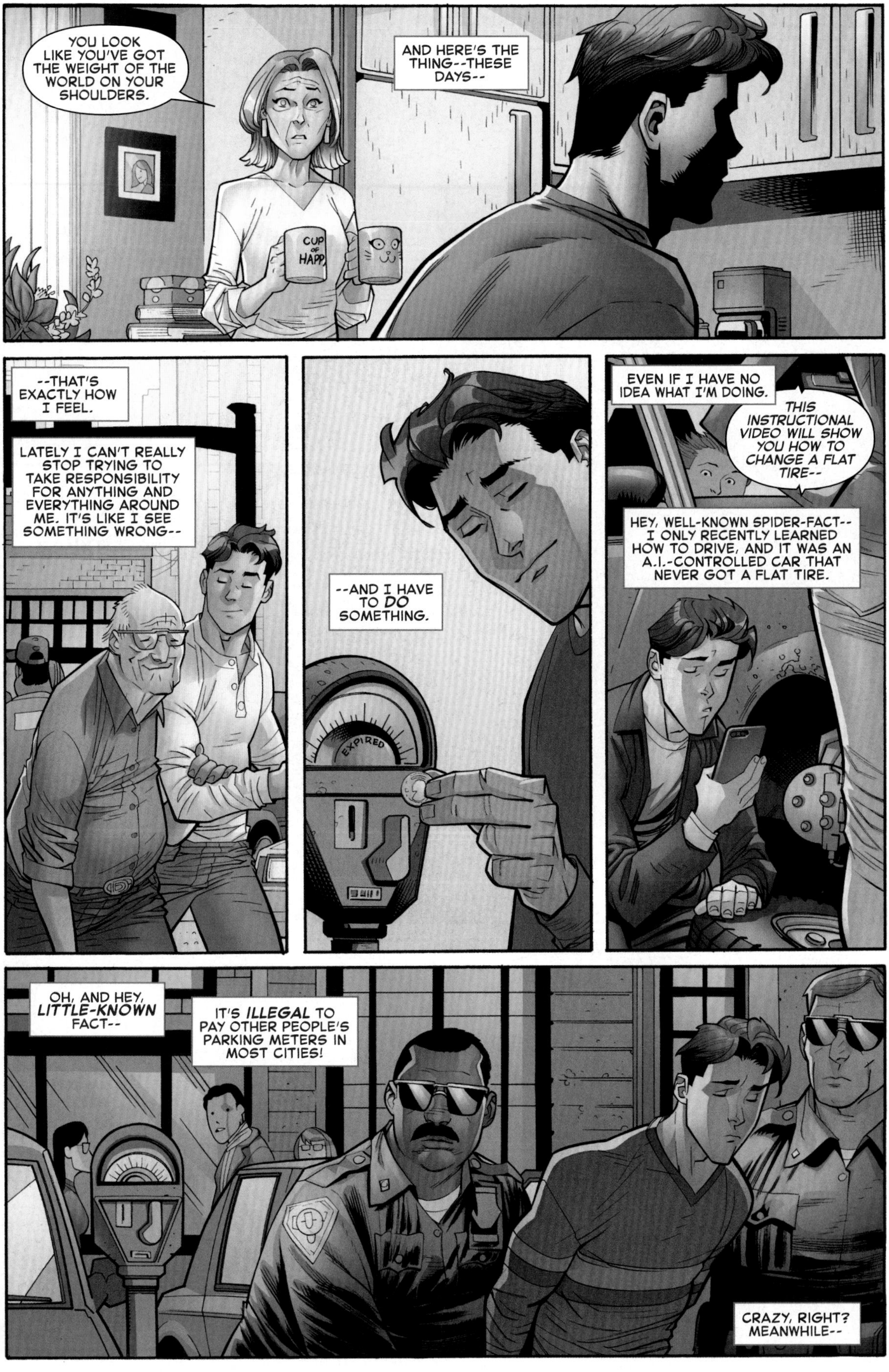
YOU LOOK LIKE YOU'VE GOT THE WEIGHT OF THE WORLD ON YOUR SHOULDERS.
AND HERE'S THE THING--THESE DAYS--
--THAT'S EXACTLY HOW I FEEL.
LATELY I CAN'T REALLY STOP TRYING TO TAKE RESPONSIBILITY FOR ANYTHING AND EVERYTHING AROUND ME. IT'S LIKE I SEE SOMETHING WRONG--
--AND I HAVE TO DO SOMETHING.
EXPIRED
EVEN IF I HAVE NO IDEA WHAT I'M DOING.
THIS INSTRUCTIONAL VIDEO WILL SHOW YOU HOW TO CHANGE A FLAT TIRE--
HEY, WELL-KNOWN SPIDER-FACT--I ONLY RECENTLY LEARNED HOW TO DRIVE, AND IT WAS AN A.I.-CONTROLLED CAR THAT NEVER GOT A FLAT TIRE.
OH, AND HEY, LITTLE-KNOWN FACT--
IT'S ILLEGAL TO PAY OTHER PEOPLE'S PARKING METERS IN MOST CITIES!
CRAZY, RIGHT? MEANWHILE--

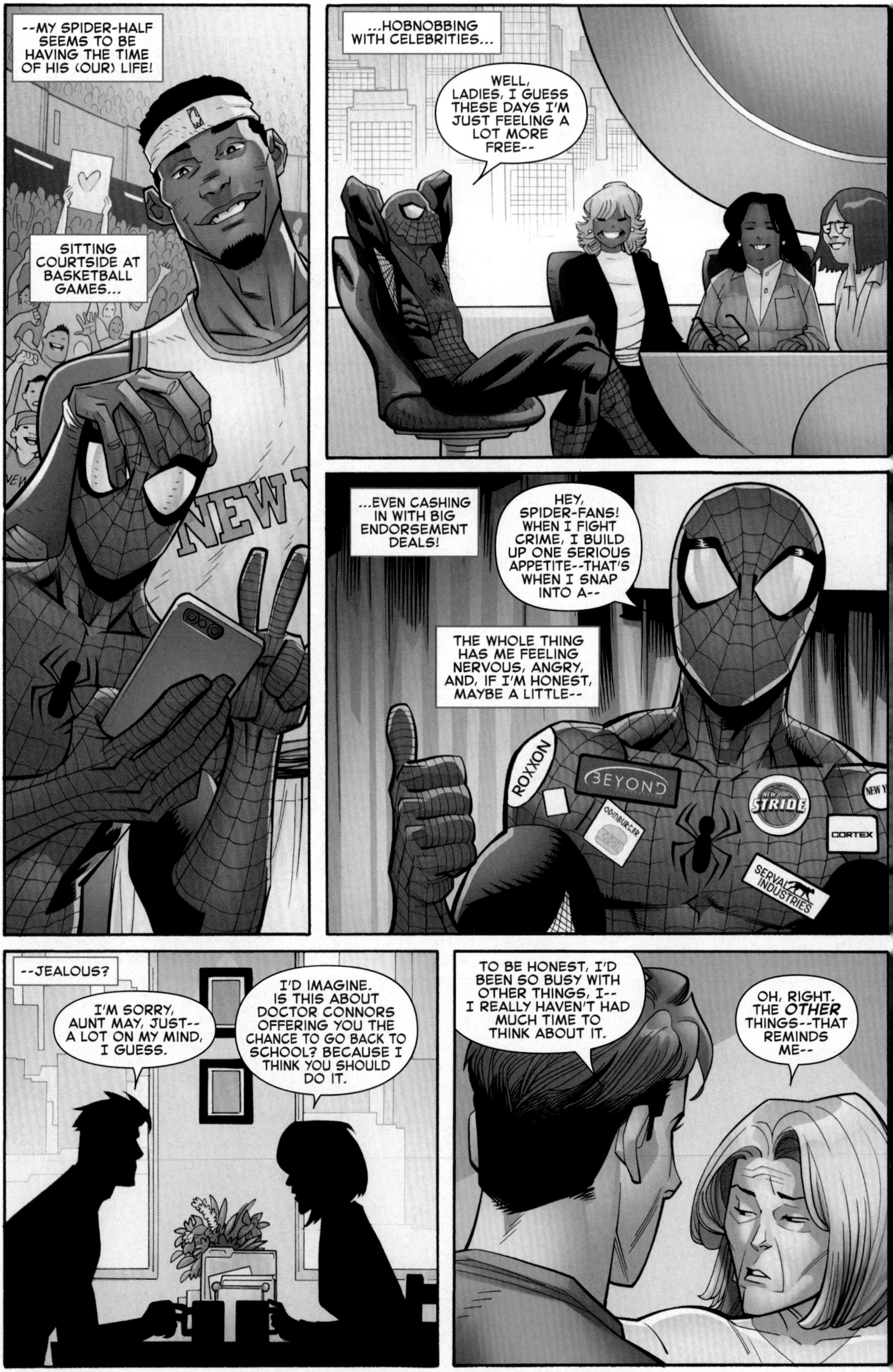
--MY SPIDER-HALF SEEMS TO BE HAVING THE TIME OF HIS (OUR) LIFE!
SITTING COURTSIDE AT BASKETBALL GAMES...
NEW Y
...HOBNOBBING WITH CELEBRITIES...
WELL, LADIES, I GUESS THESE DAYS I'M JUST FEELING A LOT MORE FREE--
...EVEN CASHING IN WITH BIG ENDORSEMENT DEALS!
HEY, SPIDER-FANS! WHEN I FIGHT CRIME, I BUILD UP ONE SERIOUS APPETITE--THAT'S WHEN I SNAP INTO A--
THE WHOLE THING HAS ME FEELING NERVOUS, ANGRY, AND, IF I'M HONEST, MAYBE A LITTLE--
ROXXON
BEYOND
ODINBURGER
NEW YORK STRIDE
CORTEX
SERVAL INDUSTRIES
--JEALOUS?
I'M SORRY, AUNT MAY, JUST--A LOT ON MY MIND, I GUESS.
I'D IMAGINE. IS THIS ABOUT DOCTOR CONNORS OFFERING YOU THE CHANCE TO GO BACK TO SCHOOL? BECAUSE I THINK YOU SHOULD DO IT.
TO BE HONEST, I'D BEEN SO BUSY WITH OTHER THINGS, I--I REALLY HAVEN'T HAD MUCH TIME TO THINK ABOUT IT.
OH, RIGHT. THE *OTHER* THINGS--THAT REMINDS ME--

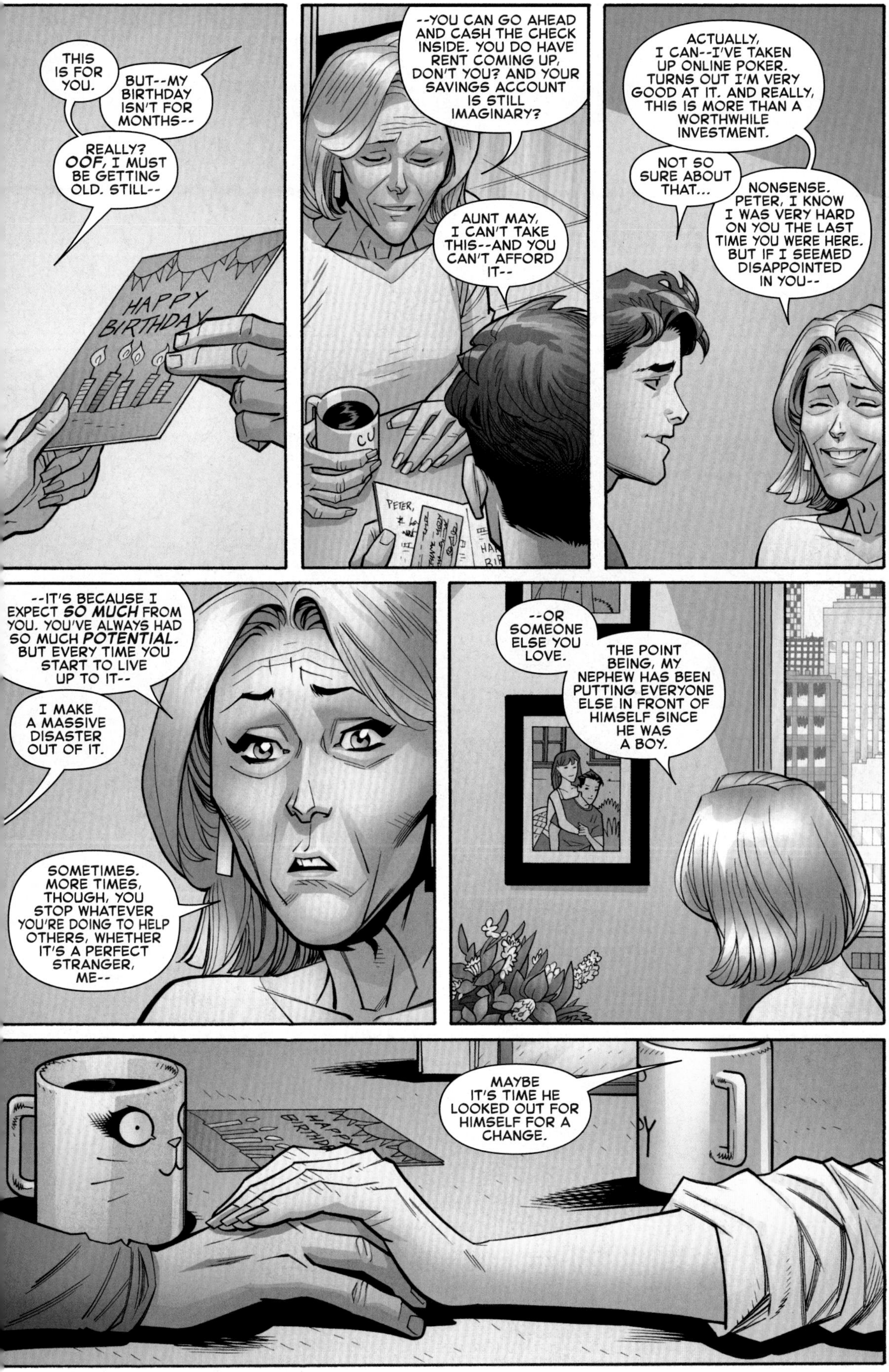
THIS IS FOR YOU.
BUT--MY BIRTHDAY ISN'T FOR MONTHS--
REALLY? OOF, I MUST BE GETTING OLD. STILL--
HAPPY BIRTHDAY
--YOU CAN GO AHEAD AND CASH THE CHECK INSIDE. YOU DO HAVE RENT COMING UP, DON'T YOU? AND YOUR SAVINGS ACCOUNT IS STILL IMAGINARY?
AUNT MAY, I CAN'T TAKE THIS--AND YOU CAN'T AFFORD IT--
PETER,
ACTUALLY, I CAN--I'VE TAKEN UP ONLINE POKER. TURNS OUT I'M VERY GOOD AT IT. AND REALLY, THIS IS MORE THAN A WORTHWHILE INVESTMENT.
NOT SO SURE ABOUT THAT...
NONSENSE. PETER, I KNOW I WAS VERY HARD ON YOU THE LAST TIME YOU WERE HERE. BUT IF I SEEMED DISAPPOINTED IN YOU--
--IT'S BECAUSE I EXPECT SO MUCH FROM YOU. YOU'VE ALWAYS HAD SO MUCH POTENTIAL. BUT EVERY TIME YOU START TO LIVE UP TO IT--
I MAKE A MASSIVE DISASTER OUT OF IT.
SOMETIMES. MORE TIMES, THOUGH, YOU STOP WHATEVER YOU'RE DOING TO HELP OTHERS, WHETHER IT'S A PERFECT STRANGER, ME--
--OR SOMEONE ELSE YOU LOVE.
THE POINT BEING, MY NEPHEW HAS BEEN PUTTING EVERYONE ELSE IN FRONT OF HIMSELF SINCE HE WAS A BOY.
MAYBE IT'S TIME HE LOOKED OUT FOR HIMSELF FOR A CHANGE.

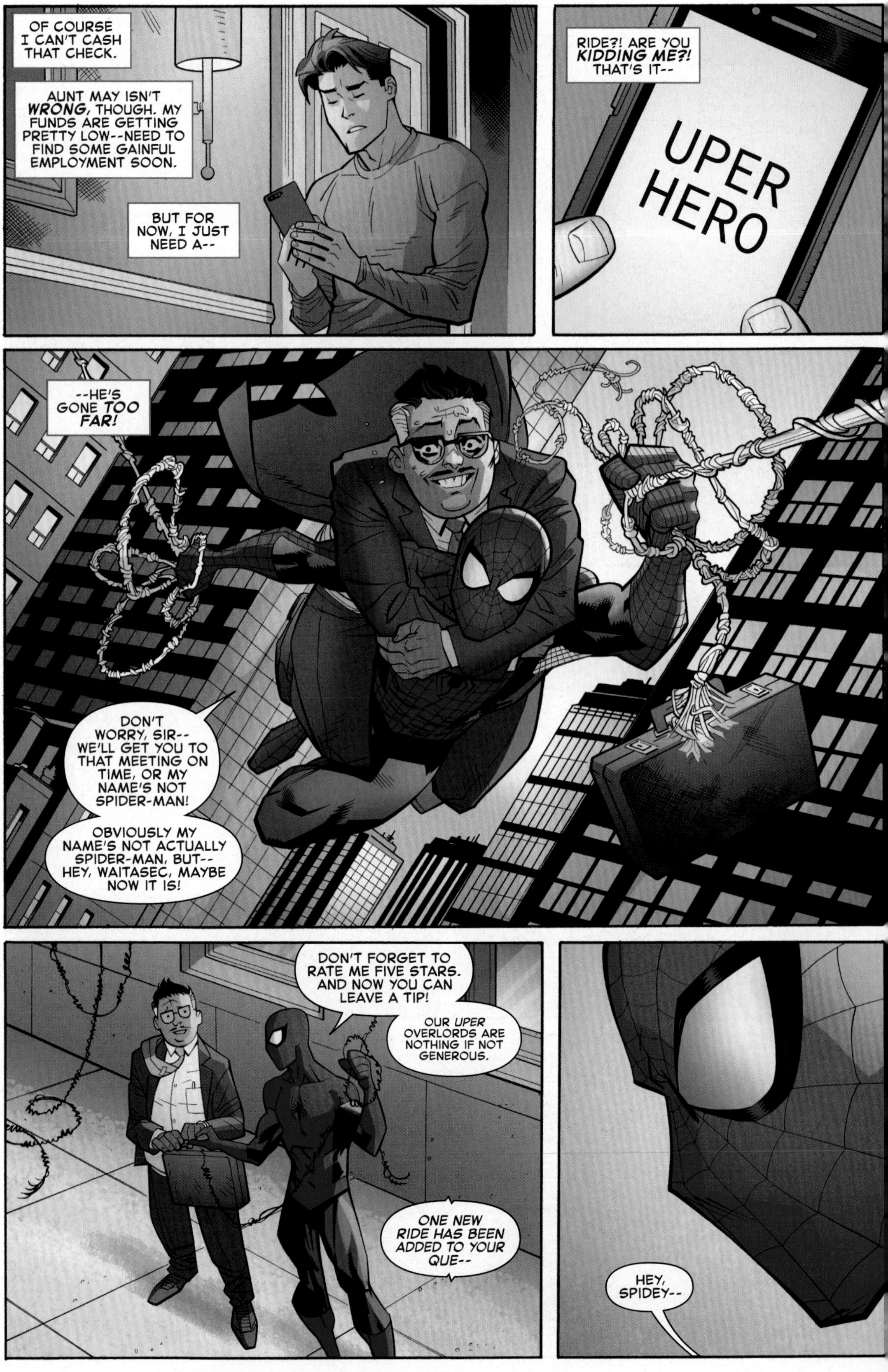
OF COURSE I CAN'T CASH THAT CHECK.
AUNT MAY ISN'T *WRONG*, THOUGH. MY FUNDS ARE GETTING PRETTY LOW--NEED TO FIND SOME GAINFUL EMPLOYMENT SOON.
BUT FOR NOW, I JUST NEED A--
RIDE?! ARE YOU *KIDDING ME?!* THAT'S IT--
UPER HERO
--HE'S GONE *TOO FAR!*
DON'T WORRY, SIR-- WE'LL GET YOU TO THAT MEETING ON TIME, OR MY NAME'S NOT SPIDER-MAN!
OBVIOUSLY MY NAME'S NOT ACTUALLY SPIDER-MAN, BUT-- HEY, WAITASEC, MAYBE NOW IT IS!
DON'T FORGET TO RATE ME FIVE STARS. AND NOW YOU CAN LEAVE A TIP!
OUR *UPER* OVERLORDS ARE NOTHING IF NOT GENEROUS.
ONE NEW RIDE HAS BEEN ADDED TO YOUR QUE--
HEY, SPIDEY--

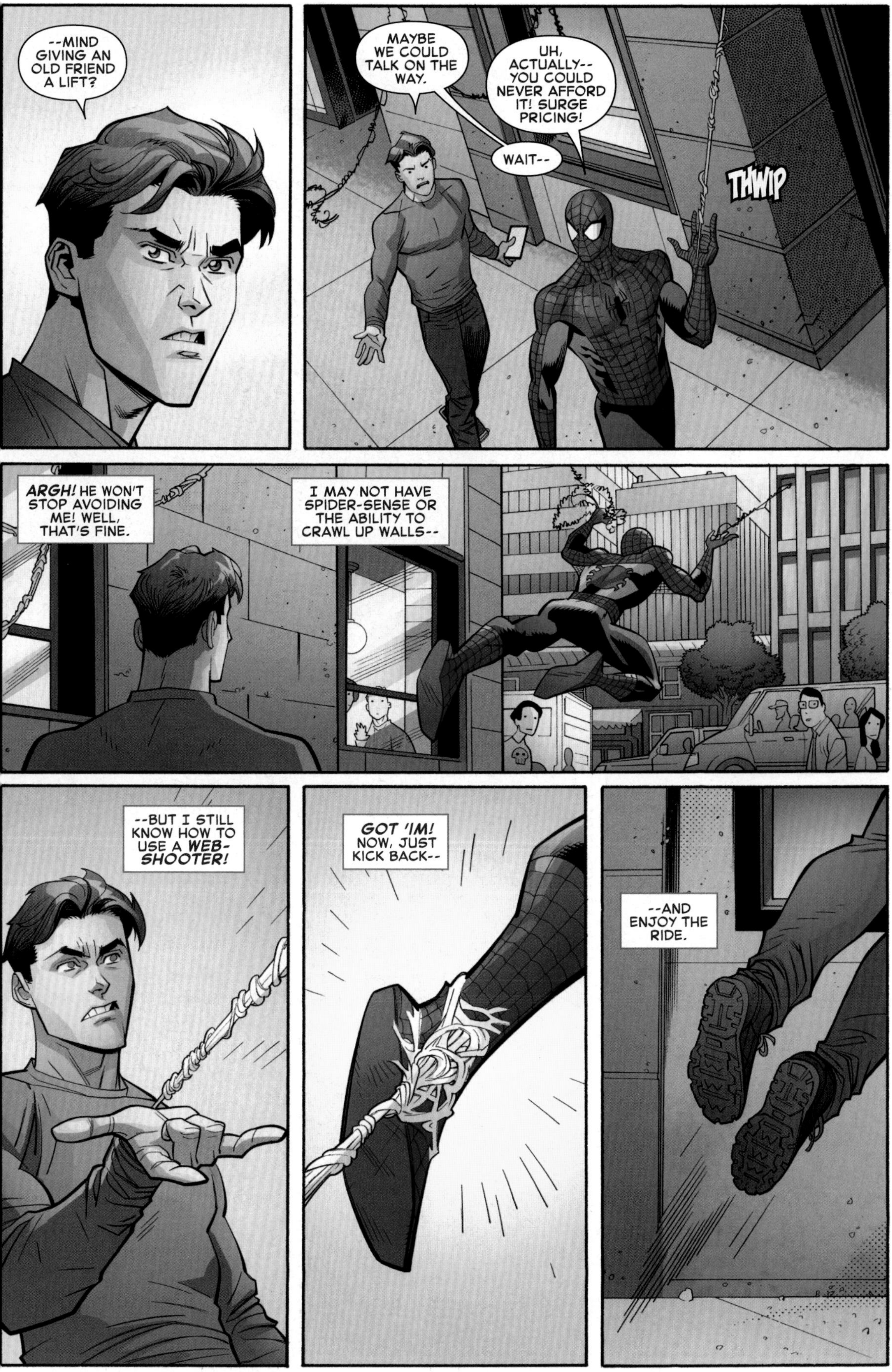

--MIND GIVING AN OLD FRIEND A LIFT?
MAYBE WE COULD TALK ON THE WAY.
UH, ACTUALLY-- YOU COULD NEVER AFFORD IT! SURGE PRICING!
WAIT--
THWIP
ARGH! HE WON'T STOP AVOIDING ME! WELL, THAT'S FINE.
I MAY NOT HAVE SPIDER-SENSE OR THE ABILITY TO CRAWL UP WALLS--
--BUT I STILL KNOW HOW TO USE A WEB-SHOOTER!
GOT 'IM! NOW, JUST KICK BACK--
--AND ENJOY THE RIDE.

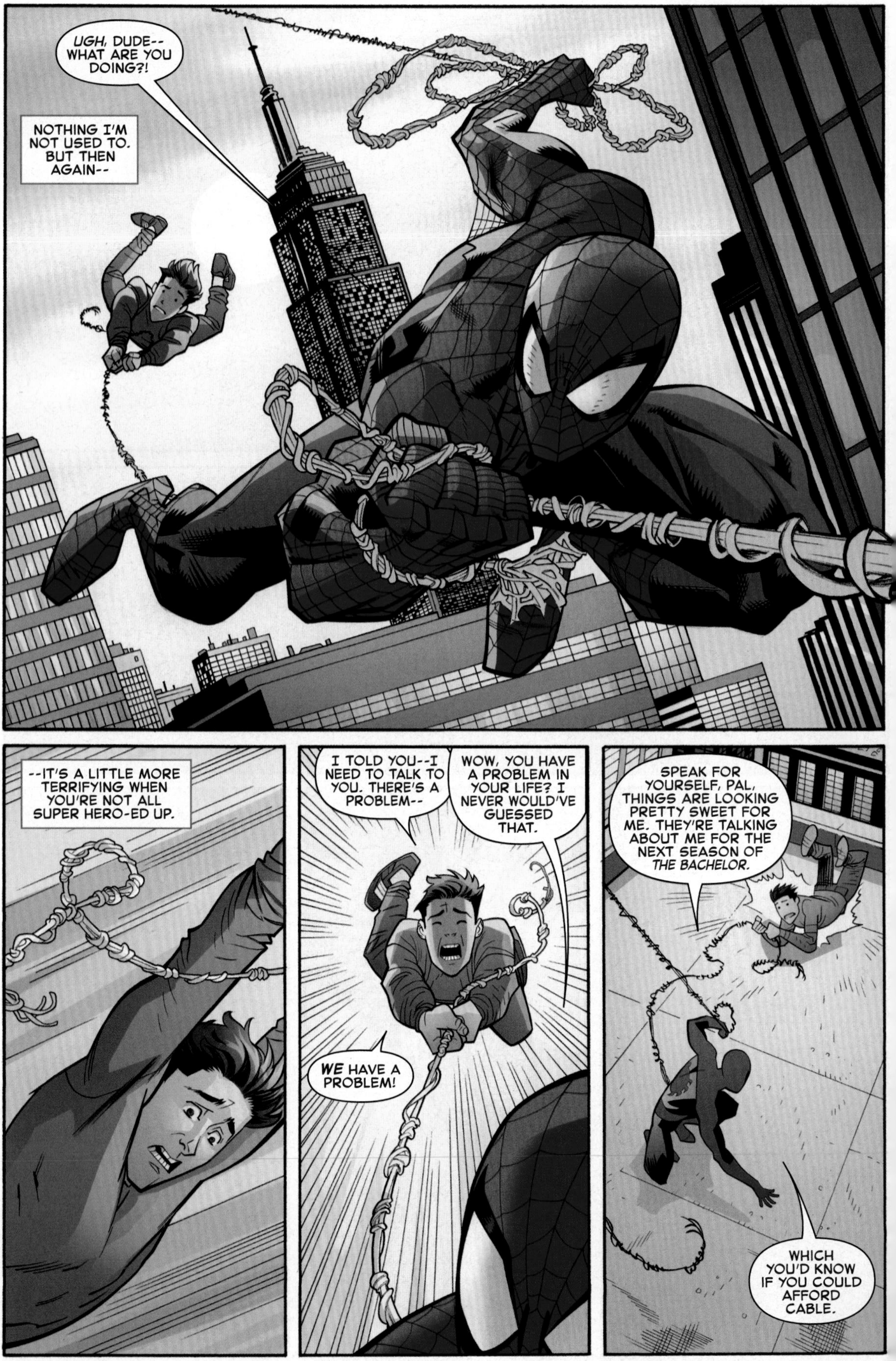
UGH, DUDE-- WHAT ARE YOU DOING?!
NOTHING I'M NOT USED TO. BUT THEN AGAIN--
--IT'S A LITTLE MORE TERRIFYING WHEN YOU'RE NOT ALL SUPER HERO-ED UP.
I TOLD YOU--I NEED TO TALK TO YOU. THERE'S A PROBLEM--
WOW, YOU HAVE A PROBLEM IN YOUR LIFE? I NEVER WOULD'VE GUESSED THAT.
WE HAVE A PROBLEM!
SPEAK FOR YOURSELF, PAL, THINGS ARE LOOKING PRETTY SWEET FOR ME. THEY'RE TALKING ABOUT ME FOR THE NEXT SEASON OF THE BACHELOR.
WHICH YOU'D KNOW IF YOU COULD AFFORD CABLE.

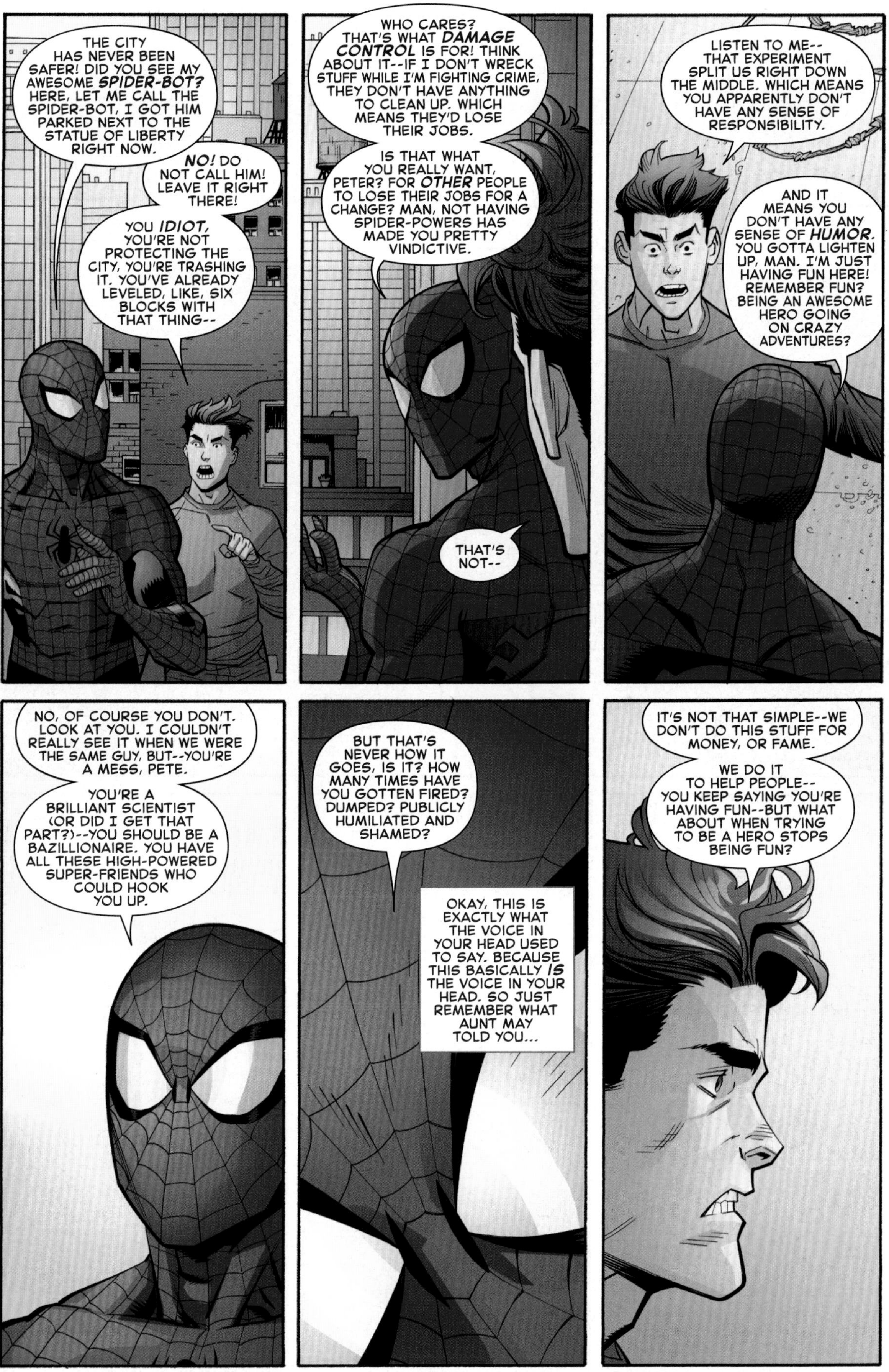
THE CITY HAS NEVER BEEN SAFER! DID YOU SEE MY AWESOME SPIDER-BOT? HERE, LET ME CALL THE SPIDER-BOT, I GOT HIM PARKED NEXT TO THE STATUE OF LIBERTY RIGHT NOW.
NO! DO NOT CALL HIM! LEAVE IT RIGHT THERE!
YOU IDIOT, YOU'RE NOT PROTECTING THE CITY, YOU'RE TRASHING IT. YOU'VE ALREADY LEVELED, LIKE, SIX BLOCKS WITH THAT THING--
WHO CARES? THAT'S WHAT DAMAGE CONTROL IS FOR! THINK ABOUT IT--IF I DON'T WRECK STUFF WHILE I'M FIGHTING CRIME, THEY DON'T HAVE ANYTHING TO CLEAN UP. WHICH MEANS THEY'D LOSE THEIR JOBS.
IS THAT WHAT YOU REALLY WANT, PETER? FOR OTHER PEOPLE TO LOSE THEIR JOBS FOR A CHANGE? MAN, NOT HAVING SPIDER-POWERS HAS MADE YOU PRETTY VINDICTIVE.
THAT'S NOT--
LISTEN TO ME--THAT EXPERIMENT SPLIT US RIGHT DOWN THE MIDDLE. WHICH MEANS YOU APPARENTLY DON'T HAVE ANY SENSE OF RESPONSIBILITY.
AND IT MEANS YOU DON'T HAVE ANY SENSE OF HUMOR. YOU GOTTA LIGHTEN UP, MAN. I'M JUST HAVING FUN HERE! REMEMBER FUN? BEING AN AWESOME HERO GOING ON CRAZY ADVENTURES?
NO, OF COURSE YOU DON'T. LOOK AT YOU. I COULDN'T REALLY SEE IT WHEN WE WERE THE SAME GUY, BUT--YOU'RE A MESS, PETE.
YOU'RE A BRILLIANT SCIENTIST (OR DID I GET THAT PART?)--YOU SHOULD BE A BAZILLIONAIRE. YOU HAVE ALL THESE HIGH-POWERED SUPER-FRIENDS WHO COULD HOOK YOU UP.
BUT THAT'S NEVER HOW IT GOES, IS IT? HOW MANY TIMES HAVE YOU GOTTEN FIRED? DUMPED? PUBLICLY HUMILIATED AND SHAMED?
OKAY, THIS IS EXACTLY WHAT THE VOICE IN YOUR HEAD USED TO SAY. BECAUSE THIS BASICALLY IS THE VOICE IN YOUR HEAD. SO JUST REMEMBER WHAT AUNT MAY TOLD YOU...
IT'S NOT THAT SIMPLE--WE DON'T DO THIS STUFF FOR MONEY, OR FAME.
WE DO IT TO HELP PEOPLE--YOU KEEP SAYING YOU'RE HAVING FUN--BUT WHAT ABOUT WHEN TRYING TO BE A HERO STOPS BEING FUN?

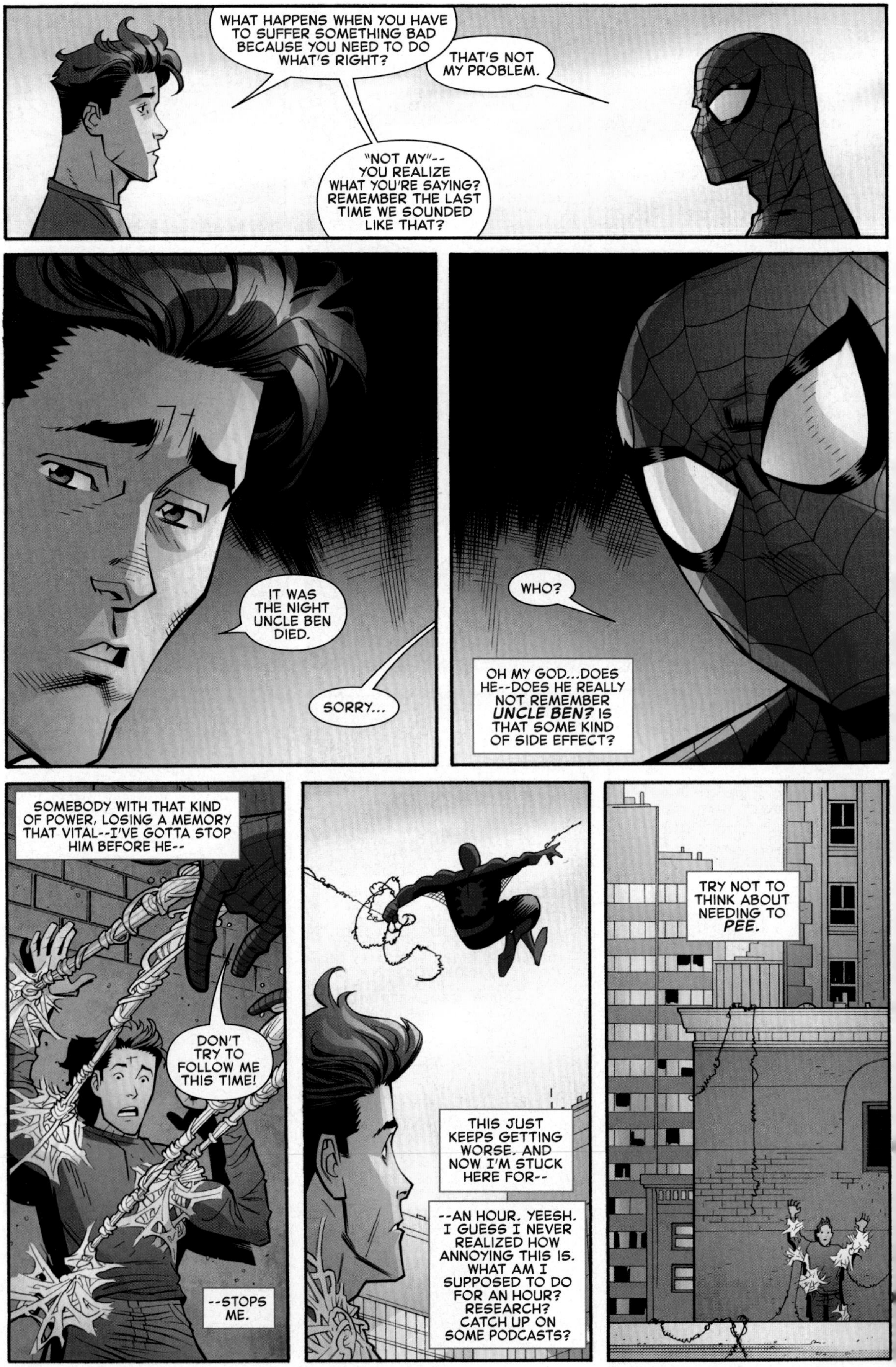
WHAT HAPPENS WHEN YOU HAVE TO SUFFER SOMETHING BAD BECAUSE YOU NEED TO DO WHAT'S RIGHT?
THAT'S NOT MY PROBLEM.
"NOT MY"-- YOU REALIZE WHAT YOU'RE SAYING? REMEMBER THE LAST TIME WE SOUNDED LIKE THAT?
IT WAS THE NIGHT UNCLE BEN DIED.
WHO?
SORRY...
OH MY GOD...DOES HE--DOES HE REALLY NOT REMEMBER *UNCLE BEN?* IS THAT SOME KIND OF SIDE EFFECT?
SOMEBODY WITH THAT KIND OF POWER, LOSING A MEMORY THAT VITAL--I'VE GOTTA STOP HIM BEFORE HE--
DON'T TRY TO FOLLOW ME THIS TIME!
--STOPS ME.
THIS JUST KEEPS GETTING WORSE. AND NOW I'M STUCK HERE FOR--
--AN HOUR. YEESH. I GUESS I NEVER REALIZED HOW ANNOYING THIS IS. WHAT AM I SUPPOSED TO DO FOR AN HOUR? RESEARCH? CATCH UP ON SOME PODCASTS?
TRY NOT TO THINK ABOUT NEEDING TO *PEE.*

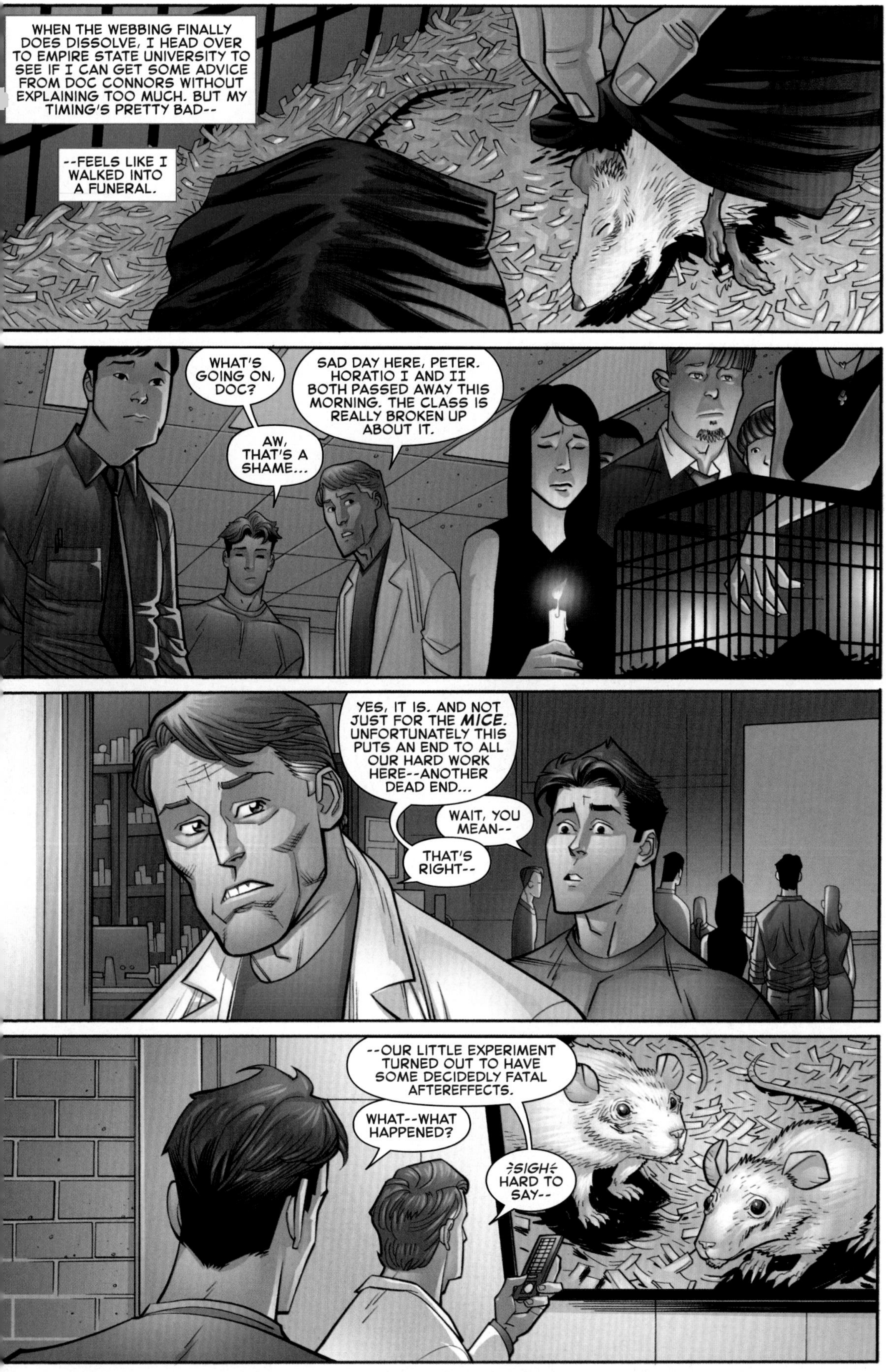
WHEN THE WEBBING FINALLY DOES DISSOLVE, I HEAD OVER TO EMPIRE STATE UNIVERSITY TO SEE IF I CAN GET SOME ADVICE FROM DOC CONNORS WITHOUT EXPLAINING TOO MUCH. BUT MY TIMING'S PRETTY BAD--
--FEELS LIKE I WALKED INTO A FUNERAL.
WHAT'S GOING ON, DOC?
SAD DAY HERE, PETER. HORATIO I AND II BOTH PASSED AWAY THIS MORNING. THE CLASS IS REALLY BROKEN UP ABOUT IT.
AW, THAT'S A SHAME...
YES, IT IS. AND NOT JUST FOR THE *MICE*. UNFORTUNATELY THIS PUTS AN END TO ALL OUR HARD WORK HERE--ANOTHER DEAD END...
WAIT, YOU MEAN--
THAT'S RIGHT--
--OUR LITTLE EXPERIMENT TURNED OUT TO HAVE SOME DECIDEDLY FATAL AFTEREFFECTS.
WHAT--WHAT HAPPENED?
SIGH HARD TO SAY--

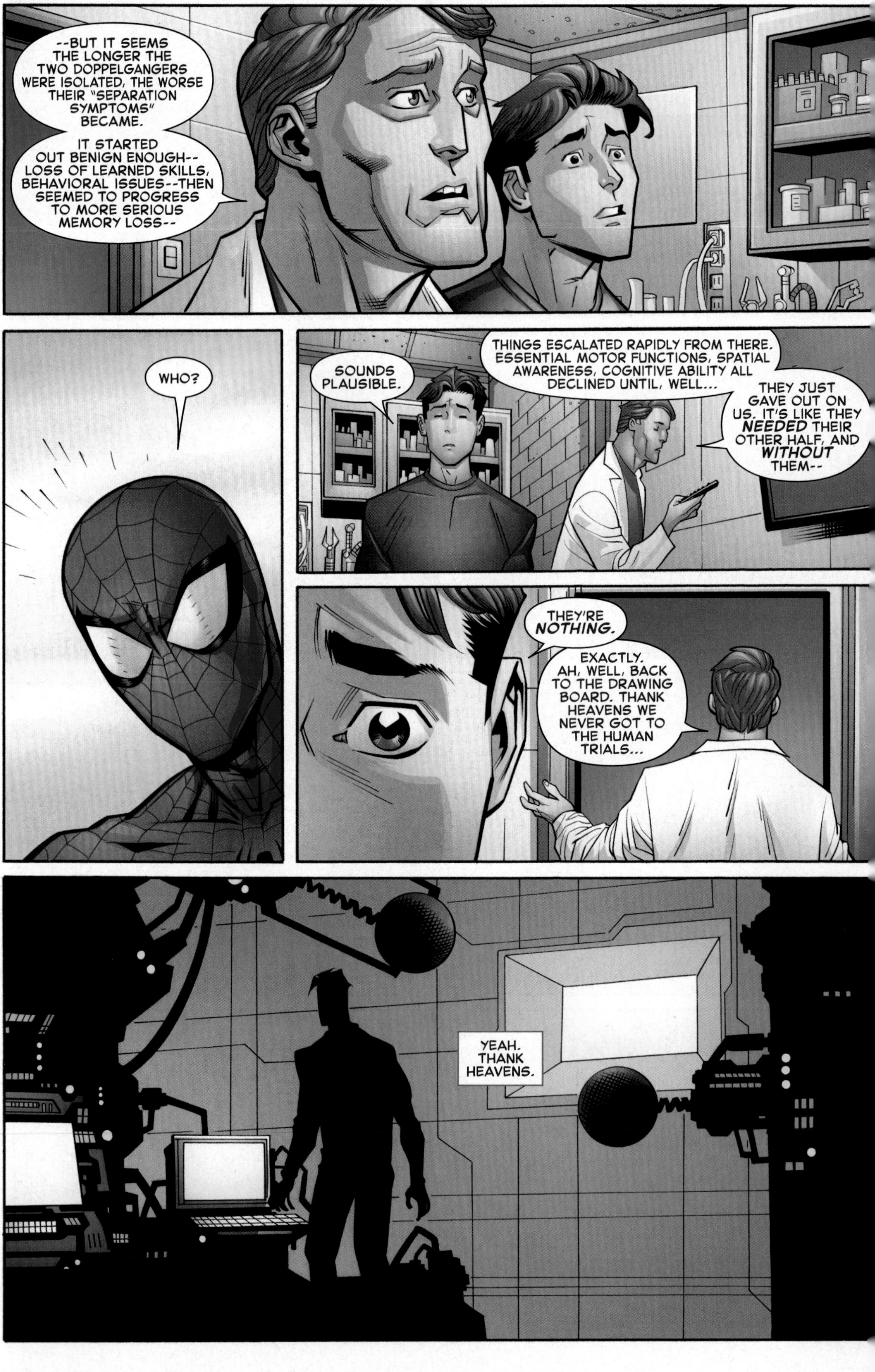
--BUT IT SEEMS THE LONGER THE TWO DOPPELGANGERS WERE ISOLATED, THE WORSE THEIR "SEPARATION SYMPTOMS" BECAME.
IT STARTED OUT BENIGN ENOUGH--LOSS OF LEARNED SKILLS, BEHAVIORAL ISSUES--THEN SEEMED TO PROGRESS TO MORE SERIOUS MEMORY LOSS--
WHO?
SOUNDS PLAUSIBLE.
THINGS ESCALATED RAPIDLY FROM THERE. ESSENTIAL MOTOR FUNCTIONS, SPATIAL AWARENESS, COGNITIVE ABILITY ALL DECLINED UNTIL, WELL...
THEY JUST GAVE OUT ON US. IT'S LIKE THEY *NEEDED* THEIR OTHER HALF, AND *WITHOUT* THEM--
THEY'RE *NOTHING.*
EXACTLY. AH, WELL, BACK TO THE DRAWING BOARD. THANK HEAVENS WE NEVER GOT TO THE HUMAN TRIALS...
YEAH. THANK HEAVENS.

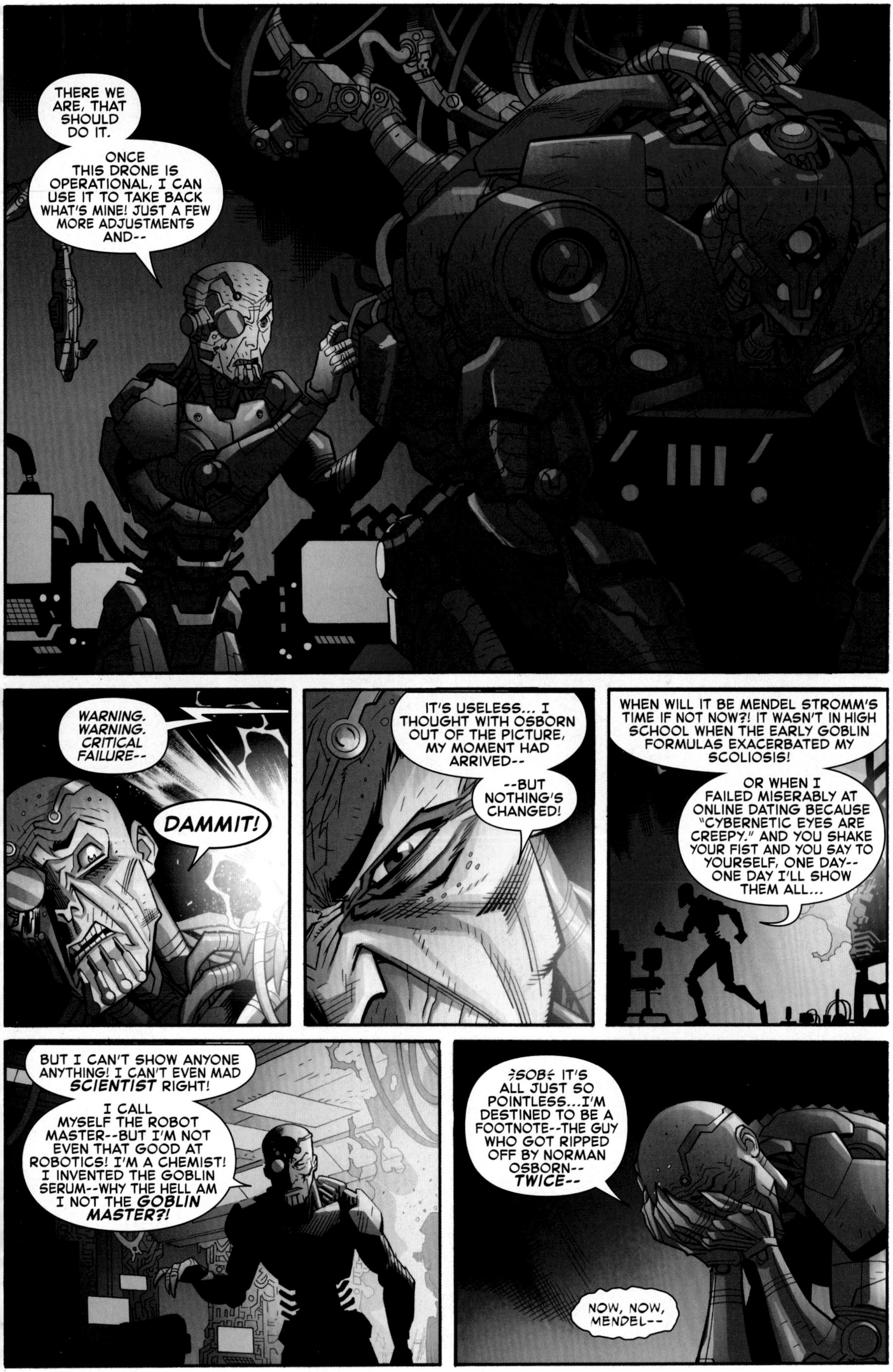
THERE WE ARE, THAT SHOULD DO IT.
ONCE THIS DRONE IS OPERATIONAL, I CAN USE IT TO TAKE BACK WHAT'S MINE! JUST A FEW MORE ADJUSTMENTS AND--
WARNING. WARNING. CRITICAL FAILURE--
DAMMIT!
IT'S USELESS... I THOUGHT WITH OSBORN OUT OF THE PICTURE, MY MOMENT HAD ARRIVED--
--BUT NOTHING'S CHANGED!
WHEN WILL IT BE MENDEL STROMM'S TIME IF NOT NOW?! IT WASN'T IN HIGH SCHOOL WHEN THE EARLY GOBLIN FORMULAS EXACERBATED MY SCOLIOSIS!
OR WHEN I FAILED MISERABLY AT ONLINE DATING BECAUSE "CYBERNETIC EYES ARE CREEPY." AND YOU SHAKE YOUR FIST AND YOU SAY TO YOURSELF, ONE DAY-- ONE DAY I'LL SHOW THEM ALL...
BUT I CAN'T SHOW ANYONE ANYTHING! I CAN'T EVEN MAD SCIENTIST RIGHT!
I CALL MYSELF THE ROBOT MASTER--BUT I'M NOT EVEN THAT GOOD AT ROBOTICS! I'M A CHEMIST! I INVENTED THE GOBLIN SERUM--WHY THE HELL AM I NOT THE GOBLIN MASTER?!
SOB IT'S ALL JUST SO POINTLESS...I'M DESTINED TO BE A FOOTNOTE--THE GUY WHO GOT RIPPED OFF BY NORMAN OSBORN--TWICE--
NOW, NOW, MENDEL--

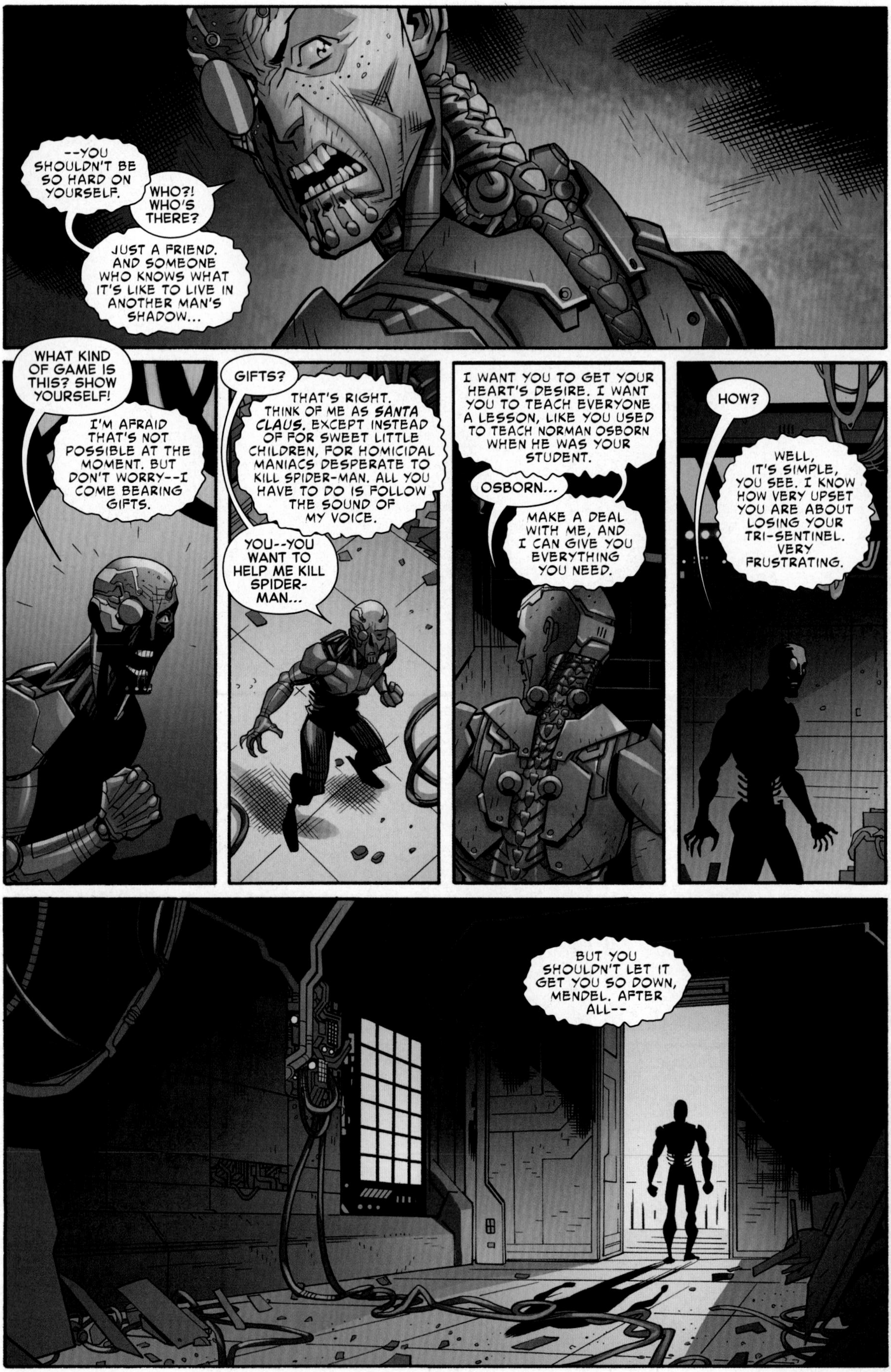
--YOU SHOULDN'T BE SO HARD ON YOURSELF.
WHO?! WHO'S THERE?
JUST A FRIEND. AND SOMEONE WHO KNOWS WHAT IT'S LIKE TO LIVE IN ANOTHER MAN'S SHADOW...
WHAT KIND OF GAME IS THIS? SHOW YOURSELF!
I'M AFRAID THAT'S NOT POSSIBLE AT THE MOMENT. BUT DON'T WORRY--I COME BEARING GIFTS.
GIFTS?
THAT'S RIGHT. THINK OF ME AS SANTA CLAUS. EXCEPT INSTEAD OF FOR SWEET LITTLE CHILDREN, FOR HOMICIDAL MANIACS DESPERATE TO KILL SPIDER-MAN. ALL YOU HAVE TO DO IS FOLLOW THE SOUND OF MY VOICE.
YOU--YOU WANT TO HELP ME KILL SPIDER-MAN...
I WANT YOU TO GET YOUR HEART'S DESIRE. I WANT YOU TO TEACH EVERYONE A LESSON, LIKE YOU USED TO TEACH NORMAN OSBORN WHEN HE WAS YOUR STUDENT.
OSBORN...
MAKE A DEAL WITH ME, AND I CAN GIVE YOU EVERYTHING YOU NEED.
HOW?
WELL, IT'S SIMPLE, YOU SEE. I KNOW HOW VERY UPSET YOU ARE ABOUT LOSING YOUR TRI-SENTINEL. VERY FRUSTRATING.
BUT YOU SHOULDN'T LET IT GET YOU SO DOWN, MENDEL. AFTER ALL--

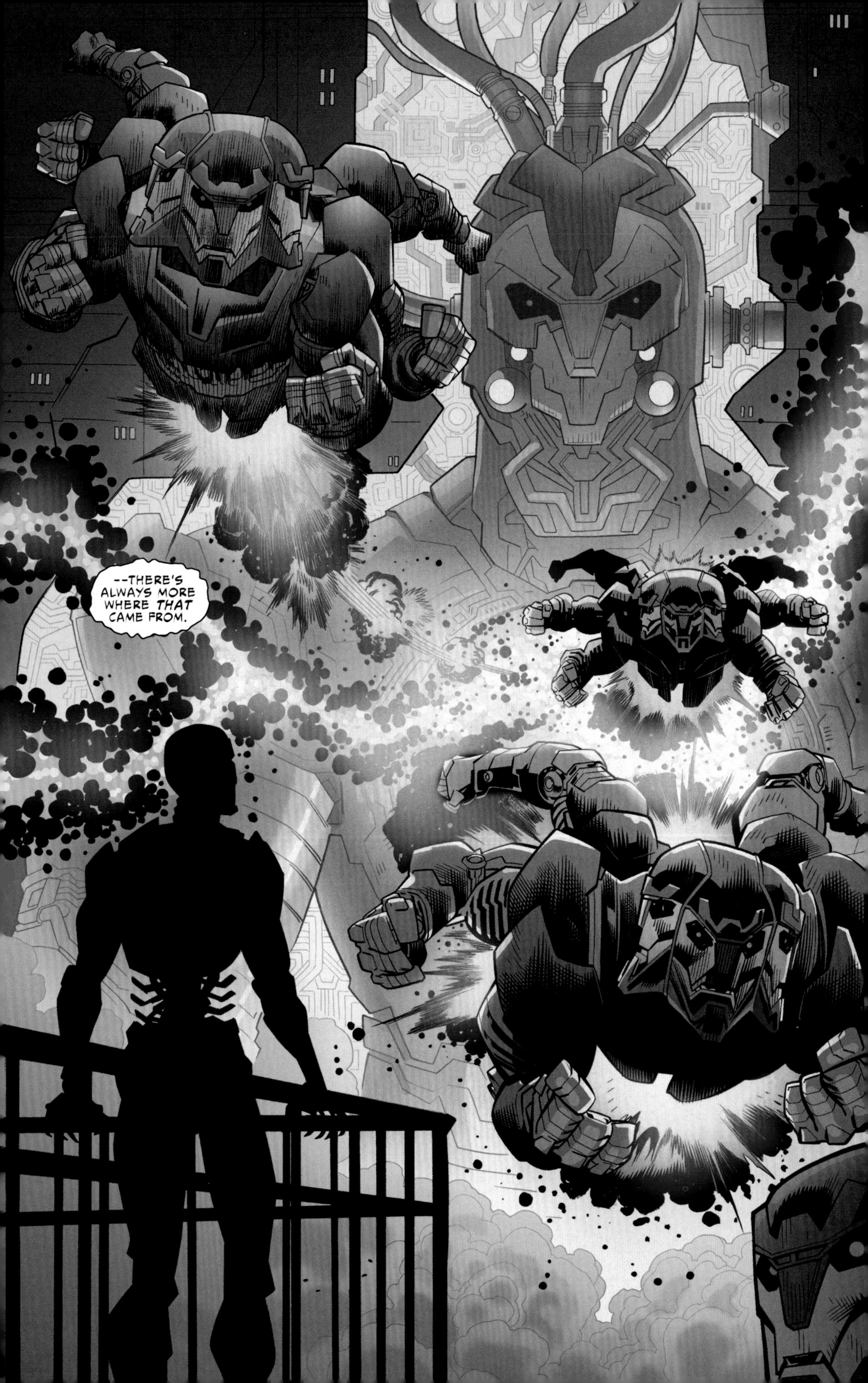
--THERE'S ALWAYS MORE WHERE *THAT* CAME FROM.

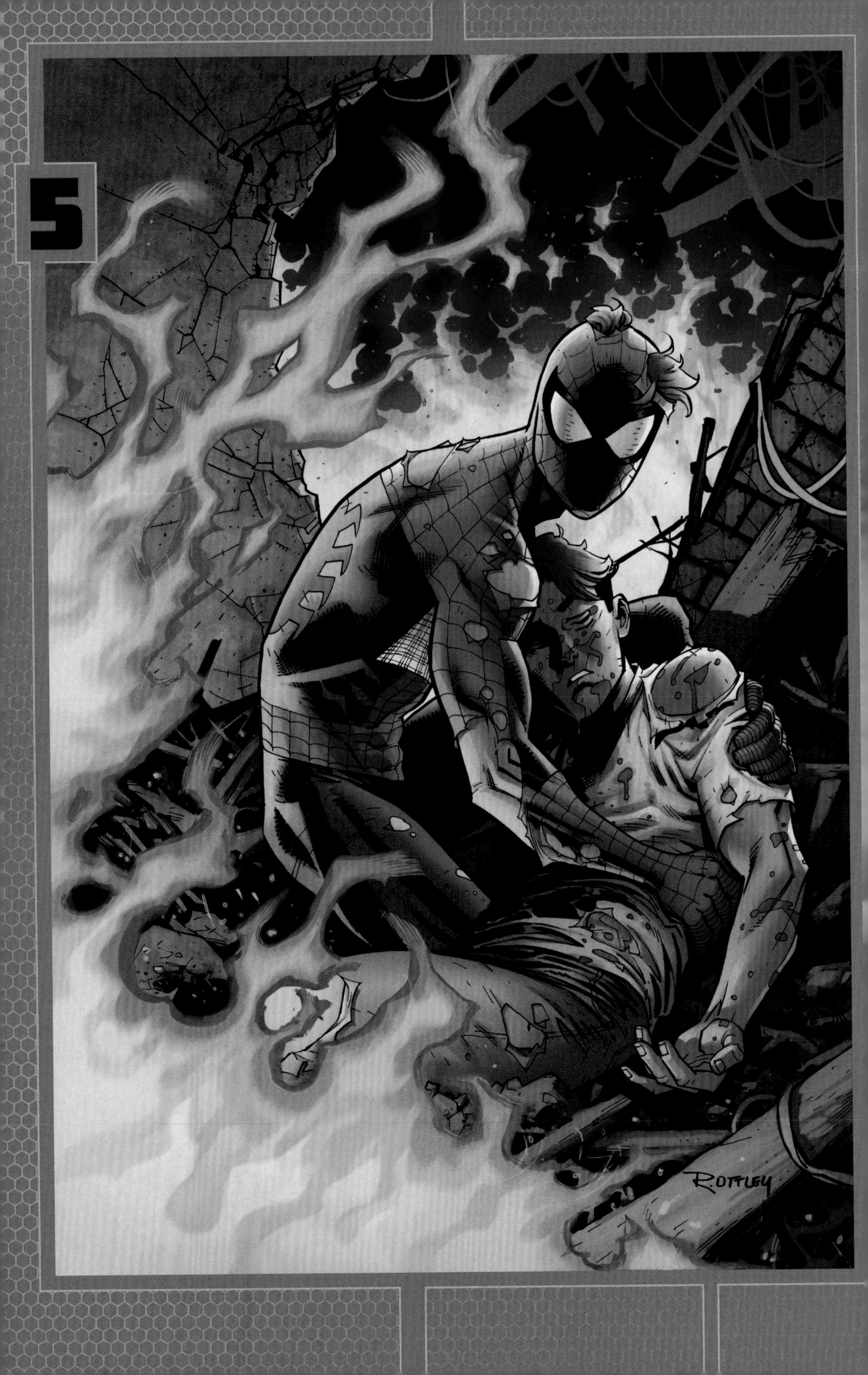
5
R. OTTLEY

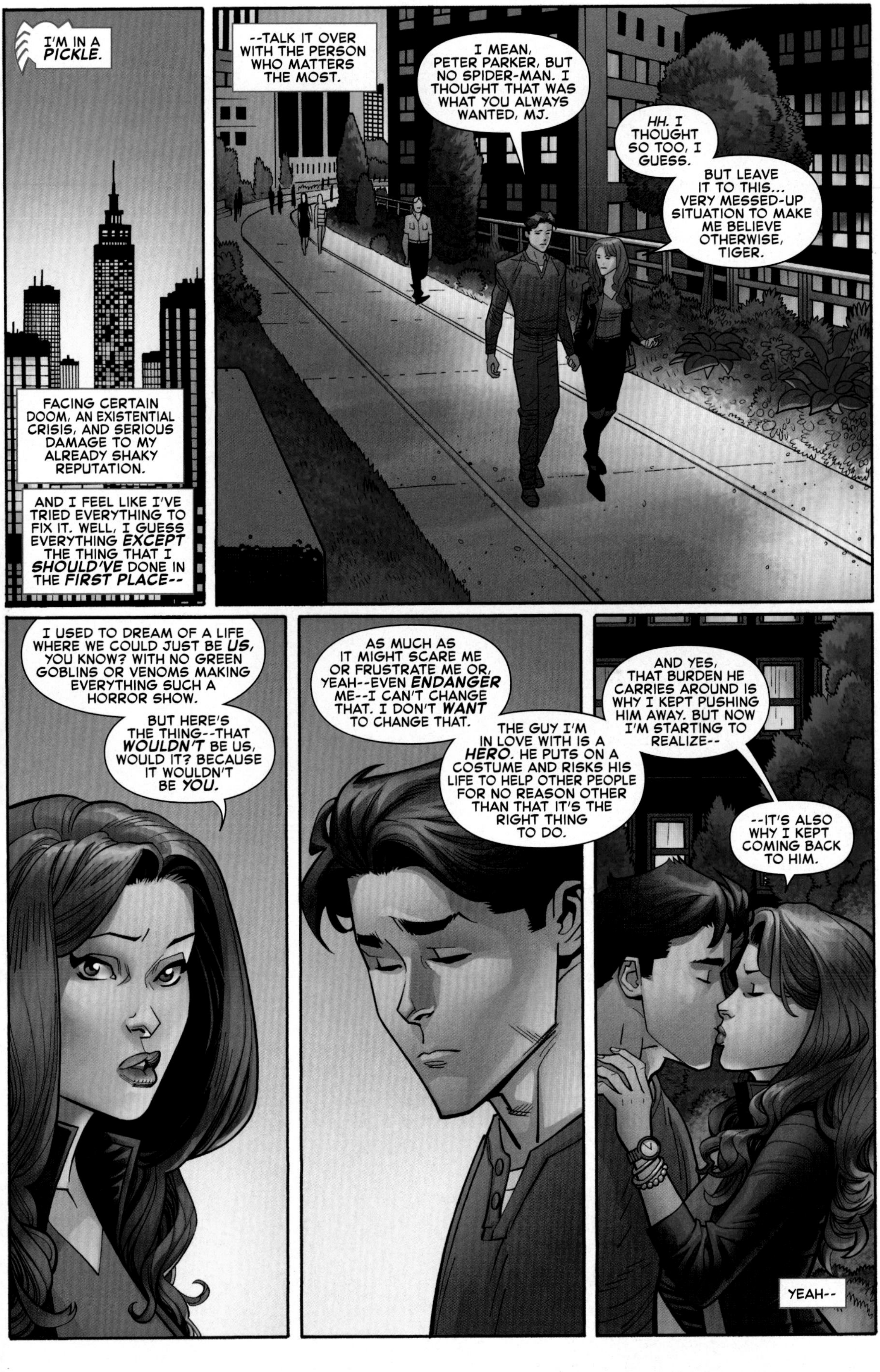
I'M IN A PICKLE.
FACING CERTAIN DOOM, AN EXISTENTIAL CRISIS, AND SERIOUS DAMAGE TO MY ALREADY SHAKY REPUTATION.
AND I FEEL LIKE I'VE TRIED EVERYTHING TO FIX IT. WELL, I GUESS EVERYTHING EXCEPT THE THING THAT I SHOULD'VE DONE IN THE FIRST PLACE--
--TALK IT OVER WITH THE PERSON WHO MATTERS THE MOST.
I MEAN, PETER PARKER, BUT NO SPIDER-MAN. I THOUGHT THAT WAS WHAT YOU ALWAYS WANTED, MJ.
HH. I THOUGHT SO TOO, I GUESS.
BUT LEAVE IT TO THIS... VERY MESSED-UP SITUATION TO MAKE ME BELIEVE OTHERWISE, TIGER.
I USED TO DREAM OF A LIFE WHERE WE COULD JUST BE US, YOU KNOW? WITH NO GREEN GOBLINS OR VENOMS MAKING EVERYTHING SUCH A HORROR SHOW.
BUT HERE'S THE THING--THAT WOULDN'T BE US, WOULD IT? BECAUSE IT WOULDN'T BE YOU.
AS MUCH AS IT MIGHT SCARE ME OR FRUSTRATE ME OR, YEAH--EVEN ENDANGER ME--I CAN'T CHANGE THAT. I DON'T WANT TO CHANGE THAT.
THE GUY I'M IN LOVE WITH IS A HERO. HE PUTS ON A COSTUME AND RISKS HIS LIFE TO HELP OTHER PEOPLE FOR NO REASON OTHER THAN THAT IT'S THE RIGHT THING TO DO.
AND YES, THAT BURDEN HE CARRIES AROUND IS WHY I KEPT PUSHING HIM AWAY. BUT NOW I'M STARTING TO REALIZE--
--IT'S ALSO WHY I KEPT COMING BACK TO HIM.
YEAH--

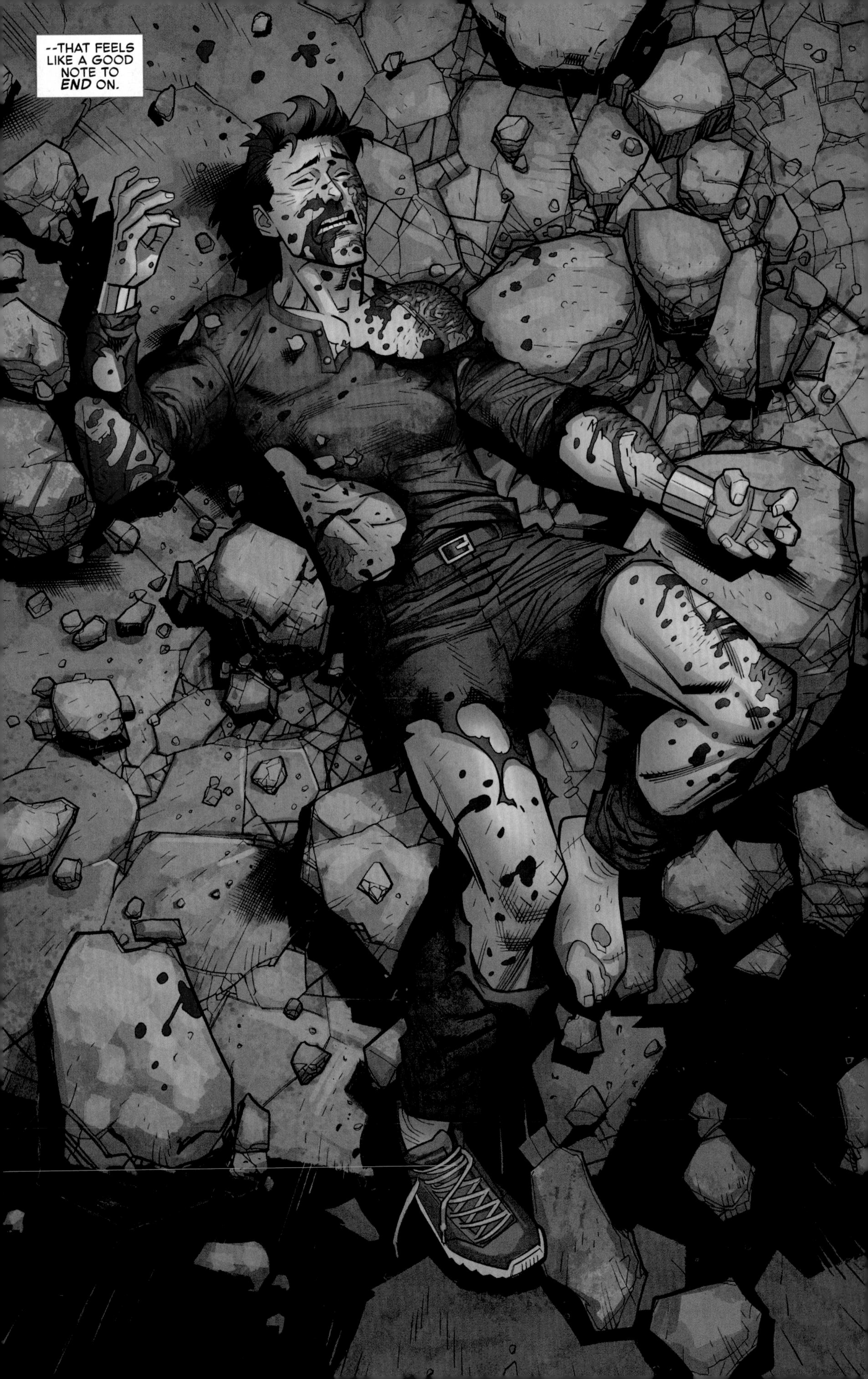
--THAT FEELS LIKE A GOOD NOTE TO END ON.

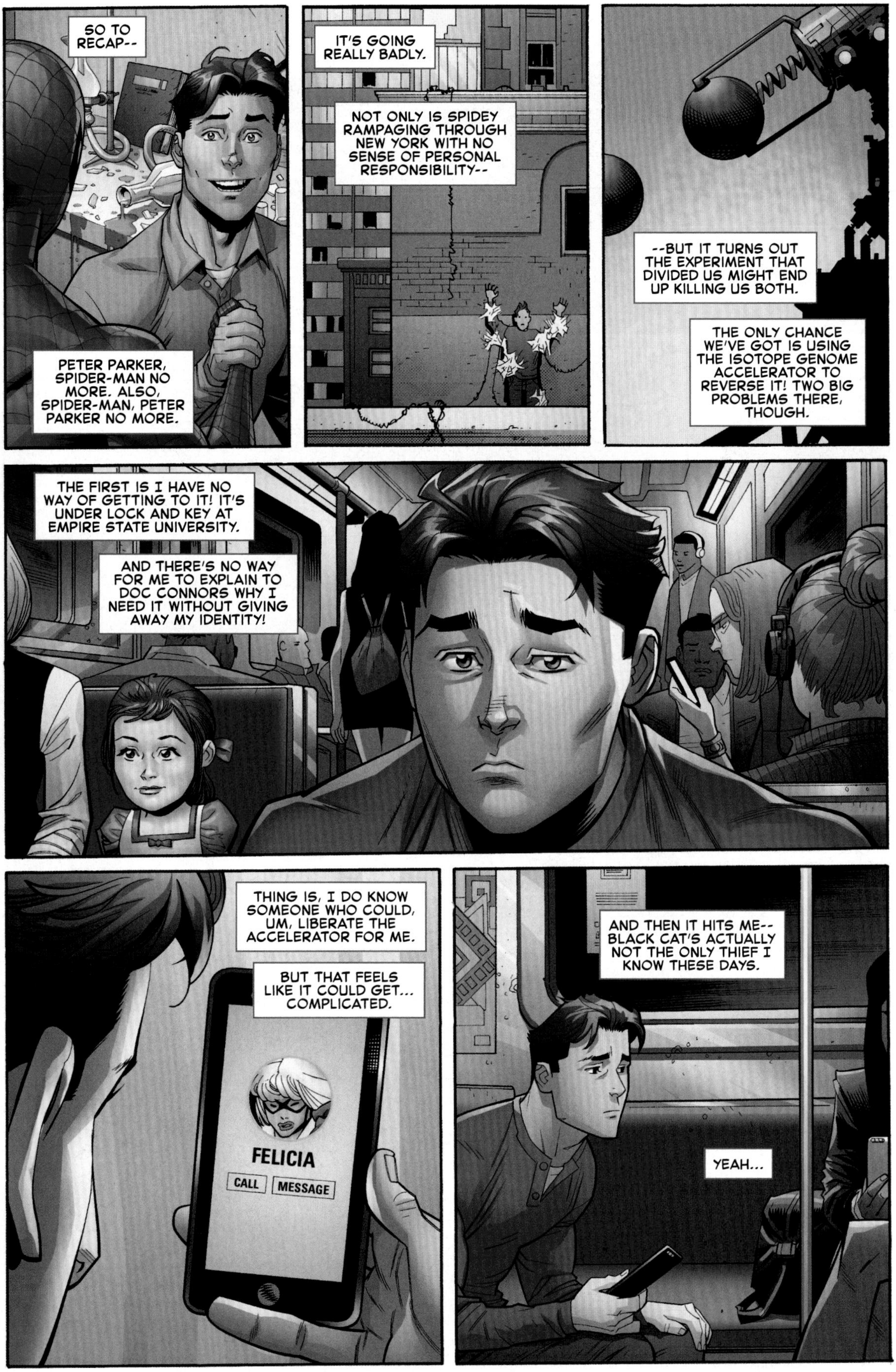
SO TO RECAP--
PETER PARKER, SPIDER-MAN NO MORE. ALSO, SPIDER-MAN, PETER PARKER NO MORE.
IT'S GOING REALLY BADLY.
NOT ONLY IS SPIDEY RAMPAGING THROUGH NEW YORK WITH NO SENSE OF PERSONAL RESPONSIBILITY--
--BUT IT TURNS OUT THE EXPERIMENT THAT DIVIDED US MIGHT END UP KILLING US BOTH.
THE ONLY CHANCE WE'VE GOT IS USING THE ISOTOPE GENOME ACCELERATOR TO REVERSE IT! TWO BIG PROBLEMS THERE, THOUGH.
THE FIRST IS I HAVE NO WAY OF GETTING TO IT! IT'S UNDER LOCK AND KEY AT EMPIRE STATE UNIVERSITY.
AND THERE'S NO WAY FOR ME TO EXPLAIN TO DOC CONNORS WHY I NEED IT WITHOUT GIVING AWAY MY IDENTITY!
THING IS, I DO KNOW SOMEONE WHO COULD, UM, LIBERATE THE ACCELERATOR FOR ME.
BUT THAT FEELS LIKE IT COULD GET... COMPLICATED.
FELICIA
CALL
MESSAGE
AND THEN IT HITS ME-- BLACK CAT'S ACTUALLY NOT THE ONLY THIEF I KNOW THESE DAYS.
YEAH...

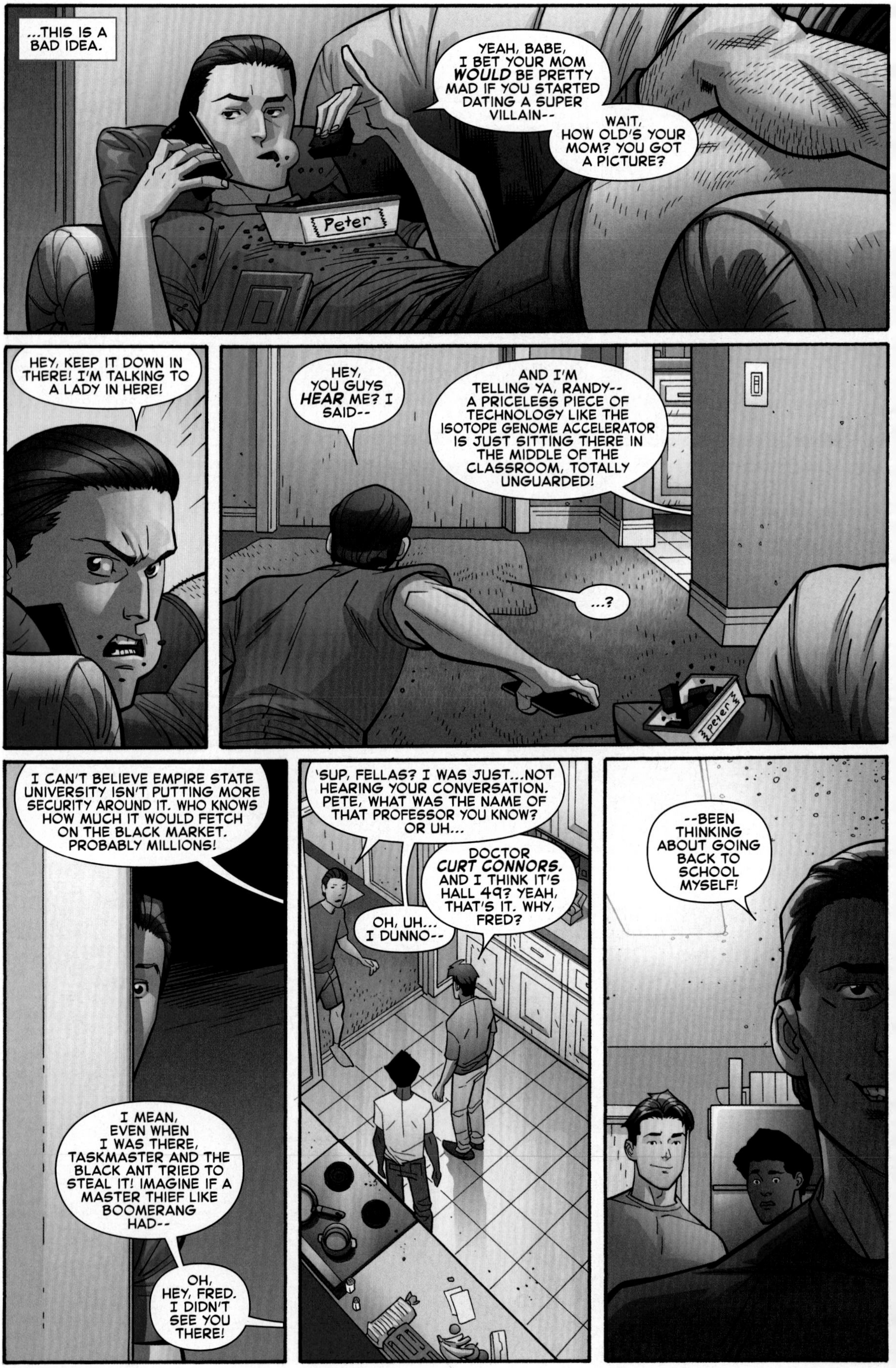
...THIS IS A BAD IDEA.
YEAH, BABE, I BET YOUR MOM WOULD BE PRETTY MAD IF YOU STARTED DATING A SUPER VILLAIN--
WAIT, HOW OLD'S YOUR MOM? YOU GOT A PICTURE?
Peter
HEY, KEEP IT DOWN IN THERE! I'M TALKING TO A LADY IN HERE!
HEY, YOU GUYS HEAR ME? I SAID--
AND I'M TELLING YA, RANDY-- A PRICELESS PIECE OF TECHNOLOGY LIKE THE ISOTOPE GENOME ACCELERATOR IS JUST SITTING THERE IN THE MIDDLE OF THE CLASSROOM, TOTALLY UNGUARDED!
...?
Peter
I CAN'T BELIEVE EMPIRE STATE UNIVERSITY ISN'T PUTTING MORE SECURITY AROUND IT. WHO KNOWS HOW MUCH IT WOULD FETCH ON THE BLACK MARKET. PROBABLY MILLIONS!
I MEAN, EVEN WHEN I WAS THERE, TASKMASTER AND THE BLACK ANT TRIED TO STEAL IT! IMAGINE IF A MASTER THIEF LIKE BOOMERANG HAD--
OH, HEY, FRED. I DIDN'T SEE YOU THERE!
'SUP, FELLAS? I WAS JUST...NOT HEARING YOUR CONVERSATION. PETE, WHAT WAS THE NAME OF THAT PROFESSOR YOU KNOW? OR UH...
DOCTOR CURT CONNORS. AND I THINK IT'S HALL 49? YEAH, THAT'S IT. WHY, FRED?
OH, UH... I DUNNO--
--BEEN THINKING ABOUT GOING BACK TO SCHOOL MYSELF!

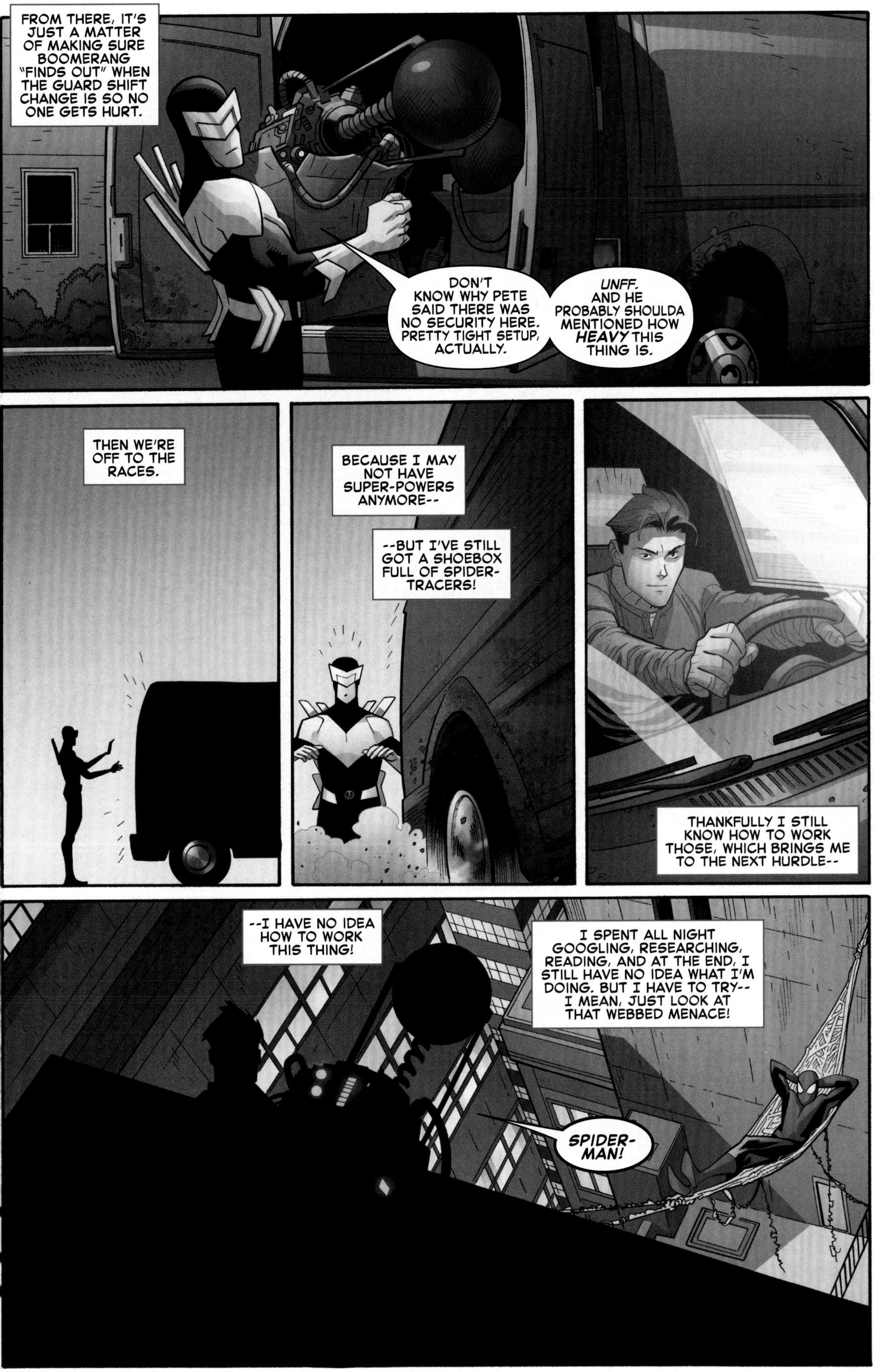
FROM THERE, IT'S JUST A MATTER OF MAKING SURE BOOMERANG "FINDS OUT" WHEN THE GUARD SHIFT CHANGE IS SO NO ONE GETS HURT.
DON'T KNOW WHY PETE SAID THERE WAS NO SECURITY HERE. PRETTY TIGHT SETUP, ACTUALLY.
UNFF. AND HE PROBABLY SHOULDA MENTIONED HOW HEAVY THIS THING IS.
THEN WE'RE OFF TO THE RACES.
BECAUSE I MAY NOT HAVE SUPER-POWERS ANYMORE--
--BUT I'VE STILL GOT A SHOEBOX FULL OF SPIDER-TRACERS!
THANKFULLY I STILL KNOW HOW TO WORK THOSE, WHICH BRINGS ME TO THE NEXT HURDLE--
--I HAVE NO IDEA HOW TO WORK THIS THING!
I SPENT ALL NIGHT GOOGLING, RESEARCHING, READING, AND AT THE END, I STILL HAVE NO IDEA WHAT I'M DOING. BUT I HAVE TO TRY-- I MEAN, JUST LOOK AT THAT WEBBED MENACE!
SPIDER-MAN!

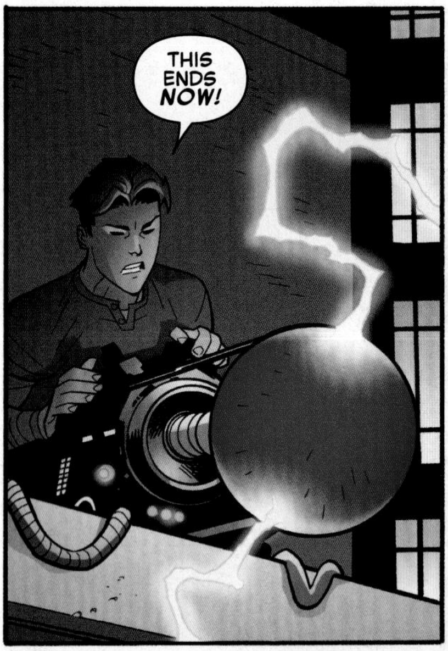
THIS ENDS NOW!

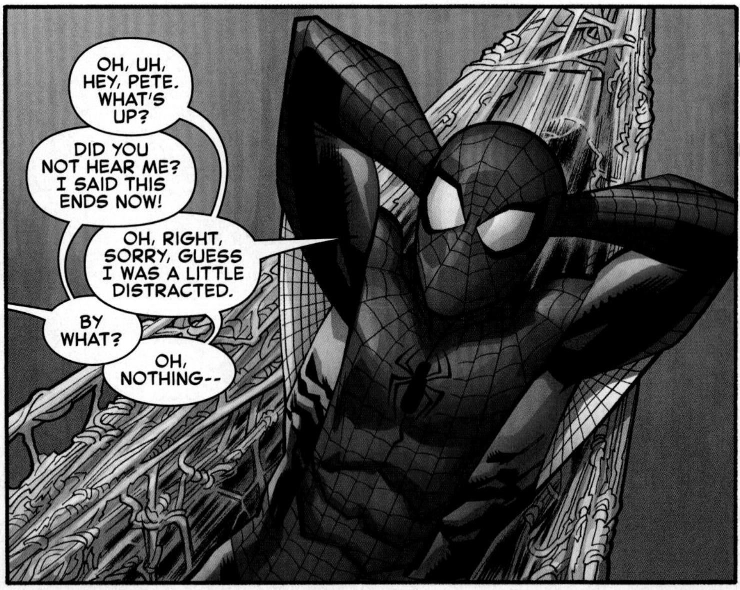
OH, UH, HEY, PETE. WHAT'S UP?
DID YOU NOT HEAR ME? I SAID THIS ENDS NOW!
OH, RIGHT, SORRY, GUESS I WAS A LITTLE DISTRACTED.
BY WHAT?
OH, NOTHING--

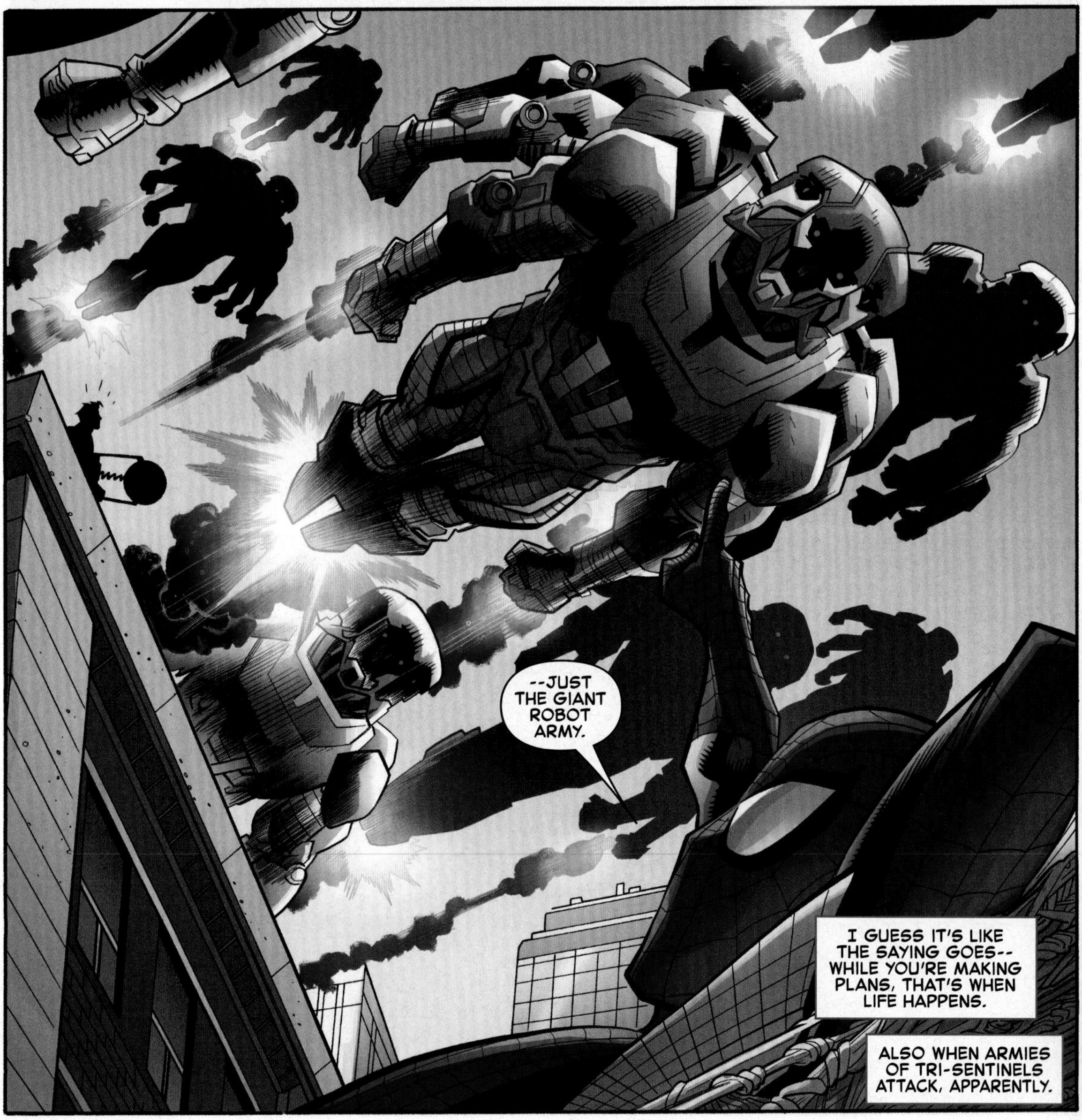
--JUST THE GIANT ROBOT ARMY.
I GUESS IT'S LIKE THE SAYING GOES--WHILE YOU'RE MAKING PLANS, THAT'S WHEN LIFE HAPPENS.
ALSO WHEN ARMIES OF TRI-SENTINELS ATTACK, APPARENTLY.

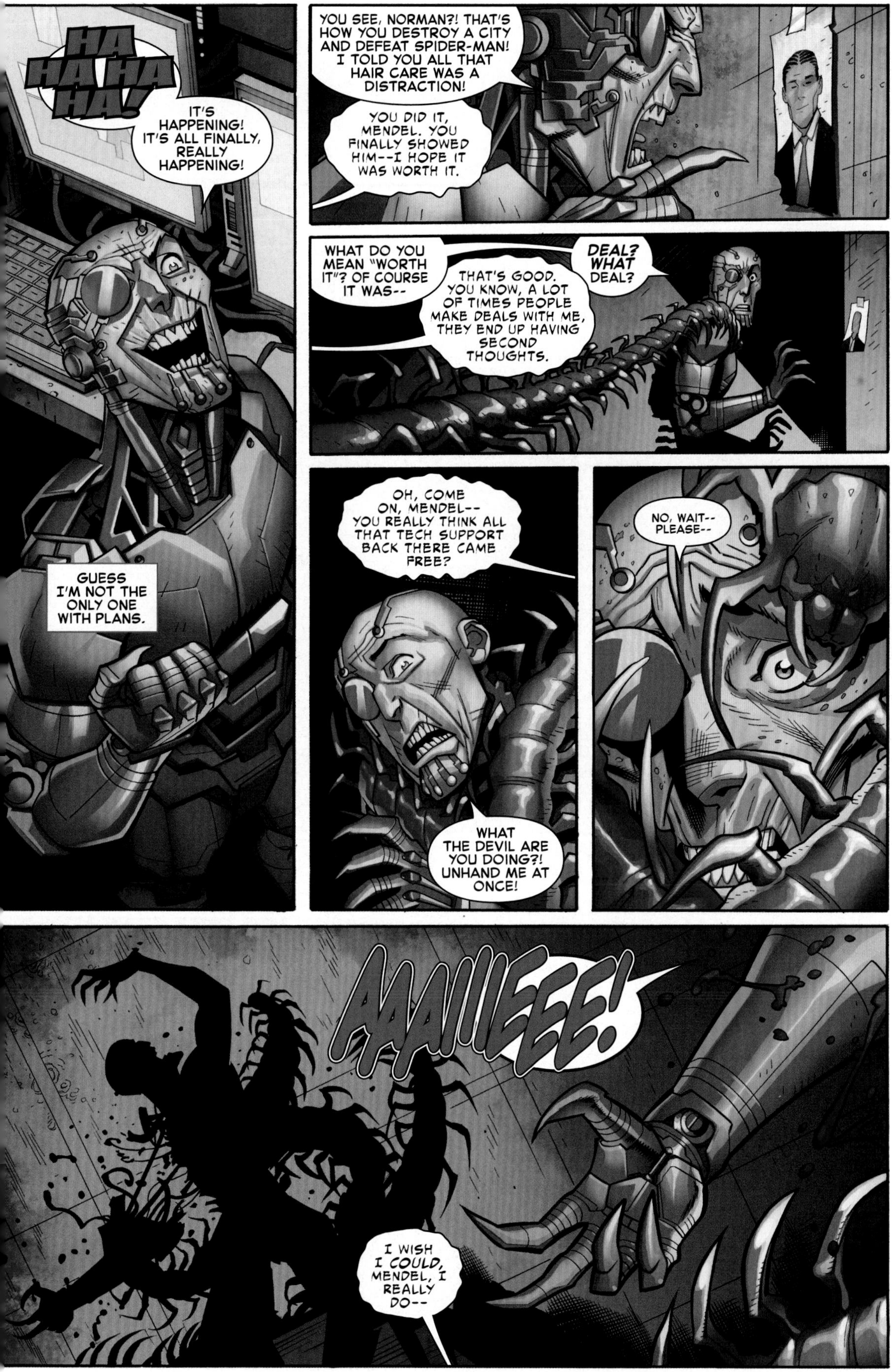
HA HA HA HA!
IT'S HAPPENING! IT'S ALL FINALLY, REALLY HAPPENING!
GUESS I'M NOT THE ONLY ONE WITH PLANS.
YOU SEE, NORMAN?! THAT'S HOW YOU DESTROY A CITY AND DEFEAT SPIDER-MAN! I TOLD YOU ALL THAT HAIR CARE WAS A DISTRACTION!
YOU DID IT, MENDEL. YOU FINALLY SHOWED HIM--I HOPE IT WAS WORTH IT.
WHAT DO YOU MEAN "WORTH IT"? OF COURSE IT WAS--
THAT'S GOOD. YOU KNOW, A LOT OF TIMES PEOPLE MAKE DEALS WITH ME, THEY END UP HAVING SECOND THOUGHTS.
DEAL? WHAT DEAL?
OH, COME ON, MENDEL-- YOU REALLY THINK ALL THAT TECH SUPPORT BACK THERE CAME FREE?
WHAT THE DEVIL ARE YOU DOING?! UNHAND ME AT ONCE!
NO, WAIT-- PLEASE--
AAAIIIEEE!
I WISH I COULD, MENDEL, I REALLY DO--

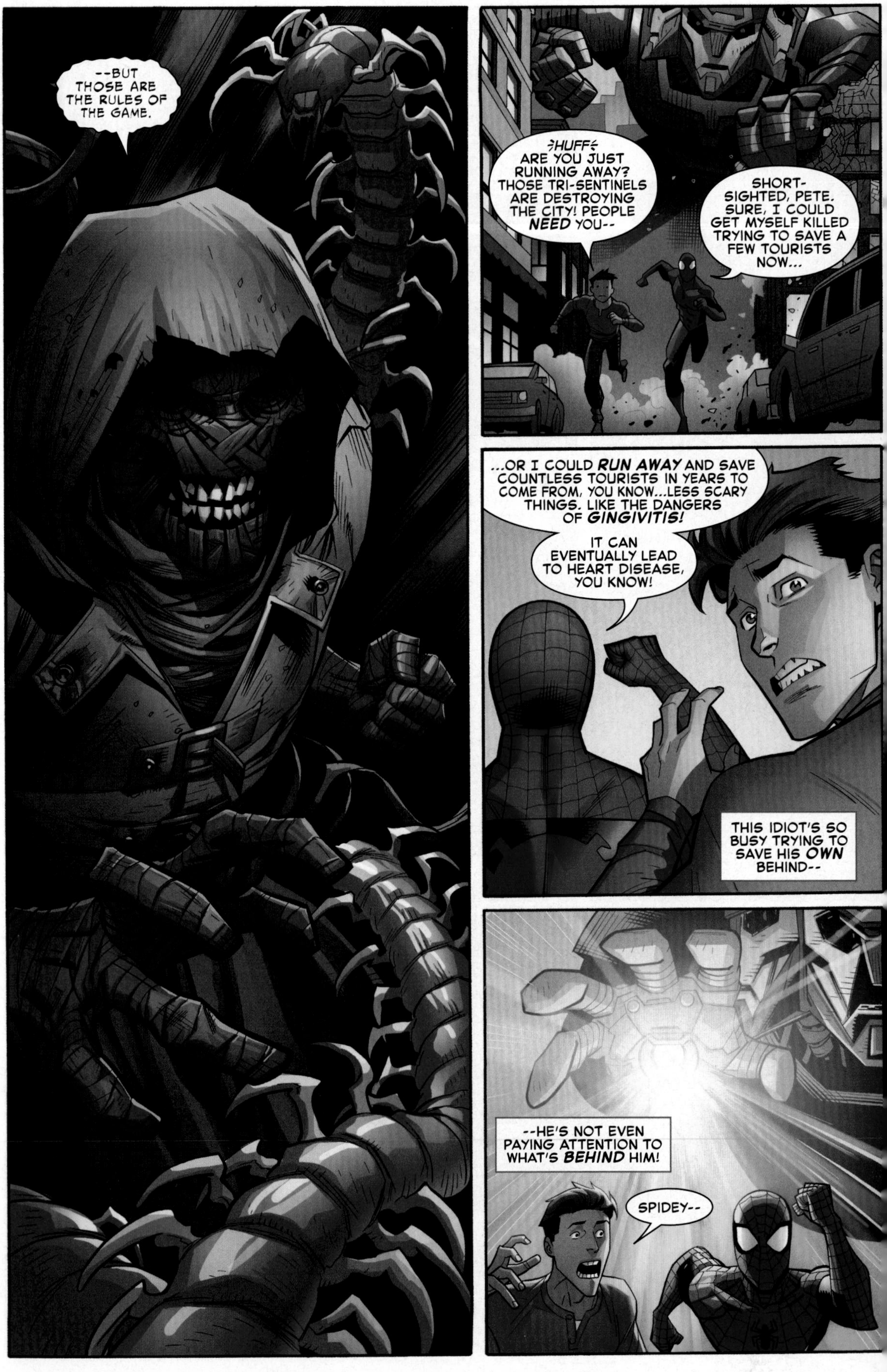
--BUT THOSE ARE THE RULES OF THE GAME.
≠HUFF≠ ARE YOU JUST RUNNING AWAY? THOSE TRI-SENTINELS ARE DESTROYING THE CITY! PEOPLE NEED YOU--
SHORT-SIGHTED, PETE. SURE, I COULD GET MYSELF KILLED TRYING TO SAVE A FEW TOURISTS NOW...
...OR I COULD RUN AWAY AND SAVE COUNTLESS TOURISTS IN YEARS TO COME FROM, YOU KNOW...LESS SCARY THINGS. LIKE THE DANGERS OF GINGIVITIS!
IT CAN EVENTUALLY LEAD TO HEART DISEASE, YOU KNOW!
THIS IDIOT'S SO BUSY TRYING TO SAVE HIS OWN BEHIND--
--HE'S NOT EVEN PAYING ATTENTION TO WHAT'S BEHIND HIM!
SPIDEY--

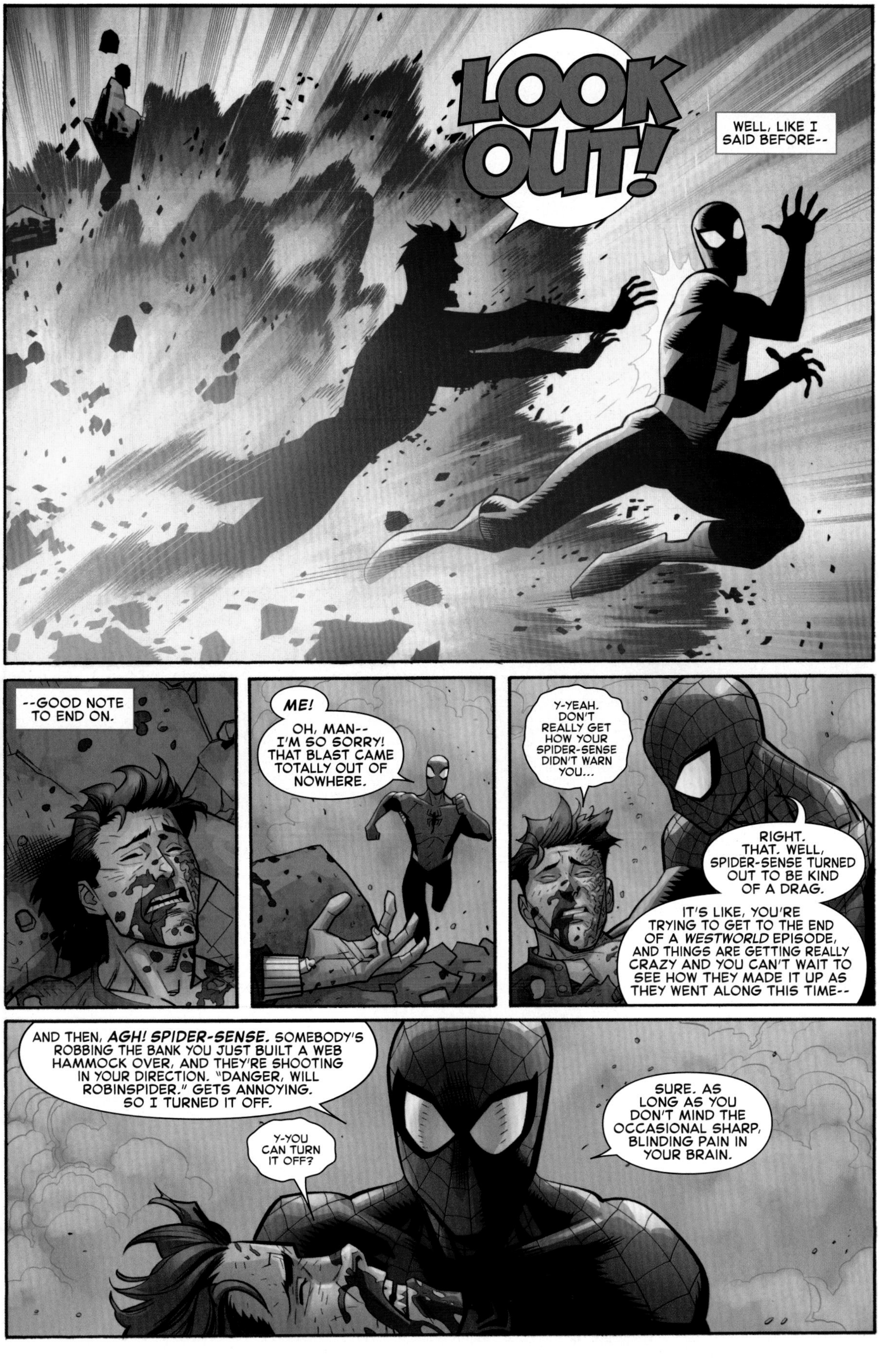
LOOK OUT!
WELL, LIKE I SAID BEFORE--
--GOOD NOTE TO END ON.
ME!
OH, MAN-- I'M SO SORRY! THAT BLAST CAME TOTALLY OUT OF NOWHERE.
Y-YEAH. DON'T REALLY GET HOW YOUR SPIDER-SENSE DIDN'T WARN YOU...
RIGHT. THAT. WELL, SPIDER-SENSE TURNED OUT TO BE KIND OF A DRAG.
IT'S LIKE, YOU'RE TRYING TO GET TO THE END OF A WESTWORLD EPISODE, AND THINGS ARE GETTING REALLY CRAZY AND YOU CAN'T WAIT TO SEE HOW THEY MADE IT UP AS THEY WENT ALONG THIS TIME--
AND THEN, AGH! SPIDER-SENSE. SOMEBODY'S ROBBING THE BANK YOU JUST BUILT A WEB HAMMOCK OVER, AND THEY'RE SHOOTING IN YOUR DIRECTION. "DANGER, WILL ROBINSPIDER." GETS ANNOYING. SO I TURNED IT OFF.
Y-YOU CAN TURN IT OFF?
SURE. AS LONG AS YOU DON'T MIND THE OCCASIONAL SHARP, BLINDING PAIN IN YOUR BRAIN.

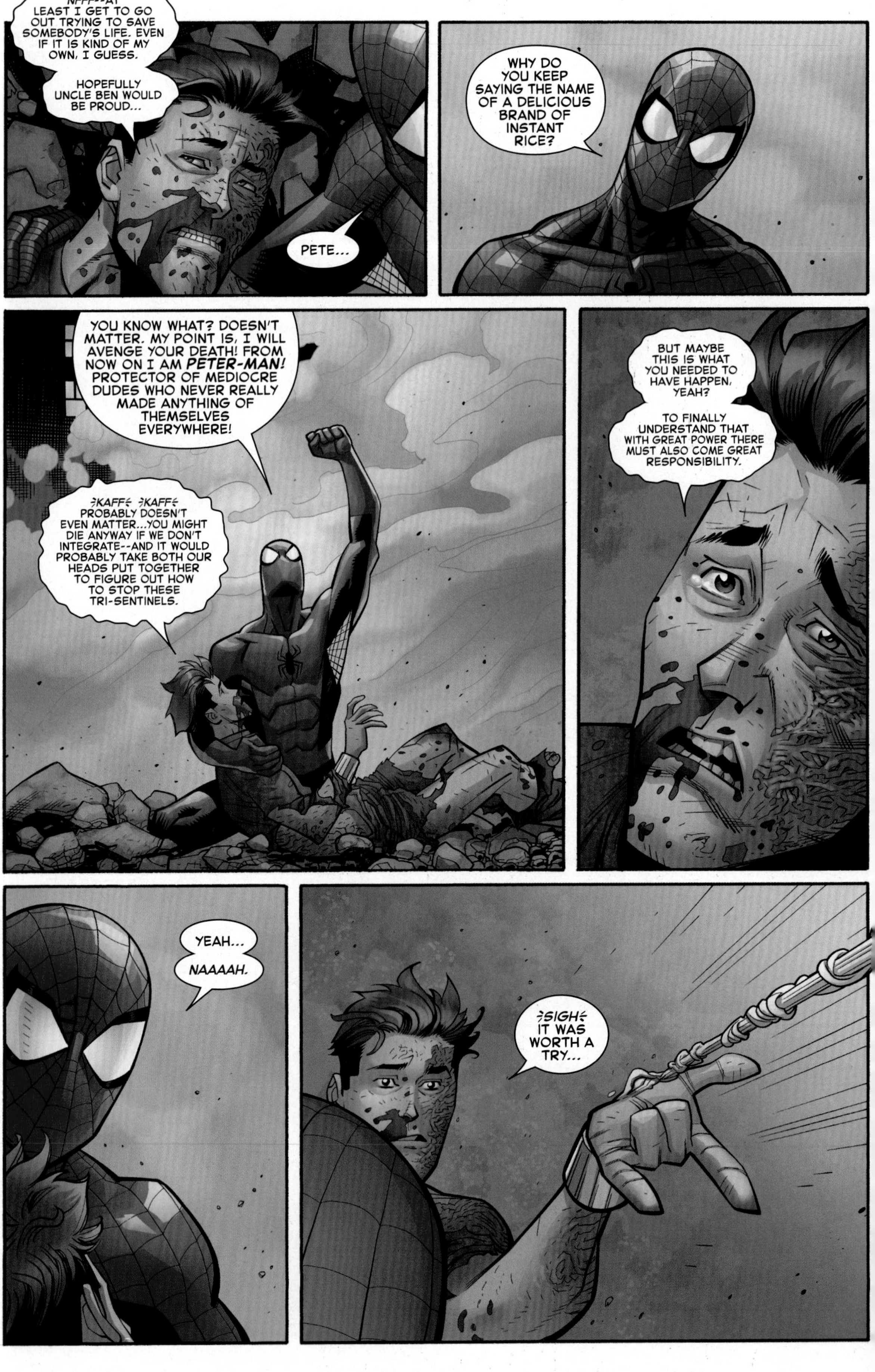
NFFF--AT LEAST I GET TO GO OUT TRYING TO SAVE SOMEBODY'S LIFE. EVEN IF IT IS KIND OF MY OWN, I GUESS.
HOPEFULLY UNCLE BEN WOULD BE PROUD...
PETE...
WHY DO YOU KEEP SAYING THE NAME OF A DELICIOUS BRAND OF INSTANT RICE?
YOU KNOW WHAT? DOESN'T MATTER. MY POINT IS, I WILL AVENGE YOUR DEATH! FROM NOW ON I AM PETER-MAN! PROTECTOR OF MEDIOCRE DUDES WHO NEVER REALLY MADE ANYTHING OF THEMSELVES EVERYWHERE!
KAFF KAFF PROBABLY DOESN'T EVEN MATTER...YOU MIGHT DIE ANYWAY IF WE DON'T INTEGRATE--AND IT WOULD PROBABLY TAKE BOTH OUR HEADS PUT TOGETHER TO FIGURE OUT HOW TO STOP THESE TRI-SENTINELS.
BUT MAYBE THIS IS WHAT YOU NEEDED TO HAVE HAPPEN, YEAH?
TO FINALLY UNDERSTAND THAT WITH GREAT POWER THERE MUST ALSO COME GREAT RESPONSIBILITY.
YEAH...
NAAAAH.
SIGH IT WAS WORTH A TRY...

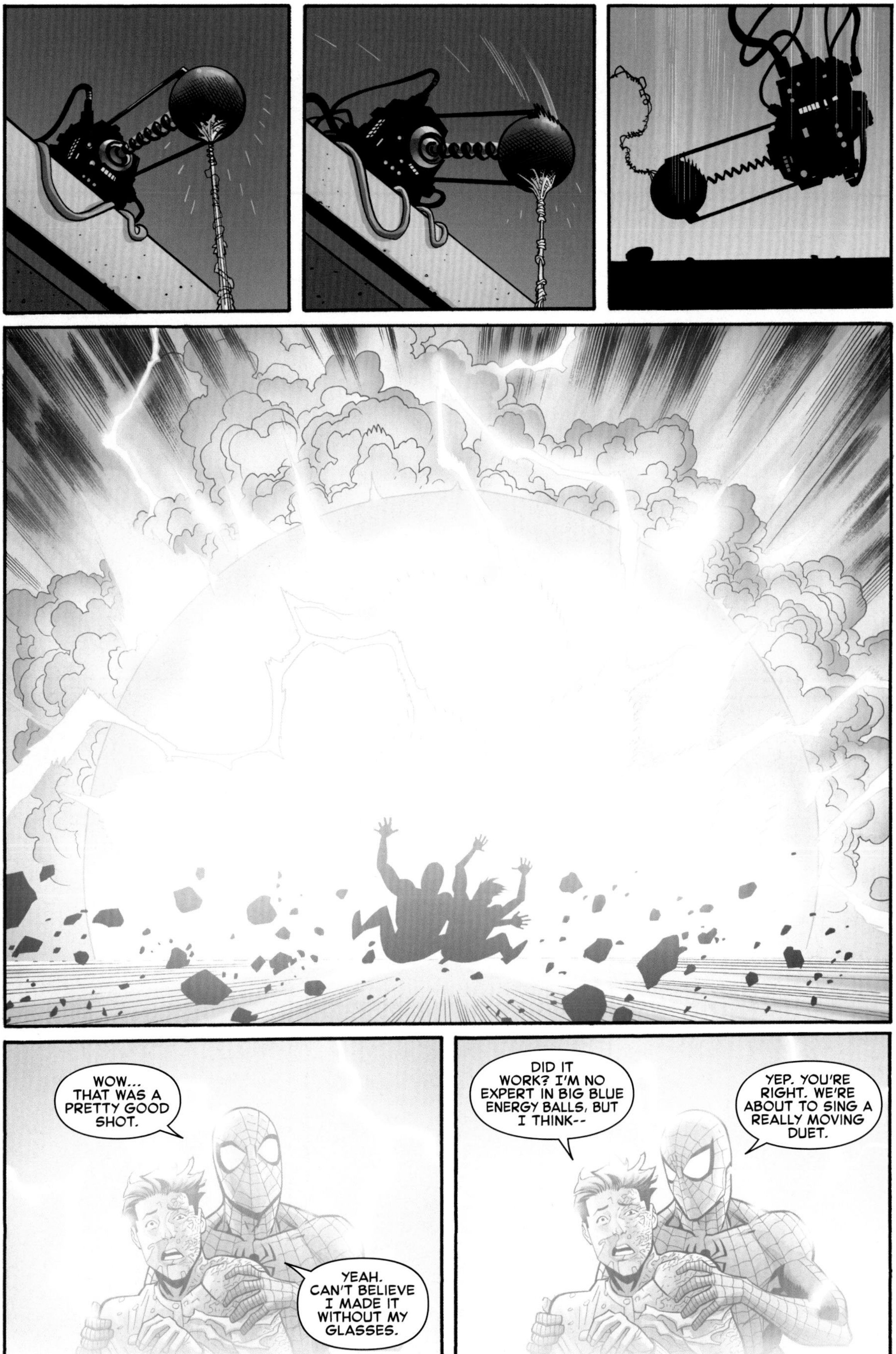
WOW... THAT WAS A PRETTY GOOD SHOT.
YEAH. CAN'T BELIEVE I MADE IT WITHOUT MY GLASSES.
DID IT WORK? I'M NO EXPERT IN BIG BLUE ENERGY BALLS, BUT I THINK--
YEP. YOU'RE RIGHT. WE'RE ABOUT TO SING A REALLY MOVING DUET.

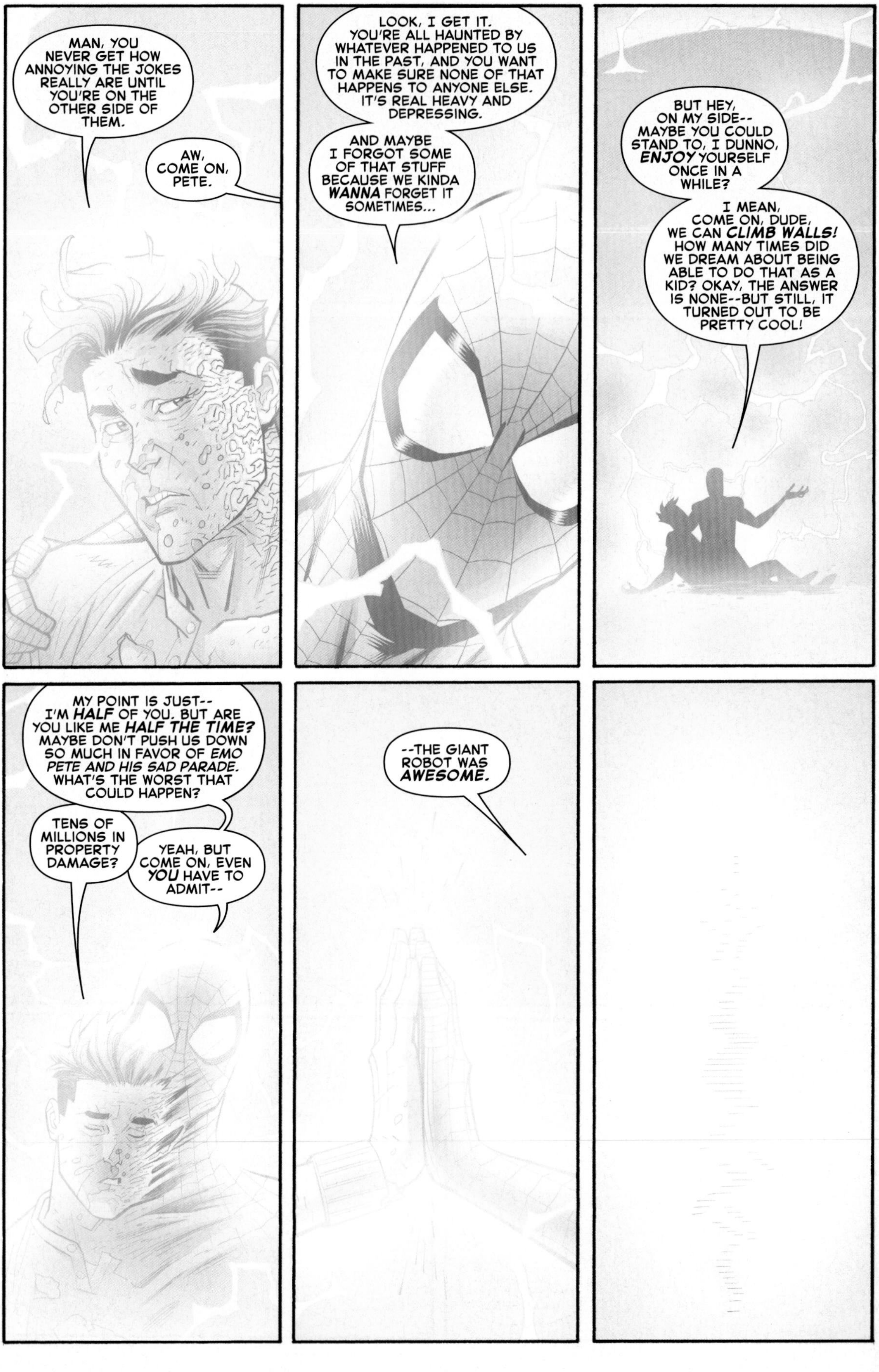
MAN, YOU NEVER GET HOW ANNOYING THE JOKES REALLY ARE UNTIL YOU'RE ON THE OTHER SIDE OF THEM.
AW, COME ON, PETE.
LOOK, I GET IT. YOU'RE ALL HAUNTED BY WHATEVER HAPPENED TO US IN THE PAST, AND YOU WANT TO MAKE SURE NONE OF THAT HAPPENS TO ANYONE ELSE. IT'S REAL HEAVY AND DEPRESSING.
AND MAYBE I FORGOT SOME OF THAT STUFF BECAUSE WE KINDA WANNA FORGET IT SOMETIMES...
BUT HEY, ON MY SIDE-- MAYBE YOU COULD STAND TO, I DUNNO, ENJOY YOURSELF ONCE IN A WHILE?
I MEAN, COME ON, DUDE, WE CAN CLIMB WALLS! HOW MANY TIMES DID WE DREAM ABOUT BEING ABLE TO DO THAT AS A KID? OKAY, THE ANSWER IS NONE--BUT STILL, IT TURNED OUT TO BE PRETTY COOL!
MY POINT IS JUST-- I'M HALF OF YOU. BUT ARE YOU LIKE ME HALF THE TIME? MAYBE DON'T PUSH US DOWN SO MUCH IN FAVOR OF EMO PETE AND HIS SAD PARADE. WHAT'S THE WORST THAT COULD HAPPEN?
TENS OF MILLIONS IN PROPERTY DAMAGE?
YEAH, BUT COME ON, EVEN YOU HAVE TO ADMIT--
--THE GIANT ROBOT WAS AWESOME.

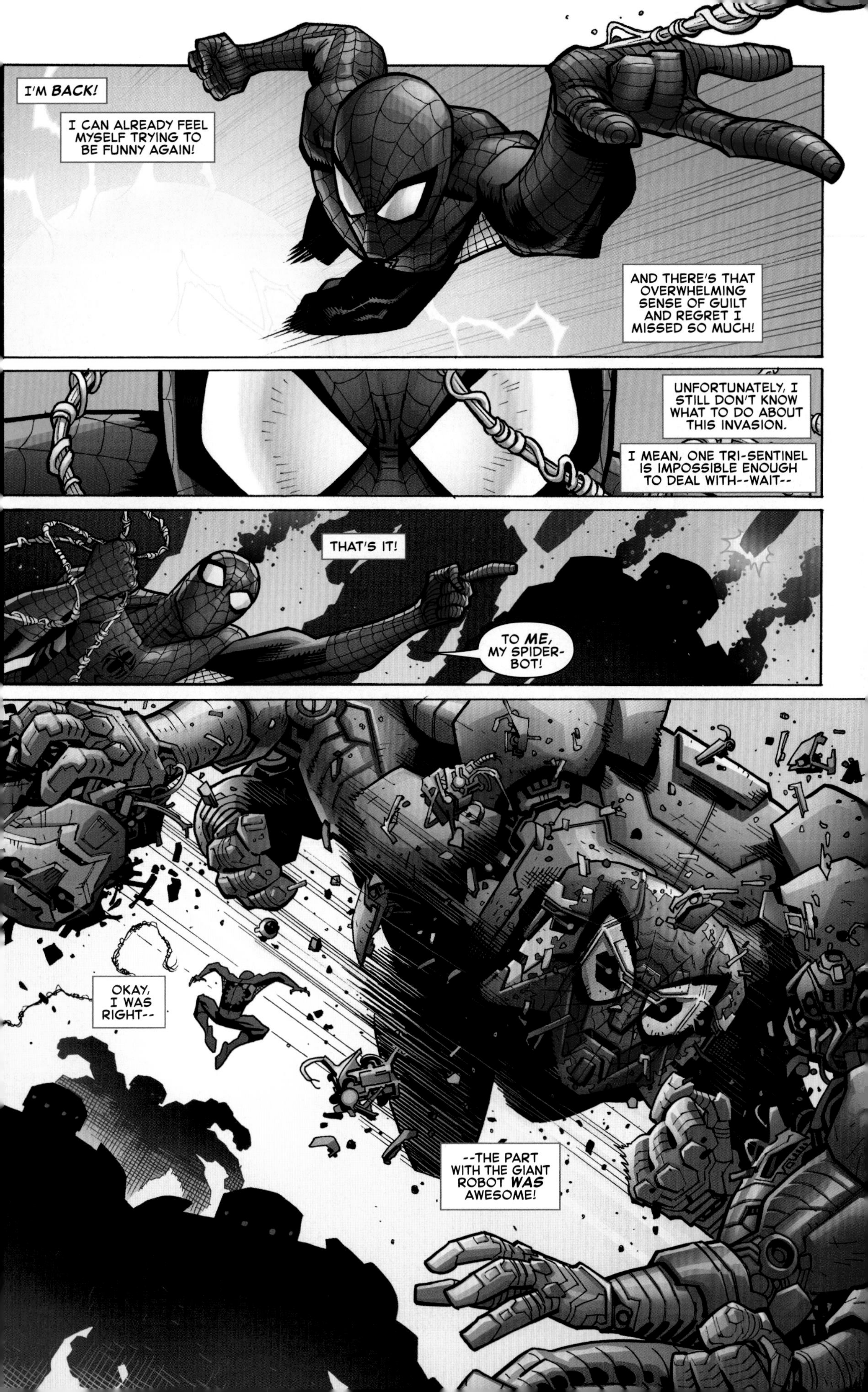
I'M BACK!
I CAN ALREADY FEEL MYSELF TRYING TO BE FUNNY AGAIN!
AND THERE'S THAT OVERWHELMING SENSE OF GUILT AND REGRET I MISSED SO MUCH!
UNFORTUNATELY, I STILL DON'T KNOW WHAT TO DO ABOUT THIS INVASION.
I MEAN, ONE TRI-SENTINEL IS IMPOSSIBLE ENOUGH TO DEAL WITH--WAIT--
THAT'S IT!
TO ME, MY SPIDER-BOT!
OKAY, I WAS RIGHT--
--THE PART WITH THE GIANT ROBOT WAS AWESOME!

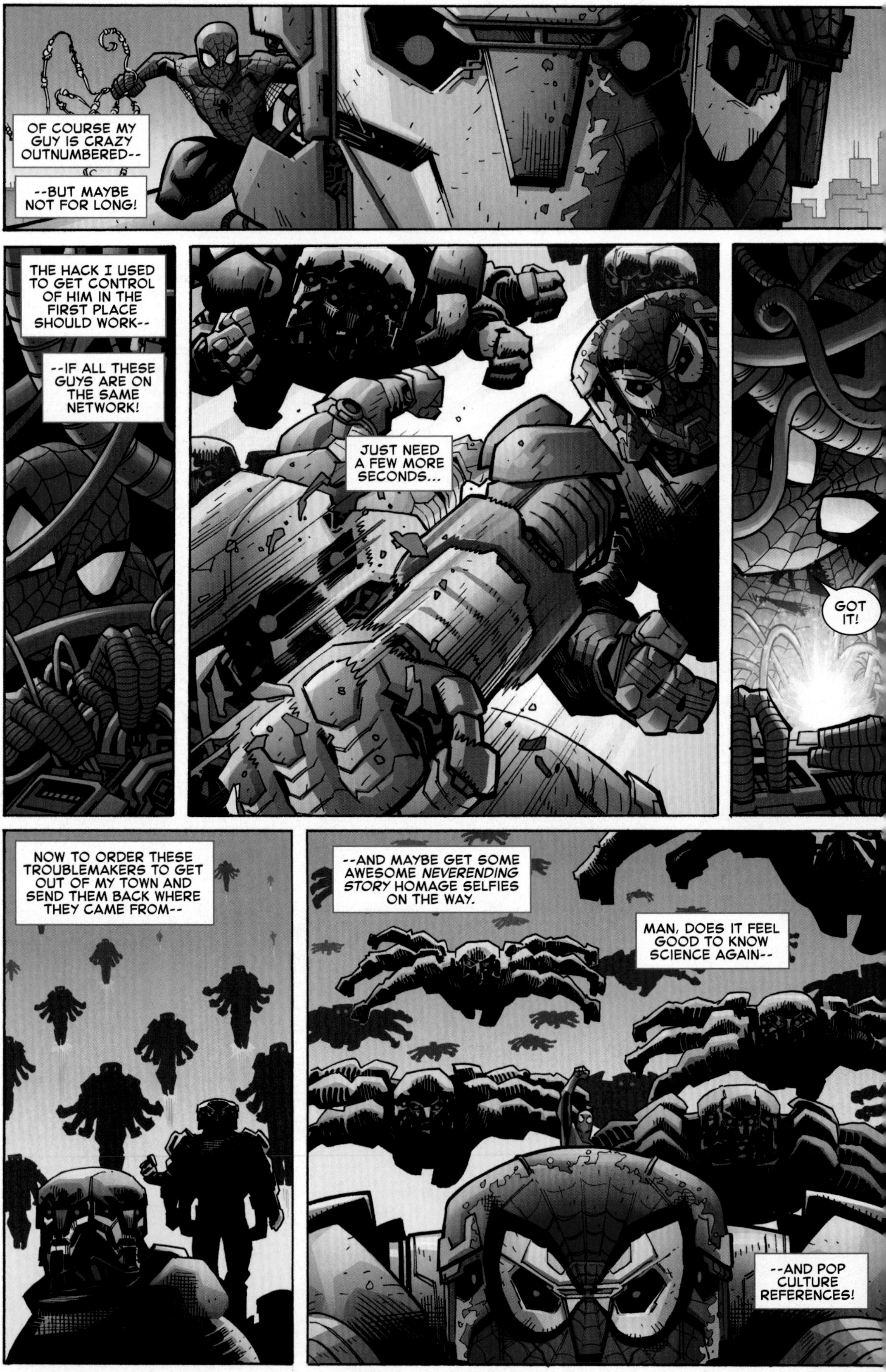
OF COURSE MY GUY IS CRAZY OUTNUMBERED--
--BUT MAYBE NOT FOR LONG!
THE HACK I USED TO GET CONTROL OF HIM IN THE FIRST PLACE SHOULD WORK--
--IF ALL THESE GUYS ARE ON THE SAME NETWORK!
JUST NEED A FEW MORE SECONDS...
GOT IT!
NOW TO ORDER THESE TROUBLEMAKERS TO GET OUT OF MY TOWN AND SEND THEM BACK WHERE THEY CAME FROM--
--AND MAYBE GET SOME AWESOME *NEVERENDING STORY* HOMAGE SELFIES ON THE WAY.
MAN, DOES IT FEEL GOOD TO KNOW SCIENCE AGAIN--
--AND POP CULTURE REFERENCES!

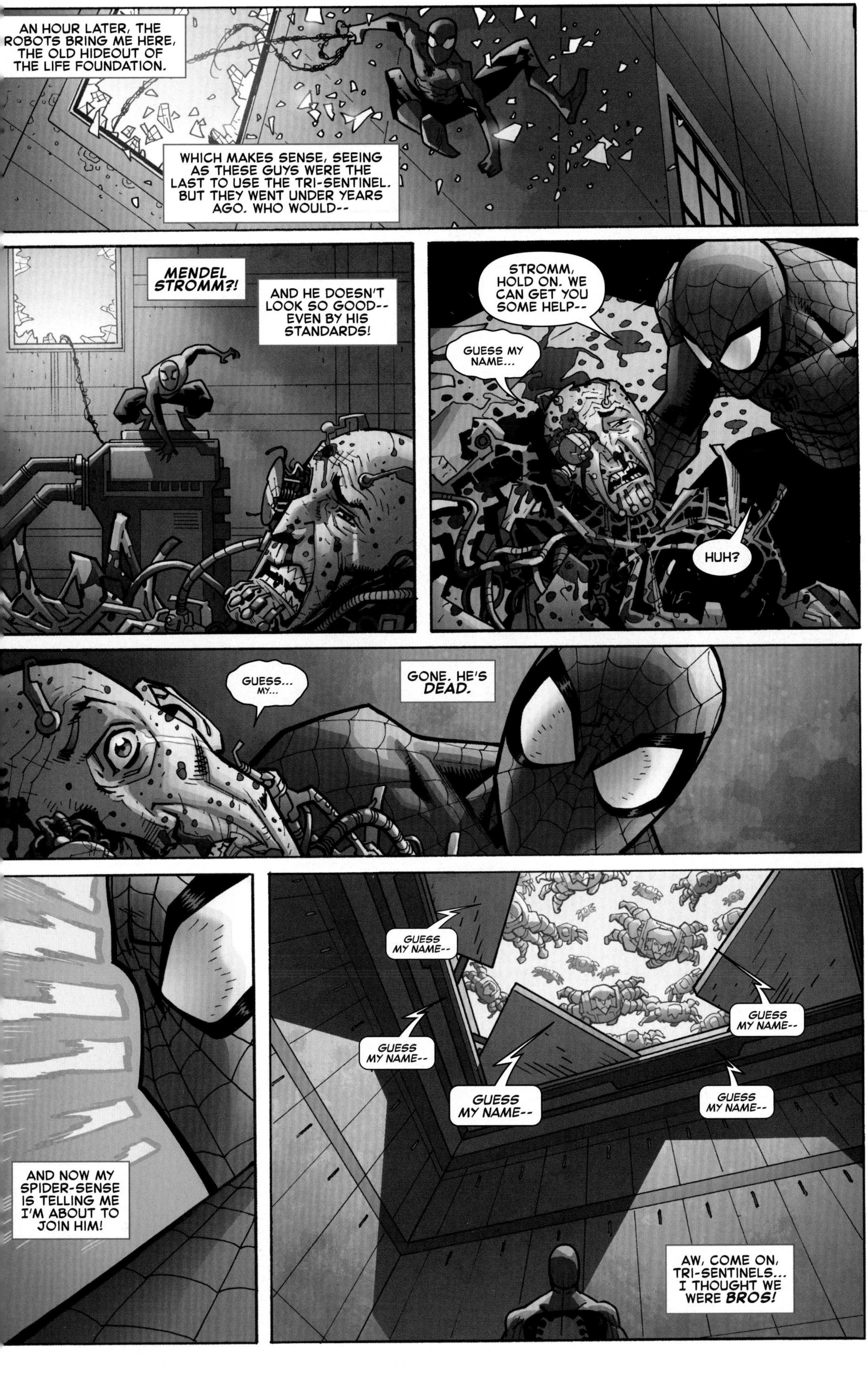
AN HOUR LATER, THE ROBOTS BRING ME HERE, THE OLD HIDEOUT OF THE LIFE FOUNDATION.
WHICH MAKES SENSE, SEEING AS THESE GUYS WERE THE LAST TO USE THE TRI-SENTINEL. BUT THEY WENT UNDER YEARS AGO. WHO WOULD--
MENDEL STROMM?!
AND HE DOESN'T LOOK SO GOOD-- EVEN BY HIS STANDARDS!
STROMM, HOLD ON. WE CAN GET YOU SOME HELP--
GUESS MY NAME...
HUH?
GUESS... MY...
GONE. HE'S DEAD.
AND NOW MY SPIDER-SENSE IS TELLING ME I'M ABOUT TO JOIN HIM!
GUESS MY NAME--
GUESS MY NAME--
GUESS MY NAME--
GUESS MY NAME--
GUESS MY NAME--
AW, COME ON, TRI-SENTINELS... I THOUGHT WE WERE BROS!

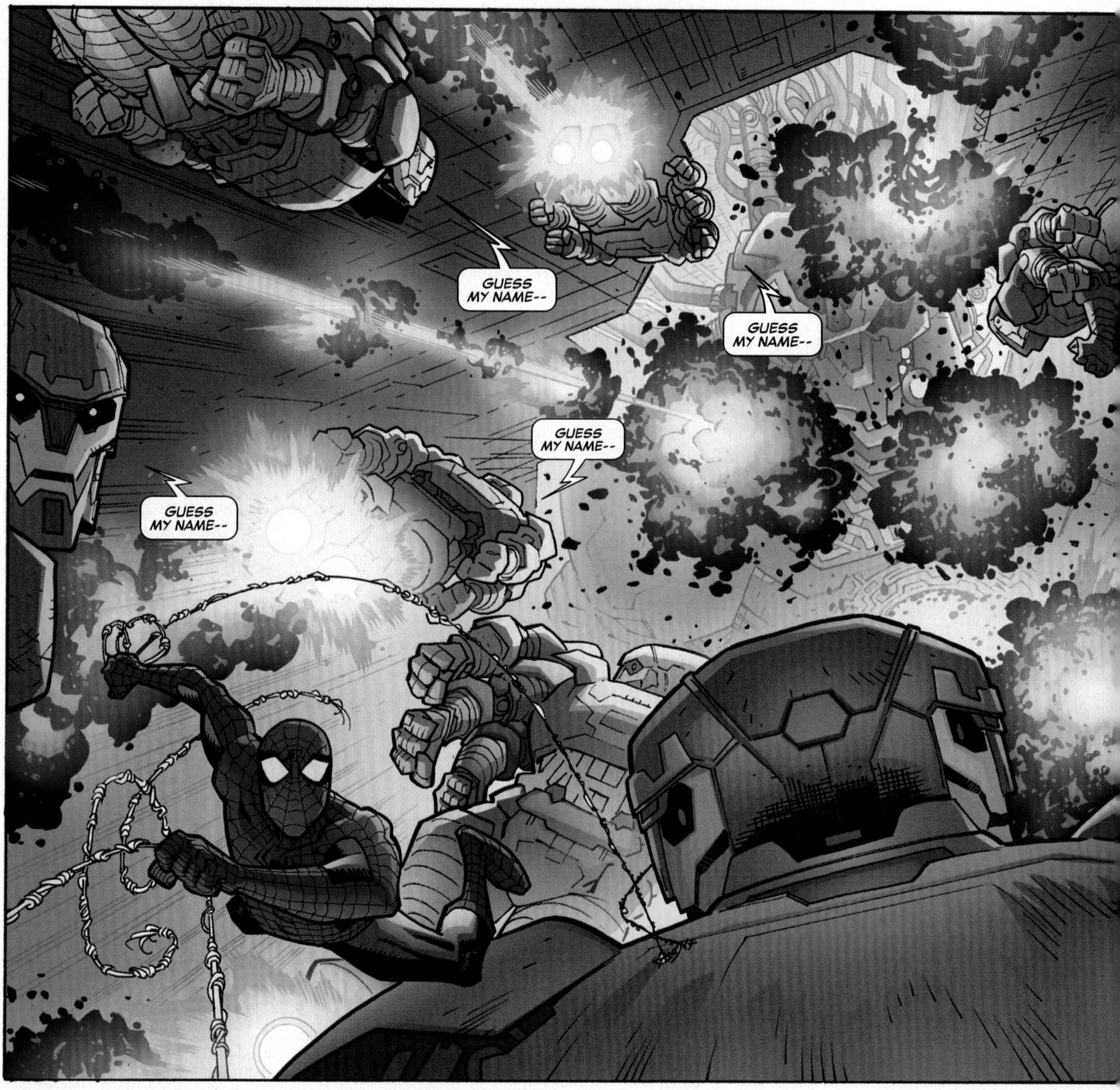
GUESS MY NAME--
GUESS MY NAME--
GUESS MY NAME--
GUESS MY NAME--

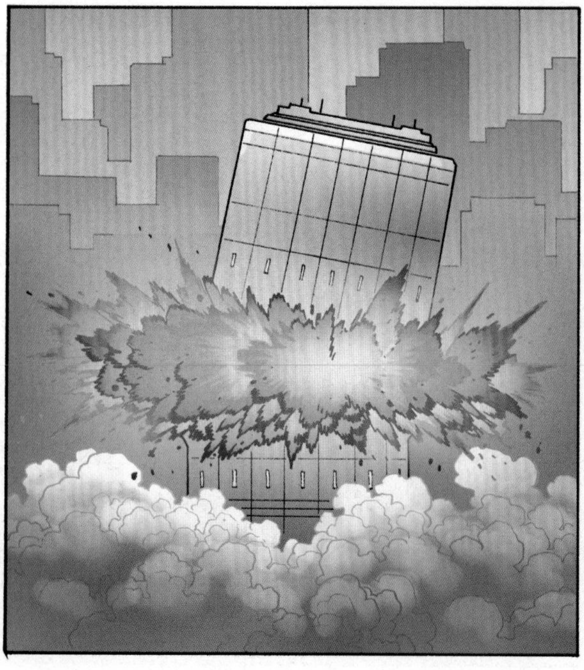

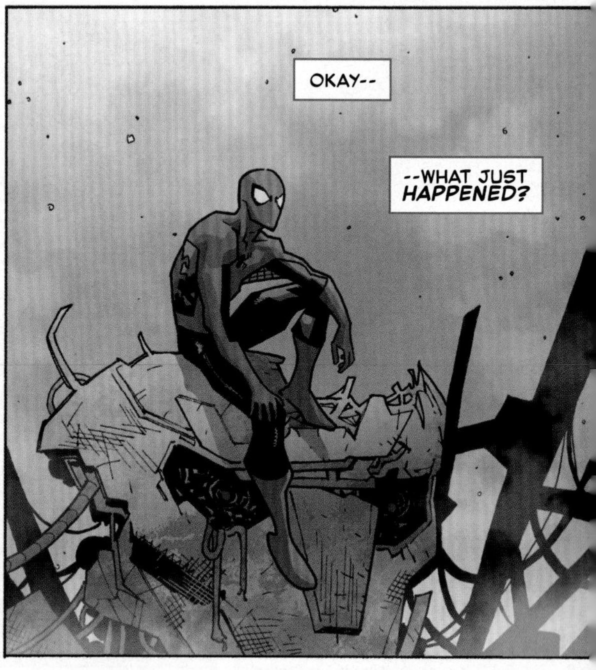
OKAY--
--WHAT JUST HAPPENED?

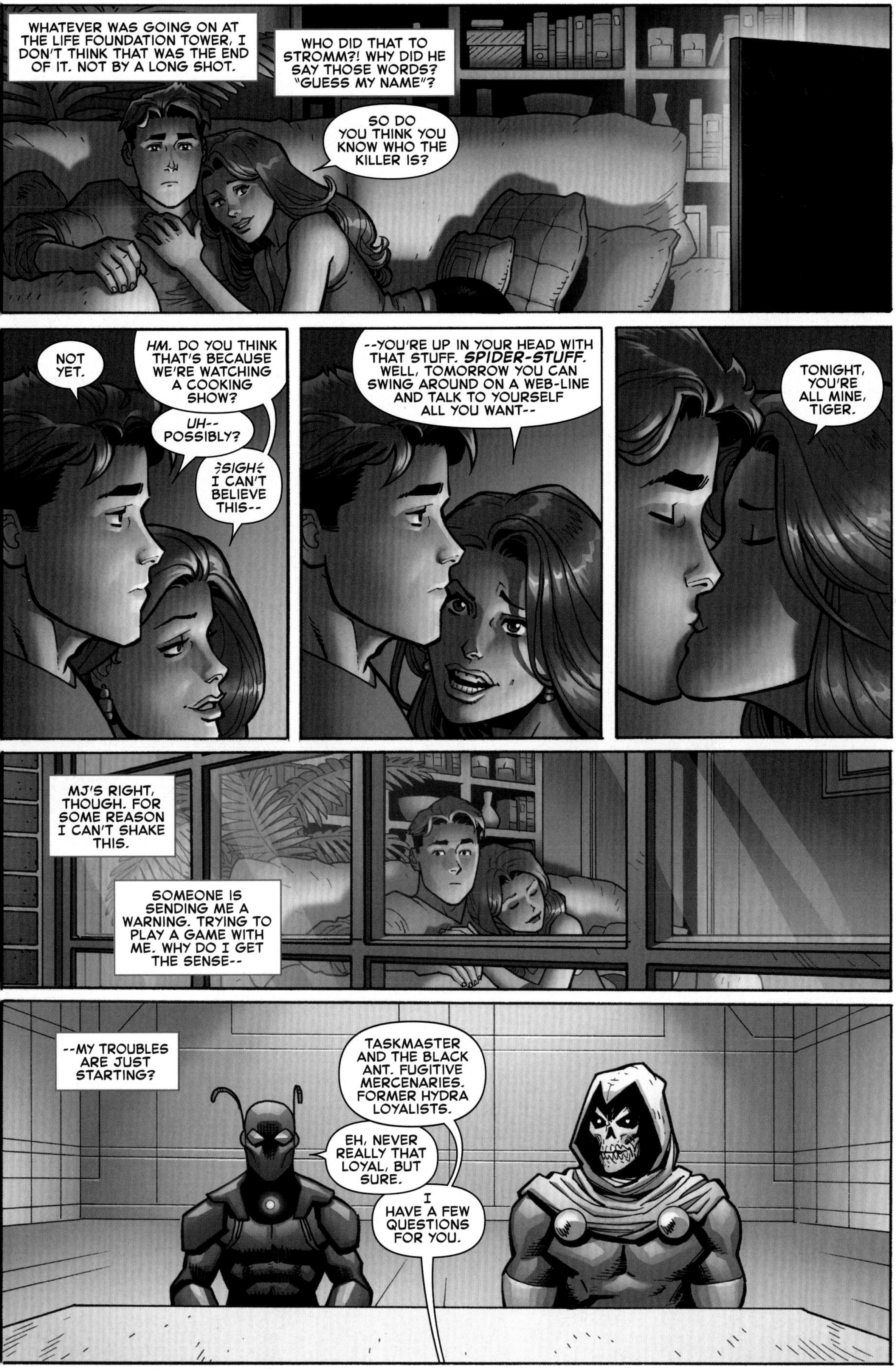
WHATEVER WAS GOING ON AT THE LIFE FOUNDATION TOWER, I DON'T THINK THAT WAS THE END OF IT. NOT BY A LONG SHOT.
WHO DID THAT TO STROMM?! WHY DID HE SAY THOSE WORDS? "GUESS MY NAME"?
SO DO YOU THINK YOU KNOW WHO THE KILLER IS?
NOT YET.
HM. DO YOU THINK THAT'S BECAUSE WE'RE WATCHING A COOKING SHOW?
UH-- POSSIBLY?
SIGH I CAN'T BELIEVE THIS--
--YOU'RE UP IN YOUR HEAD WITH THAT STUFF. SPIDER-STUFF. WELL, TOMORROW YOU CAN SWING AROUND ON A WEB-LINE AND TALK TO YOURSELF ALL YOU WANT--
TONIGHT, YOU'RE ALL MINE, TIGER.
MJ'S RIGHT, THOUGH. FOR SOME REASON I CAN'T SHAKE THIS.
SOMEONE IS SENDING ME A WARNING. TRYING TO PLAY A GAME WITH ME. WHY DO I GET THE SENSE--
--MY TROUBLES ARE JUST STARTING?
TASKMASTER AND THE BLACK ANT. FUGITIVE MERCENARIES. FORMER HYDRA LOYALISTS.
EH, NEVER REALLY THAT LOYAL, BUT SURE.
I HAVE A FEW QUESTIONS FOR YOU.

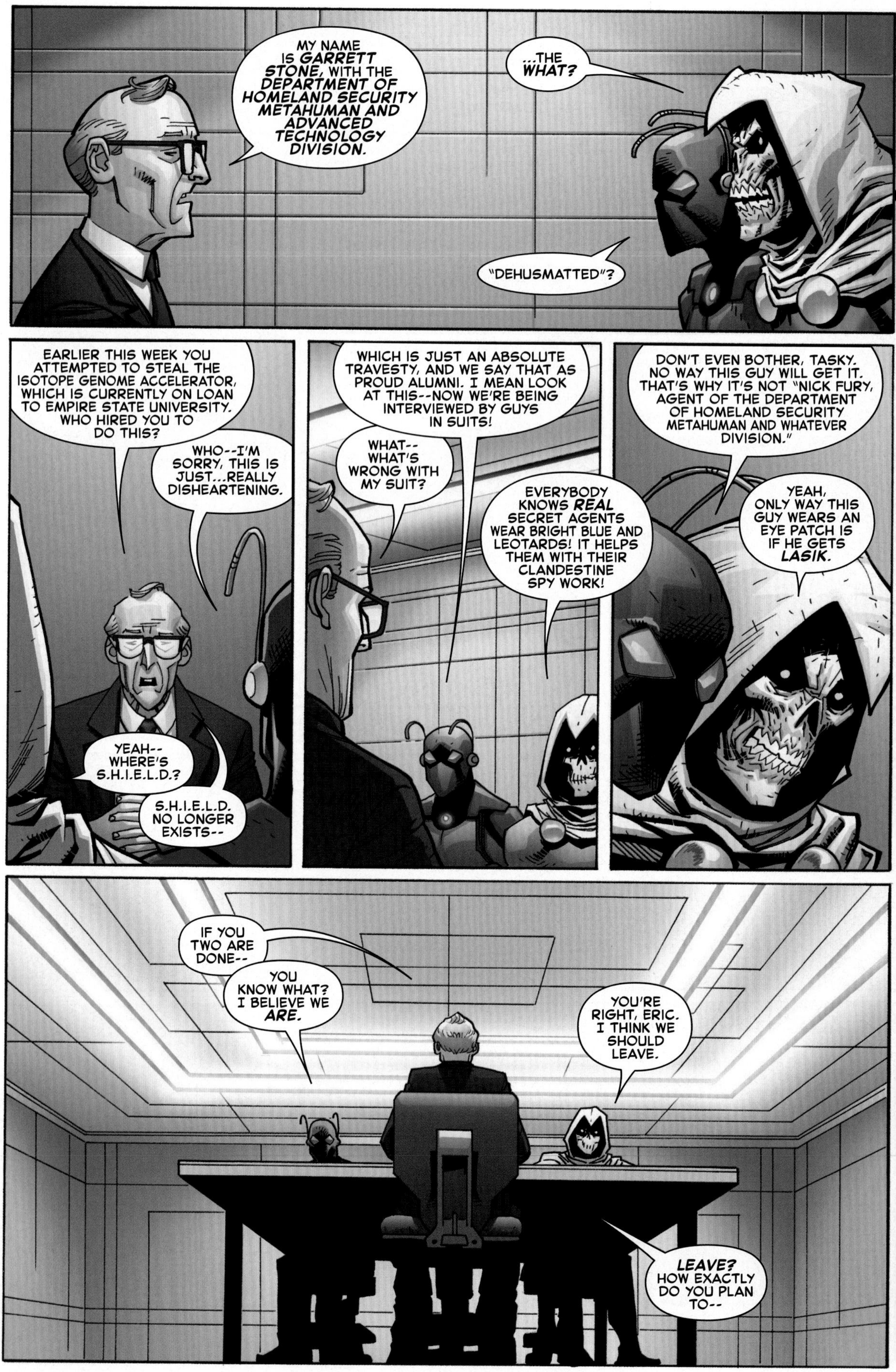
MY NAME IS GARRETT STONE, WITH THE DEPARTMENT OF HOMELAND SECURITY METAHUMAN AND ADVANCED TECHNOLOGY DIVISION.
...THE WHAT?
"DEHUSMATTED"?
EARLIER THIS WEEK YOU ATTEMPTED TO STEAL THE ISOTOPE GENOME ACCELERATOR, WHICH IS CURRENTLY ON LOAN TO EMPIRE STATE UNIVERSITY. WHO HIRED YOU TO DO THIS?
WHO--I'M SORRY, THIS IS JUST...REALLY DISHEARTENING.
YEAH--WHERE'S S.H.I.E.L.D.?
S.H.I.E.L.D. NO LONGER EXISTS--
WHICH IS JUST AN ABSOLUTE TRAVESTY, AND WE SAY THAT AS PROUD ALUMNI. I MEAN LOOK AT THIS--NOW WE'RE BEING INTERVIEWED BY GUYS IN SUITS!
WHAT--WHAT'S WRONG WITH MY SUIT?
EVERYBODY KNOWS REAL SECRET AGENTS WEAR BRIGHT BLUE AND LEOTARDS! IT HELPS THEM WITH THEIR CLANDESTINE SPY WORK!
DON'T EVEN BOTHER, TASKY. NO WAY THIS GUY WILL GET IT. THAT'S WHY IT'S NOT "NICK FURY, AGENT OF THE DEPARTMENT OF HOMELAND SECURITY METAHUMAN AND WHATEVER DIVISION."
YEAH, ONLY WAY THIS GUY WEARS AN EYE PATCH IS IF HE GETS LASIK.
IF YOU TWO ARE DONE--
YOU KNOW WHAT? I BELIEVE WE ARE.
YOU'RE RIGHT, ERIC. I THINK WE SHOULD LEAVE.
LEAVE? HOW EXACTLY DO YOU PLAN TO--

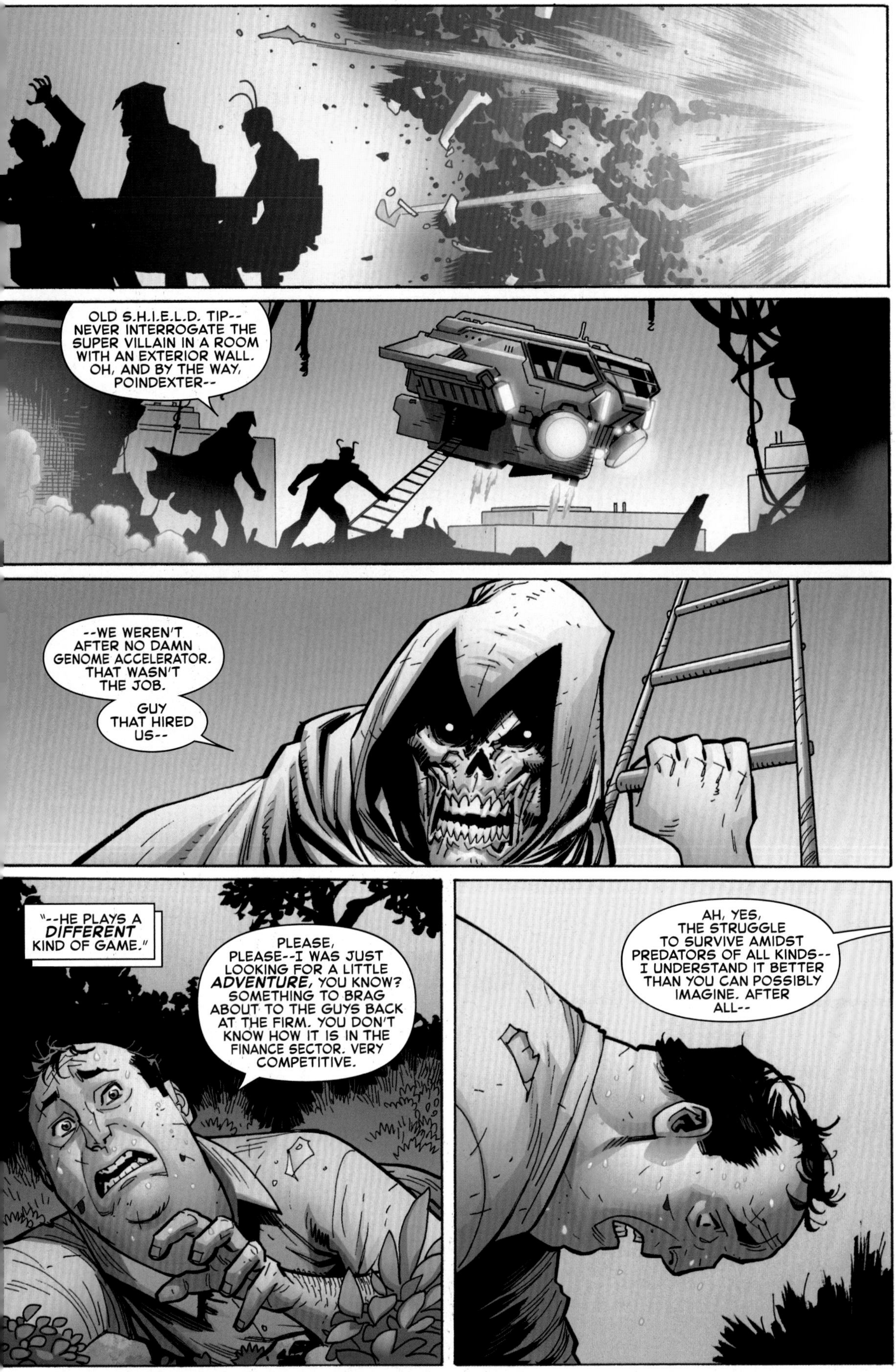
OLD S.H.I.E.L.D. TIP--NEVER INTERROGATE THE SUPER VILLAIN IN A ROOM WITH AN EXTERIOR WALL. OH, AND BY THE WAY, POINDEXTER--
--WE WEREN'T AFTER NO DAMN GENOME ACCELERATOR. THAT WASN'T THE JOB.
GUY THAT HIRED US--
"--HE PLAYS A DIFFERENT KIND OF GAME."
PLEASE, PLEASE--I WAS JUST LOOKING FOR A LITTLE ADVENTURE, YOU KNOW? SOMETHING TO BRAG ABOUT TO THE GUYS BACK AT THE FIRM. YOU DON'T KNOW HOW IT IS IN THE FINANCE SECTOR. VERY COMPETITIVE.
AH, YES, THE STRUGGLE TO SURVIVE AMIDST PREDATORS OF ALL KINDS--I UNDERSTAND IT BETTER THAN YOU CAN POSSIBLY IMAGINE. AFTER ALL--

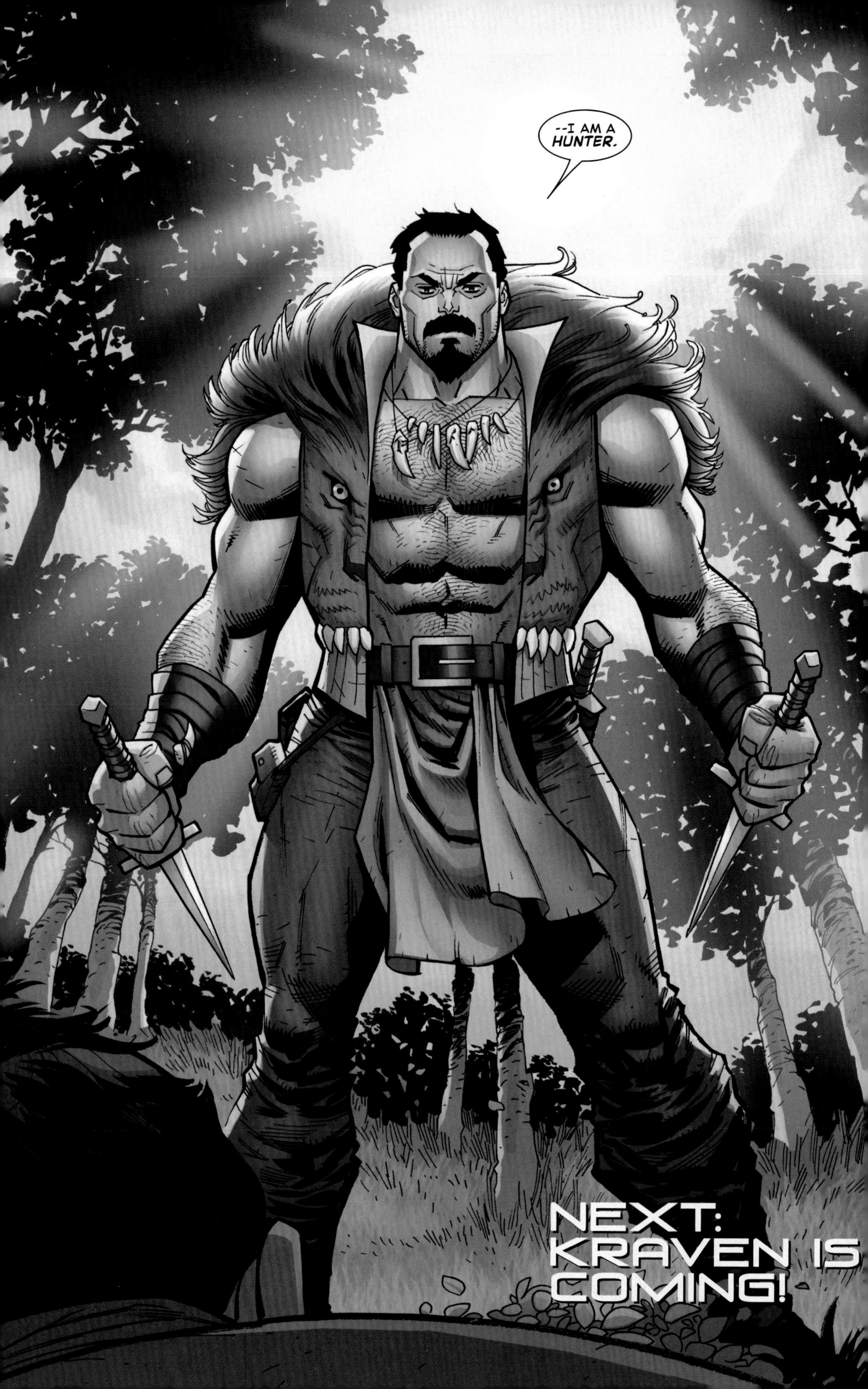
--I AM A HUNTER.
NEXT: KRAVEN IS COMING!

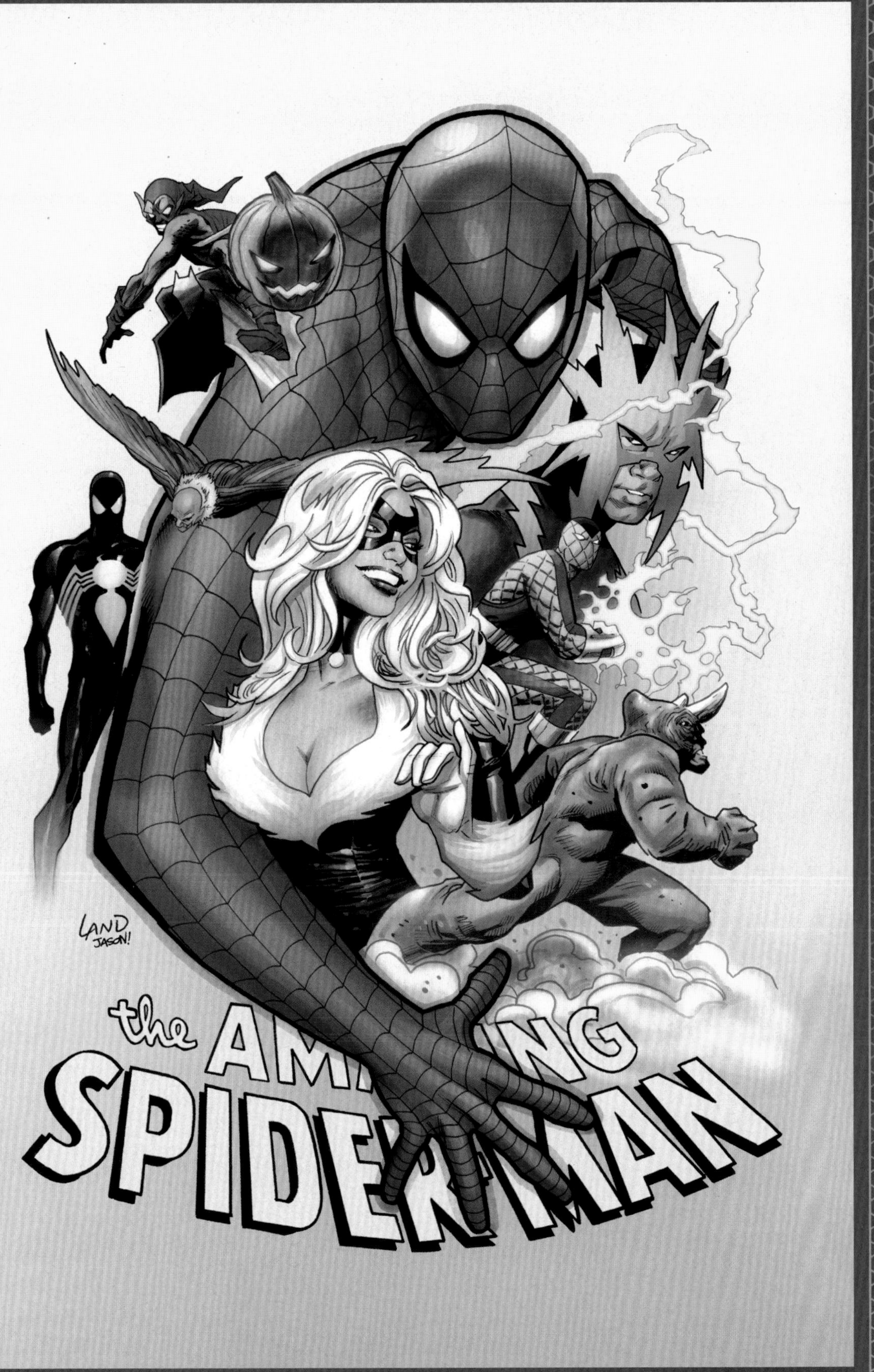
LAND
JASON!
the AMAZING
SPIDER-MAN

#1 PARTY VARIANT BY GREG LAND & JASON KEITH

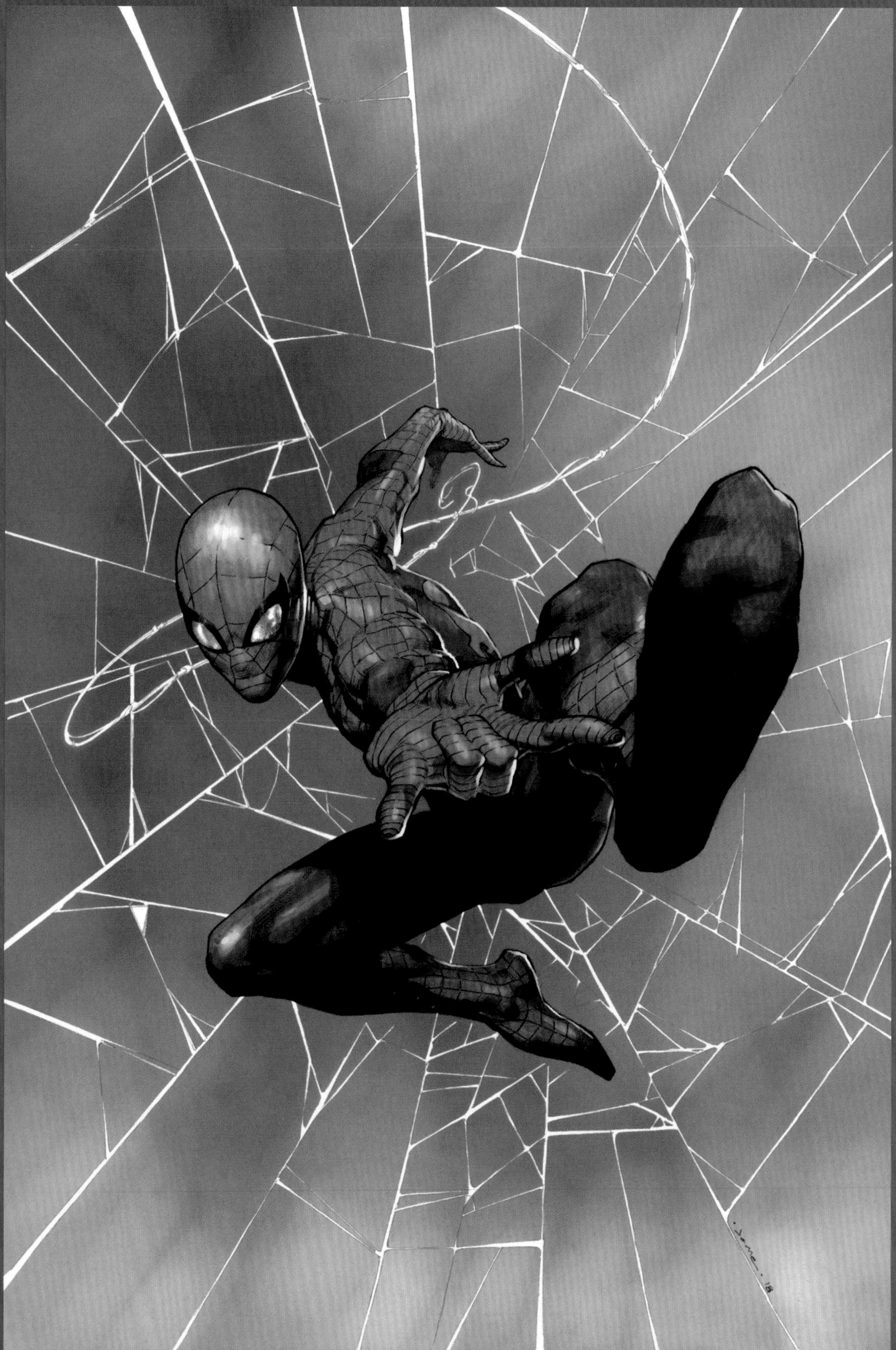

#1 VARIANT BY JEROME OPEÑA

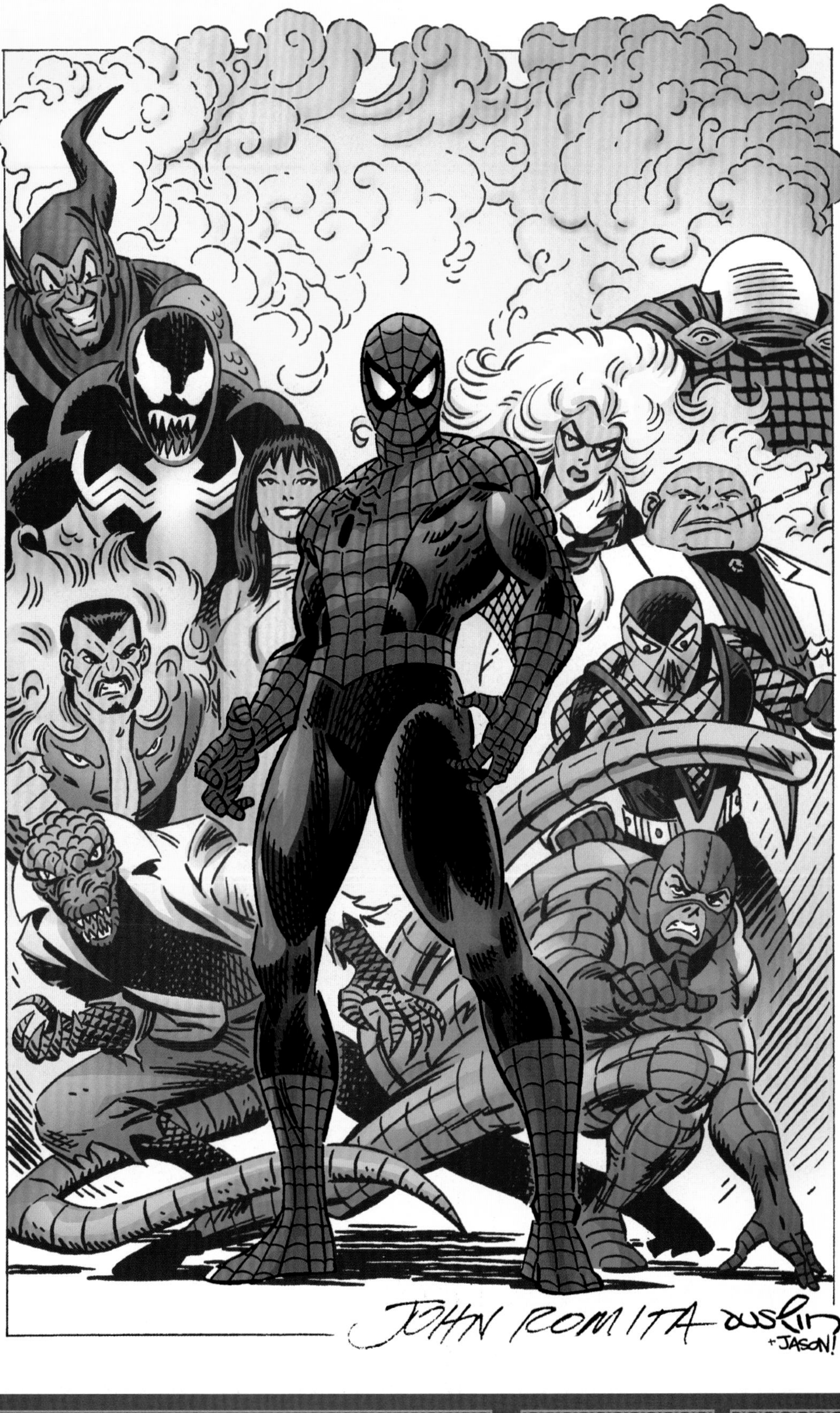
JOHN ROMITA
austin
+JASON!

#1 VARIANT BY JOHN ROMITA SR., TERRY AUSTIN & JASON KEITH

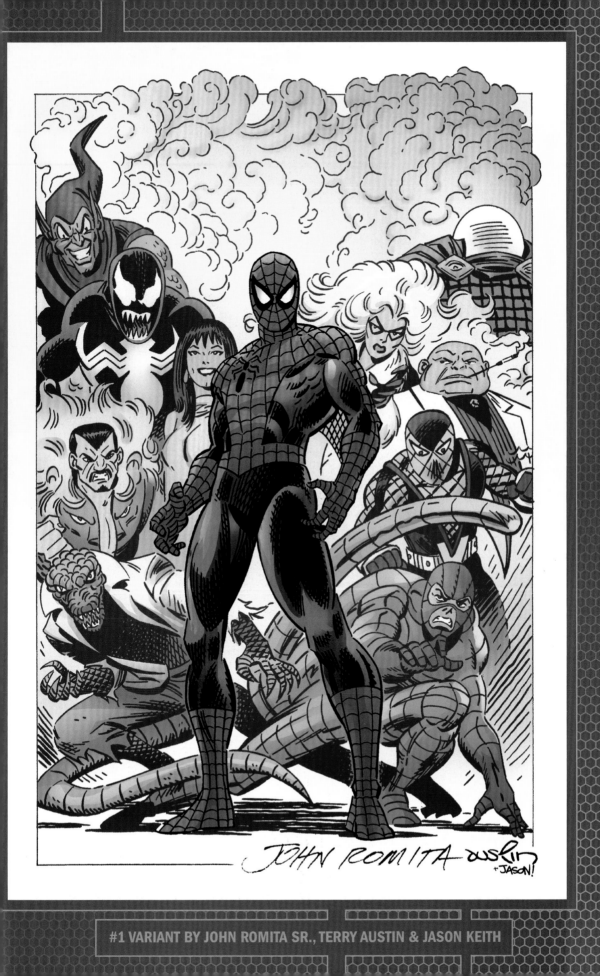

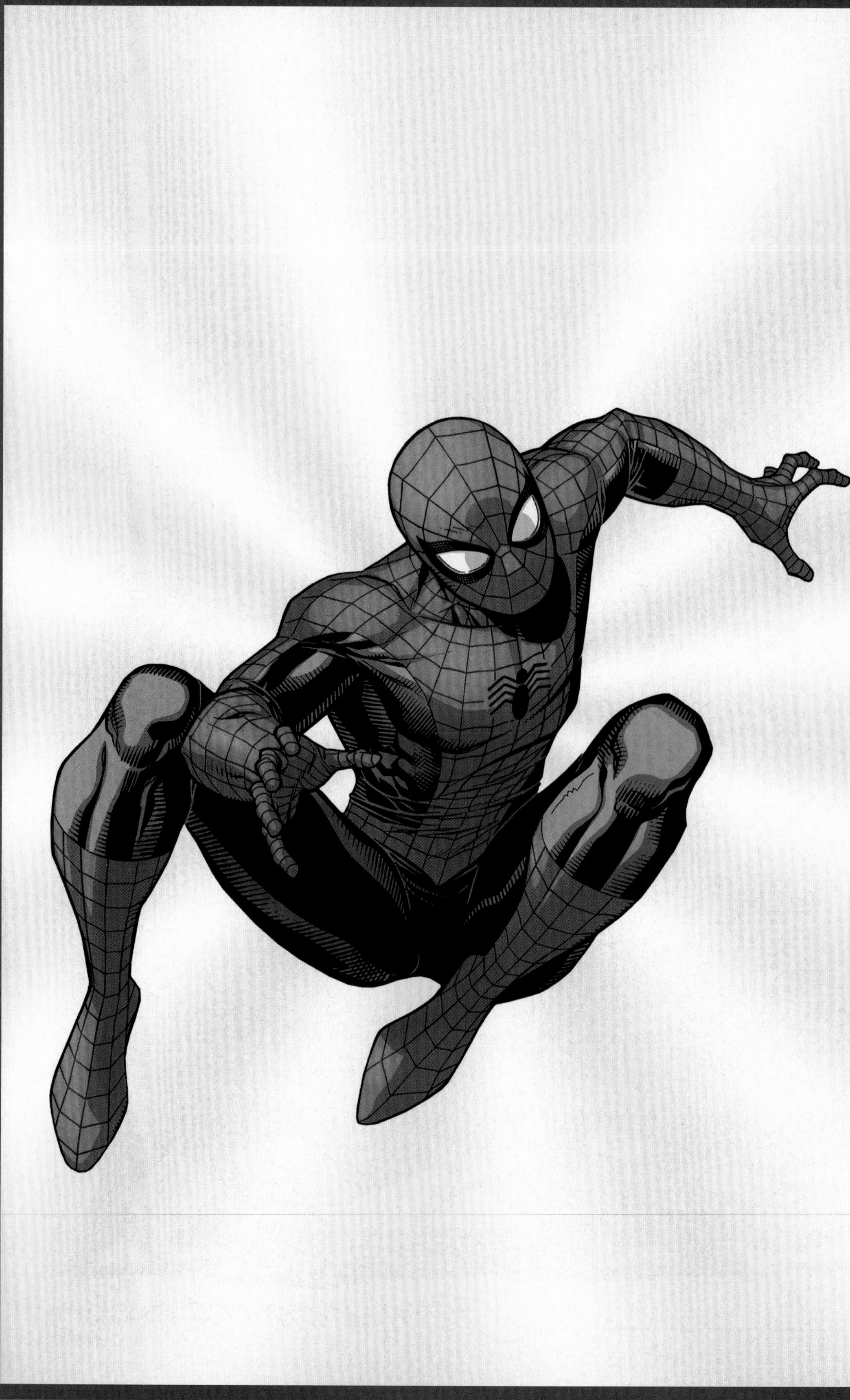

#1 VARIANT BY JIM CHEUNG & JUSTIN PONSOR

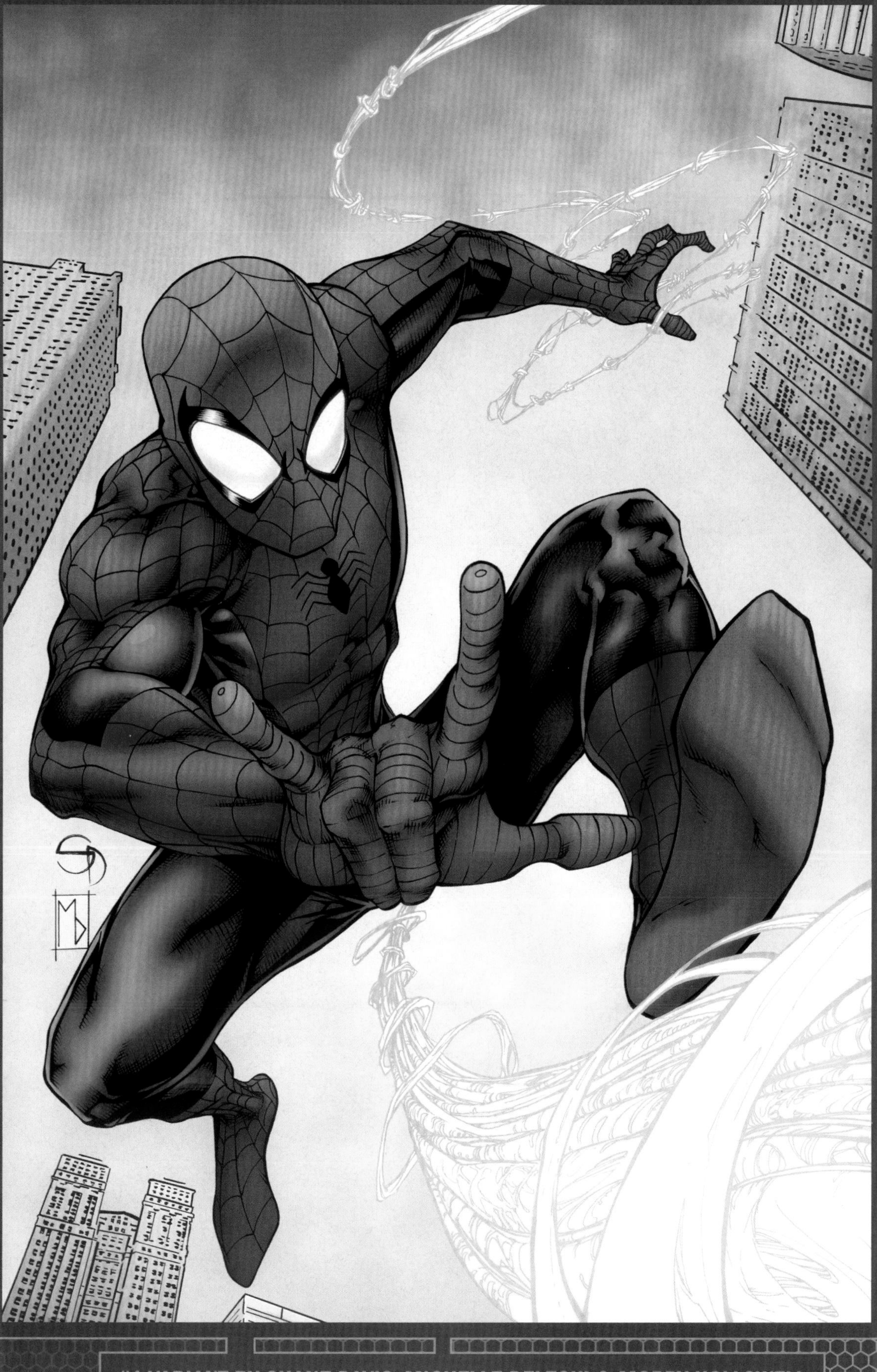

#1 VARIANT BY SHANE DAVIS, MICHELLE DELECKI & MORRY HOLLOWELL

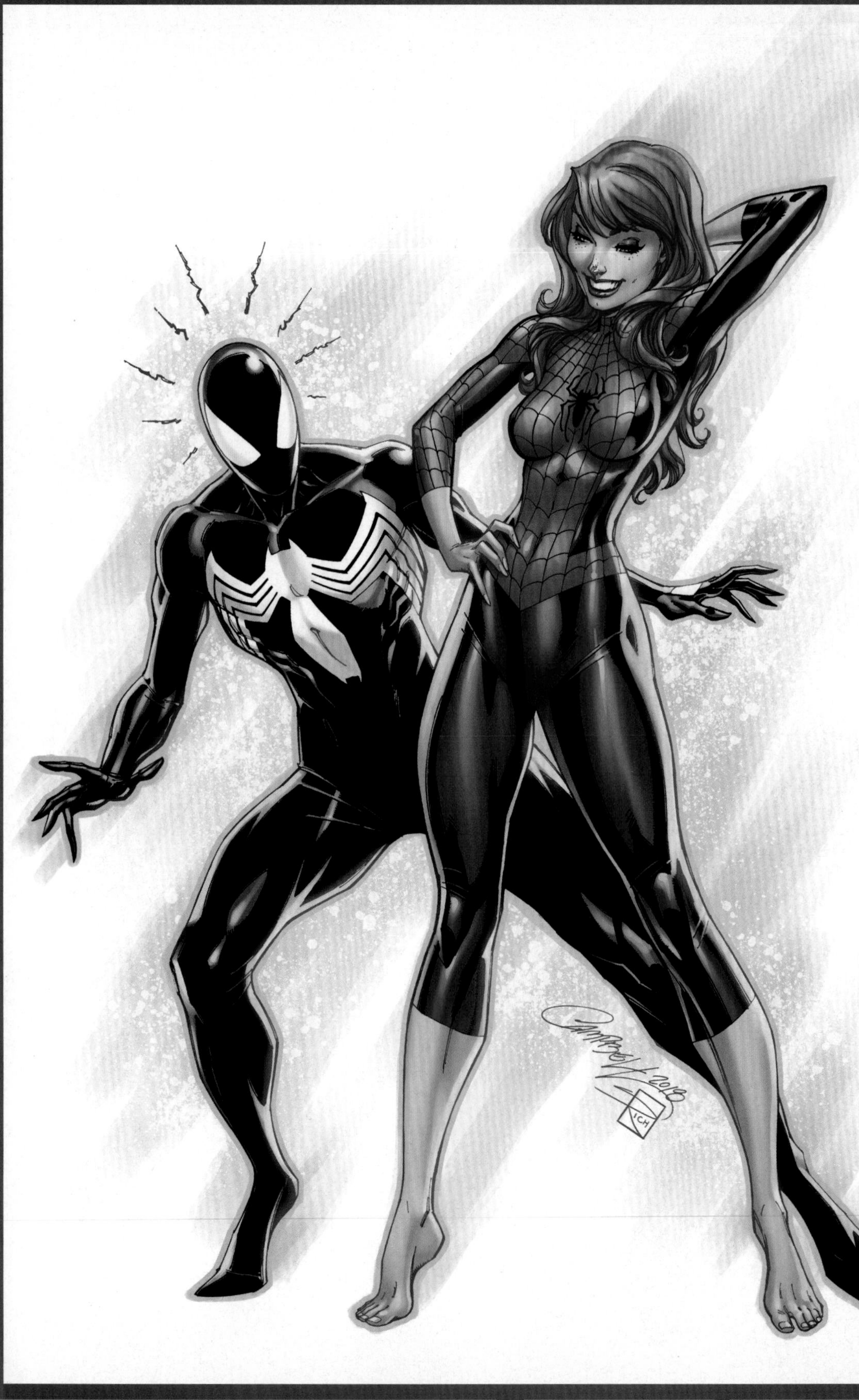

#1 VARIANT BY J. SCOTT CAMPBELL & SABINE RICH

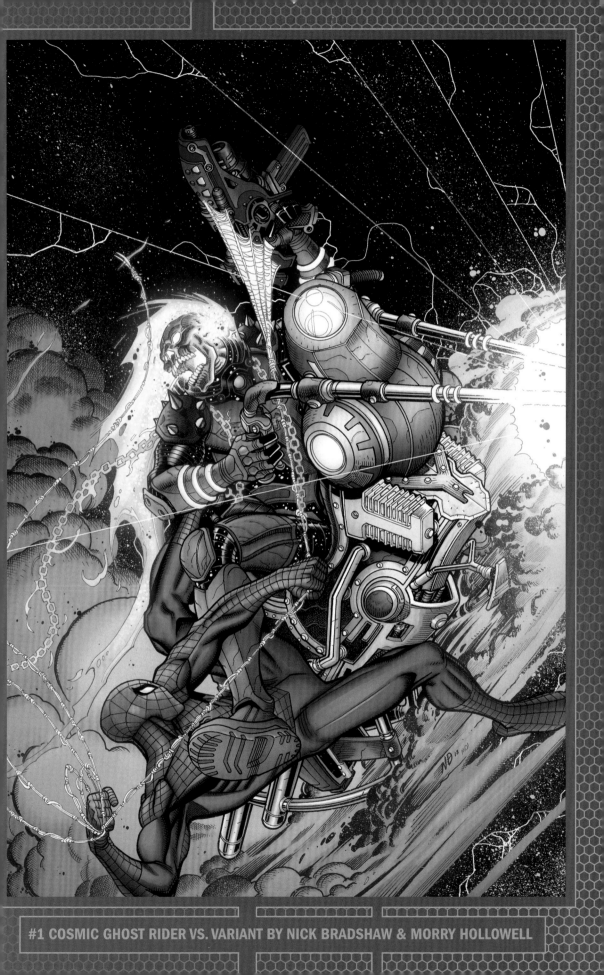

#1 COSMIC GHOST RIDER VS. VARIANT BY NICK BRADSHAW & MORRY HOLLOWELL

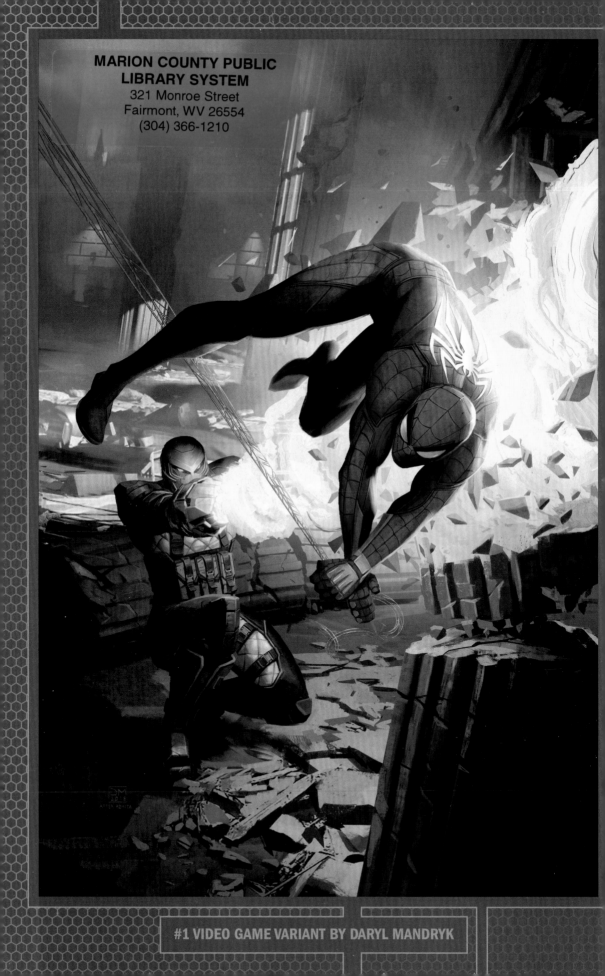

#1 VIDEO GAME VARIANT BY DARYL MANDRYK